THE SQUAD

ALSO BY RYAN GRIM

We've Got People: From Jesse Jackson to Alexandria Ocasio-Cortez, the End of Big Money and the Rise of a Movement

This Is Your Country on Drugs: The Secret History of Getting High in America

THE SQUAD

AOC AND THE HOPE OF
A POLITICAL REVOLUTION

Ryan Grim

Henry Holt and Company

New York

Henry Holt and Company
Publishers since 1866
120 Broadway
New York, New York 10271
www.henryholt.com

Henry Holt® and Ⓗ® are registered trademarks of Macmillan Publishing Group, LLC.

Library of Congress Cataloging-in-Publication Data

Names: Grim, Ryan, 1978– author.
Title: The squad : AOC and the hope of a political revolution / Ryan Grim.
Description: First edition. | New York : Henry Holt and Company, 2024.
Identifiers: LCCN 2023025162 (print) | LCCN 2023025163 (ebook) |
   ISBN 9781250869074 (hardcover) | ISBN 9781250869081 (ebook)
Subjects: LCSH: United States. Congress. House. | Democratic Party (U.S.) |
   Women legislators—United States—History—21st century. | Progressivism
   (United States politics) | United States—Politics and government—2017–2021.
Classification: LCC JK1319 .G75 2024 (print) | LCC JK1319 (ebook) |
   DDC 320.973—dc23/eng/20230822
LC record available at https://lccn.loc.gov/2023025162
LC ebook record available at https://lccn.loc.gov/2023025163

Our books may be purchased in bulk for promotional, educational, or business use. Please
contact your local bookseller or the Macmillan Corporate and Premium Sales Department at
(800) 221-7945, extension 5442, or by e-mail at MacmillanSpecialMarkets@macmillan.com.

First Edition 2023

Designed by Gabriel Guma

All emojis designed by OpenMoji—the open-source emoji and icon project. License: CC BY-SA 4.0

Printed in the United States of America

10 9 8 7 6 5 4 3 2 1

For my squad—Elizan, Iris, Sidney, Virginia, and George—
and for yours.

CONTENTS

ENDING RACISM

On April 30, 2015, a clear spring day in Washington, DC, Bernie Sanders shuffled out of the Capitol Building to a waiting collection of microphones and a C-SPAN camera. Despite his twenty-five years as the only democratic socialist serving in Congress, the U.S. senator from Vermont was far from a household name. About a dozen reporters, and no other spectators, gathered around him.

"Let me just make a brief comment. Be happy to take a few questions, but we don't have an endless amount of time; I've got to get back," the always impatient Sanders grumbled before explaining why he was announcing an improbable run for the presidency.

The country was facing a set of interlocking crises the likes of which hadn't been seen since the Great Depression. "For most Americans, their reality is that they're working longer hours for lower wages," Sanders said, explaining that people regularly approached him to ask why they were producing more than ever, yet struggling as the rich only got richer. "All over this country I've been talking to people," Sanders said. "'My kid can't afford to go to college.' 'I'm having a hard time affording health care.' How does that happen while at exactly the same time, ninety-nine percent of all new income generated in this country is going to the top one percent?"

These weren't just familiar themes coming from Sanders. They flowed straight from a left-wing zeitgeist that had found its footing in the encampments of Occupy Wall Street in the fall of 2011, less than four years earlier. Amid the rubble of the Obama administration's pivot to austerity in the wake of the 2008 financial crisis, tent cities had sprung up around the country, organized around the principle of the 99 percent against the one percent.

Occupy was an effort to create the broadest possible "we" and set it against a definable "other" in the super rich. For decades, under the pressure of neoliberalism and the Reagan Revolution—which smashed unions, suppressed wages, and challenged the very idea of the collective pursuit of a better world—the left had splintered into ever more discrete factions, pushing single issues under the umbrella of the Democratic Party. Jesse Jackson, in 1984 and 1988, attempted to organize that energy into a "Rainbow Coalition," coming shockingly close to seizing the 1988 Democratic nomination and inspiring Sanders, who, for the first time, caucused as a Democrat, leading the effort to deliver the almost all-white state of Vermont to Jackson.

Sanders, preparing for his 2016 presidential run, met with a team of progressive online fund-raisers, one of whom guessed the senator might be able to raise $25 million throughout his campaign, a sum Sanders and the rest of the team thought preposterous. Sanders nodded to that pessimism at his opening press conference. "One of the hesitancies I had in deciding whether to run or not was obviously dealing with money," he said. "I'm not going to get money from the Koch brothers, and I'm not going to get money from billionaires. I'm going to have to raise my campaign contributions through BernieSanders.com— small, individual contributions."

By the end of the day, his fund-raising team was floored. The no-frills C-SPAN affair had netted the campaign $1.5 million in the first twenty-four hours, exceeding their wildest expectations by several multiples. Something was happening out there.

Sanders started off polling at about 15 percent, but as the campaign went on, increasingly enthusiastic crowds followed him everywhere he went. People started to "feel the Bern"—a phrase conjured up by Occupy organizer Winnie Wong, who had converted her operation to draft Elizabeth Warren to run for president into "People for Bernie."

By the fall of 2015, Hillary Clinton's campaign staff were growing concerned about the momentum behind Sanders. His crowd sizes were exploding, his poll numbers were rising, and even if he didn't yet represent a threat that might snatch away the nomination, a drawn-out fight, the campaign was concerned, would drag them down in the general election. In early October, Clinton agreed to appear on *Saturday Night Live*, and that weekend, her campaign's top brass huddled to debate how to respond to the accusation made by Sanders that Clinton was too cozy with Wall Street. Another key question, which the campaign had grappled with in the previously unreported internal debate, was whether to come out publicly in favor of restoring what was known as Glass-Steagall, the Depression-era law that barred big commercial banks from gambling with their depositors' money. The Bill Clinton administration had infamously repealed the law as part of a wave of Wall Street deregulation, and it was being apportioned considerable blame for the 2008 financial crisis that was still dragging down the economy. Some on the Hillary Clinton campaign raised policy objections, wondering about the unintended consequences of breaking up such large institutions. Others argued that the move would backfire because it would come off as patently inauthentic pandering. But the third objection was the deciding one: Voters who were motivated by Wall Street corruption were going to vote for Bernie Sanders no matter what. The persuadable voters who would decide the election, the Clinton campaign determined, were more likely to vote on cultural and social issues. How to go on offense with those issues was the question.

Still, a little bit of pandering was in order, so the campaign decided that Clinton would come out for strengthening the Volcker Rule, a milder reform than reinstating Glass-Steagall, and she did so later that week.

Coming into the Iowa caucuses in early 2016, Sanders had climbed his way into a tie in the statewide polls, and Clinton emerged from the messy caucuses, replete with contested coin tosses and rampant challenges, with a narrow 2-delegate victory.

New Hampshire, home turf for Sanders, was next, on February 9, and the Clinton team decided to try to weaponize Sanders's enthusiastic young supporters against him—a bid to win over those voters Sanders's team hoped would be swayed on cultural issues. Clinton campaign manager Robby Mook and communications director Brian Fallon appeared at a "Bloomberg Politics" breakfast with reporters and first laid out the charge, with Fallon jumping in to warn Sanders against "demeaning and insulting language."

The problem, Fallon said, was Sanders's supporters—but it was also Sanders's fault for riling them up. "Distinct from the candidate and the campaign proper, there is a support base for Senator Sanders's candidacy that has been shorthanded as the so-called Bernie Bros," Fallon said. "Anyone who engages in social media in support of

Hillary Clinton has encountered this element. It can be nasty. It can be vitriolic. And I think that the Sanders campaign needs to beware the extent to which, in an effort to mobilize and galvanize their supporters, they start to let the mentality, or the crudeness, seep into their own words and criticisms that they hurl at Secretary Clinton."

Sanders himself, Fallon said, was egging those supporters on. "Senator Sanders is a very skilled and deft politician, despite efforts to hone and cultivate an image to the contrary. And he knows what he is doing when he does these little hip checks. He's injecting something into a conversation and trying to inspire a three- or four-day conversation that he knows," Fallon said, pausing to find the right words, "would be bothersome."

It was the first entry into the official record, so to speak, of the term *Bernie Bros*. At the time, the head of the Department of Labor was Tom Perez, known as the administration's most progressive cabinet secretary. The next year, he'd win a race—with Obama's backing—to become chair of the Democratic National Committee. For now, he was dispatched to both New Hampshire and Nevada to get the lay of the land. The day after Fallon's remarks, February 5, Perez reported to Clinton campaign chair John Podesta, that the Bernie Bro insight could be taken a step farther and wielded in the party's internal culture war.

The Sanders message was resonating, Perez argued, particularly among young people, whose futures were collapsing in front of their faces. Republican operative Karl Rove had pioneered the strategy of turning a candidate's greatest strength into his greatest weakness, and Perez proposed doing the same to Sanders. "I think Nevada is the firewall on a number of levels," he wrote to Podesta in an email later obtained and published by WikiLeaks.

While Clinton couldn't undermine Sanders's message, she could transform *who* people understood to be the messengers—and the audience. Nevada was an opportunity, Perez said, for Clinton to do well in caucuses that included a significant number of minority voters—Black, Asian American, and Latino—of all ages, and that meant doing well with young minority voters. "When we do well there, then the narrative changes from 'Bernie kicks ass among young voters' to 'Bernie does well only among young white liberals'—that is a different story and a perfect lead-in to South Carolina, where, once again, we can work to attract young voters of color," he suggested.

Sanders's strength was that he had people, lots of them, and they were passionate enough to volunteer, to contribute to the campaign, and to otherwise evangelize the political revolution. The goal, then, was to turn those people into a liability. Flagging the Bernie Bros as obnoxious, privileged young white men was the easiest way to do it. Sanders's support among young people, by that time, cut across race and gender, but it wasn't hard to find young, white, obnoxious men who backed him, to elevate them publicly, and then to condemn them and the Sanders campaign together.

In a riveting New Hampshire debate, Clinton took her first serious shot at fending off Sanders's charge that she was the candidate of the moneyed elite and that the support her campaign had from big-money donors and the speaking fees she personally took from companies like Goldman Sachs might have some corrupting influence. "You will not find that I ever changed a view or a vote because of any donation that I ever received," Clinton said. "So, I think it's time to end the very artful smear that you and your campaign have been carrying out in recent weeks, and let's talk about the issues." She added: ". . . I really don't think these kinds of attacks by insinuation are worthy of you. Enough is enough, if you've got something to say, say it."

Sanders refused to call Clinton personally corrupt, but he laid the point out clearly. Drug companies could raise prices at will because they had bought power in Washington. Oil companies could block climate change legislation for the same reason. Also true with the banks, and so on. "There is a reason why these people are putting huge amounts of money into our political system and, in my view, it is undermining American democracy," he responded.

In 2008, Hillary Clinton had pulled off a remarkable comeback against Barack Obama, winning the New Hampshire primary and giving life to her campaign. It wasn't to be in 2016: Sanders carried the state by 22 points and, over the next day, had brought in a staggering six-million-dollar-plus haul.

All of a sudden, the Nevada caucuses mattered. For much of the campaign, Clinton had been dismissing Sanders as a "single-issue" candidate, but at a rally in Henderson, Nevada, on February 13, 2016, a week before the caucuses, she tightened her pitch. It wasn't just that Sanders's backers were problematic, Clinton warned voters, but his platform was, too—because it didn't directly confront racism and sexism. "Not everything is about an economic theory," she said, promising to be "the only candidate who'll take on every barrier to progress."

This led her into a call-and-response that would become central to her stump speech. "If we broke up the big banks tomorrow," she asked, "and I will, if they deserve it, if they pose a systemic risk, I will—would that end racism?"

"No!" the crowd yelled back.

"Would that end sexism?"

"No!"

"Would that end discrimination against the LGBT community?"

"No!"

"Would that make people feel more welcoming to immigrants overnight?"

"No!"

Two months later, *Rolling Stone* described it as "the line that may have won Hillary Clinton the nomination."

Sanders, of course, could have countered that, for instance, breaking up the big banks and enforcing civil rights laws against them would indeed be a blow to systemic racism—redlining, after all, had been enforced and implemented by the banks. The response would have been an example of what became known as the "race-class narrative," an effort by progressive strategists to speak to people's material concerns without overlooking—and, indeed, by fully incorporating a critique of—systemic racism. Or Sanders could have noted that unchecked concentrations of capital were a threat to democracy. Or that he had been supportive of trans rights as the mayor of Burlington in the 1980s and had been far ahead of his peers when it came to what were then called gay and lesbian rights.

But Clinton's argument wasn't one of substance, so it couldn't be countered with substance. Sanders isn't as progressive as you think he is, she was telling voters, and the proof was his single-minded focus on economic security and the battle against the one percent. It was a luxury—a privilege, even—to be able to focus merely on the millionaires and billionaires and not on the intersecting forms of oppression faced in unique ways by those in marginalized communities.

The Nevada contest was tight, and got heated in several precincts. Dolores Huerta, a longtime union organizer—known, not without a twinge of sexism, as "the female Cesar Chavez"—was at one caucus site. A vocal Clinton supporter, Huerta claimed in a Twitter post, "I offered to translate & Bernie supporters chanted English only! We fought too long & hard to be silenced. Si Se Puede!"

The claim was spread widely, and the bigoted behavior just as widely condemned. It turned out to be a lie. Videos showed nobody had chanted any such thing; rather, Raymond Buckley, the neutral precinct chair and a leading figure in the New Hampshire Democratic Party, who had traveled to Nevada to volunteer, had ruled that there would be no translation at the caucus site. But the viral story of bigotry from Bernie supporters had done immense damage.

Another allegation spread from a different precinct: that enraged Sanders supporters had thrown chairs amid a caucus melee. Video later surfaced of a Sanders supporter lifting a chair over his head in anger, but then putting it back down. There was no doubt the caucuses had gotten hot, but the chair-throwing rumor was untrue. Still, the twin stories were collectively too perfect to allow debunking to suppress them. Angry, entitled young white men throwing chairs and shouting down a widely respected, elderly Latina organizer? Sounds like Bernie Bros.

Meanwhile, the party machine went to work on behalf of Clinton. Senate Democratic leader Harry Reid, who had built the Nevada machine from the ground up, called the head of the Culinary Workers Union, directing them to endorse Clinton and to urge workers to caucus. Reid then called the casinos and ordered them to give their employees time off to caucus. The orders were followed, and Clinton wound up with a 5-point caucus victory. Sanders's momentum had been blunted, but more important a narrative had been set: Bernie's movement was beset by racism and misogyny, and good progressives must support Clinton.

Days later, Sanders was blown out in South Carolina, a defeat that put an exclamation mark on the white Bernie Bro narrative. Losing both states the way Sanders did was a mortal double blow, but the campaign took many more months to bleed out, with each day of the primary driving a wedge deeper in between the party's increasingly bitter factions. The Clinton campaign, through a super PAC with which it coordinated directly, called Correct the Record, later admitted to spending at least a million dollars to get into bitter fights with Sanders supporters online, either through bots or paid accounts. When they announced this publicly in April, they said they had already "addressed more than 5,000 people that have personally attacked Hillary Clinton on Twitter." For-profit scam artists based in eastern Europe would get in the game, too, joining Sanders or Clinton Facebook groups and posting what came to be called fake news. The articles were designed to look like official American news items. The Sanders campaign had begun seeing this particular brand of news starting in early 2016, and it became digital media director Hector Sigala's job to grapple with it. "The first time that we kind of fell for it, for like two minutes, was this link from what seemed to be ABC News," Sigala said. It turned out to be ABC.com.co, a fake site that has no affiliation with the real news network. It had "reported" that the pope himself had endorsed Sanders. According to the investigation later conducted by Special Counsel Robert Mueller, an agency linked with the Russian government did much the same thing as Correct the Record and the eastern European scammers, but it used its fake troll accounts to stir anger between the party's two factions.

As WikiLeaks would later reveal, the Clinton campaign worked directly with Washington-based nonprofit advocacy groups—which universally endorsed Clinton despite their younger staff generally supporting Sanders—to ghost-write op-eds explaining how the Sanders position on this or that issue was actually sexist or racist. To the extent that the campaign tactic moved the needle at all, it likely pushed moderate voters paying only marginal attention to the campaign toward *Sanders*, who spoke like a normal person, while Clinton began ascending into what her ally James Carville would later call "faculty lounge speak." Anybody following the campaign closely, however, had no effort distinguishing which candidate among the two was more progressive. The giveaway was that one of them was openly calling himself a socialist. Former president Bill Clinton, surveying the landscape and the ham-handed efforts at identity politics, was bereft, lamenting to a longtime friend in the fall of 2016 that Hillary's campaign "could not sell pussy on a troop train."

The Clinton campaign's deft deployment of identity politics to detonate the Sanders campaign set off a chain reaction that would blow the lid off the Democratic coalition in the years to come. But Clinton's effort would not have met with such success had the conditions not been perfectly primed for it. The financial crisis of 2008, followed by the painfully slow recovery, hit Millennials especially hard. All of a sudden absent hope for a better world or a secure future, millions of people looked for purpose instead in their own moral purification. In a nation that had been founded by a radical sect of Puritans and engulfed by multiple Great Awakenings and lesser moral panics, this awakened sense of righteousness fit seamlessly into the national character. And real social progress was being made—thanks, in part, to the early petering out of the Obama administration.

Barack Obama—in no small part due to the prior machinations of his chief of staff Rahm Emanuel—was the first president in fifty years to be working with a Democratic majority more conservative than the White House. Both Jimmy Carter and Bill Clinton had faced congressional majorities that were more liberal, and they needed to triangulate and browbeat progressives in order to implement their respective agendas. Emanuel, as the 2006 chair of the Democratic Congressional Campaign Committee, assiduously recruited conservative candidates to challenge incumbent Republicans. The timing couldn't have been worse. Democrats did take the House and Senate that cycle—though whether Emanuel's strategy helped or hurt that effort is debatable—but not long after they were sworn in, cracks began showing in the bubble economy. Small-time subprime lenders, who had pumped out fraudulent loans disproportionately to Black homeowners, began going under. Big lenders followed, and in March 2008 Bear Stearns, a Wall Street giant, collapsed.

Obama, though, was surging, having caught and eclipsed the all-but-anointed Hillary Clinton. In a mirror version of 2016, it was Obama who leaned into his identity, while Clinton downplayed the pathbreaking nature of her own candidacy.

It was into this looming financial crisis that Alexandria Ocasio-Cortez graduated high school in 2007 in Yorktown, New York. In January 2008, while home from Boston University for her first winter break, she registered to vote as a Democrat and was swept up by Obama's hopeful campaign. She told me she phone-banked in between classes and tried to absentee-vote in the primary, but New York's notoriously rickety election infrastructure failed to get her a ballot in time, so she took an overnight Chinatown bus to get home to vote in person.

While at BU, Ocasio-Cortez interned for Massachusetts senator

Ted Kennedy, who had made universal health care the cause of his life. It was there that she met and began dating Riley Roberts, and the two have been together ever since, getting engaged in 2022.

At home, things were going poorly, however. Her father, Sergio Ocasio-Roman, was battling cancer at the same time that his architecture business was grappling with the housing collapse. Alexandria was in an economics class when she got a call from her mother saying he had taken a turn for the worse. She raced to a cab and caught the first flight home, making it in time to say goodbye. "Make me proud," her father told her.

Her brother, Gabriel, was still in high school, living with their mother in a house that was rapidly plummeting in value just as the family lost its main source of income. "When my father died, she was left a single mother of two, and again she had to start over," Alexandria wrote of their mother in an Instagram post after she was sworn in to Congress. "After he passed, we almost lost our home."

Their mom, Blanca, juggled odd jobs—cleaning houses, driving a school bus, answering phones. Sergio had died without a will, so the estate wound up in the local surrogate court, where lawyers prey on families in desperate situations. People Ocasio-Cortez believed were from the bank, she recalled, would pull up to the house and take pictures. All around her, people were losing their homes: 2.9 million were foreclosed on in 2009 and another 2.9 million in 2010. The number dropped to just under 2 million for both 2011 and 2012, the year the court finally cleared her family's estate. The Obama administration, as has by now been thoroughly documented, deliberately encouraged these foreclosures, with White House economic adviser Larry Summers and Treasury secretary Tim Geithner both arguing that the rubble of the American Dream would "foam the runway" for the insolvent banks, allowing them to lose money slowly rather than go bust all at once. Helping homeowners by holding banks accountable for the fraud would have been too painful for those banks and could cause them to collapse. So the Obama administration and Wall Street had agreed to slowly bleed out the homeowners to keep the bailed-out banks alive.

Once in office, conservative Democrats Emanuel had recruited in 2006 as chair of the Democratic Congressional Campaign Committee routinely bucked the Obama administration. Coupled with Obama's own instincts to go small, the result was a turn toward austerity heading into the midterms, a move that exacerbated rather than mitigated the coming losses. In order to get the votes for Obama's signature piece of legislation, the Affordable Care Act, the price tag was kept low—which drove up the cost of premiums and deductibles and delayed implementation for several years, meaning Democrats paid all the political costs up front, but got none of the benefits—and the public health insurance option that progressives saw as the ACA's linchpin was scuttled. "Look at Obamacare," Ocasio-Cortez would say later. "They really thought that a person who makes $40,000 a year can pay $200 a month in health insurance for an $8,000 deductible—and they really thought that that was insurance."

The 2010 midterm wipeout at the hands of the Tea Party reshaped what was possible for Democrats and for progressives generally. With Republicans in charge of the House, Obama's legislative window was officially closed, and he would spend the next several years locked in negotiations over how dramatically to scale back social spending, with a never-ending series of manufactured crises in the form of debt ceiling showdowns and government shutdowns. The only way to spend money is through congressional legislation, which meant that federal efforts to improve the economic well-being of the public were effectively off the table. Yet progress could still be made on the social and cultural front. Climate activists, after the failure of major legislation in 2009, converted their energy to campus protests urging divestment from fossil fuels and into direct protests against particular projects, most important, the Keystone XL Pipeline—to which Ocasio-Cortez would travel to protest—which planned to bring tar sands oil across the border from Canada.

After Ocasio-Cortez graduated from Boston University—not long after the Tea Party was sworn in—she moved into the Bronx co-op apartment where she had been born and where Sergio had run his business. At twenty-one, she started bartending and waitressing at the Coffee Shop and its sister location, Flats Fix, to help out at home and cover the expenses of her apartment. That fall, protesters took over downtown's Zuccotti Park, launching the Occupy Wall Street movement.

In the summer of 2012, Ocasio-Cortez launched Brook Avenue Press, which published educational materials for local schools and children's books that portrayed the Bronx in a positive light. In 2012, Senator Kirsten Gillibrand invited Ocasio-Cortez to a press conference, where she and others stood behind Gillibrand and other politicians as they unveiled a tax break for people who started new businesses.

Ocasio-Cortez's book publishing company was housed in the Sunshine Bronx Business Incubator, which was also featured at the Gillibrand press conference. The incubator also launched an organization called GAGEis, and named Ocasio-Cortez "lead educational strategist," a credential that remains attached to her pre-Congress life. Whatever GAGEis hoped to accomplish—or whatever it was—it flopped, and the incubator itself went belly-up, too.

Despite her earlier ambitions, by this point in her life, the proper way to understand Ocasio-Cortez was as a bartender. This was not something she was doing in the summer between semesters. It wasn't something she did on the side. It was her *job*, and she was starting to think, and to worry, that it was her career, her life. She was a living example of the millions of Millennials who were on the way to becoming the first generation in the United States to end up worse off than their parents. Capitalism was losing its luster, and with nothing left to lose, Ocasio-Cortez and others like her began to open themselves up to the message Sanders would later spread.

She recalled that dark time in a poignant Instagram post after being sworn in. "It wasn't long ago that we felt our lives were over; that there were only so many do-overs until it was just too late, or too much to take, or we were too spiritually spent," she said of her mother and herself, recalling her years trekking from the Bronx to Union Square for her job. "I was scrubbing tables + scooping candle wax after restaurant shifts & falling asleep on the subway ride home. I once got pickpocketed, & everything I earned that day was stolen. That day I locked myself in a room and cried deep: I had nothing left to give, or to be. And that's when I started over. I honestly thought as a 28 year old waitress I was too late; that the train of my fulfilled potential had left the station."

The crushing of Occupy Wall Street and the disappointment of the Obama administration's economic agenda left Ocasio-Cortez's generation believing the real forum to make progress was elsewhere—in fighting back against sexism, systemic racism, and homophobia. A good job and a raise might not be in the cards, but the culture could be rid of its bigotry.

Congress itself pointed the political way forward. In the lame-duck session of 2010, the last moment Democrats would have a majority until 2019, Congress repealed the military's "Don't Ask, Don't Tell" policy, finally allowing gay, lesbian, and bisexual people to serve openly in the military. Marriage equality cases then making their way through the courts had been significantly hobbled by the Defense Department's discriminatory policy, and legal experts on both sides of the argument believed the U.S. Supreme Court would be unwilling to draft an opinion that would dramatically change military policy. Once the policy was repealed, and LGB—though not the *T*—members began serving openly, the path toward marriage equality was cleared, particularly as there was no backlash either inside or outside the military and as openly gay and lesbian service members were quickly absorbed into military culture.

The culture was changing on other fronts, too. In February 2012, Trayvon Martin was walking to a family member's house from a convenience store in Stanford, Florida, when he was confronted by neighborhood vigilante George Zimmerman, who found Martin's hoodie suspicious. The two began fighting—we're left only with Zimmerman's account—and Zimmerman pulled out a weapon and shot Martin dead. His death sparked national fury, and when Zimmerman was acquitted in July 2013, relying on the state's "Stand Your Ground" law, activist Alicia Garza wrote a post on Facebook that finished with the admonition that "Black lives matter." The phrase struck a chord. Garza's friend and fellow activist Patrisse Cullors responded and turned it into the hashtag BlackLivesMatter, giving a name to a movement.

It was a new name but, in many ways, a very old movement. Tensions with the police had been central to the civil rights movement of the 1960s. The Watts Uprising of August 1965 was sparked when a police officer beat a Black motorist he had pulled over. The Newark Uprising, as just one more example, was similarly triggered when officers beat a motorist there in July 1967. The original name for the Black Panthers, the Black Panther Party for Self-Defense, hinted at its purpose: defense against not just rogue white citizens but also the police. In 1988, the smash hit song "Fuck tha Police," by the Compton-based rap group N.W.A., gave impolitic voice to the rage over policy brutality, with the lyrics pointing to the way a system of racial dominance could employ Black officers, too. "Fucking with me 'cause I'm a teenager / With a little bit of gold and a pager," the rap goes. ". . . But don't let it be a black and a white one / 'Cause they'll slam ya down to the street top /

Black police showing out for the white cop." The generation raised in the 1980s and '90s was politicized through hip-hop.

On Election Day in November 2020, just five years removed from Sanders's announcement of his run for the presidency but seemingly a world away, Jamaal Bowman gave me a tour of the district stretching from the Bronx to the New York State suburbs north of the city, which was about to send him to Congress—home to extraordinary wealth and extreme poverty. "I grew up in the same kind of economic segregation," he said, describing his Manhattan upbringing. "If I walked a couple of blocks to Park Avenue, you saw a whole 'nother world compared to where I was. I used to listen to a lot of political music, political hip-hop. The hip-hop was communicating what was happening in the world at that time."

When Bowman was eleven, he was on the sidewalk with some friends when police pulled up to tell them to clear out. The boys gave back a little lip, and the cops "beat the hell out of me," Bowman recalled. They threw him to the ground, dragged his face on the sidewalk, hit him with a baton. His mother picked him up at the police station. No charges were filed against him—he hadn't done anything wrong—but he and his mother never considered filing a complaint. "We just kept it movin'," he said. It was just how things were.

That didn't make it okay.

Bowman found expression in music. As he drove us toward his home, he put on a Boogie Down Productions song featuring KRS-One from the 1988 album *By All Means Necessary*, whose cover art is a tribute to Malcolm X. He played the track "Illegal Business," with the famous hook "cocaine business controls America," about a young boy selling drugs who's picked up by police and blackmailed into paying them off to stay in business. The crack trade that flourishes in the neighborhood, the song explains, does so at the behest of, and for the profit of, the police. "So, this is the music I listened to pretty much all throughout junior high school," Bowman told me. "Stuff with that sort of theme, while, like, sister being addicted to crack in real life and kids getting shot in real life and friends dealing drugs in real life," he said.

In 1999, Bowman became an educator, rising to the position of principal, and watched as a new generation of youngsters became politicized in the wake of Trayvon Martin's death, though he knew their activism was built on the back of decades of pain. This new movement was deliberately leaderless: one lesson that the left had drawn from repression of the civil rights and antiwar movements of the 1960s and '70s was that concentrating too much power in leaders left movements vulnerable to collapse in the wake of an assassination or arrest. There were early signs that the lack of direction or leadership, combined with algorithmic amplification and the instantaneous nature of the platforms, could send the energy spiraling in unpredictable ways.

One of the most visible of these signs came in December 2013, just ahead of the holidays, when an obscure public relations official named Justine Sacco strolled Heathrow airport awaiting the last leg of her flight to South Africa, where she had been born and where she visited family often. She fired off a quick joke to her 170 Twitter followers: "Going to Africa. Hope I don't get AIDS. Just kidding. I'm white!"

Sacco thought the form and the point of the quip was obvious. She was lampooning white privilege by embodying a parody of an ignorant Westerner. "I thought there was no way that anyone could possibly think it was literal," she later explained. "Living in America puts us in a bit of a bubble when it comes to what is going on in the third world. I was making fun of that bubble."

But, in the moment, she couldn't explain. She was in the air for eleven hours without internet as the world erupted below her. The slash-and-burn website Gawker had posted her tweet, and soon she was the top trending topic worldwide, with thousands of people calling for her to be fired or worse. Soon the hashtag HasJustineLandedYet began trending, with celebrities and organizations weighing in to condemn her. When she finally turned on her phone in Cape Town, she got a message from someone she hadn't seen since high school. "I'm so sorry to see what's happening," the friend texted a confused Sacco. Then her best friend texted her: "You need to call me immediately." When she called and learned what had happened, she allowed her friend to delete all her social media accounts. Sacco was quickly fired.

A few months later, in March 2014, another joke sparked a new trending war. Dan Snyder, then the owner of the team still called the Washington Redskins, had responded to pressure to change the team name by announcing the creation of the "Washington Redskins Original Americans Foundation." Stephen Colbert parodied the announcement, with his show's Twitter account posting, "I am willing to show #Asian community I care by introducing the Ching-Chong Ding-Dong

Foundation for Sensitivity to Orientals or Whatever." A young activist took offense, urging her followers to trend the hashtag CancelColbert.

The term *cancel* had kicked around as slang in young Black communities since the early 1980s, but by the mid-2010s it had migrated to Black Twitter to mean the rejection of something or somebody. American pop culture derives much of its lingo from Black culture, with cancellation being just the latest example. The concept, which had evolved from an expression of a personal dislike to an urging of complete social elimination, gave activists and those newly awakened to injustice—who appropriated another term from Black culture, *woke*—achievable targets in a world that seemed stacked against genuine progress. Its new usage coincided with a general reorientation away from the kinds of broad structural fights the Sanders campaign wanted to engage in.

And while mobilizing a global army against Justine Sacco may have been absurd, the rise of cell phone cameras continued to give online activists much more serious crimes to confront. In July 2014, Eric Garner died on Staten Island after officers—who suspected Garner of selling loose, untaxed cigarettes, a misdemeanor—slammed him to the ground and put him in a choke hold, refusing to let up even as he pleaded, "I can't breathe." Bystander video captured the scene. In August 2014, eighteen-year-old Michael Brown was killed in Ferguson, Missouri, by police officer Darren Wilson. Spontaneous protests were met with a militarized police response, and the demonstrations spread after prosecutors refused to indict Wilson for the shooting. With each shooting, subsequent news cycle, and resulting protests, more young people would be pulled from the sidelines into the fray.

In Ferguson, Cori Bush, a local nurse, saw the brutal police crackdown and decided to help however she could, volunteering as a medic night after night as the protests wore on. In Connecticut, a high school student named Alexandra Rojas showed up at a Black Lives Matter rally as the first political act in a journey that would take her to the Bernie Sanders campaign and then to a new organization called Justice Democrats, which would back Cori Bush in her bid for Congress.

In October 2014, Chicago police shot and killed seventeen-year-old Laquan McDonald as he walked away from them. (Video of the shooting confirmed the accounts of eyewitnesses but would be suppressed by Rahm Emanuel, who by then was Chicago's mayor.) In November 2014, Cleveland police shot and killed twelve-year-old Tamir Rice, again sparking protests.

In early December, though, a New York grand jury declined to indict the officer who killed Eric Garner, the result that had clearly been sought by the Republican district attorney, who parlayed the situation into a congressional seat. Weeks later, following nationwide protests, Ismaaiyl Abdullah Brinsley, claiming he was seeking "revenge" for Garner, traveled from Baltimore to Brooklyn and executed two NYPD officers at random. The shocking display of violence put a lid on the Black Lives Matter movement for several months.

But it didn't stop police violence, and in April 2015, Walter Scott, another unarmed Black man, was shot in the back and killed by police in North Charleston, South Carolina, an incident also captured on video; the footage, which went viral, showed that police claims against Scott had been fabricated. That same month, Freddie Gray's death in police custody led to protests and then riots in Baltimore. In June 2015, a white teen murdered nine parishioners at Charleston's Emanuel AME Church, a shocking massacre that blended the mushrooming crisis of mass shootings with racial injustice. In November 2015, Jamar Clark was shot by police in the Twin Cities area, sparking protests that were joined by Ilhan Omar, then an activist and rising star in the local political scene. In the summer of 2016, Philando Castile, a legal gun owner, was pulled over and shot after warning the police that he was licensed to carry a firearm. The officer was acquitted, and Omar and others again came out into the streets. She was practiced by then. In high school, she had watched in 2002 as Minneapolis police surrounded a Somali man waving a machete and showing signs of mental illness. As a crowd that included Omar gathered, he was killed on the spot, and the Somali community protested for days. Relations between the local community and the police would only deteriorate.

During the Obama presidency, public opinion was swinging rapidly in a more progressive direction on the question of race and racism. And structural advances were still being made, despite the lack of a congressional majority. In cities across the country, the Department of Justice was investigating police corruption and enforcing reforms through consent orders. On June 26, 2015, in a 5–4 ruling written by Justice Anthony Kennedy and joined by the four liberals still on the Court, marriage equality was declared a constitutional right. (The opinion was handed down just ten days after the launch of Donald Trump's presidential campaign. Three years later, Trump would tap Brett Kavanaugh as Kennedy's replacement.) The next month, the Obama administration announced that the military would allow transgender members to serve openly. With the bulk of its LGB agenda enacted culturally, judicially, or legislatively, the movement had turned in earnest toward the *T*. In February 2016, Charlotte, North Carolina, passed an ordinance allowing transgender people to use the bathroom aligned with their gender identity. The Republican state legislature responded with HB2, which became infamous as its "bathroom bill"—banning people from using the bathroom that matched their gender identity.

Chad Griffin, president of the Human Rights Campaign, flew to North Carolina to meet with Republican governor Pat McCrory. McCrory later told evangelical allies that he thought Griffin had come to negotiate compromise legislation. But Griffin had a different message to deliver: Human Rights Campaign would spend fifty million dollars in the coming election to make an example of McCrory, so that no future governor ever tried anything similar. The Obama administration issued an executive order implementing the trans-friendly ordinance passed in Charlotte, where the federal government had jurisdiction without legislation, and Griffin's organization led a boycott campaign that cost North Carolina billions and made good on Human Rights Campaign's promise by knocking McCrory out of office even as Trump carried the state. Trump, surveying the wreckage left by the boycott, said during his campaign that the bathroom bill had been wrong, another of his heterodox cultural positions.

While Bernie Sanders's campaign blended easily with climate activists—several of his top aides came directly from the movement—Hillary Clinton wasn't entirely off base to note that Sanders was indeed, as then *Washington Post* journalist David Weigel had put it, not entirely familiar with these "causes of the rising left."

Sanders stumbled at times with the new rhetoric, though Clinton did, too. In the summer of 2015, Clinton was criticized by Black Lives Matter activists for saying that "all lives matter," which they saw as her avoiding explicitly affirming that *Black* lives mattered. In a June 2015 interview with NPR, Sanders was pressed repeatedly on whether Clinton's phrasing was out of touch. He brushed off the question, pivoting instead to economics. "When we talk about issues, whether it's guns, whether it's police brutality, we should also understand something else about Ferguson. You know what the unemployment rate [is] for young African Americans in Ferguson, which virtually nobody talks about?"

"Remind us," *Morning Edition*'s David Greene said.

"Fifty percent," said Sanders. Greene asked if Sanders could return to the question on phrasing. "When the lives matter, it means we're not going to accept police brutality or illegal behavior against young African Americans *or* anybody else," Sanders said, emphasizing the *or*. "But when you talk about 'lives matter,' sometimes what we forget is when fifty-one percent of young African American kids are unemployed, are those lives that matter?"

Greene pressed again, twice, finally telling Sanders it sounded like he didn't want to use the phrase.

"Phraseology," Sanders spat, huffing audibly. "Of course I'll use that phrase. Black lives matter. White lives matter. Hispanic lives matter. But these are also not only police matters, they're not only gun control matters"—the first half of the interview had been spent knocking Sanders for a Vermont record on gun rights that was out of step with Democrats' post–Sandy Hook politics—"they are significantly economic matters.

"Wait a minute," he said as Greene tried to cut in, "let me just answer this, because it's too easy for quote-unquote liberals to be saying, 'Well, let's use this phrase.' Well, what are we gonna do about fifty-one percent of young African Americans unemployed? We need a massive jobs program to put Black kids to work—and white kids to work, and Hispanic kids to work. It's sometimes easy to say, 'Worry about which phrase you're going to use.' It's a lot harder to stand up to the billionaire class and say, 'You know what, you're gonna have to pay some taxes, you can't get away with putting your money in tax havens, because we need that money to create millions of jobs for Black kids, for white kids, for Hispanic kids.'"

For Sanders, liberals were deploying social justice rhetoric and policing phraseology precisely so they could avoid confronting the one percent yet retain their progressive credentials. Yet the Sanders quote—"White lives matter"—ricocheted around social media, and he became a target for protests. The next month, when he appeared at the annual Netroots Nation conference, a conclave of progressive operatives, Black Lives Matter protesters disrupted a town hall he was participating in. "I've spent fifty years of my life fighting for civil rights. If you don't want me to be here, that's okay," said a typically cantankerous Sanders. In Seattle that August, protesters took the stage, bumping Sanders off.

Speaking just before Sanders on stage that day was congressional candidate Pramila Jayapal, then serving as a Washington state senator. She had told the Sanders campaign she was leaning toward endorsing him, but had concerns around the issues of racial justice, gun control, and abortion rights. But he had such a dearth of endorsements from elected officials that at least being open to supporting him was enough to get her onto the stage. After the event, she and Sanders, along with his wife, Jane Sanders, and Jayapal's child, who had yet to transition, found a table at the back of a dimly lit bar, where Sanders stewed about the turmoil. "He was sort of in a bit of a stubborn place," Jayapal told me. "He's like, 'Well, I just hired Symone Sanders'"—his first Black senior adviser—"'and we're gonna work on articulating that better.' I laugh sometimes, because I think that was when he said to her, we need a racial justice agenda." Sanders recounted his time as a civil rights activist in Chicago in the 1960s. "It's not enough just to say I marched with Dr. King and I was there, which he absolutely was," Jayapal said, telling him, "That should be the basis of how you talk about your understanding of race. But you also have to think about it as it's developed over the decades." Jayapal eventually got behind him, becoming the first state elected official to endorse him, and went on to win her election to Congress.

Sanders released a statement later that day. "I was especially disappointed because on criminal justice reform and the need to fight racism there is no other candidate for president who will fight harder than me," it read.

So, when Hillary Clinton, in Nevada in February 2016, finally recast Sanders's critique of the big banks as a way for him to avoid confronting racism, the Democratic voting base had been primed to hear the attack as a reasonable one.

Still, the crowds being drawn by Sanders reflected the explosive cultural and political phenomenon that his campaign represented. Elizabeth Warren—the namesake of what had until then been dubbed the "Warren wing" of the Democratic Party—had taken a pass on the race, believing Clinton to be unstoppable and hoping to influence her personnel instead. Instead, Clinton would fall short of the White

House, and a new Sanders wing would nudge Warren out of her lead-ing role.

Yet she remained focused on her mantra that personnel was policy, planting seeds that would only grow years later. In early 2016, she sat down for what would become a pivotal dinner. She had been watching the work of Barry Lynn's anti-monopoly team with interest, and it fit with her long-standing focus on breaking up and bringing to heel the big banks. While Sanders and the Squad had risen to prominence as democratic socialists, Warren had been a Republican before evolving into a Democrat. That legacy revealed itself in the way she framed her policy critiques and proposals as aimed at supporting the development of free markets. "I am a capitalist to my bones," she famously said. "I believe in markets. What I don't believe in is theft, what I don't believe in is cheating. That's where the difference is. I love what markets can do, I love what functioning economies can do. They are what make us rich, they are what create opportunity. But only fair markets, markets with rules."

Warren reached out to Lynn to set up the dinner, and Lynn brought along a deputy named Lina Khan and an attorney named Jonathan Kanter. Khan and Kanter laid out their idea for reimagining and rein-vigorating antitrust policy, and Warren saw in it a reflection, and an extension, of her anti-corruption politics, which helpfully contrasted with a democratic socialist reluctance to embrace markets. In June 2016, she delivered a major speech on antitrust policy at Lynn's Open Markets Institute, laying down a marker in what would become a hot issue on the populist right as well as left in coming years.

But by March 2016, with Clinton's slim lead padded heavily by so-called super delegates—party elites, operatives, and lobbyists given extra votes in the nominating process—it was clear the primary was over, even if Sanders intended to soldier on. Their effort would also quickly, if accidentally, transform the Democratic Party.

2

A BRAND NEW CONGRESS

The Movement for Black Lives, which had both propelled and bedeviled Sanders, brought an entire generation of activists into politics. One of those it swept in was Alexandra Rojas, who, as a high school student, was moved to attend her first protest after a police shooting in Hartford, Connecticut. She had grown up in working-class East Hartford, the daughter of a Colombian immigrant mother and a Peruvian American father who'd been born in the United States. When Rojas was in fifth grade, her father got a good job in Glastonbury, a wealthy, white, tony village seven miles distant, but a world away from East Hartford.

That summer, when she went to Lima to visit family, she found the contrast intense. "When I showed up, they had no roof. It was like a broken building, and it just had a tarp over it, like a literal tarp instead of a roof," she said of her aunt's home. She also visited Cusco, where her extended family lived as subsistence farmers. She came home with almost nothing, having given everything she had to relatives. "As a teen, I got super angry," she said. "I couldn't go to the malls, couldn't go anywhere, because I was just, like, 'God, people are complaining about their lunch food,'" she said.

As she thought about college, Rojas learned that California allowed people who lived in the state for a year and a day to get in-state tuition. She saved money from her senior-year job at McDonald's and, before she'd even officially graduated high school, went west to plant her residency roots. There, she worked multiple minimum wage jobs to survive the next year, so she could enroll in Orange Coast College, a public community college that is a top feeder school to UC schools such as UCLA and Berkeley.

While at Orange Coast, Rojas became active in student government and fought an effort to slash programs aimed at nontraditional
students, such as one that offered classes at eight in the morning or
after work hours. But, as the time to transfer drew near, California, to
save itself money, tweaked its eligibility rules in a way that meant she
could no longer get in-state tuition.

It was around this time, in May 2015, while she was sitting in a
coffee shop, that a friend who had recruited her to student government, Lynn Hua, sent Rojas a YouTube clip that would change her life.
In it, a granddad with wild white hair and a rumpled suit, set against
the backdrop of Lake Champlain, declared a revolution.

"Today, with your support and the support of millions of people
throughout this country, we begin a political revolution to transform
our country economically, politically, socially, and environmentally,"
Bernie Sanders said. "My fellow Americans: this country faces more
serious problems today than at any time since the Great Depression,
and if you include the planetary crisis of climate change, it may well
be that the challenges we face now are direr than any time in our
modern history."

Rojas gazed at the scholarship applications she'd been contemplating. "I listened to [the video clip], and I just fell in love, and I
was just like, 'Oh my God, I've got to do everything,'" she recalled. "I
started working with [Hua] and two other kids just in our volunteer
time, organizing all the community colleges, because they're a totally
untapped resource of all these working-class people." By the fall, her
work organizing community college students across Orange County
behind the Sanders banner was noticed by senior staff on the Sanders campaign, and Rojas and three of her allies there were offered
internships.

The catch was they had to get to Burlington. "They were all working-
class people with no money in the bank; it was really hard for them to
go," said Zack Exley, a senior Sanders aide who helped bring in the
Orange County students. The four of them piled into a white Nissan
Murano, their luggage tied to the roof and hanging off the back, and
drove across the country.

Rojas didn't last long as merely a Sanders campaign intern; she
finagled her way onto the digital team, where she helped with the Text

for Bernie program and handled logistics for volunteer events known as barnstorms. "You have to remember, in the very beginning, it was very hard for the Bernie campaign to hire pros," said senior staffer Becky Bond, "because it was just very clear that you'd be totally blackballed, not just from a White House or a federal agency job, but from any of the Democratic-aligned institutions. Even vendors who weren't employed by the Clinton campaign didn't want to work for the Bernie campaign, because they were worried about not getting business in the future. The professionals that joined were really true believers, like me and Zack, and then we really had to fill out the ranks from the super volunteers who'd never worked in politics before."

Another true believer was Corbin Trent. In 2000, when Trent was twenty, he inherited two fading manufacturing companies in Morristown, Tennessee, from his grandfather B. C. Trent. "I ran the metalworking business into the ground," Trent said, citing his decision to upgrade equipment and, against objections, computerize the factory. "Maybe the old fuckers knew what they were doing."

The woodworking business lasted longer. But the company, which made component parts for other furniture makers—the curved back of a barstool, for instance—suffered as its buyers went out of business or left the country one by one. Trent understood that he was witnessing the knock-on effect of NAFTA, the North American Free Trade Agreement implemented in 1994 under Bill Clinton, and CAFTA, the 2004 version that extended the regime farther south to include Central America and the Dominican Republic.

The woodworking firm went under in 2007, as the economy was imploding, and Trent went to culinary school. But the life of a high-end chef meant catering to rich people, and seeing wealth up close was too much for him. He was cooking in tony Armonk, New York, at Restaurant North, a four-time James Beard Foundation Award–nominated establishment where lunch tabs would routinely run into the five figures.

The lunch that did it for him cost roughly $18,000, which wasn't in itself out of the ordinary. It was the wine the table ordered: a bottle of Romanée-Conti priced at around $10,000, from grapes grown by a grandfather and grandson on a small plot of land in France. Trent had been reading about the wine, known as one of the best and most expensive in the world, and he felt privileged just to be able to pour it. When the diners left, he noticed unfinished glasses and a bottle that was still half full. Boiling inside at the waste, he poured the wine back into the bottle, corked it, and quit. "I decided right there 'I'm not spending my time, talent, or energy making these people's lives any better,'" he said.

So he moved back to Tennessee and launched a successful food truck, Crazy Good Burgers. It grew to include a second truck, and when that one burned down, he pulled off an internet fund-raiser to get it going again. Then came a third truck.

When Bernie Sanders jumped into the presidential race, Trent dropped everything, selling the food truck business and organizing "Tennesseans for Bernie." He reached out to Zack Exley—finally contacting him only by guessing at every possible iteration of his email—and asked if Sanders would come to northeast Tennessee if Trent promised that five thousand people would show up. The answer was no, but Exley was intrigued at the organizing under way in the region, and the two stayed in touch.

Exley put Trent to work, first in compiling a fifty-state guide to voter registration and then in calling state Sanders chapters to help them with organizing logistics. Eventually, Trent was brought on officially as a campaign staffer.

The third true believer, and unusual and consequential hire, was Saikat Chakrabarti. After graduating from Harvard in 2007 with a computer science degree, Chakrabarti briefly worked for a hedge fund and then became the second engineer for Stripe, the fifth employee of one of the internet's dominant payment processors. When the Sanders campaign launched, Chakrabarti queried his network to find a connection inside, and like all the others that turned out to be super-connector Zack Exley. Exley brought him on board.

"We both realized that Saikat"—pronounced SHROY-cot— "couldn't just contribute as a software developer. [He] started off doing a bunch of tech stuff, but, slowly, we pulled him in and made sure that a bunch of his portfolio was actually helping us both do and manage the organizing work," said Becky Bond.

In March 2016, as Sanders was determined to fight on to the convention, Exley, Rojas, Trent, and Chakrabarti left the campaign, concluding correctly that their candidate no longer had a path to the nomination. They spent the next year—significantly, thanks to

Chakrabarti—putting together what would become Brand New Congress and, then, Justice Democrats.

In December of that year, in the wake of Trump's election, Alexandria Ocasio-Cortez cobbled together the money to travel to the Standing Rock Indian Reservation, which straddles North and South Dakota, to join the protest against the Keystone XL Pipeline. Before she headed out, her brother, Gabriel, submitted her name to Brand New Congress as a potential primary challenger to Rep. Joe Crowley, known as the "King of Queens" and widely considered the most likely replacement for Speaker Nancy Pelosi when she stepped aside. His sister hadn't objected, but she was by no means committed to the idea.

The Keystone XL protest encampment was a challenging place to be at any time, but in December 2016 it was brutally cold, and the private, militarized police working on behalf of the pipeline companies had ramped up their use of violence. Seeing the grit and the sacrifice on display on the reservation would have been enough to put anybody's circumstances in perspective, but for Ocasio-Cortez, the scene was life-altering. If the people there could fight this hard for their land, surely she could mount a bid for Congress. Something new had to be done, she thought, as neither political party was up to the challenge of the moment. And that something, for her, would be to run for that seat.

This, she understood, was what she wanted to do. "I saw a fossil fuel corporation that had literally militarized itself against American people," she said later, "and I saw that our incumbents in both parties were defending [that corporation] and were silent. And I just felt like we're at a point where we can't afford to be silent anymore, and we can't afford to sit out a political process that we may have grown very cynical over." She thought about her brother's submission of her name to Brand New Congress and decided to take it seriously.

Brand New Congress was thinking the same thing. Ocasio-Cortez fit the profile of the types of candidates the group had decided it needed. Appealing to a multiracial working-class coalition meant recruiting candidates that looked like the demographics of their districts. And shedding the Bernie Bro baggage was made easier if the candidate wasn't white and wasn't male.

When Ocasio-Cortez returned to the Bronx, she got a call from Isra Allison, a top official at Brand New Congress. A few more video calls led to a dinner in New York City with Zack Exley and Saikat Chakrabarti. They wanted to make sure she didn't have the vibe of an activist that would turn off voters. Exley was assured. "She was obviously a normal person," he said. "That might be a loaded term, but she was not a subcultural lefty or subcultural person of any weird little fringe subculture. She was a person who could communicate with anyone and make a connection with anyone."

In May, Ocasio-Cortez filed her paperwork—with Knoxville, Tennessee, listed as the location of her campaign committee, home of Brand New Congress.

Yet the hyperpolarization fueled by the Trump presidency had made running candidates in both primaries untenable. By the end of 2017, it was clear that the national coalition wasn't coming together in time; they had nowhere near the 435 hoped-for candidates across the two organizations and the national buzz they hoped would transfer from Sanders to their effort to throw out every bum hadn't materialized. They needed to pivot, and in December 2017 they gathered in Knoxville, Tennessee, to chart a new way forward.

Waleed Shahid, a progressive operative who had since joined the organization, delivered a presentation he prepared with Max Berger aimed at reorienting the movement's thinking about its path to power, a copy of which was provided to me.

The argument from the Hillary Clinton campaign that Sanders struggled with voters of color, he argued, wasn't entirely wrong. The key insight in his presentation: "Sanders lost every contest with at least a 10 percent Black population, except Michigan, and each state where Latinos make up at least 10 percent of eligible voters." That deficit needed to be confronted. "We need a narrative that weaves together race and class to put forth a new idea of America and [to] wage a fight within the Democratic Party," the text for his presentation reads over a photo of Jesse Jackson marching on behalf of jobs.

Shahid reached back to cite Georgia politician Tom Watson, who had led a multiracial populist movement in the late nineteenth century. "You are kept apart that you may be separately fleeced of your earnings," Watson had famously told a crowd of white and Black farmers. "You are made to hate each other because upon that hatred is rested the keystone of the arch of financial despotism which enslaves you both."

Shahid noted that the Rev. Dr. Martin Luther King Jr. had picked up the same analysis some eighty years later. "Many poor whites were the derivative victims of slavery," King wrote.

As long as labor was cheapened by the involuntary servitude of the black man, the freedom of white labor, especially in the South, was little more than a myth. It was free only to bargain from the depressed base imposed by slavery upon the whole labor market. Nor did this derivative bondage end when formal slavery gave way to the de-facto slavery of discrimination. To this day the white poor also suffer deprivation and the humiliations of poverty if not of color. They are chained by the weight of discrimination, though its badge of degradation does not mark them. It corrupts their lives, frustrates their opportunities and withers their education. In one sense, it is more evil for them, because it has confused so many by prejudice that they have supported their own oppressors.

Shahid's presentation was rooted in that legacy, noting that racism had been deployed to break the back of Reconstruction and then, later, the Populist movement and that it undermined the New Deal. He quoted Michelle Alexander, author of *The New Jim Crow*, to lay out the dilemma: "It's no coincidence that the democracies with the most generous social welfare programs are the most ethnically homogenous: Norway, Sweden, Denmark."

Several weeks earlier, Shahid had argued in a memo that in order to undo the narrative that the Sanders movement was just a bunch of angry young white men they needed to narrow their focus even further, given how far out of contention so many of their candidates were, and focus on a handful of races that would land like grenades in Washington. But whom should they focus on? New York's Fourteenth District, he argued, had all the pieces in place for an upset. Joe Crowley had been in office for decades as the district had transformed underneath him. He was being bandied about as the next House Speaker, so taking him down would leave a mark. "I think we should focus entirely on Ocasio as our sole OG. She needs a lot of help," he wrote in a memo, describing her as their original gangsta. "She doesn't have a lot of connections in the district in terms of either volunteers or political leads or potential donors who would donate $500 or more. It's a real problem. She doesn't have a lot of leadership of doing things inside her district that gained her respect over the years unlike someone like [Lancaster, Pennsylvania's] Jess King."

His district had changed, and Crowley was now out of touch. Indeed, the Queens native had long worried that changes to the area he represented could leave him politically vulnerable, and in the previous redistricting battle, he had come out on the losing end of a classic New York politics knife fight. Ocasio-Cortez, for her part, understood intellectually that she was the right woman at the right moment. "He can't get challenged by any down-ballot incumbent," she said during the campaign, understanding that such a challenge would be the end of the challenger's career. "Anybody who wants to keep their job in New York City would never dream of challenging Joe Crowley. It has to come from outside of Queens. It has to come from someone who's new on the political scene that they don't see coming, that they can't offer a job or pressure in another way. And it has to be somebody who represents our community in more ways than one. Basically, an insurgent, outside, grassroots candidate who's a woman of color from the Bronx."

It made sense in principle. But on the ground, they were making little progress. Ocasio-Cortez was still working four days a week at two bars, and he had to schedule calls with her while she rode the bus to work and back. *This just isn't possible*, he thought. By the end of the year, his candidate had raised just over ten thousand dollars, barely enough to fund a small-time county council race.

Shahid, who had been dispatched during the summer of 2017 to help her campaign, battled with Ocasio-Cortez over "call time"—the dialing-for-dollars every candidate needed to do to raise money in big clips. Ocasio-Cortez hated it with a passion. One afternoon, Shahid pulled up their shared spreadsheet and saw that Ocasio-Cortez hadn't entered anything from her scheduled call time.

"I texted," the Millennial insurgent explained to her Millennial campaign aide.

"That's not how it works," said a flabbergasted Shahid.

To shut him up, Ocasio-Cortez sent him a screenshot of a text conversation that ended with a voter promising to give two hundred dollars. (Shahid didn't know it, but the donor was Chakrabarti's spouse.)

Crowley, by that point in the cycle, had several million dollars in cash on hand. In December, after one of her many fights with Shahid over fund-raising, Ocasio-Cortez took to Twitter to vent.

Consultants: "Why don't more working-class people/women/people of color run for office?"

Consultants: "If you're going to run you need to raise at least $200k through your network or don't even bother."

Consultants: "Such a mystery."

The group debated the idea but didn't commit. Instead, uncertain of a path forward, Justice Democrats pulled out of her race. "I will never forget the call when they told me I was dropped and that I was on my own," she told me. "And I was like . . . but you guys promised us you'd support us if we ran. I was devastated. And they were like, 'Sorry, it just didn't turn out how we thought.' And I asked if I should close the campaign and they said that was up to me but to not expect a lot."

She was crushed and considered dropping out. "I had to figure out if I save everyone the embarrassment and close up shop or if I keep going," she said. "Basically the conclusion I came to was that by that point I had been doing canvassing and events for six months straight, and there were people who were really invested and believed in what we were doing, and I owed it to them to see it through Election Day and give it the best we got."

She said she successfully pitched the video platform NowThis on covering her campaign, which she turned into a Facebook ad, which raised enough money for a two-minute video that would go viral and raise enough for an office and two staffers. "JD had zero percent involvement in any of that part; they had pulled out," she said.

Fortunately for Ocasio-Cortez, her path to victory didn't require an extraordinary amount of money, or even that many votes. The Queens Democratic Party, aka the Queens machine, of which Crowley was the head, maintained its political dominance through the ballot—not the ballot box, but *access to the ballot itself.* Getting on it was extraordinarily difficult. The sheer number of signatures required—1,250—

wasn't the daunting part. If any mistakes were found, the entire page of signatures could be ruled invalid. Every signer had to be a registered voter in the district, and the canvassers had to be registered to vote in the district, too. The machine appointed all the local judges, and any challenges made by the machine went before those judges. The petition deadline was only two months before the primary, so a court challenge could effectively keep a would-be candidate off the campaign trail for much of that time.

Ocasio-Cortez's plan was simple: get enough signatures that a court challenge would be unlikely and then get just enough votes in a low-turnout election to win. "The default setting for the race was that Crowley was going to get almost no votes—that's how they structure it in these primaries," Exley said. The congressional primary was set for late June, while the state-level races—governor, state senator, and so on—were scheduled for September, diluting interest. The machine theory was that in a low-turnout affair the die-hard voters (mostly elderly) cast ballots and that this electorate tended to share a personal connection to or an affinity for the incumbent. It's a structure that has been extraordinarily effective at protecting forty-eight incumbents, but it has an obvious weak spot: if a challenger generated just enough votes, they could knock somebody out without needing millions of dollars. "There were two questions," said Exley. "Can we turn out some number of votes? And then the other question was: Could Crowley turn out a bunch of *additional* votes?" In other words, could the machine still fire on all cylinders?

The petition drive was organized by mom and food blogger Naureen Akhter, who had previously tried to volunteer for the local Democratic Party but was ignored. Sometimes alone, sometimes with a handful of volunteers, she scoured the district in a five-week-long sprint, not stopping until the last moment. The campaign turned in more than five thousand signatures, well more than they needed, but enough, they hoped, to overcome the expected lawsuit from Crowley. For years, the way incumbents had kept challengers off the ballot was by suing to invalidate signatures on technicalities in front of the machine-appointed local judges. "Here we are, April twelfth, 2018, and we're on the ballot," Ocasio-Cortez told a documentary camera crew following her, after dropping off her petition. "Unless he sues us."

In a decision he likely regrets to this day, Joe Crowley did not sue, and the sprint to June 26 was on. Suing would have been a bad look for a man seeking to maintain enough progressive cred to become Speaker, which may have influenced his decision not to. "If he were running against an older white man, he'd probably have sued," Akhter guessed.

In January, Chakrabarti put the all-in plan in motion, stepping down from Justice Democrats and moving to New York to work full-time on Ocasio-Cortez's campaign. In the spring, Rojas and Trent left Knoxville for New York. Trent handled press for her, Rojas managed the field program. "It was a chip-pushing-in moment. If that didn't work, our whole thing was done," Trent said. "Justice Dems just went all in and just diverted it all to her." The group had a list of about 330,000 members, and they pounded away to fund-raise for Ocasio-Cortez and find people willing to canvass and work the phone bank. "We stopped raising money for anybody else, including ourselves," Trent said.

That, as Chakrabarti had feared, led to some deeply bruised feelings among the other candidates Justice Democrats had recruited and trained, including Cori Bush in Missouri. There would be no national movement. "We abandoned them—promised the world and delivered shit," Trent acknowledged, though he agreed with the difficult decision. "This thing, while it's amazing, was a complete and utter failure for the original idea. I'm not saying it wasn't an insane idea, but that was the idea we were selling people. This is utter, abysmal failure."

Chakrabarti hadn't realized how successful his organization's efforts were to convert the email list into activists until he arrived in the district. Justice Democrats might not have built exactly the movement it had foreseen, but there was indeed something of a movement afoot. A number of the candidates and their teams were in touch throughout 2017, swapping campaign innovations. A critical one was developed by the field team behind Jess King in Pennsylvania and shared with the Ocasio-Cortez crew. (King had beaten a DCCC recruit in the primary, but the district was redrawn by the courts mid-race and turned deep red.) It was, like all such innovations, simple in hindsight. Working from the voter files, they found local residents on social media rather than at their physical residences. They then targeted them with digital ads. Now voters knew who Jess King was and had a sense that there was something substantial behind her, because her name was popping up in their feeds. Having made a potential voter aware of the campaign, they would then follow up by sending a canvasser to knock on their door. The combination of the digital ad and the door knock added up to more than the sum of its parts, as the voter was much more receptive to King's message than they would have been with just a cold call.

With about a month before the election, Ocasio-Cortez's two-minute, format-busting campaign video went viral. "This race is about people versus money," she intones in it. "*We've* got people; *they've* got money. It's time we acknowledge that not all Democrats are the same, that a Democrat who takes corporate money, profits off foreclosure, doesn't live here, doesn't send his kids to our schools, doesn't drink our water or breathe our air, cannot possibly represent us," she says in the ad, whose power lay in its sophisticated approach to the intersection of class and identity.

Just running as a progressive wasn't enough, though. "In the very beginning, I was running with a very strong progressive base and a very strong progressive coalition," Ocasio-Cortez said. "But that alone was not enough to take me over the top. And it was when I really leaned in on this broader message and crafted a progressive message that was rooted in my life story that we were able to really capture a much wider electorate, even though my progressive message was still the same. And so, I think it's important that we don't ignore the power of identity, because it is very powerful."

One week after the video launch, Ocasio-Cortez sat for a video interview with reporter Glenn Greenwald, who asked her to expound on her idea of identity politics. "There are a lot of Trojan horses," she said. "There are a lot of folks who say, 'Vote for me. I am this intersection of different identities,' but at the same time they still try to advance, or are primarily financed by, special interests, so it doesn't necessarily get us to where we need to be."

Identity can't be ignored, she added. "A lot of the problems we sometimes have here—our current social problems—are due to the fact that we've ignored a lot of the history of the United States around issues of race, religion, class, and creed, and because we don't want to discuss the fact that, for example, slavery has essentially evolved [in]to Jim Crow, which has evolved into our mass incarceration system. To pretend that mass incarceration is not tied to race, to pretend that current immigration policy is not tied to racism or xenophobia, is also a mistake," she said. "It's not the fact that I'm a Hispanic woman that allows me to better represent this district; it's the fact that that's a lens that I have to better organize and communicate with the people who live here."

Ocasio-Cortez added that it might be a different question if Crowley had pushed seriously for comprehensive immigration reform, criminal justice reform, or had even bothered to learn Spanish or live in the district. (He lived in Virginia full-time.) "Our identities, whether we like it or not, are a lens. We can never take that lens off," she said. "It's a factor, but it's not *the* factor. At the end of the day, I'm a candidate that doesn't take corporate money, that champions Medicare for All, a federal jobs guarantee, the abolishment of ICE and a Green New Deal."

Crowley didn't help himself on the campaign trail. At one gathering with Queens Millennials—meant to be outreach to the cohort of the community currently turning on him—he stood before a group of about two dozen and made his case for why he should be returned to Congress for a tenth term. In his view, it was "destiny." "I was born for this role," he boasted at the May 20 meet and greet. His opponent was trying to make the campaign "about race"—a strategy he called "unnecessarily divisive" at a time when the party needed to be "fighting Republicans, not other Democrats."

"I can't help that I was born white," he lamented at one point.

Panicked, he also publicized an endorsement he had long ago received from California representative Ro Khanna, before there had been a competitive race. Khanna had been elected in 2016 and quickly became a Justice Democrat; he was later named cochair of the 2020 Sanders campaign. He was mercilessly pummeled online for his Crowley endorsement. Active on Twitter, and responsive to criticism from the left, Khanna rethought his endorsement in real time. After several hours of awkwardly explaining himself, he announced that he was *also* offering an endorsement of Ocasio-Cortez. "If we'd have scripted the whole thing, we couldn't have done it better," Corbin Trent later told me. As absurd as a "dual endorsement" may be, the way the drama unfolded in real time put a brighter spotlight on the race than a simple endorsement could ever have. Khanna wound up being the only member of Congress to endorse Ocasio-Cortez.

That summer, news broke that President Trump had been systematically separating children from their parents and caging them at the border. On June 13, Crowley and other members of Congress, led by civil rights legend Rep. John Lewis, planned to commit civil disobedience at the office of Customs and Border Patrol, to get arrested in protest of Trump's cruel detention policy. But the police ignored the members of Congress, refusing to arrest them. So they marched to the White House, in the hope that the Secret Service would be more obliging. But it was a brutally hot day, and a profusely sweating Crowley wobbled and fainted while walking up Fifteenth Street. It made headlines back home.

Crowley's private polling had him up by 30 points, but in such a low-turnout environment, it didn't feel safe with the surging energy around Ocasio-Cortez. "The campaign just grew exponentially" in those last several weeks, recalled Naureen Akhtar. Crowley started blanketing the airwaves with TV ads, filling mailboxes with glossy flyers, and robocalling Democratic voters. He also agreed to a debate.

At their only candidate debate, on Friday, June 15, neither side delivered a knockout blow, but Ocasio-Cortez more than held her own. In some significant ways, the debate took place on the challenger's political turf. She had embraced a position that was popular online among progressives—that the government ought to "Abolish ICE," that is, shut down the Immigration and Customs Enforcement agency. As with "defund the police," the policy behind the saying was nuanced, but the blunt language gave party operatives heartburn and allowed the right to caricature the position. But rather than Ocasio-Cortez's call to abolish ICE becoming a liability, Trump's caging of children made *Crowley*'s refusal to call for its abolition a problem. Crowley had referred to ICE as fascist—why, Ocasio-Cortez wondered aloud to the local television audience, was it controversial to shut down a fascist agency?

The pair was scheduled for a second debate, to be held on the following Monday, this one hosted by Ocasio-Cortez's neighborhood newspaper, the *Parkchester Times*. Before it started, Ocasio-Cortez spotted Crowley's spokeswoman, Lauren French, in the venue and assumed that Crowley had shown up. Instead, she learned, he was in Queens at a community meeting. Citing a scheduling conflict, he had sent a surrogate instead, Annabel Palma, a former city council member.

In Washington, the conventional understanding of Crowley's loss was that he had been caught sleeping. Exhibit A was his skipping the Bronx debate. That point misses, though, given that he had just debated Ocasio-Cortez on television—so it's not as if he were ignoring her—and it also misunderstands *why* he skipped the debate. Crowley believed, tactically, that he potentially had more to lose by showing up. That this blew up in his face does not change the fact that he thought skipping was the smarter move. It was a poor political decision, but one made not because he considered Ocasio-Cortez a lightweight. On the contrary, he had a genuine sense of the threat, and he responded by trying to minimize it.

An editorial that ran in the *New York Times* that Tuesday had a major impact on the race. "When asking New Yorkers for their vote, most candidates would begin by showing up," the broadside began. "Not Representative Joseph Crowley." It ended with just as much of a bang: "Mr. Crowley is far from the first candidate to decline to debate a challenger he is heavily favored to beat," the *Times* editorial board noted. "But his seat is not his entitlement. He'd better hope that voters don't react to his snubs by sending someone else to do the job."

In the final weeks, a flood of small-donor dollars from across the country poured in, as people began to believe Ocasio-Cortez could actually pull this thing off, Khanna's unusual dual endorsement having triggered a tsunami of money. The cash was immediately pumped into paid canvassers, who buttressed the sidewalk-weary volunteers who'd been pounding on doors for months. "It felt like the cavalry had arrived," Akhter recalled.

With troops on the ground the weekend before the election, Ocasio-Cortez pulled something unusual: she left. She flew to Tornillo, Texas, and took part in a demonstration outside a temporary detention facility holding children who were seeking asylum. Her call to abolish ICE intersected with the moment in a way nobody could have predicted, as the country was hitting a moral rock bottom. A photo of her leaning against a Texas fence, crying as she looked on, would become both iconic and a meme deployed against her in the years to come.

That same weekend, Crowley aide Lauren French met a friend for drinks, and the friend, intrigued at the online enthusiasm for Ocasio-

Cortez, asked if the insurgent had a chance of toppling French's boss. "She'll get ten percent and get a job with *The Young Turks*," French quipped. Ro Khanna's communications director had been friends with French before the primary, but after the election, French told them, "Never talk to me again."

As the sun was setting on June 26, 2018, Election Day, canvassers reconvened in the Bronx and swapped stories about what they'd seen. With no exit polling, anecdotes were all they had—but they were adding up to something that warranted optimism.

Many of the voters had appeared, to the canvassers, like stereotypical young Bernie Sanders supporters. According to a precinct-by-precinct analysis of the results, Ocasio-Cortez's success can be attributed, in large part, to the strategy of mobilizing so-called drop-off voters, folks who had voted in the 2016 presidential campaign but who rarely voted in midterms. The drop-off voters, it seemed, hadn't dropped off, and the analysis undercut the prevalent media narrative, which suggested that Ocasio-Cortez won only because she was Hispanic and got the votes of Hispanics. In fact, it was presumed that Crowley, Irish American and from Queens, would perform better there than Ocasio-Cortez, who was expected to carry her home borough. The analysis, having mapped out votes across the district, found the exact opposite of the pundits' conclusions: Crowley was crushed almost everywhere, but he did better in the Bronx than in Queens.

Gentrifiers, even among gentrifiers, remain an unpopular demographic, and so it can be uncomfortable to acknowledge the role they played in Ocasio-Cortez's win. (Though Trent, ever the straight talker, had no such compunction: "It was the gentrifiers," he said.) But while the economic resources traditionally possessed by gentrifiers often exacerbate the financial pressures felt by long-term residents, after the 2008 global financial crisis and the Great Recession, crushing student debt and soaring rents meant that many of these new residents of Queens and the Bronx were decidedly downwardly mobile and had political interests that aligned more closely with those of longtime residents.

In the car on the way to the billiard hall hosting her Election Night watch party, Ocasio-Cortez wouldn't let anyone look at their phones, even as the clock struck nine and the numbers began coming in. She couldn't look. As they approached the hall, though, she saw something startling: reporters sprinting to get into her party. She stepped out of the car. On the sidewalk, she and Riley paused for a long embrace. "Whatever happens, I love you," he told her.

Just moments after she entered, the crowd exploded in celebration as the chyron on the TV screen behind the bar flashed her victory. She cupped her hands to her mouth. "Oh my God," she said. Without hesitation and with nothing prepared and no expectation that she was going to win, she stepped onto a barstool and delivered a barn-burning speech to a crowd that was small—maybe fifty to seventy-five people—but overcome by a mixture of shock and ecstasy.

"This victory tonight belongs to each and every single person in this room," she declared, gesturing around the small, tightly packed bar. "Every person out here this evening changed America tonight. And what I wanna make very, very clear is that this is not an end; this is the beginning. This is a beginning because the message we sent the world tonight is that it's not okay to put donors before your community.

"And what you have shown is that this nation is never beyond remedy, it is never too broken to fix," she said. "We will be here, and we are going to rock the world in the next two years."

"Rock it!" Trent shouted.

"Because every person in this room is going to DC with me," Ocasio-Cortez continued. "We have to dedicate ourselves each and every single day to this fight, cuz I can't do it alone. So, not only do I need to get elected, but we've got a whole bunch more primaries to go. And when we get to November, we should be electing a caucus of people on these beliefs and on this change. So I'mma tell you right now—I'mma tell you right now—we've got Ayanna Pressley in Massachusetts, we got Cori Bush in Missouri, we got Chardo Richardson in Florida, we got a whole bunch of more races." Confused shouts of "O-A-C!" mingled with "A-C-O!" until the crowd finally fixed the rendering, producing the first public chants of "AOC! AOC!"

After her speech, having been transformed into AOC, her phone began buzzing nonstop with calls from political figures who hadn't known her name five minutes earlier and who had managed to find her number, as well as from friends who had had no idea she was even running for Congress. It would take her months to get through the messages, but for the moment, she handed off her phone to Trent, whose own phone was exploding with calls from the press.

Saikat Chakrabarti had been heading for the party as the returns started coming in. When the first votes dropped, showing his candidate ahead, he turned around and sprinted back to the campaign office to watch the returns from there with Rojas and the field team. When he arrived at the party, he found bedlam. "I see Corbin, and he's, like, crying in a corner, basically," Chakrabarti said. "I mean, he's just like being bombarded with everything. He was trying to answer her phone and his phone, and I tried to help him with that a little bit. Everybody reached out all at the same time, and we picked up none of their calls just because it was impossible."

Rebecca Katz, a Cynthia Nixon aide, found Trent and marveled at the lack of reporters at such a historic event. "They're on the sidewalk," he explained to her. Trent, in the glow of victory, had no plans to allow the media, which had ignored the campaign, to have any part in the celebration. "They didn't RSVP," he told her, "so I'm not letting them in."

The campaign team huddled to decide how to capitalize on the moment. Comparisons to the 2014 upset of House Republican leader Eric Cantor were already being made publicly. "This seems big," the campaign team agreed, said Chakrabarti, "but we're not sure how big. Maybe this is going to be Eric Cantor, so, in that case, we really need to make use of the next, like, two days, because then it's probably not gonna be news anymore. Corbin was basically trying to make the case for 'We should just do news tomorrow and try to get on TV.' AOC understandably was, like, 'I am dead tired. I want to take off,' but she kinda got convinced that this might be a special moment."

The next few days were a blur of TV hits, press interviews, and avoided phone calls. Despite the calls that had come in on Election Night, very few politicians knew how to get in touch with Ocasio-Cortez, and the few who managed to locate a number found their calls largely going to voice mail. "Hillary Clinton called. Heads of state were calling. It was ridiculous," Chakrabarti said. Trent, who was setting up the calls, said the same thing, though he added that AOC had agreed to take one brief call, from Nancy Pelosi, who used it to take a swipe at Crowley, who had been organizing a challenge to her for the Speakership. "We already have too many old white men here in Congress," she quipped to AOC, looking to bond with her over a shared passion for taking on powerful men.

Otherwise, though, like a true Millennial, Ocasio-Cortez sent every call to voice mail. "She just doesn't pick up the phone," said Trent. "So, during orientation and the months leading up to that, there was no contact with sort of *the system*. The contact with the Man didn't occur until she was on the floor of the House," Trent said. "So, there's this moment where everything was working, but it was a confluence of things that made it possible, and then, yeah, DC sort of brought her in."

"For three days, she just didn't sleep again," Chakrabarti said, "would wake up at like six a.m., and just did media, and in the middle of all that, we're trying to figure out 'What is the big message you're trying to get across in this moment?' And, at the time, AOC did want to get this message across that it wasn't just her; there was this huge movement that's running with her, and she would take every chance she got to call out the [insurgent Democratic] campaigns coming, happening right afterward."

Ocasio-Cortez didn't recognize at the time the effect the interviews she was giving would have on her soon-to-be colleagues in the House. Upsetting Joe Crowley was one thing. Everybody's entitled to run in a primary, even if incumbents might not like it. And plenty of members of Congress—not many, but some—had themselves gotten there by challenging an incumbent in their own party. That was part of the game, if a quite small part. But encouraging an entire movement to take on incumbent Democrats across the country? That was another thing entirely. "Now that you've gotten elected, everyone tells you you should spend the rest of the summer staying in your district and talking to people, making your political connections," Chakrabarti said. That would not be AOC's approach.

During her call with Bernie Sanders, the two bonded over their commitment to build a true multiracial majoritarian working-class coalition. To that end, there was a primary still under way where they felt they could make a statement. The left has been passionate about Kansas since before it became a state, when New England elites funded antislavery advocates to move there and build enough of a population to make it a Free State. The Rev. Henry Ward Beecher, the nation's most famous preacher—and relative to activists, educators, and authors, including Harriet Beecher Stowe—excoriated his flock to go west. Antislavery bankers and merchants funded an endless supply of what became known as Beecher's Bibles—the rifles the men and women were given to defend themselves and with which they were sometimes to go on the offense in a war among proslavery, abolitionist, and Free State contingents that became known as Bleeding Kansas. A half century later, Teddy Roosevelt launched the modern Progressive movement with a landmark speech in Osawatomie, Kansas, and a century after that, Obama returned to Osawatomie at the height of Occupy Wall Street to meet the moment, at least rhetorically.

Kansas had taken on even deeper mythological importance for liberals after the 2004 publication of the bestselling book *What's the Matter with Kansas?* Comparing present-day Kansas to its prairie populist, antislavery roots, author Thomas Frank asks why it was that white working-class voters consistently voted against their own economic interests.

Sanders and AOC believed that with the right message and the right messengers, these voters could be won back. They decided to travel to Kansas together, where labor lawyer and unapologetic progressive Brent Welder was running in a three-way primary for a Republican-held swing congressional seat that was trending blue. If a left-wing challenger flipped this seat, it could prove their theory of the case.

The Kansas City race would be the duo's first clash with the surging power of identity politics in the Democratic Party. Welder was a former Obama delegate, but he was also a straight white man. The second major candidate in the race was Sharice Davids, a Native American woman, lesbian, twenty-year U.S. Army vet, former mixed martial arts fighter, and White House fellow under President Obama. For suburban Democratic primary voters, she was a dream candidate. Where she stood politically was less clear, but there was no question she was running to the right of Welder. By the time of AOC's victory, which came six weeks before the Kansas primary, Davids had raised less than three hundred thousand dollars, while Welder had pulled in more than seven hundred thousand, much of it from small donors. Once it was clear that AOC and Sanders planned to make the race a priority, EMILY's List, the Democratic establishment group that backs pro-choice women candidates, quickly began spending hundreds of thousands of dollars through its super PAC in the race.

The day before the Kansas City rally, the venue had to be changed to accommodate the overflow interest. Ocasio-Cortez, staring out at four thousand roaring Kansans, was triumphant. "And they said what we did in the Bronx, no one would care about it in Kansas," she said, before riffing on Obama's famous "hope and change" mantra. "Hope is not something that's found; it's something that's made," she said. "Change takes courage. Change takes guts."

On social media, the race got ugly quickly, with Sanders accused of racism and sexism for challenging what would be the first Native American woman ever elected to Congress. The attacks were centered largely on Sanders, as the center hadn't yet settled on how to confront Ocasio-Cortez over questions of identity politics.

The day after the rally, AOC made good on a promise and headed to St. Louis to rally with Cori Bush, a fellow Justice Democrat and Black Lives Matter activist, who was challenging Democratic incumbent William Lacy Clay Jr. The Clays had held the seat for nearly half a century. Both primaries were held in early August, and Clay bested the massively outspent Bush. On Election Day in Kansas, Welder cleaned up in the minority-heavy urban precincts, while Davids dominated the suburbs. The white candidate was beaten by white voters, losing by 3.5 percent, which amounted to just over 2,000 votes. By the end, Davids had gotten a decisive amount of super PAC support, totaling more than seven hundred thousand dollars.

AOC's first live meeting with Pelosi came in July 2018, when she and Chakrabarti lunched with Pelosi and her daughter Christine at a restaurant in San Francisco. Pelosi spoke for nearly the entire lunch, dishing out her trademark looping, run-on sentences to her bewildered companions. "She just keeps talking; it's a fascinating thing," Chakrabarti recalled. "We were eating, and she just talked the entire time without even taking a break. And I wasn't sure exactly what she was saying, but I was like, 'Huh, okay.'" Getting Pelosi's unfiltered thoughts was both eye-opening and disturbing. Ocasio-Cortez, who had made the slogan "Abolish ICE" central to her challenge to Crowley, was particularly perplexed to hear Pelosi say that the phrase had been injected into American political discourse by the Russians and that Democrats needed to quash it. AOC wondered, *This is how the leader of the party thinks?* The next time Pelosi came to New York, she tried to connect with Ocasio-Cortez, but AOC's staff slow-walked things long enough to dodge the meeting, and they ducked efforts to schedule calls. And so, from her June victory to her November orientation, AOC largely charted her own course, free of pressure from party leadership, not because she was able to resist it, but because she had sidestepped it.

In Michigan, Justice Democrats had another candidate on the ballot—in fact, on two ballots. The twin races run by Rashida Tlaib to replace John Conyers, who'd been representing Detroit since first winning office in 1964, offer perhaps the clearest example in electoral politics of the way small margins and unpredictable decisions can change the course of history. Because Conyers resigned amid a MeToo scandal, a special election was needed to fill out his term, and another election was needed to replace him for the following term. The special election for his remaining term and the primary to succeed him the following year were held on the very same day.

Voters got identical ballots for both races, save for one pivotal difference: Coleman Young II, the son of the iconic former mayor, and former state representative Shanelle Jackson decided to run only in the primary election for the next term, not the special election to replace Conyers for just a few weeks. This meant that the Black establishment vote was divided further in the primary than in the special election. In the primary, Young pulled in 12.5 percent of the vote, while Tlaib won 31.2 percent, and Brenda Jones, the city council president, carried 30.2 percent. Tlaib, having won the primary, was guaranteed a seat in Congress the next year.

We don't have to wonder if Young and Jackson served as spoilers. In the special election, which didn't include either, Jones beat Tlaib by 2 percentage points and served out the remaining weeks of Conyers's term.

The narrow election gave Justice Democrats its second victory, though not one it had gone all in on, and sent half the members of what would come to be known as "the Squad"—a brand name that came from a throwaway Instagram caption AOC used after the general election underneath a photo of all four—on their way to the House. The next week, freshman state representative Ilhan Omar, also running with a Justice Democrats endorsement, won her primary in Minnesota. Whereas Sharice Davids's story of overcoming adversity as a Native American woman in Kansas had played well in a Democratic primary, so had Omar's journey from Somali war refugee to activist to elected official. Identity, it was clear, could work both for the center and for the left in their intramural battles.

This left Ayanna Pressley, whose Boston primary against incumbent Mike Capuano came in early September. Pressley, unlike the three leftist outsiders who'd already won their races, was a convert to the Justice Democrats cause. As an at-large city councilor, she'd been progressive but not in a way that set her apart in Boston. In the 2016 presidential campaign, she'd been a surrogate for Hillary Clinton, bashing Sanders and trashing Medicare for All. And her opponent had a strong progressive record, particularly on foreign policy. Pressley ran heavily on her identity and her life experience, making the argument that "those who are closest to the pain should be closest to the power," a mantra of her stump speech.

In its rush to endorse as many candidates as possible, Justice Democrats hadn't noticed Pressley's outspoken opposition to Medicare for All and hadn't spotted the corporate and lobbying contributions littered throughout her city council fund-raising. But then, with just over two weeks to go before the election, Pressley's record was laid bare in an article by the nonprofit news organization the *Intercept*. Reading the story, the leaders of the group were livid, but Alexandra Rojas was particularly infuriated, feeling betrayed. She wanted to publicly rescind the endorsement, a move that risked tanking Pressley's campaign, but one that would send a message about what Justice Democrats was willing to tolerate.

Others in the group suggested phoning Pressley to hear her defense and get a renewed commitment that whatever her previous politics, she was now a comrade in the political revolution. The call was tense, but Pressley made her case and promised that she believed fully in the progressive vision being laid out by Justice Democrats. She also pledged to issue a new statement vowing to refuse corporate PAC money after the primary.

"We did that—or, I did that. And it was really tough," Rojas said when I asked her about the last-minute doubts. "My philosophy is we have to hold them accountable every step of the way. It doesn't matter if it's a week before your primary: if you take corporate money, that's a litmus test for us. Based on what we found and what they said, we felt like that statement was sufficient, and they proved that their donations were clean—for the congressional."

AOC's victory had put a national spotlight on the race, and Pressley ended up blowing Capuano out. The Squad was in place.

But while Joe Crowley's loss amounted to an earthquake inside the insular world of House Democratic caucus politics, it turned out that nationally and even internationally Ocasio-Cortez's win was the bigger story. In the days after her victory, she was consistently a presence on national TV, creating viral moments that sent her star rising farther with each one. On Twitter, her clapbacks were feasted on by a rapidly growing social media following. Her direct-to-camera Instagram dispatches were bringing a rawness to politics that young people were craving. "She was just hitting homer after homer and kept doing these interviews and just blowing it out of the park," said Chakrabarti. "And every time she would do one, we'd get bigger and bigger people asking her to come on. And then, at some point, all the late-night shows were asking to have her, but then, they have this weird competition thing, where you can't be on one and then also the other; they get really mad about that." Still, the toll of her popularity was about to hit its limit. "A mistake we made early is we did not do enough to just figure out how to keep AOC from not getting exhausted. I mean, it's incredible she didn't have a nervous breakdown."

In the middle of July, the stress finally caught up to Ocasio-Cortez, and she did the unthinkable: she took on the Israel-Palestine question unprepared. "Corbin and I put her in a bit of a vulnerable position," Chakrabarti said, "on a topic that wasn't her thing. She never really talked about Israel-Palestine, and that's just not something she'd ever really thought a lot about, other than a little bit during the campaign." Ocasio-Cortez was still surging in celebrity when she agreed to a sit-down interview on PBS's *Firing Line*. In the midst of the primary campaign, she had attracted attention with her full-throated criticism of the Israel Defense Forces, which had fired on Palestinian demonstrators, killing many.

Her criticism hadn't been a commentary on the politics of the region, she said, but merely a defense of the right to protest without being killed. "This is a massacre," she had posted in May 2018, as Israeli forces continued to kill protesters in Gaza, with the numbers of dead climbing north of two hundred. "I hope my peers have the moral courage to call it such. No state or entity is absolved of mass shootings of protesters. There is no justification. Palestinian people deserve basic human dignity, as anyone else. Democrats can't be silent about this anymore."

But among Puerto Rican families, the issue just doesn't come up all that often, outside of those who are heavily engaged in geopolitics, and if it does, there's a reflexive solidarity with the Palestinians. "Puerto Rico is a colony that is granted no rights, that has no civic representation," AOC told Glenn Greenwald in an interview during the primary campaign. "If sixty of us were shot in protest of the U.S. negligence in FEMA, I couldn't imagine if there were silence on that."

Her *Firing Line* interviewer, Margaret Hoover, brought up AOC's use of the term *massacre* and asked a broad question: "What is your position on Israel?"

"Well, I believe absolutely in Israel's right to exist," Ocasio-Cortez began, adding that she supported "a two-state solution."

She then said that she was merely looking at the killings through her lens as an activist. "If sixty people were killed in Ferguson, Missouri, if sixty people were killed in the South Bronx, unarmed, if sixty people were killed in Puerto Rico—I just look at that incident more through . . . just as an incident, and as an incident, it would be completely unacceptable if it happened on our shores."

Ocasio-Cortez, in equating the lives and dignity of Palestinians with others around the world, was treading unusual terrain for a New York politician. "Of course," Hoover cut in, "the dynamic there in terms of geopolitics and the war in the Middle East is very different than people expressing their First Amendment right to protest."

AOC paused and took a deep breath. The First Amendment might not *legally* cover unarmed Palestinian protesters, but it certainly did from a *moral* perspective. She stood her ground. "Well, yes," she allowed, "but I think what people are starting to see, at least, in the occupation of Palestine is just an increasing crisis of humanitarian condition, and that, to me, is where I tend to come from on this issue," she responded, now visibly nervous.

"You used the term 'the occupation of Palestine,'" Hoover pressed, leaning forward. "What did you mean by that?" From one perspective, it could mean the entire state of Israel was an illegitimate occupation of the nation that is truly Palestine—though this was ruled out by AOC's initial assertion of her support of the right of Israel to exist. From another perspective, it could merely refer to the ongoing occupation of Palestinian territory, an occupation recognized as illegal by international law. But Ocasio-Cortez wanted none of the discussion.

"Oh, I think—what I meant is, like, the settlements that are increasing in some of these areas and places where Palestinians are experiencing difficulty in access to their housing and homes," she said, clearly suggesting she was referring to the latter definition.

Hoover wanted more. "Do you think you can expand on that?"

But Ocasio-Cortez was tapped out. "I am not the expert on geopolitics on this issue," she said, laughing at herself. "I just look at things through a human rights lens, and I may not use the right words. I know this is a very intense issue . . . I come from the South Bronx, I come from a Puerto Rican background, and Middle Eastern politics was not exactly at my kitchen table every night, but I also recognize this is an intensely important issue."

Her team decided to take a break from national interviews. "To me, the scary thing about that whole Israeli-Palestinian thing wasn't that she got an answer wrong," Chakrabarti said. "That was the first time she had a bit of a confidence hit because she didn't do incredible in an interview. Up until that moment, she was doing incredible at every interview, and that's a scary thing for someone like her, who really runs on her ability to command the room and [possess] confidence and belief in herself."

After the *Firing Line* interview, she was slammed from all directions—from the left for being too soft on the occupation, from the right for "attacking Israel," and from all sides for the cardinal sin of admitting to not knowing about something. But Ocasio-Cortez had not run for Congress to become a voice on the Israeli-Palestinian conflict. At the time, she betrayed a visceral sense of just how treacherous the issue could be for her, but she could never have guessed how significantly she had underestimated it.

The excitement of the primaries gave way to the general election, with anti-Trump fervor sweeping Democrats into control of the

House. The Squad would be coming to Washington as members of the new majority party. They had shown they had an unprecedented ability to generate news coverage, which was everything in America's current attention economy. Their question now was what they could do with it.

3

OCCUPATION

Alexandria Ocasio-Cortez awoke in her room in the Omni Shoreham in northwest Washington, a hotel that had played host to inaugural balls, presidents, and corporate conferences of every kind. It was now the temporary home of the sixty-two-member freshman Democratic class of the 116th Congress. They had all been elected exactly one week earlier, on November 6, 2018, in a wave that swept the party into power. The class was here for freshman orientation, learning the ins and outs of federal lawmaking, along with the basics of putting together a staff, what kind of budget was available (not much), the housing situation (not good), and the all-important lottery, at which incoming members would draw lots to determine who won the least-bad freshman offices.

But Ocasio-Cortez had something bigger on her mind that morning, and she was wondering if she had the courage—or, perhaps, the stupidity—to go through with it. Her plan to occupy the office of the incoming Speaker of the House had not been put through much of a deliberative process. Yet neither had much else, and here she was, weeks away from being sworn in as the youngest woman ever to serve in Congress, already an international rising star. So why overthink it now?

The previous Friday, Evan Weber, the political director for the obscure youth climate group Sunrise Movement, had a thought. Sunrise was planning to march on Pelosi's office, and Weber wondered aloud if Ocasio-Cortez might be willing to back the demonstration, maybe with a post on Twitter or a statement of support to the press.

It was worth asking, the group's leaders agreed, given that Sunrise had been one of the few national organizations to endorse AOC's long-shot bid against Crowley. Had Crowley won, he'd have been prowling the halls of the Omni rounding up votes for a potential challenge to Pelosi. Instead, he was taking meetings with corporate lobbying firms, his involuntarily early retirement plan.

Weber didn't have a direct way to get to Ocasio-Cortez, so he called Zack Exley, who at forty-eight was an elder in the scrappy progressive movement that had grown up around the internet dating back to MoveOn.org, the blogosphere, and the Howard Dean campaign. Weber asked Exley if he could connect them with somebody in AOC's orbit, telling him about the plan for the coming occupation on Tuesday.

"What're the demands?" Exley asked Weber.

"A green jobs guarantee," Weber told him.

"That's pointless," Exley said, and explained why. Nancy Pelosi was already on record in support of green jobs. Who wasn't? And the part about the "guarantee" would get lost in the press coverage, and they would have wasted everybody's time—at best. Weber said he didn't necessarily disagree with that analysis, but that that's where the politics of coalition building had come in. A whole bunch of other progressive groups had endorsed the action, and getting consensus, he said, drove decision-making down to the lowest common denominator. Everybody was okay with a green jobs guarantee. Also, coalitions were not nimble. Changing the demands over the weekend would be impossible.

"Ah, but what if Alex wants it changed?" Exley asked, using the name by which everyone on Ocasio-Cortez's campaign knew her. If she led, he argued, the groups would follow. He reminded Weber that AOC had run on a Green New Deal—a much cleaner, clearer, and bolder demand. (Exley's latest organization, a small think tank called New Consensus, was building the policy infrastructure for that campaign promise on the fly.)

"Okay," Weber said, "but would she do that?" He thought Exley was bluffing and that he wouldn't be able to get the idea to Ocasio-Cortez in time anyway, but there was little risk in trying. He didn't realize that a little less than two years earlier, it was Exley who had sat down in a Union Square Thai restaurant with his friend and colleague Saikat Chakrabarti to try to talk a young bartender into running for Congress—and who had had to decide whether their organization, at the time called Brand New Congress, would get behind her.

Now, two years later, Chakrabarti would soon be her chief of staff. With Weber on the line, Exley hit Add Call, and to Weber's surprise

Chakrabarti picked up. He quickly agreed: the Green New Deal was a better thing to ask for. He took the idea to Ocasio-Cortez. "Sunrise is doing this protest," he recalled telling her. "It's in Pelosi's office, and they were just hoping that you could, like, tweet about it or something to support them, but, you know, maybe you could even join them, but I know that'd be kind of crazy. And she was like, 'What? Yeah, that sounds awesome.' And she was, like, really into wanting to join them."

The radical activists were taken aback. "Are you guys sure?" Sunrise cofounder Varshini Prakash wondered when she learned Ocasio-Cortez would be joining them.

"Like anyone else, she had some moments where she wasn't entirely sure. She was trying to figure out a way to do it that wasn't just seeming like she's yelling at Pelosi as her first action," said Chakrabarti. "I could tell she was sort of fading a little bit, so Sunday, Corbin and Zach and the Sunrise kids were at a church, doing this all-day rally, and Corbin and Zack were like, 'You just need to bring AOC here. She'll get so revved up,' and that's exactly what happened." At the church, AOC felt the pulsing energy of the young people—most of them younger than her—and her shaky resolve to go through with the occupation stiffened.

That night, still revved up, Ocasio-Cortez saw the news that Amazon had completed the national sweepstakes it had been running to pick a home for its second headquarters. The most likely contenders were always going to be Washington, DC, where Jeff Bezos owned the local newspaper and needed friendly lawmakers on his side, and New York City, and Amazon announced that it would be splitting its so-called HQ2 between the two cities. At 11:40 p.m., Ocasio-Cortez fired off a Twitter thread that would derail the project. "She had not realized the AOC effect yet," Chakrabarti said. "The thing she actually tweeted was something much more qualified than what it got turned into."

She had written: "We've been getting calls and outreach from Queens residents all day about this. The community's response? Outrage. Amazon is a billion-dollar company. The idea that it will receive hundreds of millions of dollars in tax breaks at a time when our subway is crumbling and our communities need MORE investment, not less, is extremely concerning to residents here."

At 12:20 a.m., as her tweet and its thread rocketed around the internet, she added that her complaints were not limited to Amazon and that she wasn't trying to pick a fight but, rather, was just the messenger for her community: "Lastly, this isn't just about one company or one headquarters. It's about cost of living, corp[oration]s paying their fair share, etc. It's not about picking a fight, either. I was elected to advocate for our community's interests—& they've requested, clearly, to voice their concerns." Amazon would soon pull out of New York, with Ocasio-Cortez's opposition cited by many observers as the proximate cause.

The next morning, on less sleep than she'd like to have gotten, Ocasio-Cortez was most definitely not sure about the Green New Deal protest anymore. In fact, she felt she might vomit. What if she took the momentum that millions of people had built collectively and squandered it all for nothing? It felt like too much responsibility. The very fate of the planet was at stake. And she was running late.

About five miles away, outside the Cannon House Office Building, about two hundred climate activists, many of them high school and college students, had been split into two groups, had gone through security, and were waiting in the building's basement for the signal to march on the office of the Speaker. That morning, they'd gathered at Spirit of Justice Park, a green roof constructed on top of a congressional parking garage across the street from Cannon, where they were met by Rashida Tlaib, soon to be sworn in to represent Detroit. Tlaib handed out Jolly Ranchers and rallied the crowd, telling the story of her own civil disobedience, which had led to the locking up of a corrupt Detroit billionaire. From there, she headed off to orientation, wishing the activists strength.

Corbin Trent and Alexandra Rojas were on the sidewalk outside. Trent had nothing but contempt for the orientation process Congress was pushing new members through. "If I were gonna be an asshole, I'd say [AOC]'s providing *them* with an orientation," he told me as I loitered with him and Rojas.

He, Rojas, and Chakrabarti had all devoted themselves full-time to Ocasio-Cortez's campaign in the home stretch—Trent doing communications, Rojas covering field organizing and door knocking, and Chakrabarti overseeing the whole. They knew AOC well. "She's looking in the mirror, saying, 'Come on, Alex, you can do this!'" Trent quipped by way of explaining Ocasio-Cortez's tardiness.

Would she do it?

"She'll be here," he promised.

Back at the Omni, Ocasio-Cortez was getting it together. So far, she had been challenging the Democratic Party from afar—on cable news and through Twitter and Instagram, but not face-to-face. Now she was on their turf. Meanwhile, New York City mayor Bill de Blasio and New York governor Andrew Cuomo were fuming about her unwelcome intervention in the Amazon HQ2 debate.

Ocasio-Cortez filled a to-go cup of coffee, took a deep breath, and climbed into a cab with Chakrabarti. "In this context, where she had just pissed off all of the New York leaders, we're about to maybe go piss off Pelosi," Chakrabarti recalled. "That was what's sort of going through her mind. How I felt, I was just like, 'Man, I hope I'm not convincing this person with this really bright political career to just throw her entire future away for no reason.'"

Arriving at what they thought was Capitol Hill, AOC asked the driver to pull over at their destination, at First and D. "Are you sure?" he asked. He was no stranger to tourists and other out-of-towners who didn't realize Washington is organized into quadrants, and therefore has four First and Ds.

Out of the cab, AOC called Trent and learned her mistake. They were a very long walk—with Ocasio-Cortez in heels—from where they needed to be. She and Chakrabarti trudged up Capitol Hill, past the interminably long Rayburn House Office Building, built in the 1950s during the postwar boom, when Congress had outgrown its square footage, to finally arrive at Pelosi's building.

Reunited with Rojas and Trent, the group passed Rep. Jan Schakowsky, a progressive Democrat from Illinois, who gave a head nod and a smile and might have wondered why Ocasio-Cortez wasn't at orientation. As we rounded the corner toward the stairs leading to the entrance, AOC said she wasn't thrilled about the coming confrontation, but she believed it was the only viable path forward. "The way things are done has not been getting us any results for the last twelve years," she said, referring to 2006, the last time Democrats had swept into power in Congress. "So we have to find new methods." . . . "I'm open to the possibility" of getting arrested, she also said, but concluded— with a grin that seemed to recognize the privilege that came with her new status—that it was highly unlikely.

The group ascended the marble stairs to Cannon and pulled open the double doors, where security was waiting. Members of Congress at the time had the privilege of bypassing the X-ray machines manned by the Capitol Police, but Ocasio-Cortez hadn't been sworn in yet; nor did the cops seem to recognize who she was. She took off her stylish black coat and ran it, along with her handbag, through the metal detector.

We cleared security and headed down the hallway.

"Hey!" an officer shouted. "Somebody's coffee," he said, pointing to Ocasio-Cortez's cup. She sheepishly reclaimed it and tossed it into the nearest trash can.

Now the group had to find Pelosi's office. After wandering aimlessly, they stopped to ask a young woman who appeared to be an intern—and who promptly pointed them in the entirely wrong direction. In the interest of efficiency, I decided to pierce the journalistic veil. "It's right up these stairs," I told them.

At the top of the staircase, we pushed through a swinging set of double doors and were met with the crashing bulbs of a crush of reporters and a bank of television cameras. The secret hadn't held. The office was already occupied.

A roar rolled down the hallway as the endlessly stretching occupiers realized AOC had arrived. Ocasio-Cortez planted her feet for an impromptu press conference.

A CNN correspondent got in the first query: "Did you have a hard time finding your way here?"

She was then asked the obvious political question: Is joining the protest a direct challenge to Pelosi?

"One of the things I admire so much about Leader Pelosi," AOC responded, "is that she comes from a space of activism and organizing, and so I think that she really appreciates civic engagement. And really what I'm here to do is just to support the folks who are here."

By the time Ocasio-Cortez made her way inside Pelosi's office, protesters were already squatting on nearly every available square inch. AOC found a space in the middle of them, standing on the plush beige carpet inside an emblem of the seal of the United States, her heels digging into the claws of the eagle. Behind her was a sign that had clearly been made before she switched the demand: "Green Jobs for All." Over her shoulder was one that read "Step Up or Step Aside."

"Should Leader Pelosi become the next Speaker of the House, we need to tell her that we've got her back," Ocasio-Cortez told her young audience. The way to do that, she argued, was to capture the energy in the room and use it to push "the most progressive energy agenda that this country has ever seen." They were not there to attack Pelosi, she said, but to support her.

Down the hall, I spied Drew Hammill, Pelosi's deputy chief of staff, who was red in the face, livid. "Can you tell them we support every single thing they're protesting us for?!" he said. I noted that one of their demands—that Democratic candidates refuse to take fossil fuel money—was an area of disagreement. For Hammill, this was nonsense. Whether an individual member of Congress took fossil fuel money was up to them, he argued.

Ocasio-Cortez did not stay around to get arrested—she was in and out. Pelosi told the police to let the young people go free, too. Leaving Cannon, I told AOC that Hammill had complained that they were protesting the wrong person, that Pelosi wanted all the same things she did.

"That is absolutely true," she said. "What this just needs to do is create a momentum and an energy to make sure that it becomes a priority for leadership."

Ocasio-Cortez's speech, and the decision to protest inside Pelosi's office, marked a critical moment for understanding the irreconcilable contradiction that has been AOC's approach to politics. While somebody like Obama wants to be *seen* as being all things to all people, Ocasio-Cortez actually thinks she can *be* all things to all people, even while leading a political revolution. She believed she could occupy the Speaker's office *and* have Pelosi appreciate it—if not immediately, then at least down the road.

Aside from her election, the occupation was AOC's first great triumph. It launched her as a power player and put the Green New Deal on the global map. Within days, the Green New Deal would find dozens of congressional supporters; within a few months, it would become a resolution introduced in both chambers of Congress, would dominate the political conversation, and would receive endorsements from almost every serious Democratic presidential candidate for 2020. By May 2019, Democratic voters would tell pollsters that climate change was their top issue of concern. Later that year, Spain would implement its own Green New Deal, inspired by Ocasio-Cortez, and the notion would spread around the world.

But Ocasio-Cortez's day was just starting. Next on the agenda, she noted: a luncheon for the freshman class, hosted by Nancy Pelosi. "That should be interesting," she predicted, a smile showing that the commonsense part of her knew the truth: that despite her insistence that she had been with the protesters merely to support and empower Pelosi, Pelosi did not necessarily appreciate what she had just done.

Thanks to the size of the freshman class, the luncheon was large enough not to be overly awkward, and Pelosi had to leave for her meeting with the members of the powerful Ways and Means Committee to talk about their 2019/20 agenda.

Pelosi told the assembled members of the committee that she wanted a focus on infrastructure and a review of Trump's tax cuts, which required their obtaining a copy of his tax returns. Before she left, she added one more item. "And we need to deal with the environment," she said, "because the teenagers want us to do something."

Pelosi later called Ocasio-Cortez in to meet about the protesters' key demand: a select committee on the climate crisis. "Who knows what she actually felt, but she took it as, like, 'Oh, I already want to do this climate select committee, and your protest actually gives me some political capital to make it stronger,'" Chakrabarti recalled. "She wasn't super hostile."

On the Saturday after the sit-in, Ocasio-Cortez joined a public Justice Democrats conference call designed to encourage people to run for Congress. It was the same message Obama had sent two years earlier—grab a clipboard and get in the game—but coming from AOC and Tlaib (who released a statement of support but didn't join), it read as a threat to the party establishment. Every Democrat in the House who would later see a primary challenge—and there would be more than one hundred—would blame Ocasio-Cortez, even though she ended up endorsing only a handful.

On the Saturday video call, she made clear that she and Justice Democrats would continue challenging incumbents, but only in safe blue districts where the sitting representative wasn't representative enough of the district, whether ideologically or demographically. "All I'm asking you to do is throw your hat in the ring, say 'What the heck,'" she said. She also brought up the recent protest. "If I made people mad, they could have put me on the dog-walking committee," she said. "They still might."

She was, however, in someone's doghouse. The conventional wisdom in Washington is that every member needs an issue. In 2016, Washington State had elected Pramila Jayapal to Congress. An outspoken progressive organizer, she had been making climate her issue. She was also a rising star with ambitions for a party leadership role and soon would become cochair, and then the sole chair, of the once-moribund Congressional Progressive Caucus, committed to turning the CPC into a political force to be reckoned with.

Born in India, Jayapal didn't get to the United States until she was sixteen. After the terrorist attacks of September 11, 2001, she was inspired to get into activism, she said, by a lonely, courageous speech delivered by Rep. Barbara Lee, who stood up against the invasion of Afghanistan and the crackdown on civil liberties that came from it. Jayapal founded the group Hate Free Zone to push back on the xenophobia directed at Muslims and other immigrants in the wake of the attacks, and she went on to be elected to the Washington State Senate in 2014 before coming to Washington, DC, two years later.

Now, in a flash of breaking news alerts and cable segments, the role of climate champion had been firmly usurped by Ocasio-Cortez and the idea of a Green New Deal. Pelosi would later drive a wedge into a relationship that was by turns partnership, mentorship, and rivalry, delighting privately that Ocasio-Cortez and Jayapal "were vying to be the 'queen bee' of the left." Jayapal told me that any gossip about interpersonal beef was just that. "It constantly happens, where people try to set us up against each other." After Pelosi's comment was reported publicly, AOC reached out to Jayapal. "Alex texted me after that with some lovely message, like, 'You'll always be my queen bee,'" Jayapal said. Still, it opened an opportunity for Jaypal. For decades, the lead champion of Medicare for All had been civil rights icon John Conyers of Michigan, but he was no longer in Congress.

Jayapal picked up the Medicare for All bill and transformed it from the short messaging bill it had been under Conyers into a serious piece of legislation she would draft in collaboration with Bernie Sanders in the Senate.

4

THE THUMB

The day after the New York State primaries, Ocasio-Cortez was asked a question by the *Washington Post* she hadn't given much thought to: Would she be supporting Pelosi for Speaker? She told the paper it was indeed time for "new leadership," but she wasn't sure who was even in the mix to replace Pelosi. "I mean, is Barbara Lee running? Call me when she does!"

Lee, by this time in her career, had become something of a matron saint of the progressive movement. A congresswoman from Oakland, California, she had volunteered with the Black Panthers' Free Breakfast for Children program and had worked on Shirley Chisholm's groundbreaking 1972 presidential campaign. A year later, she'd worked on Black Panther cofounder Bobby Seale's bid for Oakland mayor. She had worked on the staff of Ron Dellums, the first member of the Democratic Socialists of America to serve in Congress, and had played a leading role in both of Jesse Jackson's presidential campaigns, in 1984 and 1988. She was elected to Congress herself in 1998 and would soon cast the vote that would define her career. In the wake of the attacks of September 11, 2001, she was the lone vote against going to war in response, delivering a searing and prophetic speech.

Since then, Lee had become a close ally of Pelosi's, and the notion that she would directly challenge her was a fantasy. Her radical roots were real, but she had always been interested in being an inside player—you don't work as a staffer for a member of Congress or a mayoral candidate if you don't have some faith that working inside the system can deliver results.

After the Democratic takeover, it quickly became clear that nobody was going to mount a challenge from Pelosi's left. Her right, however, was a different story. Waiting to ambush her was New Jersey representative Josh Gottheimer, cochair of a group called the Problem Solvers Caucus. Gottheimer had founded the caucus in 2017, his freshman year, under the guidance of the group No Labels. (It had initially been formed by No Labels in 2013, but after Gottheimer's election, he helped make it an official caucus recognized by the House of Representatives.)

Problem Solvers, made up of an equal number of Democrats and Republicans, held the title for receiving the most bipartisan mockery, but over the years it had become a funnel for a growing amount of super PAC spending, which required it to be taken seriously. (The super PACs, which themselves went by names like Forward Not Back and United Together, operated under the umbrella of No Labels.) Ostensibly, it claimed it would solve problems by bringing together moderate Democrats and reasonable Republicans to find commonsense solutions. In practice, it was simply a vehicle for blocking any type of tax increases on the private equity moguls and hedge fund executives who funded the dark-money groups No Labels sponsored.

No Labels, for its part, was founded after the Tea Party wave of 2010 and publicly sought to "cool the temperature," striving to bring bipartisan groups of centrists together to fend off the extreme elements of both parties. To fund the endeavor, founder Nancy Jacobson and her husband, Mark Penn, the notorious operative who rose to prominence as the whispering devil on President Bill Clinton's shoulder, turned to a who's who of hedge fund barons, private equity executives, and other moguls. Many of the donors Jacobson and Penn recruited to fund No Labels also maxed out donations to Gottheimer.

It was a role Gottheimer had been preparing for his entire career. His first job out of college was as an intern in Bill Clinton's White House, where he rose to a speechwriting position under Penn. The pollster-slash-operative Penn took the up-and-comer under his wing, training Gottheimer in the dark arts of palace intrigue. Gottheimer, quite short, both in size and temper, with a rabid dedication to weight lifting, quickly took on the nickname "Pocket Hercules" among his Clinton administration colleagues.

Penn and Gottheimer stayed close, and when Penn worked to nudge Hillary Clinton into the 2004 presidential campaign, he brought Gottheimer with him to work on the effort as a consultant. He wound up as a speechwriter for John Kerry, where he picked up his second nickname, "The Thumb," a nod to the squat stature and high forehead that made him look like one. Following the campaign, Gottheimer became director of strategic communications for Ford Motor Company, where Penn was a consultant.

Penn had become CEO of the consulting firm Burson-Marsteller in 2006, long one of the PR outfits working closest with Saudi Arabia, and that year, he hired Gottheimer as an executive vice president. ("He was a terror there," said one of Gottheimer's employees.)

Burson-Marsteller, as MSNBC's Rachel Maddow laid out while Penn was running it, had long been a reliable voice for the worst of the worst. "When Blackwater killed those seventeen Iraqi civilians in Baghdad, they called Burson-Marsteller," Maddow said. "When there was a nuclear meltdown at Three Mile Island, Babcock and Wilcox, who built that plant, called Burson-Marsteller. Bhopal chemical disaster that killed thousands of people in India—Union Carbide called Burson-Marsteller. Romanian dictator, Nicolae Ceauşescu—Burson-Marsteller. The government of Saudi Arabia, three days after 9/11—Burson-Marsteller."

She continued: "When evil needs public relations, evil has Burson-Marsteller on speed dial. That's why it was creepy that Hillary Clinton's pollster and chief strategist in her presidential campaign was Mark Penn, CEO of Burson-Marsteller." (Penn, at the time still serving as CEO, disputed the characterization.)

Penn's most notorious strategic advice was that Hillary should paint Barack Obama as un-American, the true birth of birtherism. He was explicit about the strategy, penning a 2007 memo with a section titled "Lack of American Roots." Arguing that Obama's "roots to basic American values and culture are at best limited," he urged Clinton to draw a contrast by noting in every speech that she was "born in the middle of America to the middle class in the middle of the last century."

"Let's explicitly own 'American' in our programs, the speeches and the values. He doesn't," Penn wrote. Publicly, he advised, they had to pull this off "without turning negative." Privately, the Clinton camp circulated images of Obama in African garb and of his minister, Jeremiah Wright, intoning "God damn America!" in a sermon. The Clinton team whispered to reporters of an audio recording of Michelle Obama bashing "whitey." The rumors of the recording would turn into a scream on the right, where black-bag operatives and conspiracy nuts would spend years looking for the nonexistent "whitey tapes." Among right-wing radio and TV audiences, it simply became an article of faith that the tapes existed. (There's zero evidence that they do.)

As for Gottheimer, he was known during the Obama-Clinton primary to be one of the more vicious knife fighters in Hillary's camp—a hatchet man's hatchet man. Every foul thing that emanated from the campaign was presumed by the Obama team to be the handiwork of Penn as executed by Gottheimer, and the latter earned the universal enmity of Obama's staff. Yet, in 2010, Gottheimer copublished a book called *Power in Words: The Stories Behind Barack Obama's Speeches, from the State House to the White House.* The gall was breathtaking, and simply mentioning that book today to Obama alumni is enough to trigger a range of emotional reactions. (For all that, the book sold fewer than a thousand copies across all formats, according to Book-Scan.)

In the summer of 2010, Gottheimer became senior counselor at the Federal Communications Commission, just as Penn was joining Microsoft, which was engaged in a major battle with the FCC. Gottheimer's reputation as a brutal boss to work for carried over to the FCC. "Josh Gottheimer is the biggest douche I have ever worked for ever," said one former FCC employee, calling him a "poor man's Rahm," a reference to former Chicago mayor Rahm Emanuel. While there, Gottheimer helped ease through the controversial NBC-Comcast merger. "He wrote slimy press releases touting Comcast's broadband for poor people that was basically dial-up for ten dollars," the employee recalled. Gottheimer served for two years before Penn pulled him back through the revolving door to join him at Microsoft.

In 2015, Gottheimer became a consultant with the Stagwell Group, a Penn-owned private equity firm, according to a 2017 financial disclosure. Between 2015 and 2017, while Gottheimer was consulting for Stagwell, Saudi Arabia paid Targeted Victory, a digital company owned by Stagwell, more than a million dollars to spread pro-Saudi disinformation on Twitter. ("The congressman has never done any work for Saudi Arabia," a Gottheimer spokesperson told me.)

In 2016, Pocket Hercules ran for Congress in a Republican-held swing district in his home area of northern New Jersey. In the campaign, he played up his close ties to the pro-Israel lobby, noting that he was active with both the American Israel Public Affairs Committee and NorPAC, an organization even less hospitable toward Palestinian rights than AIPAC. Donors connected to NorPAC made up his largest source of campaign cash, and he's been a regular speaker at AIPAC's annual conference.

These ties, paradoxically, were aided by Penn's longtime work on behalf of Saudi Arabia. For the prior several years, Saudi Arabia and the United Arab Emirates had built an alliance with the Israeli lobbying operation in Washington, DC. Israel won Arab cred from the two autocracies even as its settlements in occupied Palestinian territory were rapidly expanding. And the autocracies were helped by association with one of Washington's most powerful lobbies, while at the same time beginning to form cyber warfare and military technology connections that would later blossom into the Abraham Accords under President Trump.

"Israel and the Arabs standing together is the ultimate ace in the hole," a high-level official at the Israeli embassy told me in 2015. "Because it takes it out of the politics and the ideology. When Israel and the Arab states are standing together, it's powerful." The United Arab Emirates and Saudi Arabia were spending tens and sometimes hundreds of millions of dollars per year to influence Washington, but because of the limited number of Saudi or Emirate immigrants with U.S. citizenship, and with very limited sway over the American Muslim community, they had little ability to contribute directly during elections. Israel had no such handicap.

Israel's highest priority that year was blocking the Obama administration's Iran nuclear deal. It was in the Iran deal fight that Mark Mellman, later to found Democratic Majority for Israel, sharpened his intra-Democratic knife-fighting skills. Though he and Gottheimer would lose the first round of that fight, with the Iran deal approved and Congress unable to stop it, they would win later when Trump ripped the deal up. Gottheimer became the most reliable ally of the Saudi-Emirati-Israeli nexus in Washington, with Mark Penn and Mark Mellman as his patrons. One of Gottheimer's earliest fund-raisers in 2015 was hosted by Don Baer, an ex-Clinton aide who replaced Penn as CEO of Burson-Marsteller.

In Washington, a handful of law and lobbying outfits are registered as agents on behalf of Saudi Arabia. In his first reelection cycle, Gottheimer was among the top recipients of cash from those firms' lobbyists and lawyers, according to Ben Freeman, an analyst at the Center for International Policy's Foreign Influence Transparency Initiative. This made Gottheimer one of the top twenty biggest recipients of Saudi agent cash in either party, but that number is deceptive, as the rest of the list includes party leaders and veterans. Nobody as junior as Gottheimer came anywhere close to that level of donation. The alliance between him, the two Gulf states, and Israel would become a major force in Washington, taking direct aim at the Sanders-AOC wing of the party.

Gottheimer quickly began building on his Pocket Hercules reputation. In January 2017, he got an invitation to the eightieth birthday party for a senior member of his state's delegation. The area that Rep. Bill Pascrell represented abutted Gottheimer's district in New Jersey, but it couldn't have been more socioeconomically different, anchored by the working-class city of Paterson. Pascrell was hosting the party-slash-fund-raiser at a favorite hometown bar, Duffy's, something of a dive on the outskirts of town.

Paterson wasn't the type of place where Gottheimer spent much time, but it wasn't an actively dangerous spot. Not only was the bar a regular haunt of the local congressional representative, but it was owned by Terry Duffy, a town freeholder, the state's version of a county council member. Gottheimer agreed to brave the journey to Paterson to celebrate his colleague, but when he arrived, it was clear that he'd taken a confounding set of precautions: he was accompanied by an off-duty police officer and showed an unusual amount of bulk under his shirt.

"Are you wearing a bulletproof vest?" Pascrell asked his first-term colleague. Gottheimer acknowledged that he was, but he went on to say, by way of explanation, that he had been doing a ride-along earlier with the officer and had worn the vest for that. The explanation, even if it was true, failed to explain why he was still wearing the vest at the party. A round of heckling and wisecracking ensued, drawing the attention of Terry Duffy.

The freeholder was not amused and ordered Gottheimer out of his bar. "Duffy told him to get the hell out, 'You're mocking us,'" Pascrell confirmed to me. "I said, 'He's not intelligent enough to mock you.' So, he says to me, 'Should I leave him in?' and I said, 'Yeah, you're not going to get anything by throwing him the hell out.'"

This kind of approach to his colleagues led to an unusual level of hazing for Gottheimer, and the ribbing at the weekly New Jersey delegation meetings began immediately. Members of the delegation simply couldn't bring themselves to stop giving Pocket Hercules a hard time, whether it was Rep. Albio Sires turning on his phone's stopwatch whenever Gottheimer arrived, to time how long it took him to leave—the "Gottheimer Timer" never ran very long—or Pascrell and Don Norcross mocking him for barely being a Democrat.

Gottheimer's voracious fund-raising was inextricably linked with his legislating. At a Financial Services Committee hearing early in his tenure, he objected to a small reform put forward by Rep. Steven Lynch, a Massachusetts Democrat close to Big Labor. The top-ranking Democrat, Rep. Maxine Waters, called for a private huddle of Democrats to sort the mess out. In that side room, Gottheimer's colleagues were first introduced to his legendary temper. He excoriated Lynch and Waters, an extraordinary display for a freshman, and warned that the legislation would kill him back home among his financial industry backers. He pulled out his phone and dialed Pelosi, certain she'd have his back. Explaining his predicament, he asked her to intervene on his behalf. "Josh, it sounds like a reasonable amendment. I think you should support it," Pelosi told him before hanging up. The awkward meeting broke up and, that afternoon, his personal office would feel the brunt of his fury.

Gottheimer also began picking up a reputation for telling little lies. Once, he reached out to Pascrell's office to pitch a joint event in his district with the American Postal Workers Union. It wasn't his idea, he said; the union wanted to do it. So Pascrell's team called the union rep, who told them Gottheimer, in fact, had pitched the idea and then had asked him to lean on Pascrell to make it happen. It was the whitest of lies—who cares whose idea a banal union event was? But it seemed to define Gottheimer for his colleagues.

His treatment of staff and fear of his own constituents quickly became legend within the Democratic caucus. In the wake of Trump's election, spontaneous demands sprang up around the country that members of Congress hold town hall meetings so they could hear the frustrations of those they represented. It was the last thing Gottheimer wanted to do, but after extensive negotiations, he eventually agreed to hold one, in Teaneck, at the Ethical Culture Society of Bergen County, on the condition that no press be allowed and that all questions be written down.

The Teaneck Democratic Municipal Committee meeting on May 8, 2017, is now seared into the memories of those who witnessed it. The event was going well until Gottheimer's staff noticed an elderly Teaneck resident in the audience taking notes. The man, Jim Norman, had been thinking of starting a community newspaper, a weekly that he planned to call the *Teaneck Independent*. As it was, he occasionally posted his community dispatches online. Gottheimer's aides tried to get the representative's attention, to warn him that a potential member of the fourth estate was in the audience. They also told Norman that no press was allowed at the event, but he told them that it was a public event and that the press couldn't be barred.

Norman said that Ron Schwartz, the committee vice chair, stood up for Norman's right to be there as a member of the press, saying that the committee would not bar press from a public event. "A little disagreement was developing around me," Norman said. "I declined to leave."

When the event ended, Gottheimer's aides let him know that it had gone terrifically, but they flagged the fact that the would-be community reporter had been taking longhand notes. A switch flipped, and Gottheimer moved into war mode. Get me those notes, he demanded, growing increasingly agitated as his aides advised against this. As he grew louder, sprinkling in profanity, his staffers nudged him into a corner, where they hoped his outburst would be less of a scene for the audience members who'd lingered and were now seeing an encore. It didn't work, so an aide went to find state senator Loretta Weinberg.

Gottheimer's aides briefed her on the situation, and Weinberg, who was the state senate's majority leader, tried to intervene. Weinberg had known Norman for years, and she assured Gottheimer that if he wrote anything at all, it would be a straightforward, community newspaper–style write-up of the event. Weinberg, when asked about being brought in by Gottheimer's staff to try to calm him down at the Teaneck gathering, said, "I really don't have anything to add."

Gottheimer wasn't reassured by Weinberg, and he stormed outside, where, now in the middle of the street, he could go on an even louder diatribe. His aides continued to gather around him, working to calm him down, as the Teaneck Democrats filed out and rubber-necked the perplexing scene.

Pocket Hercules ordered two aides to confront Norman and demand his notes. Norman, who had recently been part of a mass layoff at the *Bergen County Record*, told me that he stood firm under pressure from the staff. He said he was aware that Gottheimer was angry at his presence, though the representative never spoke to him directly. (Norman confirmed that he has indeed known Weinberg for years and that the two had worked on a number of local issues together, including a fight to protect one of Teaneck's largest trees.)

Gottheimer's aides, Norman said, told him that they would need to review anything he wrote before it was published, a condition Norman rejected. Furious, Gottheimer spotted the car of the staffer who had driven him to the event and channeled all his rage on it, raining blow after blow down upon its roof.

He then developed a new battle plan. He wanted his remarks transcribed that night, so his team would be prepared to rebut whatever the old man might post. Gottheimer's staff did transcribe his remarks, but they were never needed. Jim Norman posted an 817-word dispatch on his now-defunct website, TeaneckIndependent.com, and, indeed, it reads like a straight community newspaper write-up of a town hall meeting, summarizing Gottheimer's talk and including positive quotes from attendees.

The crowd, according to Norman, generally approved of Gottheimer's positions. "I think he's a good middle-of-the-road Democrat, even if he does not understand why we should be pushing for single-payer health care," said Mark Fisher, a member of the sponsoring organization.

"I think he's a good, centrist, reach-across-the-aisle congressman who knows a lot of his constituents are Republicans," said committee vice chair Ron Schwartz.

For Gottheimer's staffers, the episode was one of the most extended, public expressions of the madness they'd come to know in private. Gottheimer's more extreme outbursts were often followed by quasi-apologies. One in particular, during his first year in Congress in 2017, stood out. After multiple staffers quit or threatened to quit, Gottheimer agreed to do a conference call with his staff to apologize for his general behavior—except, on the call, he never quite apologized, instead telling his aides that they should be proud of the work the office was doing. That was fine enough, but it was the specific work he identified that had staffers shaking their heads. Take deep pride, he told them, in how much money we're raising. But nobody in his congressional office had gotten into politics to break fund-raising records—as Gottheimer does routinely. The staffers simply stared at one another in disbelief. Raising money, several aides said, appeared to be the only thing Gottheimer genuinely cared about. To talk about it with staff in a congressional office crossed the ethical boundaries most members had set—and was also likely a violation of the law separating fund-raising and official congressional work.

Gottheimer cycled through staff at a startling speed. Of the 535 members of the House and Senate, he had the tenth highest turnover rate in 2018, according to LegiStorm's ranking of "worst bosses." He was the only freshman member of Congress to burn through enough staffers that quickly to make the top ten. But the ranking is somewhat generous, as four of those ranked as worse than Gottheimer retired that year, which better explains the exodus of staff from their offices.

Aside from the campaign cash Gottheimer raked in from the pro-Israel and pro-Saudi lobbies, he cultivated Wall Street openly. This tendency was on unusually obsequious display at an April Financial Services Committee hearing, where the CEOs of America's major banks testified, including JPMorgan Chase's Jamie Dimon, Bank of America's Brian Moynihan, Goldman Sachs's David Solomon, Morgan Stanley's James Gorman, and Citigroup CEO Michael Corbat.

At the hearing, titled "Holding Megabanks Accountable," Waters, the committee chair, showed a rotating series of slides highlighting antisocial banking practices. When it was Gottheimer's turn to question the bankers, he borderline apologized to them, flattering them and telling them how much he appreciated their work. "Mr. Dimon, can you describe some of the work that your firm has done in the small business lending arena and how those loans are helping to facilitate small business growth?" he fawned.

Rashida Tlaib, sitting in front of Gottheimer at the hearing, was startled. "I had to pause, because he was on our side of the aisle," she told me. "I was taken aback by his strong stance for megabanks. There's a way to do it that doesn't undermine the leadership of the committee."

Throughout 2018, it became increasingly apparent that Democrats would take over the House of Representatives, setting up Pelosi to become Speaker again. That cycle, Nancy Jacobson of No Labels vowed to raise and spend fifty million dollars to defend centrists in both parties, though the group ended up spending roughly twice as much on Republicans as Democrats. And some of what they spent on Democrats was in defense of the party's most retrograde remaining member. Rep. Dan Lipinski of Illinois had been gifted his seat by his father, a "Chicago machine" boss, and governed so far to the right that in the 2010 redistricting, he successfully fought to make his district more conservative. His politics—outspokenly anti-LGBT, opposed to a fifteen-dollar minimum wage, and against abortion rights—had skated by in the oblivious years before Trump, but once Democratic voters were awakened in 2017, Lipinski's days were numbered.

Marie Newman, a small business owner who'd become an anti-bullying activist to defend her trans child, challenged Lipinski, and she had not just the support of Justice Democrats but, eventually, and belatedly, also the broader progressive infrastructure, including NARAL Pro-Choice America, which put together a coalition to take on Lipinski. Yet Planned Parenthood and EMILY's List, uncomfortable challenging an incumbent Democrat, were both slow to join the race, getting in only a few weeks before the election.

As her run picked up steam, Newman got a call from the top federal affairs official for AIPAC in Washington, who happened to be a friend of her nephew. She told him he was wasting his time, that she didn't agree with AIPAC's posture on the Israeli occupation or its support for endless military aid with no conditions attached. "Well, you're really gonna lose a lot of fund-raising," she recalled him telling her. "And I said, 'Okay. Are you trying to scare me? Because that's not working.'"

Newman probably should have been scared. Founded in Illinois, AIPAC, as we know it today, was born thanks in large part to the work of Chicago businessman Robert Asher, who pushed in the 1970s to transform the committee into a political powerhouse, becoming one of the so-called Gang of Four board members who helped set strategy and organize a national network of donors. They first tested their theory of the case on Republican representative Paul Findley, whom they viewed as too sympathetic to the Palestinian cause.

In the 1980 election, Asher sent scores of letters to AIPAC donors around the country and chipped in his own money, targeting Findley in both the GOP primary and the general election. A young Rahm Emanuel took time off from college to volunteer for his first campaign that year, becoming chief fund-raiser for the Democrat challenging Findley, raising some three quarters of a million dollars. It was the first attempt to unseat a member of Congress by fund-raising on the issue of support for Israel, and Findley survived, but the model was in place.

In 1982, Asher and his AIPAC allies recruited Dick Durbin to challenge Findley and helped make the race the costliest ever in Illinois. "If I hadn't been a persistent critic of Menachem Begin, I wouldn't have had a real contest this year," Findley told the *Washington Post* then. This time, he lost by less than 1 percent, and the message was sent that showing sympathy for the Palestinians or wavering in one's full support of Israel could be politically costly, even in districts like Findley's, with a significant Arab population. (Bridgeview, Illinois, is known as "Little Palestine.")

The next cycle, AIPAC recruited Democrat Paul Simon to take on Sen. Charles Percy, whom the group also deemed too sympathetic to Palestinians. Simon won. Thomas Dine, AIPAC's executive director, called it a warning. "Jews in America, from coast to coast, gathered to oust Percy," Dine said at the time. "And American politicians—those who hold public positions now, and those who aspire—got the message."

Asher, thirty-eight years later, was still sending letters, but now in the form of emails. The *Times of Israel* reported that he went into overdrive on behalf of Dan Lipinski, telling allied donors that Marie Newman was "catering to the anti-Israel population in the district," a reference to Bridgeview's Palestinian Americans. "They are well aware of where there are strong Arab and Muslim American communities, they are intensely aware of it," said Newman.

Gottheimer's ally Nancy Jacobson worked closely with AIPAC, she told *Washington Jewish Week* magazine, and she and Gottheimer's mentor, her husband, Mark Penn, were able to raise and spend a million dollars through various super PACs linked to No Labels, saving Lipinski by just a few thousand votes.

It was a significant win, but it came at a cost beyond just the money: defending an incumbent who was opposed to reproductive freedom and hostile to marriage equality angered some in the No Labels community, one of whom fired off an angry email to Jacobson. She responded by saying that despite Lipinski's views, it was worth defending him in order to push back against the Sanders wing of the party. "I see a whole new crop of Democratic challengers—like Marie Newman—who see Bernie—WHO IS NOT EVEN A DEMOCRAT—as a model worthy of emulation," Jacobson wrote (using all caps in the original), apparently oblivious to the irony that she was attacking a politician for eschewing a label—No Labels' implicit goal. "But I don't think we need more people in Congress on either side who rile up their bases and then actually achieve nothing."

During the campaign, according to emails I obtained, No Labels deliberated making Pelosi a "boogeyman" in its communications strategy, but ultimately decided against doing so. No Labels chief strategist Ryan Clancy argued that the time wasn't right. The group "is probably going to go to war with Pelosi. And it probably should," Clancy wrote in an email. "I don't know that now is the time to do it, especially when we have a perfectly good villain to use in Bernie."

The time to do it would come. In June 2018, No Labels launched the "Speaker Project," aimed at expanding the power of a small group of centrists if Democrats took power in the House of Representatives. The project pushed for a rules change that would give a clear path to a floor vote for any legislation that met a certain threshold of bipartisanship. It was easy for K Street to round up small bipartisan groups, meaning the reform, if passed, would effectively hand control of the floor to corporate interests. "There's a problem-solvers group that is looking to have some influence, if the result is close, in terms of changing the rules and naming the Speaker," Penn said in September 2018 on Fox News's *Tucker Carlson Tonight*, declining to mention his central role in that group.

The demands were absurd in the extreme, and the group knew they'd be rejected by Pelosi, which would then give them a public rationale to oppose her. Gottheimer attempted to execute the Speaker Project in the run-up to the new Congress, organizing the Problem Solvers Caucus to withhold support from Pelosi. He worked in tandem with Rep. Seth Moulton, a Massachusetts Democrat who had been raising money furiously and backing veterans running for Congress in the hope of building a bloc of power he could use to oust Pelosi.

But in the Trump era, in the shadow of the Women's March, with women forming the backbone of the party's support, it was absurd to think the two men could oust Pelosi and replace her with another man. They needed a woman, and they didn't have one. At a minimum, they needed a viable candidate, and they didn't have that, either. "You can't beat somebody with nobody," Pelosi's allies noted repeatedly during the contest, deploying what was an accurate, if not exactly inspiring, campaign slogan. Had Joe Crowley been reelected, the week after Thanksgiving in 2018 could very well have been the day the Democratic Party nominated him to be House Speaker. Crowley had long been viewed as the Democrat most likely to take Pelosi's spot when she retired or was pushed aside. Throughout 2018, his operation seeded stories in the political press about his ambitions, while he publicly insisted he wouldn't challenge Pelosi directly if she ran again for the gavel.

But Crowley had been ousted by Ocasio-Cortez, so the Pelosi opponents publicly attempted to recruit Rep. Marcia Fudge of Ohio. But Pelosi was able to offer her a subcommittee chairmanship, and that threat was neutralized. As it became clear that she had the votes, and Moulton and Gottheimer didn't, Pelosi began taunting them publicly. She offered some modest concessions, and Gottheimer folded.

The threat from the left, such as it was, was massaged by Pelosi, and Barbara Lee ran for caucus chair instead, spying an opening in the loss by Crowley, who had held the position. She would be running against Crowley's protégé, a Brooklyn machine politician named Hakeem Jeffries.

Jeffries had his own radical past, but it came through his father. Marland Jeffries was a New York state substance abuse counselor and, in his free time, an active Black nationalist in a period when there was intense energy behind the Black Power movement. Leonard Jeffries Jr., Marland's brother, became the subject of a national controversy and debate over free speech and academic freedom when the City University of New York tried to remove him as chair of the Black Studies Department for claims he'd made about the Jewish role in the

African slave trade (incidentally, the same outlandish and genuinely anti-Semitic claims that tore apart the leadership of the 2017 Women's March).

Out of this cauldron, Hakeem Jeffries emerged with a visceral hostility toward the radical left. During an interview in the fall of 2021, Jeffries said that one of his sons came to him and said he wanted to participate in some upcoming protests. "Are they marching on me?" Jeffries said he asked him. He was joking—sort of.

Elections for caucus leaders began on the morning of Wednesday, November 28, 2018, and in a twist of narrative fate, Joe Crowley, still chair of the Democratic caucus until the new Congress was sworn in, oversaw the proceedings. Staff was barred from the private session, resulting in something of an intimate atmosphere inside the main auditorium at the U.S. Capitol Visitor Center. After ten long years, Democrats would finally retake control of the House.

The longest-serving member from each state introduced each new freshman. Eliot Engel, who represented parts of the Bronx and Westchester County, took the stage to introduce the new members of Congress from New York. "Haha they had the region deans announce all the new members and give everyone a rousing, long intro," AOC texted. "Engel had to introduce me and I got golf claps."

After the caucus acquainted itself with its new members, Crowley moved to the election for his own soon-to-be-vacant leadership position, chair of the caucus.

Congress is like high school in many ways—one being that it is saturated with rumors. Shortly after Jeffries entered the race, the talk among Democrats turned toward the role of Pelosi in his decision to run. Some of Pelosi's opponents in the caucus had been hoping Jeffries would make a bid for Speaker. Jeffries was a natural Plan B. A number of members of Congress who supported Lee, as well as some who backed Jeffries, were convinced that Pelosi had recruited Jeffries to run against Lee—not necessarily to undermine her Bay Area ally, but to prevent Jeffries from running for Speaker.

In either event, Jeffries's bid was a boon to the trio of septuagenarians in the top three leadership positions, as it offered a release valve for the pressure in finding younger faces among the brass. Concern that Pelosi was behind Jeffries mounted as the race tightened. With her vaunted whip operation, it was assumed that if she wanted Lee to win, she had the tools to make it happen, but she didn't lift a finger to help Lee.

Brian Higgins, a New York representative who backed Jeffries, suggested that Crowley had a hand in nudging Jeffries into the race against Lee. "To what extent, I don't know, but I do know that he's a mentor, and I think he helped him develop a strategy to succeed," Higgins told me. "Joe Crowley is the most popular guy on campus, with Democrats and Republicans."

Lee, meanwhile, made her own miscalculation. Convinced by responses from her colleagues that she had enough votes to win, she demanded that the city's progressive groups—including MoveOn, NARAL, Color of Change, and Democracy for America—stay out of the race rather than call in favors.

Headed into the auditorium that morning, both Lee and Jeffries believed they had the commitments they needed to win. What Lee didn't know was that Crowley had been doing more than emceeing the proceedings. In the run-up to the vote, he told a number of House Democrats that Lee had cut a check to Ocasio-Cortez, painting Lee as part of the insurgency that those in the room considered a viable threat. Supporting a primary challenge against the beloved Crowley was a treasonous act.

Lee's campaign did indeed cut a thousand-dollar check to the campaign of Ocasio-Cortez, but it did so on July 10, two weeks *after* AOC beat Crowley. Since then, Steny Hoyer, Raúl Grijalva, and Maxine Waters, as well as the PAC for the Congressional Progressive Caucus, had all given money to Ocasio-Cortez's campaign committee. It's not unusual—a way to welcome an incoming colleague—but Crowley's framing linked Lee to the growing insurgent movement, despite her decades of experience in Congress. But even if Crowley had been strictly honest about the timing of the donation, the fact of it at all would have been disturbing to many Democrats. The "golf claps" represented the profound distrust Ocasio-Cortez's new colleagues felt toward her, and it was true that the group coming to be known as the Squad was supporting Lee. So Lee had to be beaten.

Lee took the stage with some thirty members of Congress, and a half dozen gave speeches on her behalf. Her mistake, members of Congress argued to me afterward, was that her message was flat. Her campaign, and the speeches that day, made two points: that Black women powered the Democratic Party and should be in leadership and that Lee had cast that lone courageous vote against going to war in 2001.

There was universal acclaim for both points, but Lee didn't bother to make a case beyond that. And the fact that her opponent was also Black, albeit a man, diluted the potency of her pitch. Jeffries, meanwhile, made his case based on "generational change" and cited his ability to go toe-to-toe with Trump on cable TV. Implicit in his generational argument was that elevating him to caucus chair would put him in line for Speaker. And nobody in the room thought there was any chance he'd support primaries against incumbents (except, perhaps, against Ocasio-Cortez or others in the Squad).

The votes were cast by secret ballot, and as the counting began, Crowley returned to the stage to say goodbye. On the night of his primary loss, Crowley queued up a song at his watch party, "Born to Run," that he'd been playing for years at events and had planned to play at his victory party. Instead, he dedicated it to the insurgent who'd beaten him, mispronouncing her name. As the votes to replace him in leadership were being counted, he again broke out in song. This time it was what multiple members said sounded like an Irish funeral dirge.

As Crowley sang his mournful tune, one member of Congress leaned over and captured the mood of the room, saying quietly, "It's such a shame. This isn't right." The congressman looked up and realized—or, perhaps, pretended to realize—that he was talking to Ocasio-Cortez. She texted me about the exchange, adding a laughing-crying emoji 😂 and "Belly of the beast baby!"

It took more than an hour, but when the votes were tallied, Jeffries prevailed 123–113. I found Lee in the hallway later that day and asked her about Crowley's spreading the rumor about her check to Ocasio-Cortez. "Those rumors took place, and that was very unfair," Lee said. "I didn't even know [Crowley] had a primary."

Crowley, following Jeffries's victory, congratulated him. "I've been honored to work alongside Hakeem as we both fought for the working- and middle-class families of New York," he said in a statement. "As chair, I know he'll continue that fight and serve as a champion for all Americans by protecting their health care, their voting rights, and their livelihoods. I am incredibly proud that a fellow New Yorker and my friend will help lead the Democratic caucus. New York, and the country, are in good hands with Hakeem."

Roughly half of Jeffries's campaign money had come from political action committees—including from the spheres of real estate, finance, law firms, entertainment, and the pharmaceutical industry—and he was one of the most outspoken defenders of the most aggressive Israeli policies inside the Democratic caucus. Jeffries had broken with Democrats to back Wall Street on key votes, including one high-profile measure written by Citigroup lobbyists in 2013. He had also been one of the most vocal supporters in Congress of charter schools and a close ally of not just Crowley, but also New York governor Andrew Cuomo. A prominent supporter of Hillary Clinton during the 2016 campaign, he savaged Sanders in particularly aggressive terms, dubbing him a "gun-loving socialist" who provided "aid and comfort" to Donald Trump.

After the vote, I asked Jeffries what specific ideas he and Lee disagreed on during the contest of ideas. "Well, the question for many was 'How do we get the right mix of experience and generational change,'" he said, deploying a phrase he would return to over and over. "I focused a lot on the work that I've done in the past with Blue Dogs, New Dems, and progressives; and with Republicans, at least as it relates to the criminal justice bill, and in a divided government context, [I] made the case that I was reasonably well positioned to get things done, working with Republicans in the House and in the Senate and with a Republican administration in the White House."

Orientation was just getting started. In a tradition that stretched back generations, veteran members of Congress used the period after the November elections and the start of the new session in January as an opportunity to school incoming freshmen on the ways of the institution. The break also offered an opportunity for powerful interests to shape impressionable new congressional minds.

The House has been continuously in operation more or less since its first session in March 1789, and the chamber has evolved the type of complex and overlapping ecosystems you'd expect in a still-functioning two-hundred-plus-year-old institution. In order to orient members of Congress in the proper direction, they must first be *dis*-oriented. Finding one's place in that teeming mass of 435 bodies is a challenge, but luckily for new members, they can turn to the former ones for guidance—former members still hanging around but now serving as lobbyists.

For candidates who oust a member of their own party, there's no sharing of institutional knowledge. Crowley's staff was as surly as possible with AOC's, and Michael Capuano, who had lost to Pressley, dragged his feet as long as possible in sharing anything helpful.

The Democratic Congressional Campaign Committee used the orientation process to hammer home to its members the importance of immediately beginning to fund-raise for the next election. The DCCC had put together a PowerPoint presentation for freshmen, and a version that had been used in previous cycles was leaked to me. The daily schedule they recommend contemplates a nine- or ten-hour day while members are in Washington. Of that, four hours are to be spent in "call time," and another hour is blocked off for "strategic outreach," which includes fund-raisers and press work. An hour is walled off to "recharge," and three to four hours are designated for the actual work of being a member of Congress—hearings, votes, and meetings with constituents. If the constituents are donors, all the better. The presentation assured members that their fund-raising would be closely monitored; the Federal Election Commission requires members to file quarterly reports.

The schedule back in the home district allowed for a more leisurely fund-raising pace. Members were expected to put in a workday of only eight hours, three of which were to be spent on call time, three to four on community events, and one on strategic outreach.

"What's my experience with [call time fund-raising]? You might as well be putting bamboo shoots under my fingernails," Rep. John Larson of Connecticut told me. "It's the most painful thing, and they're no sooner elected and they're down there making phone calls for the [next] election."

Tom Perriello, who as a populist Democrat represented a right-leaning Virginia district in the consequential Congress of 2009/10, spoke with Ocasio-Cortez after her primary victory, as she was looking for young progressives who could give her some insight into the chamber and its occupants. For Perriello, the fund-raising demands had warped the institution. He told me that the four hours indicated in the presentation may even be "lowballing the figure so as not to scare the new members too much."

Perriello also said that the drive for fund-raising winds up containing "an enormous anti-populist element, particularly for Dems, who are most likely to be hearing from people who can write at least a five-hundred-dollar check. They may be liberal, quite liberal in fact, but [they] are also more likely to consider the deficit a bigger crisis than the lack of jobs." The time spent fund-raising, he added, also "helps to explain why many from very safe Dem districts who might otherwise be pushing the conversation to the left, or at least willing to be the first to take tough votes, do not—because they get their leadership positions by raising from the same donors noted above."

Congressional hearings and fund-raising duties often conflict, and members of Congress have little difficulty deciding between the two—occasionally even raising money from the industry covered by the hearings they skip. It is considered poor form in Congress—borderline self-indulgent—for a freshman to sit at length in congressional hearings when the time could instead be spent raising money. The purpose of being on a good committee—a "money committee," as they're known—is to be able to fund-raise from the industry the panel oversees.

Over the course of the House's history, power had gradually been concentrated into the hands of the leadership and, specifically, of the Speaker. Once upon a time, individual chairs of committees held sway over their own fiefdoms, and those competing fiefdoms allowed entrepreneurial backbench members of Congress to have at least the tiniest amount of leverage. Much of that is thanks to Rep. Phil Burton, who served in Pelosi's seat from 1964 until his death in 1983. Burton was instrumental to Pelosi's rise, though Pelosi resists the descriptor of mentor, seeing it as a suggestion that she needed a man to get where she is. In truth, she also needed a woman: Burton's wife, Sala, took his seat after his passing. As she herself lay dying in 1987, she delivered a deathbed endorsement of Pelosi that eased her into the seat.

Phil Burton, known as "the fighting liberal" and one of the most consequential members of the House in the twentieth century, successfully went to war with the southern Old Bulls who had a lock on the House committee structure. He invented a new power structure—no longer would seniority reign; money would—and pioneered the practice of raising money and then sharing it with colleagues to build personal power and rise through the ranks, the system that persists to this day.

Pelosi now had a lock on most sources of big money, and she oversaw a super-committee that operated in secret, which controlled who got on what congressional committee. The money-est of all money committees is Ways and Means, which has jurisdiction over tax and revenue policy, but also over tax credits, which have increasingly become the way the government spends money. The panel has always reserved at least one seat for a member from New York City, and that seat had been Crowley's. It was now up for grabs, with only two eligible candidates: Ocasio-Cortez and Tom Suozzi, a Long Island Democrat whose few blocks of Queens technically made him eligible. The seats almost never went to freshmen, but AOC decided to try for it. "Well, fuck," Suozzi told me when I called to tell him Ocasio-Cortez was making a bid for the seat.

The jockeying went on all throughout orientation and was particularly heated as the freshman class traveled to Boston for one of the bipartisan capstone events. The newly elected members attended the gathering hosted by the Harvard Kennedy School's Institute of Politics not because it was required, but because it was the thing everybody else was doing. Looking back later, Ocasio-Cortez recalled the ordeal as surreal. "That retreat is so weird," she told me. "It's not 'official,' but it's so engrained in everything that it seems like it is, but it actually isn't. So, everyone goes because you just got elected and have no idea what's going on and don't want to miss anything important, and then it's like an MLM for the ruling class," she said, referring to multi-level marketing. But, she added, "it is really weird, though, because it's not totally unofficial either—House admin is involved."

She was in Cambridge that week for a bizarre series of panels organized in part by the House of Representatives, but underwritten by corporate-backed think tanks. The Cambridge event was cohosted by the American Enterprise Institute, the Center for Strategic and International Studies, and the Congressional Institute. AEI is a corporate-funded, right-wing think tank; CSIS is a foreign policy think tank funded by corporations, foundations, and foreign governments, many with horrific human rights records, like the United Arab Emirates; and the Congressional Institute is a largely Republican-run, corporate-funded operation that throws retreats for members of Congress, allowing lobbyists access while skirting ethics rules that bar them from funding such activities directly.

The trip to Boston was also a chance for Ocasio-Cortez to return to her college stamping grounds a conquering hero—she had graduated from Boston University just a few years earlier—and to see Ayanna Pressley in her Boston element.

The first week of December, Ocasio-Cortez, Pressley, Omar, and Tlaib filed into seats to listen to panel after panel of business leaders and lobbyists telling them how Washington works. One panel, called White House Congressional Relations: How to Advocate for Your Priorities, was led by lobbyists Dan Meyer and Anne Wall of the Duberstein Group; the top lobbyist for CVS Health, Amy Rosenbaum, a former aide to both Obama and Pelosi; and Josh Pitcock, Oracle's top lobbyist, a former aide to Vice President Mike Pence. Another panel included Gary Cohn, former president of Goldman Sachs, who had been an economic adviser to Trump.

Ocasio-Cortez couldn't hold back anymore. "This Harvard 'orientation' is a corporate indoctrination camp and it's infuriating," she texted me. About an hour later, she shared a similar sentiment online: "Right now Freshman members of Congress are at a 'Bipartisan' orientation w/ briefings on issues. Invited panelists offer insights to inform new Congressmembers' views as they prepare to legislate," she tweeted.

# of Corporate CEOs we've listened to here: 4

# of Labor leaders: 0

Aside from Cohn, the incoming members had heard from General Motors CEO Mary Barra, Johnson and Johnson CEO Alex Gorsky, and Boeing CEO Dennis Muilenburg.

"Our 'bipartisan' Congressional orientation is cohosted by a corporate lobbyist group. Other members have quietly expressed to me their concern that this wasn't told to us in advance," she tweeted. "Lobbyists are here. Goldman Sachs is here. Where's labor? Activists? Frontline community leaders?"

Members of Congress had been writing memoirs for two hundred years, but none had ever exposed the banal corruption at the heart of the enterprise with such a brutal flick of the thumb in real time. AOC's words were retweeted more than 25,000 times and liked more than

100,000. Like nothing House Democrats had ever seen, her tweet was a moment of radical opportunity, as if the public had sneaked somebody inside Troy and they were now opening the gates. "Even if it is off record, I didn't say what they said. Just who wasn't there," Ocasio-Cortez recalled later. "I never got a rebuke for that, surprisingly. I think because it was so blatantly embarrassing and indefensible[,] they didn't have a straw to grasp at."

Once it became clear what the event's agenda truly was, the four—Ocasio-Cortez, Pressley, Omar, and Tlaib—began skipping out on events. Some dropped in on a fossil fuel divestment protest at Harvard. AOC went to watch Pressley participate in her final city council hearing.

When transportation secretary Elaine Chao—the wife of Mitch McConnell and heiress to a Chinese shipping fortune—spoke at the orientation session, Pressley led Ocasio-Cortez and Tlaib outside for a rally and press conference, a rebuke of the bipartisan comity being urged on them. "We need to shake this nation awake," Ocasio-Cortez told the assembled reporters, flanked also by Rep. Andy Levin, a Michigan Democrat who would go on to be a leading voice of labor in the House.

"I did attend a lot of the panels[;] don't get me wrong!" Ocasio-Cortez added later, ever the diligent student. "But after a while it was repetitive[,] and I got the gist. 'Bipartisan' = neoliberalism conference."

One evening, she walked the short distance from her hotel to a nearby bar to meet friends from college. While she may have been returning to town as a conquering hero, she was not yet a universally recognized one.

"ID," said the server.

Ocasio-Cortez fumbled around, realizing she'd left her license back in her room. At twenty-eight, she was the youngest woman ever elected to Congress, and in person she looked it. The server was skeptical, and Massachusetts has rules. It took Ocasio-Cortez all her powers of persuasion to talk her way out of an ejection.

She would have less luck with the Ways and Means Committee. The seat ultimately went to Suozzi.

5

INSIDE-OUTSIDE

Ilhan Omar was born a fighter and born into fighting. She opens her memoir, *This Is What America Looks Like*, with a scene in which she's grinding the face of a bully into the dirt outside her elementary school. Omar is often described in the United States as a political insurgent, but she was driven out of Somalia as a young girl by actual insurgents.

Her father, Nur Omar Mohamed, was a colonel in the Somali military under the presidency of Siad Barre, who took over in a 1969 coup and established a Soviet-aligned, Marxist-Leninist dictatorship. In 1977, Barre launched a war with Ethiopia. It was a fatal mistake for Somalia. Several months before the invasion, Cuba's Fidel Castro had flown to Aden, Yemen, to try to stave off a war between the two ideologically opposed nations. He proposed a united Ethiopian-Somali-Yemeni socialist federation that would bring together the three powers situated at the mouth of the Red Sea and the Gulf of Aden. The idea got no traction, and the invasion went ahead, ultimately plunging all three countries into crisis for the next half century.

Ethiopia was also a Soviet ally, and the USSR, along with much of the rest of the Communist bloc, sided with the aggrieved party against the aggressor. The Soviets largely cut Somalia off and gave technical and military support to Ethiopia; the Cubans sent some 15,000 troops, and after early victory, Barre was routed and sent back to Somalia. With great fanfare, he announced that he was breaking ties with the Soviets and would align instead with the United States, which began flooding weapons into Somalia.

The 1982 border war between Ethiopia and Somalia put those weapons to use, further destabilizing the country and laying the groundwork for an insurgency turned civil war against what had become a brutal Barre dictatorship. Like many in the Barre regime at the time, Omar's father was trained in the Soviet Union.

Nur Mohamed "played a significant role in the war," according to Yusuf Ismail Faraton, another colonel in the Somali military, who spoke to the Minnesota-based outlet *Sahan Journal.* Omar would grow up without her mother, who died when she was just two, after giving birth to seven children.

Omar describes being raised in a guarded compound in Mogadishu in the 1980s. When she was just five, Barre unleashed a genocide against the Isaaq people, systematically slaughtering upward of two hundred thousand civilians in what has become known as the "forgotten genocide." The Somali Civil War eventually came to Omar's doorstep, as insurgents assaulted the family's compound amid the collapse of the Barre regime in 1991. Relying on her grandfather's connections—he was a minister in the Barre regime—the family made their escape to a Kenyan refugee camp when Omar was just eight years old. Barre escaped to Nigeria. Omar spent the next four years in the refugee camp before the family successfully won asylum, with some of them arriving in New York in 1995 and, later, in the Twin Cities area, home to the country's largest Somali diaspora.

In her teens, Omar became heavily active both in social movements and in electoral politics. She helped elect multiple local candidates and became a leading figure in the local Movement for Black Lives, which became one of the most vibrant in the country and also the focus of national attention with the killings of Jamar Clark in 2015 and Philando Castile in 2016. That same year, Omar was elected to the state legislature, making national headlines.

Not long after winning her primary against a twenty-two-year incumbent, and assured of a general election victory in the Democratic district, she saw her victory marred by a *Star-Tribune* headline atop a story that gave mainstream credibility to conservative allegations that she had at one point married her brother in order to commit immigration fraud and that she was married to two people at the same time.

The story of Omar's marriages is a case study in the complete divorce between the media ecosystems on the right and the left. On the left, the allegation was seen as absurd on its face and shot through with racism and Islamophobia, playing into African tropes around polygamy. On the right, it was accepted as simple fact.

Omar has spoken publicly about the difficulty of proving a negative, and she showed the *Star-Tribune* paperwork indicating that upon her arrival in the United States, none of her siblings was named "Ahmed," evidence that her second husband, Ahmed Nur Said Elmi, wasn't her brother. Conservative media, though, has Ahmed Elmi first finding asylum in the United Kingdom—not coming with Omar to the United States—but then doing a year of high school in Minneapolis and then college in North Dakota with both Omar and her previous husband, Ahmed Hirsi, whom she had married in a religious ritual, but not officially. (Omar and Hirsi remarried legally in 2018, divorcing in 2019.)

In February 2020, Abdihakim Osman, a Somali immigrant in Minneapolis who knew Omar, Hirsi, and the man claimed to be her brother, Ahmed Elmi, would say in an interview with the conservative tabloid the *Daily Mail* that Omar had been open about helping her brother get his paperwork so that he could obtain student loans for college, but that she didn't say anything about marrying him. "She said she needed to get papers for her brother to go to school. We all thought she was just getting papers together to allow him to stay in this country," said Osman. "Once she had the papers they could apply for student loans."

Legally, Elmi and Omar married in 2009, and she says they divorced, though didn't complete the paperwork, in 2011. That fall, she graduated from North Dakota State University with a degree in political science. She says she then rekindled a relationship with her first partner, Ahmed Hirsi, with whom she has three children. She didn't file the divorce paperwork until after the press coverage years later, and she had to pay a fine to fix her previous tax records, as she had filed with Ahmed Hirsi listed as her husband while still legally married to Ahmed Elmi.

The right argues that she never legally left her first husband and that she married Elmi only to help him with his immigration situation. Investigations by Minneapolis newspapers have been inconclusive, reporters unable to debunk the notion or to prove it, so it has just lingered as Fox News fodder while being effectively ignored on the other side.

The scandal didn't slow Omar down. After Trump's election, one of the few members of Congress to have endorsed Bernie Sanders announced that he would run for chair of the Democratic National Committee. Keith Ellison, who represented Minneapolis, was also one of the only Muslims in Congress, and his run was seen as a way to bring the Bernie wing of the party into a true coalition. Immediately, Sen. Chuck Schumer endorsed Ellison, as did outspoken Clinton ally Randi Weingarten, head of the American Federation of Teachers, signaling that a rapprochement was under way. Instead, as a parting shot at the progressive wing of his party, outgoing president Obama recruited his labor secretary, Tom Perez, to run. Fresh off his concoction of the strategy to label Bernie's supporters as bigots, Perez argued that Ellison's day job as a congressman meant he'd be distracted from the work of the DNC, so Ellison pledged to resign if he won. With some arm-twisting by Obama, Perez eked out a win, but in June of the next year, Ellison stepped down anyway to run for Minnesota attorney general. This opened up the seat, and Omar won the crowded primary.

The day after her primary win, she got a congratulatory call from Nancy Pelosi. Omar used it to press a critical request: House rules originally written to prevent men from wearing hats in the chamber banned headgear on the floor. A crazy-hat-wearing Democrat, Frederica Wilson, had previously challenged the rule as unfair to her flamboyant Floridian style, but personal style concerns weren't enough to override the tradition. Omar was concerned the rule would similarly bar her from wearing a hijab and keep her off the floor. Pelosi told her not to worry about it, that they would win the majority and she'd rewrite the rule. Pelosi and Omar checked in nearly every week between her primary and the election, and Omar brought the topic up each time. Each time, Pelosi assured her she'd get it done.

The vote on the rules package that would allow head coverings was scheduled for January 3, 2019. The rules package, the committee assignment process, and the elections for party leadership positions all fell around the same time, turning the lame-duck period into a biannual horse-trading bazaar. It made for a complex series of negotiations, because each member has different priorities, whether it's a committee seat, a change to the rules, or support for a bid for leadership for themselves or an ally. What Pelosi wanted in return was their support for the Speakership and their approval of the rules package, which was necessary to start the session.

Jayapal had just taken over as cochair of the Congressional Progressive Caucus after Raúl Grijalva stepped aside, and she and Mark Pocan, a Democrat from Wisconsin, set about attempting to build the CPC into a force with real power. The caucus was first organized in 1991, with just five progressives, and chaired by freshman Bernie Sanders. This was a time when the Democratic caucus wouldn't allow Sanders to join, with rural Democrats afraid of any association with a democratic socialist. He was given committee assignments as if he were a Democrat but barred from joining meetings.

For its first two decades, the CPC was mostly a place for beleaguered progressives to socialize and commiserate. "It was a glorified Noam Chomsky book club," Grijalva told me. During the fight over the Affordable Care Act, the caucus was disorganized and marginalized. "When I arrived in Congress in 2017, I was surprised to see how little power was really leveraged among progressives," Jayapal wrote in her subsequent memoir.

She and Pocan took three new steps to beef up the caucus: they increased dues, so they could hire more staff; with funding from the network of philanthropies financed by George Soros, they launched the Congressional Progressive Caucus Center, which would serve as part think tank and part liaison with outside progressive groups; and they grew the CPC PAC, so they could back up their politics with financial support for progressive candidates and incumbents.

On the afternoon of November 15, 2019, Jayapal and Pocan met Pelosi to lay out their demands. Gottheimer and a gang of centrists were pushing either to shove Pelosi aside or to strip her of power, and Pelosi was shoring up support. Wendell Primus, her longtime senior aide, met them in the lobby. "I'm hearing from the groups that they want to see how this meeting goes before they will give their support. I see you're playing hardball here," said Primus, who was known among Democrats as "Speaker Wendell" for the power he'd developed through his longevity with and devotion to Pelosi.

The "groups" was a reference to Indivisible, MoveOn, and other progressive outfits that had teamed up with the CPC to withhold support from Pelosi until concessions were leveraged. The groups were divided, though, over how much to push for and what to accept.

Another faction, led by Social Security Works—a group pushing to expand Social Security, increase legislative support for Medicare for All, and cut drug prices by allowing the government to negotiate—was working with the CPC and the Squad for specific committee assignments. One of them was for Jayapal, who currently served on the Judiciary Committee but wanted to add Ways and Means. The two most important committees in the House were that and Energy and Commerce, and Jayapal's Medicare for All cosponsor was already on the latter committee. A foothold on Ways and Means would grow her power and also be a step forward for the bill. But to claim the seat, she needed a waiver from leadership, without which she couldn't sit on both Judiciary and Ways and Means. Ocasio-Cortez was also gunning for Ways and Means. Omar, hoping to go to war with U.S. imperialism, wanted the House Foreign Affairs Committee.

The first demand that Jayapal, Pocan, and all their outside allies agreed on was that progressives needed a minimum of 40 percent of seats on so-called A committees, or money committees—Appropriations, Ways and Means, Energy and Commerce, Financial Services. Leadership preferred to give those seats to moderate and conservative Democrats who were more likely to serve in swing districts—known as "frontliners"—so they could use the plum spots as fund-raising vehicles. That dynamic then tilted the balance of power in the caucus to the right, as the powerful committees were stacked with people more conservative than the average Democrat. Progressives, meanwhile, would be tucked away on the Judiciary Committee or on Education and Labor, where they could make speeches about criminal justice reform and the rights of workers while actual policy was made elsewhere.

"Progressive members themselves never tried to get on the [powerful] committees," said Alex Lawson, executive director of the member-based progressive organization Social Security Works. "It was just, hippies you go there, corrupt Dems, you go there." Simply requesting that progressives—including freshmen!—get onto A committees was a stark break.

The second demand was the creation of more leadership posts, so that progressives could run for those and get a seat at the leadership table.

The third demand was around PAYGO, a Reagan-era budget rule

that made it very hard for Democrats to launch new spending or design new programs. And here Pelosi was less flexible, agreeing only to discuss it further before it was implemented.

Still, Pocan and Jayapal were happy to win two out of three, and they texted the outside groups the results. "We strongly support and call on all members of the Democratic caucus to support @NancyPelosi for Speaker," MoveOn quickly tweeted, "Dems must reject attempts to defeat her and move the caucus to the right." MoveOn followed with a tweet reiterating its support for Barbara Lee for caucus chair.

But the faction led by Lawson continued fighting, teaming up with labor lobbyists who also had a list of demands—not about whom they wanted on particular committees, but whom they did not want to get particular chairmanships of various committees or subcommittees.

Pelosi deployed her daughter Christine to put down the uprising. For that, she zeroed in on billionaire couple Steven and Mary Swig, major donors to the organization. It's hard to find a family more closely tied to Pelosi than the Swigs. Steven Swig had served as treasurer for Pelosi's reelection campaign each cycle since 2012, and the Swigs' niece was even working for Pelosi at the time as a staff assistant. At home, the Swigs owned mugs with Pelosi's mug on them—before it was hip to glorify Donald Trump's bête noire—and organized their social calendars around the Speaker's many events and fund-raisers.

The Swigs were funding Social Security Works for its effort to cancel all student debt and never had any intention of getting on the wrong side of Pelosi. But they began receiving messages, including from Christine Pelosi, that they needed to sever ties with Lawson and SSW.

The committee fight was linked to another battle Social Security Works was waging, an effort to drag the House prescription drug negotiation bill to the left. Since at least 2006, Democrats had been promising to allow Medicare to negotiate drug prices, and for just as long Big Pharma had been fighting back—and Democrats had been backing off the pledge. But a coalition of outside groups, with SSW in a leading position, was putting pressure on Democrats finally to deliver on it, now that even Trump claimed he was for it. Pelosi was being led on the issue by her top aide, Primus, arguably the second most powerful person in the chamber.

"I've never seen them more mad than when we were organizing to get AOC on Ways and Means," Lawson said. "It was super shocking to me, because I've been doing this for a long time. I'm used to pissing off politicians to get stuff." He was soon being asked around Washington about his "Christine Pelosi issue."

In Washington, the social scene is an extension of the struggle for power, and glossy magazines cover its ups and downs in the same way tabloids cover Hollywood, but with an eye toward what it means about who is on top in town. Lawson watched as those associated with his organization began getting chopped up on that social scene. His highest-profile activist supporter was Jon Bauman, who had been famous in the 1970s and '80s as a greaser character in the doo-wop cover group Sha Na Na. Bauman had become something of a mascot for Washington progressive groups and was routinely asked to kick off meetings or conference calls with a ditty, which he was all too happy to do. All of a sudden, "Bowzer" from Sha Na Na was banned from organizing calls and began getting disinvited from events. Pelosi was making herself heard.

She came at the group's donors, too.

In politics, proximity to power is everything. Palace intrigues dating back thousands of years have hinged on nearly imperceptible cues from a ruler toward those in court. Some signals are starker than others, and Pelosi made sure one pair of Lawson's donors didn't miss hers. At a fund-raising dinner that was a pillar of the Bay Area's social calendar, key Lawson donors were moved from Pelosi's table and conspicuously relegated to table two—a cataclysmic social assassination.

While the group's donors faced social ostracism by Pelosi, the group itself had its survival put at risk. Trying to cut off an organization's financing is one of the primary tactics leading politicians use to keep those groups in line, and it was a favorite move deployed by Rahm Emanuel when he was chief of staff to President Obama. The pressure flips donor-politician relationships on their head. Instead of donors and organizations made up of active citizens making demands of politicians—power built on the outside and flowing into Congress— politicians make certain those demands *aren't made* by concentrating power internally and expressing it outward. With fewer demands coming from the outside, politicians are then not on the hook to accomplish as much.

Lawson and the Swigs mutually decided to part ways, recognizing what they were up against. "The Pelosis are really good at what they do," said Lawson, before correcting himself. "Christine is not good at what she does, though. Nancy Pelosi is good at what she does. Christine—I gave Christine, like, fifteen opportunities for us to just be like, 'Dude, we agree on like ninety-two percent of things, and I'm the lefty who actually understands that Pelosi is the best we can get right now, right?' It did not make any sense for her to try to destroy me. First, she couldn't accomplish it. And second, she didn't know she couldn't accomplish it." (Pelosi's daughter is widely known to be angling to replace her mother in Congress when she steps down in 2024.)

What makes this such a perfect tale of how Washington works is how pointless it all was. Pelosi still planned to push a drug-pricing bill, but Primus wanted to do it his way, without the embarrassment of a well-funded organization calling his effort too soft. For Lawson's part, he recognized the problem that came with having too much of his organization's fate in the hands of donors, who themselves could be pressured by politicians, so his organization launched a digital consulting and fund-raising firm, with the profits designated to support the nonprofit organization. This gave it a buffer against future efforts to undercut it.

Pelosi's pledge to give the Congressional Progressive Caucus 40 percent of the committee seats turned out to be illusory, because it gave Pelosi too big a box to play in. The CPC had never had any ideological litmus test for membership, and plenty of members were also part of the business-friendly New Democrat Coalition, so Pelosi stuck New Democrats on the committees, and as long as they were members of the CPC, they counted toward the quota. In multiple instances, people who hadn't been CPC members joined after the fact so they could be counted as such.

Pelosi didn't mind negotiating over the numbers, but it was the specific demands to elevate specific members that turned her hostile. "Pramila has a megaphone and actually knows how to make noise," Lawson said. "That's what [Pelosi] was worried about with AOC. That's what she was worried about with Pramila—is that these are two people who are clearly going to make a thing on the committee, and they're going to wield the committee, not as a place to accrue corporate cash for Democrats, but to advance lefty stuff, and that's what pissed her off so much." Jayapal's waiver request was rejected, and Ocasio-Cortez was kept off of Ways and Means.

But the efforts weren't a total failure. For years, the money committee for stashing vulnerable freshmen was Financial Services, where they could raise money from banks and insurance giants. But the hangover from the 2008 financial crisis had made Wall Street money toxic, and deregulating banks a political vulnerability. So, for the most part, freshmen looking for cash weren't interested in a seat on that committee. Those who didn't need bank money were happy to take the seats, and Katie Porter, Pressley, Tlaib, and Ocasio-Cortez all won spots.

Omar got her own top choice: the House Foreign Affairs Committee, where she wanted to fight against debilitating sanction regimes, the drone war, and a broadly belligerent U.S. foreign policy. She also won a rules change that would allow head coverings on the House floor.

In the 1980s, as President Ronald Reagan blew up the deficit by cutting taxes and increasing military spending, Democrats thought they had a clever way to combat the "tax-and-spend liberal" weight yoked around their necks. Rep. George Miller, a Bay Area Democrat who would later be a top lieutenant of Pelosi's, proposed a rule that all new spending must be paid for with either tax increases or spending cuts elsewhere. Known as "pay as you go," it was shortened to PAYGO.

After the 2006 blue wave that brought her to power for the first time, Pelosi implemented the PAYGO rule she and Miller had long been talking about. Demand can create supply, and the new rule created an industry of what became known as PAYFORs—spending cuts or tax policies that reduced the deficit according to the official score-keepers at the Congressional Budget Office. If a surtax on, say, a particular chemical discharge could raise a billion dollars over a ten-year period, then a member of Congress could use that PAYFOR to be in compliance with PAYGO for a program that spent a billion dollars.

Most of the painless PAYFORs—essentially, budget gimmicks—were quickly identified and catalogued by leadership. In order to use one in your legislation, you needed the permission of leadership, or your bill wouldn't move forward. The other option was to get a waiver from leadership. Effectively, this meant that in order to move a piece of legislation, a member of Congress needed a ticket to ride that could be given out only by House leaders, further concentrating power in the hands of the Speaker and giving that person an added disciplinary tool.

In 2010, after Republicans took over the House, they amended the rule to "CUTGO," meaning new spending could be offset only by cuts made elsewhere, with no tax hikes allowed. When Pelosi took over again in 2018, she was intent on reinstituting PAYGO.

Jayapal and Pocan had hoped to make progress on rolling it back, but in their talks with Pelosi, it became clear the rule was a priority of hers. Besides, with Trump in office, it wasn't as if they'd be passing any big-ticket items. Pelosi assured them they'd have her blessing to get waivers, and they moved on to other items.

With just two days to go until the vote over the rules package, a PAYGO war broke out on Twitter. As obscure a rule as it may seem, it was central to the contest between Reagan-era neoliberalism and the type of robust, New Deal–inspired agenda the left wanted to push. Reagan couldn't be buried until PAYGO was dead and gone. Warren Gunnels, the longtime spokesperson for Bernie Sanders, was often able to tweet without the approval of his boss, a privilege enjoyed at the time only by him and AOC's staffers. He took advantage of the freedom with a series of tweets urging the House to vote the rules package down for its inclusion of PAYGO. Ro Khanna surprised his staff by publicly agreeing with Gunnels. "I will be voting NO on the Rules package with #PayGo. It is terrible economics. The austerians were wrong about the Great Recession and Great Depression. At some point, politicians need to learn from mistakes and read economic history," Khanna tweeted.

Ocasio-Cortez followed: "Tomorrow I will also vote No on the rules package, which is trying to slip in #PAYGO. PAYGO isn't only bad economics, as @RoKhanna explains; it's also a dark political maneuver designed to hamstring progress on healthcare+other leg," she posted. "We shouldn't hinder ourselves from the start."

Other progressives began to consider voting it down, not wanting to get on the wrong side of the outside energy pushing for a no vote. Pelosi was now at risk of losing her first vote of her new legislative session. Rules Committee chair Jim McGovern called Jayapal "in a panic," she writes in her memoir. "Look," she said. "I will try to help, but we need something in exchange for this." McGovern had given his promise that PAYGO would be routinely waived, but Jayapal needed more. "Help me get the Speaker to commit that I will be able to have hearings on my Medicare for All bill," she told him.

"I can do a hearing in Rules," he responded. "It's not typical, but I'll do it."

Jayapal thanked him and said she'd also need a hearing in a major committee, as a hearing in Rules was a nice gesture but a bit gimmicky. Over the next twenty-four hours, she and McGovern went back and forth, with McGovern checking in with Pelosi's staff on what he could offer. Finally, Pelosi called Jayapal and offered a hearing in Rules as well as in the Budget Committee and promised to help ease the Medicare for All bill into a bigger committee like Ways and Means. In exchange, Jayapal agreed to keep the CPC in line.

Despite the win, Jayapal was privately furious at having been embarrassed publicly. She lit into Khanna while Pelosi's staff worked over Ocasio-Cortez and her chief of staff, Chakrabarti. Drew Hammill was sent to push Chakrabarti. "He just kept making shit up. It was amazing," Chakrabarti said. "It's so hard in that situation, because you're a freshman member of Congress, the rules are complicated, so you don't really know what you know or don't know. And of course, there's no other members who're actually researching about the rules, because you don't need to. If all you do is follow leadership, you never actually learn how to be a congressperson."

Hammill told him not to worry, that PAYGO would be waived routinely anyway.

"Well, then, why can't we just get rid of it?" Chakrabarti asked.

"This is a really important issue for all our swing district Democrats," Chakrabarti remembered Hammill arguing, unconvincingly, as far as he was concerned. "I couldn't imagine that half of those freshmen who got elected even knew what PAYGO is," Chakrabarti said. Hammill also argued that a PAYGO statute would allow Trump to cut Medicare. But this was in conflict with his other argument: If the rule could be routinely waived, then a statute on it could be dealt with in the bill itself. If the statute couldn't be dealt with, then the rule waiver was meaningless.

"It was rarely full-on lies, but it's usually stuff where they're just omitting the way to get around it," Chakrabarti said.

These types of conversations would come to characterize his and the Squad's interactions with leadership, where an asymmetry in the knowledge of congressional procedure could easily be deployed in service of an agenda. Omar, at least, had served a term in the Minnesota legislature, and Pressley and Tlaib had served on the Boston City Council and in the Michigan legislature, but for AOC it was all new.

Pelosi worked on Ocasio-Cortez. "Pick your fights later, but don't tank the rules package, because a lot of work has been put into it," she told her, according to Chakrabarti. "She told AOC something in effect, like, 'You're dead to me if you vote against this,'" he said.

On the morning of January 3, Ocasio-Cortez headed from her office in Cannon with Chakrabarti to get sworn in and start voting. By then, it was clear she had lost on the PAYGO fight and had also come up short on her demand for a special committee on climate change that would have subpoena and law-writing authority. The question now was whether she'd cast a hopeless no vote, laying down a marker even as it cost her with party leadership.

In the Capitol basement as we headed toward the elevators, I asked AOC about those losses. "I think there are a lot of wins that we've had so far policy-wise," she said, referring to the gains made by the CPC in the rules package. "When you look at what's considered a loss, whether it's the select committee or whether it's PAYGO, I see them as short-term losses, because in the long run, what we've accomplished is we've put these issues on the map."

I asked her how her view of politics and Congress had changed since she'd won her primary. "I think coming through this process from the background of organizing, and as an organizer, it really makes you think of the political process as—it really opens what that field looks like, of what change is possible. So, it's not just about whipping votes or getting someone to a yes or no—although all of those are critical elements of the job—but the other part of it is really shaping the landscape of what we think is possible," she said.

When the vote came, just three Democrats rejected the package—AOC, Khanna, and Tulsi Gabbard of Hawaii. The gap between AOC's power outside the Capitol and the display of it on day one inside could hardly have been greater.

To reshape that landscape, she was rapidly sacrificing her relationships with colleagues. Her most successful organizing effort so far had been the Sunrise Movement– and Justice Democrats–led occupation of Pelosi's office during orientation. Aside from Pelosi, she had also alienated Jayapal in the process. Now she had done it again with both.

Jayapal called Ocasio-Cortez and Chakrabarti to a meeting in her office. She didn't scold AOC, instead directing her ire at Chakrabarti. She finished by suggesting AOC needed to keep her staff in line. "Pramila was so annoyed, and so was Pocan," Chakrabarti confirmed. "I went to the principal's office."

To colleagues, Jayapal complained that Ocasio-Cortez, who touted herself as an organizer, had very little track record of actually organizing, whereas Jayapal had been a genuine organizer for more than ten years before coming to Congress. The growing hostility toward AOC was built upon already strong wariness on the part of her colleagues, who saw in the celebration of the Squad a challenge to their own integrity or progressivism.

The climate committee AOC had proposed ran into turf issues, too. Frank Pallone, the powerful chair of the Energy and Commerce Committee, saw it as a threat, and lobbied Pelosi to strip it of power. He took the issue so personally that he later blocked a bill authored by Ro Khanna from moving through his committee, as retribution for Khanna's support of the rival climate committee. Pelosi offered Ocasio-Cortez a seat on the diminished panel, but she refused.

"When AOC chose not to be on the committee, that upset Pelosi even more than the sit-in—that and the vote on the rules package," said Chakrabarti. Pelosi later told her biographer that she had told the Squad members that once they crossed the threshold of membership in Congress, it was time to leave the activism behind. "I say to them, as advocates, outsiders, it is our nature to be relentless, persistent, and dissatisfied," she told Susan Page, Washington bureau chief for USA Today. "When you come in, cross that door, take that oath, you have to be oriented toward results. Have confidence in what you believe in, have humility to listen to somebody else, because you're not a one-person show. This is the Congress of the United States." Page would soon invite Ocasio-Cortez to a salon at her home with other journalists. Scanning the room after introductions, Ocasio-Cortez whispered, "There are more people named Susan here than there are Black people." (I recall at least three Susans.)

As Chakrabarti, Ocasio-Cortez, and I walked through the basement of the Capitol toward the swearing-in, I thought back to a summer happy hour hosted by the CPC shortly after Ocasio-Cortez's victory over Crowley. The members there were consumed with the question of whether she thought them progressive enough. Did she plan to form a new caucus? What, they asked me, had she said about them? For some, AOC was a walking spotlight on the gap between their ideals and how they had come to practice politics. It was easier to get angry at the light than to close the gap. She told an interviewer not long after she won the nomination that the Progressive Caucus was too large and unwieldy to be an effective fighting force, and that she hoped to put together a "sub-caucus" that would vote as a bloc and extract concessions with the resulting leverage.

It was becoming clear, though, that if every win Ocasio-Cortez notched on the outside simply created more distance between her and her colleagues on the inside, organizing an effective progressive majority would be impossible. But something was happening. A security guard by an elevator spotted AOC coming and threw his arms out for a hug, embracing her as other members of Congress walked past.

6

DOING THE THING

Heading into the 2018 midterms, President Donald Trump settled on twin themes to try to salvage his Republican majority in Congress: Kavanaugh and the caravan. Republicans had become infuriated at the "unfair treatment" of Supreme Court nominee Brett Kavanaugh, who faced allegations of sexual assault toward the end of his confirmation process—some highly credible, like that from Christine Blasey Ford, and some ludicrous, such as one brought forward by attorney Michael Avenatti, a con man who briefly rose to prominence in Democratic circles before he was imprisoned for fraud.

The caravan was an organized march of asylum seekers making their way from Central America, through Mexico, and toward the southern U.S. border. Trump hoped that backlash over #MeToo and hostility to migrants could combine to bring enough voters back out to counteract the Democratic resistance, but the strategy failed, and Democrats won a sizable majority.

The election did nothing to dampen Trump's enthusiasm for a southern border wall, and in fact it only increased his sense of urgency, as he would soon be losing control of a chamber of Congress needed to fund the project. That he had so far failed to build his wall was an intolerable humiliation, and he made obtaining the money the central focus of the 2018 lame-duck session.

Yet congressional Republicans were in no mood for Trump's border antics. They struck a deal on government funding that included, as Democrats demanded, not a penny for the wall. So, on December 22, 2018, Trump shut down the government at midnight. He wouldn't open it again, he pledged, until Congress funded his wall.

The shutdown dragged into the next year, and the new class of freshmen was sworn in to office with the government still closed. On

January 22, a month into what would become the longest government shutdown in U.S. history, House Democrats made a bid to open things back up, unveiling legislation to fund only the agencies under the Department of Homeland Security. There would be no wall money, but some supplemental funds would go toward improving conditions at the border for detained migrants.

Six months earlier, Ocasio-Cortez had been at those facilities and had been shocked by what she saw. The treatment of the migrants, she said, was fascist. Photos of her pained emotional reaction had become synonymous with Democratic outrage over Trump's policy. In her televised debate with Joe Crowley, she had savaged him for his hypocrisy on the issue, arguing that while he had called Immigration and Customs Enforcement "fascist," he wouldn't do anything about it. "If you think this system is fascist," she asked him, "then why don't you vote to eliminate it?"

He had no answer. There is no good answer. But now it was her responsibility to offer one. She sat down with her staff and opened the discussion: Do we vote against this funding proposal? She laid out the terms of the debate to her team. The bill includes money for things we don't support, and we might be the only vote against it. Meanwhile, a lot of this is symbolism: the party is trying to reopen the government, and it's not like this bill will pass the Senate and get signed by Trump. It's a messaging bill, and the message is that Democrats are being the adults in the room, while Trump is having a tantrum.

Assembled that day was most of her team, including Chakrabarti; Trent; her legislative director, Ariel Eckblad; and her new legislative aide, Dan Riffle. Ocasio-Cortez noted that eventually she would have to vote for a CR—short for "continuing resolution," a bill that continues to fund the government on the same terms as it had been funded. The CR would include the money not just for Homeland Security, but also for many other agencies whose mission she supported. Drawing a line in the sand now, she said, would mean voting against all future government funding bills, even when it came to actually reopening the government. "Where do we draw that line?" she asked. "What is enough?"

Before she could finish the question, Trent interrupted with an answer in the form of his own question: "Yeah, what is enough to fund a fascist agency that cages children?"

Nobody had an answer. "We all just kind of looked at each other," Riffle recalled. "Like, nothing. Nothing is enough. So, we're a 'no' on this."

Trent's intervention had ended the conversation, but it was clear that what they were trying to do was going to be a challenge. "You could see not just her, but me, everybody in the office, sort of like *doing the thing*," Riffle said. "It's going to be hard," he realized. "It's going to be hard for us to be principled here."

As the month ground on, Ocasio-Cortez mused to her staff that she should threaten to endorse Republicans who wouldn't reopen the government, which their primary opponents could then use against them to vote them out of office. She wasn't serious, but the focus on her and the Squad from the right certainly was. Fox was covering AOC nearly every hour, and her name identification was higher in surveys among Republicans than Democrats. The same was true for Ilhan Omar, but with her, the coverage took on a more hateful edge. Summing up the posture of the conservative movement toward each, one analyst who spent his days consuming right-wing media said the divide was becoming clear: the right had a twisted, sexualized fascination with Ocasio-Cortez, but with Omar it was pure fear; they just wanted her dead. Many on the right also said they wanted Ocasio-Cortez dead. One typical email her staff forwarded to Capitol Police had the subject line "Can I join the revolution?" but its contents read, "Fuck You Bitch! I will fucking kill you and, hump your dead body!" A separate threat against Omar was so direct and explicit that authorities were able to prosecute the case.

The Squad huddled and agreed to vote as a bloc, making up the only four "no" votes on the bill. A few days later, Trump caved, and the House voted on a measure that was actually meaningful, the bill that would reopen the government . . . and ICE, the fascist agency AOC wanted abolished. This time it wasn't a messaging bill; this funding would actually get to ICE.

AOC stuck with her "no" vote. On the way to the House floor, she shot an Instagram video. Walking beside her was Riffle, and she introduced him to her followers. "He's 'Every Billionaire Is a Policy Failure' on Twitter. So, yeah," she quipped, a reference to his handle, which had recently sparked a national conversation about whether the claim was fair.

She subtitled the video with an explanation of her vote. "Most of our votes are pretty straightforward, but today was a tough/nuanced call," she wrote. "We didn't vote with the party because one of the spending bills included ICE funding, and our community felt strongly about not funding that."

When the roll was called, precisely one Democrat voted "no," Representative Ocasio-Cortez. The rest of the Squad had gone along.

Casting the vote was draining. She'd been pressed on the floor by party leadership to switch, told by whip staff she'd be put on "a list"—what kind of list, nobody said, but it didn't sound like a good one. She'd been called in for a personal meeting with Steny Hoyer. Everyone had told her that what she was doing was wrong, that it was hurting the team. It weighed on her.

The final vote came late into the night, past midnight, and Chakrabarti walked AOC back to her apartment. As they passed Capitol Hill's famous Mexican restaurant Tortilla Coast, a worker was leaving, having just closed it down. "Alexandria, is that you?" he asked.

She told him it was.

"I just wanted to say thank you for standing up for me and my family. It means so much," he told her. The weight, for just that moment, lifted.

7

THE BENJAMINS

Not long after Rashida Tlaib and Ilhan Omar were sworn in to Congress, they began hearing from their new colleagues that one member of the House Democratic caucus, Josh Gottheimer, had particularly strong views about each of them. Many of his colleagues had particularly strong views about Gottheimer, but as far as they knew, he was just another member of the Democratic caucus. They would soon learn there was much more to him.

Gottheimer had an intense hostility to the left wing of the party—he dubbed them "the herbal tea party"—and considered the progressive movement generally to be poisoned by anti-Semitism. But he had particular animosity toward Tlaib and Omar. The pair were far too rough to Israel in their rhetoric, he complained, taking his beef to Majority Leader Hoyer on the House floor. Hoyer told Gottheimer to work out his problems with the two members directly, which Gottheimer took as a blessing from the party leadership to go to war with them.

When Gottheimer reached out to meet with Tlaib, she was eager to take the meeting, hoping that a personal connection would help bridge their differences. On the day of the meeting, February 6, 2019, Gottheimer arrived with a colleague, freshman Elaine Luria from Virginia—and a white binder. Luria began by saying that she had met with Israeli prime minister Benjamin Netanyahu six weeks earlier. Tlaib tried to break the ice with a joke: "How's the two-state solution going?" Netanyahu had recently been making it explicit that he was never serious about a two-state solution and that his real aim was to stall for time while Israel gradually annexed Palestinian land.

The joke fell flat.

Gottheimer pulled out the binder, opening it to show Tlaib the contents. It was a collection of printed-out articles, with quotes from her and other lines highlighted. He began going through it line by line, occasionally misattributing quotes by Omar or other activists to Tlaib.

Tlaib tried to reach Gottheimer on a personal level, telling him about her grandmother, who lives in occupied Ramallah. He wasn't interested. "He was using a very stern tone, like a father to a child. At that moment, I realized he's a bully," Tlaib later told me. "He had a goal of breaking me down. I left feeling exactly that way."

Walking out, she pulled out her phone and found the contact for Ilhan Omar. When Omar picked up, she could tell that Tlaib had tears streaming down her face as she recounted the meeting's blow-by-blow. "If he asks you to meet, don't do it," Tlaib warned her. "Don't do it."

Four days later, Israeli media reported that Kevin McCarthy, the House minority leader, had promised "action" against Tlaib and Omar for their criticism of Israel. My colleague at the time Glenn Greenwald posted the news on Twitter, adding "GOP Leader Kevin McCarthy threatens punishment for @IlhanMN and @RashidaTlaib over their criticisms of Israel. It's stunning how much time US political leaders spend defending a foreign nation even if it means attacking free speech rights of Americans."

Omar then shared Greenwald's post on her time line, adding the commentary "It's all about the Benjamins baby ♪♩," a reference to the hip-hop song of that name. Asked to clarify whose Benjamins she was claiming had influenced McCarthy, she responded, "AIPAC!"

All hell broke loose.

Omar had never thought she was on dangerous, anti-Semitic territory because she was talking about the Irish American McCarthy, arguing that his approach on the issue was influenced by campaign cash. It was a naïve assumption, but one with some logical backing: the very purpose of large financial contributions, of course, is to influence politicians. (What nobody, including Omar, noticed at the time was that the Diddy song to which her "Benjamins" remark had alluded included an explicitly anti-Semitic line: "You should do what we do / stack chips like Hebrews.")

Gottheimer seized his chance, demanding not just an apology but official action from the House of Representatives. The Squad was a month into their first term and facing the first test of solidarity.

Outside Congress, the elections of Omar and Tlaib had generated their own reaction. In late January, pollster and Democratic strategist Mark Mellman announced the formation of the group Democratic Majority for Israel (DMFI), which Mellman said in a statement would stand up for Israel inside the "progressive movement." And as Mellman set up shop, he linked up with LinkedIn billionaire Reid Hoffman, who was similarly invested in undermining the party's left flank. Hoffman's concern, he said, was pragmatic and electoral—he believed that politicians like Omar were bad for the Democratic brand—while Mellman's focus was Israel, but the two aligned on goals and began sharing office space and more or less uniting their two operations.

Mellman told me his work against the party's left was meant to undermine the Israeli right. "I have substantial direct experience in Israeli politics, having helped bring down Netanyahu," he said, referring to the former prime minister, also known as Bibi. "The simple fact of Israeli politics is that the right uses attacks from the U.S. and Europe to its great and consistent benefit. That's correct. Anti-Israel forces in the U.S. do vastly more to help the right than to hurt it. They enable Bibi to run as the guy who will stand up to the U.S. and the world to protect his country. That has been a key element of most of his campaigns . . . The anti-Israel far left has propped up the Israeli right and done tremendous damage to the prospects for peace between Israel and the Palestinians."

In his efforts to beat back Netanyahu, Mellman had worked as a key election consultant to Yair Lapid, an Israeli politician at the head of a center-right political party, Yesh Atid, which would surge several years later, under Mellman's guidance, making Lapid prime minister of Israel. Democratic Majority for Israel provided a forum for Lapid's first call with an American Zionist organization after his election, during which he declared his intention to reinvigorate Israel's ties to American political parties.*

Mellman was also a veteran AIPAC strategist, and DMFI was an effort to do something of a rebrand for AIPAC within Democratic circles. AIPAC itself had become a toxic brand inside the Democratic Party after the organization worked to torpedo Obama's signature foreign policy achievement, the Iran nuclear deal. Mellman's firm, the Mellman Group, had consulted for AIPAC's dark-money group Citi-

---

* Netanyahu returned to power in December 2022 atop a far-right government.

zens for a Nuclear Free Iran. The Mellman Group was also the second largest contractor for AIPAC's educational arm, the American Israel Education Foundation, in the year it fought the Iran deal. The biggest contractor that year was a travel business then owned by Sheldon Adelson, a casino mogul and Republican mega-donor.

Mellman's new organization was rolled out with a splashy *New York Times* profile and supportive comments from Majority Leader Hoyer, whose biannual congressional trips to Israel AIPAC sponsored and AIEF organized; caucus chair Hakeem Jeffries; Senate Foreign Relations chair Bob Menendez; and Arizona's freshman Democratic senator, Kyrsten Sinema. (Sinema has since left the party, calling herself an independent.) DMFI may have been a rebranding of AIPAC within Democratic circles, but it would also be able to deploy different tactics. Before *Citizens United*, AIPAC had grown its power not simply with the wealth of a handful of mega-donors, but through genuine and sustained grassroots organizing. Synagogue to synagogue, from the 1980s onward, AIPAC organized powerful local support for politicians who voiced unqualified backing for Israel and ran high-profile campaigns against those who deviated. Much like the NRA, its strength lay in its numbers and in its narrow focus on a particular issue. Post–*Citizens United*, AIPAC could skip the grassroots organizing component—which was fortunate for DMFI, as blind support for the occupation of Palestinian territory and the refusal to grant Palestinians any semblance of human rights were unpopular stances in Democratic primaries—and go straight to big-money efforts directed through super PACs. It was joined in many of its efforts by the big money flowing into Washington from the state treasuries of the United Arab Emirates and Saudi Arabia, which struck up an alliance inside Washington against the progressive wing of the Democratic Party, which all three of these factions considered a threat to the status quo in the Middle East.

Breaking down Tlaib, Omar, and their allies on the left had been one of Gottheimer's primary goals since the November elections. After taking control of the House, Democratic opponents of the war in Yemen, led by Rep. Ro Khanna, introduced a War Powers Resolution to end U.S. support for the Saudi-led war. In the Senate, Bernie Sanders teamed with Republican Mike Lee to do the same.

The Yemen resolution became a key flash point, pitting progressives against their newly arrayed opponents in the form of Saudi

Arabia, the UAE, and Israel. As progressives in the House neared a historic achievement, Gottheimer organized behind the scenes to take the resolution down, in part by attempting to make it a referendum on support for Israel.

Gottheimer tried to play hardball with his own party's leadership with a parliamentary maneuver that would link the fate of the Yemen war resolution to public support for Israel, the most aggressive linking together of the interests of the Gulf States and Israel in the history of the U.S. Congress. Claiming that he had "the votes in [his] pocket," he approached Majority Leader Hoyer on the floor, sources involved in the fight told me. Gottheimer would allow the War Powers Resolution to pass, he said, only if Hoyer agreed to hold a vote the same day on a bill targeting the BDS movement. Short for "boycott, divestment, sanctions," BDS—depending on the definition to which one subscribes—encourages businesses and individuals supportive of Palestinian rights and opposed to the Israeli occupation not to do business either with Israel or with Israeli companies operating in the occupied territories.

Hoyer was a fierce opponent of BDS and one of the lower chamber's most vocal supporters of Israel. He had lashed out at Omar in a fiery speech at AIPAC's annual conference, which was held just as the Yemen debate was coming to a head. Nobody would have confused him for a supporter of a boycott on behalf of Palestinian rights, but Hoyer was all in on the Yemen war resolution, so Gottheimer had a real fight on his hands. He may have prevailed had two forces, Hoyer and the Congressional Progressive Caucus—unaccustomed to being in full alignment—not come together to resist his effort. Hoyer called Gottheimer's bluff. As the votes were tallied, only four Democrats voted with Gottheimer. One of them, Jeff Van Drew, a machine politician and freshman from New Jersey, would later switch parties and become a Republican. Another was Gottheimer's ally in every fight against the Squad: Elaine Luria.

The bill's supporters out-organized Gottheimer, and in April 2019, Congress sent a War Powers Resolution to Trump's desk. He vetoed it, rejecting Congress's demand that he stop backing the Saudi-led war, but the congressional action did in fact lessen hostilities, as the Pentagon agreed to stop refueling Saudi warplanes midflight, drastically cutting down the bombing campaign.

Gottheimer's rearguard action against the Yemen resolution, and his attempt to link the issue to Israel, was perhaps the most aggressive move any Democrat made against the Democratic caucus and its leadership that session—and the intensity with which he approached it made clear he was working to establish himself as a leading player in the years to come and would be doing so in league with the forces arrayed behind, and funded by, Saudi Arabia, the United Arab Emirates, Israel, and their allies in the United States. Yet it would be the members of the Squad who would routinely be labeled by party leadership as disloyal.

The blustering battle between the Squad and Gottheimer—sometimes with leadership on his side, sometimes not—would come to define the next several years of House Democratic politics, reaching its zenith in the battle over Build Back Better, Biden's major climate and social spending package, more than three years later. But, for now, Gottheimer had the "Benjamins" post to worry about. He began organizing a letter demanding that Democratic leaders condemn Omar, and the newly formed advocacy group Democratic Majority for Israel marshaled its outrage against her.

The day after the Benjamins post, Pelosi had called Omar. There's an informal rule in Congress that before publicly criticizing somebody, the proper etiquette is to give them a private heads-up. Omar told Pelosi that regardless of her call, she had already made the decision to apologize, and Pelosi let her know there'd still be a joint statement coming. Pelosi worked to soften the blow, explaining that she was under intense pressure to condemn her and really had no choice, but that it shouldn't be taken as a personal attack. Omar came away from the conversation feeling no ill will toward Pelosi.

Omar, who had been taken aback by the avalanche of charges of anti-Semitism, had been shaken after speaking with longtime allies who told her they had been genuinely offended by her post, saying that it played squarely into the tropes about conniving Jews using money to manipulate things behind the scenes. Omar raced to post what was a genuine apology, not wanting be seen as having been forced to do so by her bosses. Her statement and the one from leadership landed around the same time. "Anti-Semitism is real," Omar said, returning to Twitter, the scene of the crime, "and I am grateful for Jewish allies and colleagues who are educating me on the painful history of anti-Semitic tropes." She continued: "We have to always be willing to step back and think through criticism, just as I expect people to hear me when others attack me for my identity. This is why I unequivocally apologize."

The joint statement signed by Pelosi, Hoyer, Jeffries, and their lieutenants read:

> Legitimate criticism of Israel's policies is protected by the values of free speech and democratic debate that the United States and Israel share. But Congresswoman Omar's use of anti-Semitic tropes and prejudicial accusations about Israel's supporters is deeply offensive. We condemn these remarks and we call upon Congresswoman Omar to immediately apologize for these hurtful comments.
>
> As Democrats and as Americans, the entire Congress must be fully engaged in denouncing and rejecting all forms of hatred, racism, prejudice and discrimination wherever they are encountered.

That wasn't the end of it. What Gottheimer and his allies wanted was a resolution on the House floor condemning Omar, an extraordinary step to take against a representative not yet through her second month in office. Gottheimer's letter, signed by him and Luria, was sent on February 11, just days after their collective browbeating of Tlaib, so they made sure to make their complaints plural. "As Jewish Members of Congress, we are deeply alarmed by recent rhetoric from certain members within our Caucus, including just last night, that has disparaged us and called into question our loyalty to our nation," they wrote. "We hope that our Caucus will take swift action to address these issues in the coming days by reiterating our rejection of anti-Semitism and our continued support for the State of Israel."

Democrats had come into the House promising to be a bulwark against Trump and to model what a just and progressive government would look like under Democratic control if voters were generous enough to bestow them with it in two years. Instead, the rest of the month was spent battling over whether Omar's comments demanded a full censure on the House floor or if her apology was sufficient. Democrat upon Democrat was pressed by cable news on whether they supported the resolution condemning the freshman congresswoman from Minnesota.

During the third week of the debate over her comments, on February 27, Omar appeared at the DC bookstore and restaurant Busboys and Poets for an event with Jayapal, Pocan, and Tlaib. Earlier that day, Jayapal had introduced her Medicare for All bill, and much of the event focused on that. Omar got a question from Busboys owner Andy Shallal, a leftist Iraqi American activist, about the Benjamins controversy and the allegations of anti-Semitism. Tlaib answered first. "This conversation is about human rights for everyone, this conversation around what this looks like is not centered around hate, it's actually centered around love," she said.

Omar spoke about her conflicted feelings on the fallout. "I know what intolerance looks like, and I'm sensitive when someone says, 'The words you use, Ilhan, are resemblance of intolerance,'" she said. "And I am cautious of that, and I feel pained by that."

Her odd phrasing—"resemblance of intolerance"—was another reminder that English wasn't her first language. And yet, there she was, dancing through fields of linguistic land mines known to have blown up even the most balletic critics of the Israeli government. Her next word, fatefully, as it often is, was *but*.

"But it's almost as if every single time we say something, regardless of what it is we say, that it's supposed to be about foreign policy or engagement, our advocacy about ending oppression, or the freeing of every human life and wanting dignity, we get to be labeled in something, and that ends the discussion, because we end up defending that, and nobody ever gets to have the broader debate of 'What is happening with Palestine?' So, for me, I want to talk about the political influence in this country that says it is okay for people to push for allegiance to a foreign country. I want to ask, why is it okay for me to talk about the influence of the NRA, of fossil fuel industries, or Big Pharma, and not talk about a powerful lobby that is influencing policy."

The comments were clipped and posted online, and Omar was once again blasted as anti-Semitic for her line about "allegiance to a foreign country." The Anti-Defamation League fired off a letter to House leaders demanding a resolution condemning her. House Foreign Affairs Committee chairman Eliot Engel called it a "vile, anti-Semitic slur," as other colleagues piled on. Gottheimer and Luria added Rep. Brad Schneider to their group and penned a column for CNN attacking Omar.

The resolution was drafted, but this time there was significantly more pushback. Large numbers of Democrats thought that singling out Omar was wrong and pushed the resolution to condemn all forms of bigotry. The resolution came to the floor on March 8. After tense negotiations, it had been redrafted to condemn bigotry broadly. Some two dozen Republicans, angry that the resolution didn't go directly after Omar, voted against it. Omar stood mostly in the back of the chamber, glancing at her phone and, as *Politico* would later write, "seemingly oblivious to the remarkable rebuke being leveled at her."

When Omar saw Jayapal on the House floor, she bounded over to her. Jayapal told her she had sprouted a new batch of gray hairs over the past week, all of them thanks to Omar. The two laughed hard, becoming the center of attention and further infuriating Gottheimer and the Republicans.

Congress was more than two months old and still focused primarily on the question of whether Omar was anti-Semitic, rather than on any substantive legislative agenda or effort to challenge President Trump. It was not the fight that Justice Democrats had envisioned for the Squad or one that anybody was prepared for. If psychologist Abraham Maslow had developed a political hierarchy, alongside his famous hierarchy of needs, surviving an onslaught of scandals would probably have been the first order of business, coming well before the organization of an alternative power center capable of advancing an agenda. The repeated cycles of outrage and reaction left less room for the Squad to strategize together toward a shared objective. Still, it raised the question of whether there *was* a shared objective, or whether each of them was pursuing their own priorities and the interests of their districts while learning how to navigate the complex dynamics of the House. "We're not an entity," Omar once told me when I asked if the Squad held any regular meetings. "It's a media creation." Pressley would tell her Squadmates: "At the end of the day, you vote alone, and you're voting for your district."

8

IT IS A DREAM

Not long after Ocasio-Cortez won her primary, Saikat Chakrabarti and Corbin Trent ventured to DC to scope things out. Both were planning to work on AOC's official side, with Chakrabarti as chief of staff, able to take just $55,000 in a salary, thanks to his Silicon Valley days. The first question everyone they ran into asked the two was the same, a question born of both curiosity and a sense of competitiveness: What committees does Ocasio-Cortez want to be on?

Several members of Congress gave advice related to her "legacy" twenty or thirty years down the road. What does she want her legacy to be? She should figure that out first, they told Chakrabarti and Trent, and then work backward from there to figure out what committees she needs and what alliances she must form to make that legacy a reality.

I met both men in the lobby of the Hyatt on Capitol Hill, and they relayed their revulsion at the notion. "Twenty years?" said Trent. "Christ, if we're still here in twenty years, we'll be total failures."

"We have, like, a decade to turn this entire thing around," said Chakrabarti, who was evangelizing about a book on the World War II mobilization that turned a peacetime economy into a wartime industry capable of producing the armaments, ships, planes, bombs, and vehicles that defeated fascism. *Freedom's Forge: How American Business Produced Victory in World War II*, written by Arthur Herman, a scholar at the conservative American Enterprise Institute, focused, as its subtitle suggests, on the role of business in winning the war. But the book itself teaches a different lesson: that it was Roosevelt who used every tool at his disposal to engineer the top-to-bottom redevelopment of the economy. The same would have to happen this time, Chakrabarti suggested. Let *that* be AOC's legacy.

For all her eagerness to continue raising money from the fossil fuel industry, Pelosi had been early in warning of the dangers of climate change, and the first thing she did when she took the House in 2006 was create a select committee on the climate with real teeth and subpoena power and then appoint then representative Ed Markey, a true believer, to chair it. She also backed her ally Henry Waxman, another climate hawk, in his successful effort to oust the Big Auto–friendly John Dingell Jr. from the chairmanship of the Energy and Commerce Committee, specifically so Waxman could ram through a climate bill. He did so, at significant electoral cost to Democrats in swing seats, and the House passed the bill, only to see it die without a vote in the Senate. Obama had declined Reid's suggestion to use budget reconciliation—a 50-vote process—to pass the climate bill. Had the country started that year in reducing carbon emissions, the picture a decade later would have looked much different.

What happened to that climate committee? Chakrabarti and Trent wondered. Given the history, they both said, it seemed reasonable to push for it to be rebuilt and be the vehicle to turn the Green New Deal from a vision into legislative text, so that if and when the party took power fully in 2021, they'd have a bill ready to go.

Creation of a Green New Deal Committee became the central demand of the occupation of Pelosi's office, though the method had been a gamble. On a personal level, Pelosi didn't want to be pushed into doing anything, lest it chip away at the image of toughness she had effectively cultivated. She went out of her way to belittle the Green New Deal. "It will be one of several or maybe many suggestions that we receive," she told reporters. "The green dream, or whatever they call it. Nobody knows what it is, but they're for it, right?"

The "green dream" had started as a Google Doc put out by Sunrise, AOC, and the other groups behind the march on Pelosi's office, and while the idea of a Green New Deal took off, the document itself came in for immediate criticism, both from the AFL-CIO, which warned that it would cost union jobs in the fossil fuel and pipeline industries, and from climate justice activists, who thought it didn't go far enough in redressing the systemically racist impacts of climate change and pollution.

Moving from dreamland to Google Doc to a congressional resolution (which is significantly short of legislation) required much more compromise than might be expected in an aspirational document. Work on it began in December 2018, before AOC had any staff. The joke was that Evan Weber of Sunrise, who had made the fateful ask that Ocasio-Cortez support the sit-in, was her interim legislative director. The first task was to find a cosponsor in the Senate, and they immediately ruled out anybody potentially running for president, a good chunk of that chamber. "We knew if we had a presidential candidate, it would just be their thing, and we wanted it to be everybody's thing," said Weber.

After the Sunrise protest, Ocasio-Cortez had felt isolated, having gone out on a radical limb on her own, breaking all sorts of norms and customs in Congress. Sen. Ed Markey of Massachusetts was one of the few who reached out to her with an encouraging word, congratulating her on what she'd done and probing her about the new youth movement. Markey was facing reelection in Massachusetts, with rumors that Rep. Joe Kennedy or Attorney General Maura Healey might challenge him. As a senator, Markey was liked well enough, but he'd been in Congress since 1976 and knew he was vulnerable to the question of why he deserved another term. What was he fighting for?

Recalling Markey's service as chair of the previous special climate panel, and his authorship of Waxman-Markey—the American Clean Energy and Security Act of 2009—the only major climate bill ever to clear a chamber of Congress, Ocasio-Cortez asked him to be her lead sponsor in the Senate. He eagerly accepted.

By mid-January, working closely with Sunrise, which coordinated with outside groups, AOC's office had consulted an endless number of organizations, including the Sierra Club, the AFL-CIO, the Service Employees International Union, the BlueGreen Alliance, Climate Justice Alliance, and New Consensus, the think tank backed by Chakrabarti and helmed by Zack Exley, where Rhiana Gunn-Wright, an up-and-coming radical policy writer, was taking the lead in drafting the resolution.

An exchange between Sunrise and the NAACP was indicative of the difficulties they faced. A week before the unveiling, an NAACP official, Katherine Egland, wrote to Sunrise. The NAACP's objections:

> It isn't that we want or expect a perfect bill or resolution, but that we are fundamentally opposed to carbon capture sequestration, by any name or concept; and we are vehemently against any form or theory of carbon taxing, credits, dividends, etc.

This is shocking to many of our partners and fellow advocates. They feel that they know better and that our opposition is from a lack of understanding. However, we fully understand all aspects. We have discussed and debated them ceaselessly and continue to stand firmly grounded in our position. We unapologetically believe that these two particular proposals will do more harm than good—especially as it relates to the very people it proposes to uplift. So while we understand the well meaning intent behind them, we vehemently differ.

Sunrise's Evan Weber forwarded the note to Markey's and AOC's teams. "Wanted to make sure you both had this from the NAACP. My opinion is that it would be very bad to not have them with us, and their concerns will be shared by other environmental and climate justice advocates as well," Weber wrote, recommending that they remove the "true cost of emissions" bullet—which, to many in the know, Weber understood, signaled "carbon pricing."

Putting a price on carbon allows renewables to compete on a more level playing field, as carbon is now asked to pay for its pollution rather than sticking the public with the tab. But this setup also raises the price of gas and utilities, and no amount of credit or rebate scheme is enough to persuade people, the NAACP worried, that they won't be paying more at the pump to satisfy the vanity of environmentalists. The Yellow Vests protests in France in 2018 had sounded the death knell for such an approach, as it became clear the working class weren't willing to pay for what they saw as a problem they hadn't created.

The term *climate justice* was relatively new to the mainstream lexicon, with *justice* standing in for the idea that the disproportionate impact a particular policy had on particular people needed to be taken into account. Reproductive justice, for instance, drawing on the analysis of intersectionality, confronted the way that abortion restrictions were more oppressive to those already racially and economically oppressed. For the NAACP, carbon capture and sequestration—the idea that emissions could be captured or sucked out of the air and sequestered back into the ground—was seen as a scam by the fossil fuel industry to continue to burn coal in Black neighborhoods and call it clean. A 2018 NAACP resolution referenced a clean-coal debacle in a Black community in Mississippi, in which the state spent $7.5

billion on a Kemper County project with little to show for it but higher electricity rates and no reduction in pollution. The resolution observed that "low income and minority populations are the most disproportionately impacted by the production of fossil fuel based [*sic*] energy and continue to be the least able to combat the adverse effects due to less financial resources and inability to pay discriminatory fixed and grid access costs."

When it came to carbon pricing, another NAACP resolution, which had recently been reaffirmed in 2018, had cast it as insufficient to the scale of the crisis, while putting too much burden on Black communities. Lost on nobody involved was the NAACP's significant support from the fossil fuel industry, whose leading companies sponsored the group's conventions and otherwise kicked in support.

Yet dropping some form of carbon pricing could risk losing supporters on the left, who would see the resolution as mere wish-casting. "This is the kind of response we will likely get if we keep the carbon pricing thing as is," Chakrabarti wrote in a subsequent email to Weber about the NAACP response. Carbon pricing was dropped.

The final document was a result of wheeling and dealing the likes of which hadn't been done by the left in Washington since Lyndon B. Johnson was president and the final product had a stunningly broad coalition behind it. The unveiling of the resolution was set for February 7. "We got everyone in the right place. We had the Big Greens lined up, and they were happy because AFL was in a good place," said Weber. "AFL-CIO was planning to put out a positive statement on the whole thing."

And then came the FAQ—and the cow farts. "We spent months really carefully negotiating between all these interests," Weber recalled years later. "Honestly, this is like one of my biggest political regrets, is what happened around the FAQs."

Several things happened around the frequently asked questions document the office prepared, but what first set the resolution veering off course, Weber said, was an article in *Politico*—or, as Weber called it, "pain-in-the-ass-fucking-*Politico*." (I started my political journalism career at *Politico* and can confirm that it is a pain in the ass.) The story, based on sources who had seen a late version of the resolution, landed on Monday, February 4, and was headlined, "Green New Deal Won't Call for End to Fossil Fuels."

The story came from frustrated elements on the left of the climate world who insisted that the only rational path forward was to shut down the burning of fossil fuels and worry about the rest later. Weber understood the irony: nearly everyone in the Sunrise leadership came from the divest-and-shut-it-down side of organizing. These were *their* people, and now they were getting attacked by them. The Sunrise team was barely into their mid-twenties and were already being called sellouts.

"It's the movement that many people in Sunrise came out of, but our whole thesis was that that kind of campaigning was ineffective both because it was an unpopular message with the public—that saying no to everything doesn't actually give people something to believe in—and it was really bad for coalition building," Weber said, noting that it's impossible to get labor on board with a policy position that will eliminate jobs, even if you promise a world full of other types of jobs in the future.

Indeed, the *Politico* story—as if to make Weber's point—quoted the policy director for the climate group 350.org (where some of the Sunrise brass had started their careers or journeys into activism) criticizing the resolution for using the term *clean*, which indicated a "keep the door open" approach to carbon capture and sequestration, allowing fossil fuels to continue to be used.

The rationale for the blanket opposition to any carbon technology is a bit elliptical. The carbon industry supports investment in clean-tech infrastructure cynically, as a way to stave off its own demise, the argument goes, and the technology isn't actually able to do what its proponents have claimed it will one day be able to do. Therefore, support of clean tech only strengthens the fossil fuel industry. Forcing carbon reductions to be achieved exclusively through renewable sources, meanwhile, channels investment in that direction and moves us closer to a genuinely carbon-free economy. In this telling, carbon, rather than carbon emissions, is the real enemy.

But there are kinks in the logic. If a technology's current state equaled its promise, both wind and solar would have been shut down long ago and we would never have seen the exponential technological bursts that have led both to become cheaper sources of energy than fossil fuels. It also ignores the reality that carbon capture technology does work—at least at a small scale and in theory. Whether it can be scaled fast enough to meet the crisis is an open question, but it's not out of the question.

More to the immediate political point, if it's an open question but a green coalition rejects it, that coalition won't include organized labor, and that coalition will not enact legislation—legislation needed to reverse the climate apocalypse. The *Politico* article quoted Sean McGarvey, president of the North America's Building Trades Unions, saying that oil and gas industry jobs paid solid, middle-class wages while work in the renewable field still did not. "They're talking about everything except the workers that are doing the work," he said. McGarvey made the comments at an event alongside Mike Sommers, a lobbyist for the American Petroleum Institute, who gleefully drove in the wedge, claiming that one-third of construction jobs are in the oil and gas industry.

Spooked by the article, AOC's team began walking away from some of the concessions they had made. But instead of rewriting the resolution, they began tweaking the FAQ and other material that described it. Where the resolution left room for carbon tech and the possibility of nuclear power to play a role, for instance, the FAQ blasted the concepts. And it was the FAQ that the media used to shape its coverage. Weber lamented that the retreat away from the compromise they had agreed upon came in the face of everything they'd done to reorient their politics toward coalition building, reaching the masses, and expanding the tent of environmentalism with the aim of actually passing a Green New Deal. "We believe that really deeply in our bones. It was one of the whole reasons why we broke off 350.org and the rest of these groups and started Sunrise in the first place, and we were really thrilled to find alignment with AOC and the New Consensus folks," he said. "And basically, the second this *Politico* article hit, we sort of got scared, and I think it was eve-of-launch jitters."

Overconfidence had crept in, as AOC and Sunrise had become the It kids of Washington. "I think we had done such a good job, up until that point, of massaging the language that there was kind of an arrogance of, like, 'We can actually appease everyone here,' instead of sticking to our guns and making a real choice about charting a different direction and keeping our eyes on the prize," Weber said. "And so, the decision was made by AOC's team to write that FAQ, and they very rapidly and haphazardly put it together without any sort of process, like the one that we went through to write the resolution."

There was also an execution error with the FAQs, with Trent sending the document out to the media before it was fully ready. That it was in draft version was clear from the first bullet point, which included this parenthetical that made no sense to include in a final document: "We will begin work immediately on Green New Deal bills to put the nuts and bolts on the plan described in this resolution (important to say, so someone else can't claim this mantle)." It then called for "economic security for all who are unable or unwilling to work," which led to rounds of guffaws on Fox News and headshaking within the Democratic Party.

The arrogance came through in the first FAQ, along with the reflexive defensiveness kicked off by the *Politico* article. "Why 100% clean and renewable and not just 100% renewable? Are you saying we won't transition off fossil fuels?" the document asked.

"Yes, we are calling for a full transition off fossil fuels and zero greenhouse gases," the answer read, going beyond the carefully negotiated resolution. It continued:

> Anyone who has read the resolution sees that we spell this out through a plan that calls for eliminating greenhouse gas emissions from every sector of the economy. Simply banning fossil fuels immediately won't build the new economy to replace it— this is the plan to build that new economy and spells out how to do it technically. We do this through a huge mobilization to create the renewable energy economy as fast as possible. We set a goal to get to net-zero, rather than zero emissions, in 10 years because we aren't sure that we'll be able to fully get rid of farting cows and airplanes that fast, but we think we can ramp up renewable manufacturing and power production, retrofit every building in America, build the smart grid, overhaul transportation and agriculture, plant lots of trees and restore our ecosystem to get to net-zero.

"Farting cows and airplanes." Trent's plainspoken, no-bullshit approach, and his frustration with and contempt for the norms of Washington, DC, had helped him slash and burn his way through the swamp. Trent and Ocasio-Cortez's team were trying to have it both ways: to expose the absurdity of the zero-emissions approach. How will you fully eliminate cow farts? Or campfires? How to replace a fleet of jet-fueled airplanes with electric ones when the latter didn't exist yet?

The answer had to lie in the technological capacity to capture and sequester carbon emissions. But they couldn't say that. "We, at the last minute, buckled under this pressure from the left," Weber said. "The actual people that we were responding to are like sixty nonprofit professionals, but who we have relationships with, and so, I was like, 'Oh, we don't wanna piss off our friends.'"

The bungling gave an opening to the right and to Fox News. Weber recalled that the Green New Deal was polling at the time with 80 percent approval, and even 56 percent approval among conservative Republicans. "It's a layup, a political coup d'état," he said. "In kowtowing to this small corner of the left who was literally fighting over words and phrases, even though we are all basically aligned on the goals, we threw a lot of that away."

The FAQ brought up carbon capture specifically, asking, "Are you for CCUS [carbon capture, utilization, and storage]?"

The resolution plainly left the door open for that technology, and Trent, in the *Politico* article, had even reiterated as much. But the FAQ document got weasely, and instead of referring to the resolution, it stepped back to ask what its authors believed, which is a different question: "We believe the right way to capture carbon is to plant trees and restore our natural ecosystems. CCUS technology to date has not proven effective." The answer leaves wiggle room for CCUS tech but is clearly trying to close the door—not what unions were looking for. The FAQ document added that while the Green New Deal didn't ban fossil fuels or nuclear fuel, it might as well: "The Green New Deal makes new fossil fuel infrastructure or nuclear plants unnecessary."

The AFL-CIO, which had prepared a supportive statement, was livid, and issued a skeptical statement instead. Major environmental groups like the Sierra Club panicked. Fox News delighted in the entire affair. "We just fucking served them up this thing on a silver platter," Weber said of Fox. "They go wild with the cow farts and the antinuclear and all this sort of stuff. We lose the support of AFL-CIO, they are freaking out. Their freaking out almost caused these Big Greens to pull out of the thing at the last minute. This is all happening while the press conference launching the thing is taking place. It's just a total shitshow disaster. Months of some very delicate planning, years of strategic thinking and correction for mistakes, sort of gone in like, less than forty-eight hours."

But the PR stayed strong. At the press conference outside the Capitol, Ocasio-Cortez pulled off one of her more impressive jujitsu moves when a reporter asked her about Pelosi's swipe that it was just a "green dream or whatever they call it." AOC disarmed the attack by adopting it. "No, I think it is a dream," she said, going on to defend the Green New Deal as the full aspiration of the public.

From there, the Green New Deal took off on two separate tracks. On one, it was ridiculed by the right and dismissed by Democratic leaders as unserious. But on the other, it became a global sensation. The Canadian government adopted a version of the Green New Deal, as did the Spanish government. The German government, unfamiliar with the American context of FDR's New Deal, mixed up the words and pledged to implement a New Green Deal. And Democratic presidential candidates from the center to the left rushed to embrace it. Joe Biden, who would go on to become the Democratic nominee and then president, rejected the moniker as part of his effort to differentiate himself from the progressive wing, but the context of his platform was wildly more ambitious than anything Hillary Clinton had put out in 2016 and became even more so after he named AOC and Sunrise head Varshini Prakash to a committee charged with crafting his climate agenda.

The capitulation to the environmental left had set back the cause of winning over organized labor and the party's center, but the entire effort succeeded in reshaping the climate zeitgeist. "One of the main things we wanted to accomplish was to have Green New Deal be one of the questions that gets asked in a debate," said Trent. "And we far and away achieved that goal. Like, the Canadian government is running Green New Deal shit. It literally took it across the world. And so, I felt like it was an accomplishment. I really don't think [Ocasio-Cortez] does. I think she was embarrassed by the Green New Deal. She didn't feel like it was serious enough," he said. "That's not what she wanted to do."

He noted that AOC pivoted after the rollout to something she called the Just Society series, a suite of six pieces of legislation that addressed housing, immigration, criminal justice reform, and other progressive priorities. "She wants to do the serious work of Congress, getting things in the record, on the record in committee, and things like that," Trent said. She was there to help the party succeed in living up to its principles, she believed, not there to tear it down, and was frustrated that her colleagues and the party leadership couldn't see it. What she wanted, said Trent, was "that they'd accept her as a sort of normal rep, that she would be one of the team. That just wasn't never gonna happen."

Whereas her colleague Ilhan Omar thrived on conflict, as long as it was somewhat within her control, Ocasio-Cortez was deeply conflict-averse, a painful trait for a radical in Congress. Her colleagues began to pick up on her vulnerability, her interest in their approval, and would play off it. "It's built into the whole way they deal with her," Trent said. "They keep her back on her heels, they keep her feeling this utter vulnerability and failure, this constant sense that she's failed at something. And she lets it in her head. She really takes that shit to heart. And if you live on Twitter, and take negativity to heart, it makes it hard."

By convincing her to judge herself by the same metric as rank-and-file members of Congress, rather than as a political superstar, her congressional colleagues nudged her away from the place where she was most dangerous to them. "That's how they judge themselves and each other, because if they judged themselves in any other way, they can't compete with her. Like, did you get anything passed this last Congress? Well, what the fuck did this last Congress pass besides Covid stuff?" Trent said. "She has twelve million Twitter followers, doesn't have that great of committee seats, though. Where does her power lie?"

Trent said he would often warn Ocasio-Cortez that because of the way she had burst onto the scene, and because of the threat she represented to others, her hope of being accepted as a member in good standing would always be frustrated. "Disarming will not make them happy," he said. Even if she left politics and became merely an influencer or an MSNBC talking head, he argued, they'd still hunt her until the end of time. "The funny thing is it still wouldn't prove to her that it won't work," he said. "'I just have to get a little smaller, so nobody thinks I'm a threat. Okay. Sorry again, guys. Sorry again for all this trouble.'"

Her staffer Dan Riffle, who served through the first two years, also watched the burn-it-down image that had developed around AOC clash with her more conciliatory approach to her colleagues. "Despite her having beaten Joe Crowley and her public-facing persona," Riffle said, "she is a very conflict-averse person, more so than a normal person I think. And you add in all of the very real shit that she has to deal with and the very difficult decisions that she's faced with as a then-twenty-nine-year-old female."

At the end of her first term, AOC produced and posted a video noting all her accomplishments, and the Green New Deal gets roughly as much time as the fact that she "Introduced more amendments than 90 percent of freshman lawmakers" and "cosponsored 78 pieces of legislation that passed the House, 14 that were signed into law."

"If you go back and look at the stuff she actually focuses on, to me it's not the really fucking useful stuff she did," said Trent.

The rollout of the Green New Deal and Trent's screwup with the cow farts opened up a rift between the two, even as they stayed bonded through their shared experience of the campaign and AOC's launch to stardom. "My dad used to always talk about how Peyton Manning was good at never blaming other people on the team—took the blame and gave away the credit," Trent said. "[Alex] used to love to talk about how—well, not love, but she would literally throw me under the bus all the time for fucking up that rollout, as she put it, or she'd say things like 'Well, it didn't go as smoothly as we'd like.'"

The Green New Deal rollout bundled together all the contradictions at the heart of Ocasio-Cortez's politics and personality, tying her up in knots. In a profound way, she had found herself in a tortured position: a consensus builder and a people pleaser thrust into the role of rebel; a science fair champion, a congressional intern, and a loyal progressive Democrat cast as a burn-it-down radical because she had come from outside the system—had been forced to come from outside, because there was no other way in. And she was cast as unrealistic—a green dreamer—because she grasped the reality of the crisis.

9

BURN IT DOWN

Later that month, March 2019, former President Obama came to the Capitol for a private meeting with the House Democratic caucus. In his talk, he didn't mention the Squad by name but left no doubt whom he was referring to, using the opportunity to skewer them, arguing that their big ideas, like a Green New Deal and Medicare for All, would undermine Democrats.

As Obama delivered his broadside, coming as it did after a month-long battle over anti-Semitism, Ocasio-Cortez could feel the room turning against them. "Party's coming for us hard now. I feel a tide change," she texted that evening. "I just feel more hostility. They think I'm making them look bad and intentionally targeting swing districts with primaries, instead of safe Dems who should do better."

Her colleagues saw her as a threat, she said. "They all think I'm coming after them. Because the few who should be afraid are turning the whole caucus against me," she added. "It's pretty bad. They read the news and believe the narratives even though I'm sitting right next to them."

That gap—between the AOC of the news who was said to want to burn it all down and the real-life colleague who wanted a collegial relationship with (most) other members—wasn't helped by Ocasio-Cortez's personal warmth. Multiple members told me it made them even more suspicious of her. They could accept, and even have a working relationship with, somebody from a different party faction, even a different party, but to engage in factionalism while claiming not to was an even greater sin, they said. They simply didn't believe that Ocasio-Cortez, through Justice Democrats (which her colleagues believed, wrongly, was effectively part of her operation), didn't plan to oust them. Her outspoken staff contributed to the struggle. "You've gotta open the brunch or the birthday party by apologizing for that tweet your chief of staff sent yesterday, or your legislative assistant sent last week," said Riffle, her legislative assistant, guessing at what her interactions must have been like. "Great to see you, sorry about my legislative assistant calling you a real piece of shit the other day, saying that all your staff are leaving to go to K Street and don't care about anyone. But anyway, on to that bill I wanted to talk to you about. You interested in cosponsoring?"

Ocasio-Cortez's curse was her desire to win consensus and persuade her colleagues that she was there to help, coupled with her radical politics. She wanted to remake the system and to be thanked for doing it. She took any resistance as a personal challenge. "I used to think if she had one vote against her in the district that she'd spend the next two years and twenty million dollars trying to convince that person to vote for her next time, and how much of a liability that kind of thinking is in building power rapidly, especially in the House. Because if you're trying to convert these people over to liking you—if that's literally one of your goals—first of all, it ain't gonna happen. It's elusive as hell, and you can just spend all this time and get nothing," Trent said. "It also just makes you do some crazy-ass shit," he added, using a freshman colleague as an example. "Like, why'd you do that? Well, it turns out Cindy Axne asked me to do that at brunch. Why does she want me to do that? I don't know."

AOC's legislative aide Dan Riffle said that he would routinely hear from staff at other offices, looking to ink the support for whatever-it-was that Ocasio-Cortez had just pledged on the House floor to the staffer's boss. "Sorry," Riffle would tell them. "it's not happening." The same problem came up with requests to appear at events. In the beginning, Ocasio-Cortez would eagerly agree to lend her presence, but then, when the date arrived, she'd insist to staff she had never signed off on it and didn't want to do it. Chakrabarti eventually developed a system whereby AOC had to approve an event twice and sign her name affirmatively until it was scheduled, creating a paper trail for the later backtracking. One effect of this was that far fewer events got approved. Ocasio-Cortez also began to put into practice a philosophy she said she had learned from her late father, who would say that once he was in the apartment at night, he wasn't going back out. That's fine for an architect, but it's a challenge for a rising star with ambitions for the highest office. The rejection of so many invitations from so many Washington-based groups, who, she rightly guessed, wanted to use her for fund-raising purposes, undermined her standing in the influential Washington insider world, depriving her of some would-be allies, though also giving her some distance from the hive mind that can be contagious.*

I asked Ocasio-Cortez in March 2019 if she was considering leaving the House and launching a primary challenge to Senator Chuck Schumer. "I haven't the slightest idea," she texted. "There's a full-time conspiracy machine on me, so I don't even know if it'll even be a viable path tbh. The conservative media machine is intense and powerful, and they actually put resources into generating tons of new media, establishment media, and social media. So I really have no idea what the landscape will be like in a few years." She added, "Maybe I'll just go to grad school. 😩"

She had also infuriated the DCCC, which had expected her to become a fund-raising cash cow for the party but, instead, she was refusing, given the campaign arm's embrace of corporate money. She also declined to pay DCCC dues, worried about whom the party would support with her money. In a call with Pelosi, one of the two or three times they spoke by phone, she told the Speaker that even though she had beaten Joe Crowley, who relied on DCCC vendors and consultants, nobody had reached out to hear how she had done it. "I told her DCCC campaign vendors sucked and that it was strange that after I beat Crowley not a single person bothered to ask how I beat him when he used Dem vendors; and how I think we should pay attention and ask questions when that happens to spot weaknesses," she told me. "She got so mad at me." To demonstrate that she did have loyalty to the party, however, she decided to raise money directly for members in swing districts whose positions aligned with her own.

---

* When Ocasio-Cortez decided to attend the Met Gala in 2021, wearing a dress with the message "Tax the Rich" painted on it, she infuriated every organization that had ever either been told she couldn't attend their event or, more commonly, simply been ignored by her office. An ethics investigation later chided her for not paying the rental cost for the dress and other accessories until after the probe had been launched. Her office had not responded to repeated requests from the vendors to be paid, joining a long line of allies, constituents, and even members of Congress unable to get through to them.

She picked Reps. Jahana Hayes of Connecticut and Katie Hill and Mike Levin of California. All three were backers of Medicare for All and the Green New Deal. "Jahana fears nothing," AOC told me. "She's the best."

One afternoon that March, the two were getting into an elevator in the Capitol together. "Some *Politico* or Hill reporter was incredibly rude to [Jahana] in the elevator and asked me for a quote when we got out," AOC said, "and I said no because she was mean to Jahana. She got so shook. The classism and racism gets to be too much sometimes."

Ocasio-Cortez raised around thirty thousand dollars for each candidate in just a few hours. "I think there are a lot of good eggs in this class, but I see how a lot are, like, at this tipping point of getting indoctrinated."

The Squad and the broader left couldn't just expect House Democrats to align with them out of goodwill. There needed to be a scalable path toward political power and campaign financing for candidates who weren't national stars. Otherwise, they'd have to rely on the DCCC model as the only viable path. "We literally have to build it for them—that's what DCCC did even with call time," AOC said. "Like, no one can conceive of any other way, and [email] list fund-raising hasn't worked for anyone else."

She counted just thirty-five Democrats who had sworn off corporate money, but party leaders were working on ways to win them back to it, urging members who did take corporate money to set up leadership PACs that would then funnel that money to vulnerable Democrats. The donation wouldn't come from a corporate PAC directly, but would, instead, appear in Federal Election Commission records as coming from a different member of Congress. "I basically consider most of those [thirty-five members] to be up for grabs in some way— not all, but most," AOC said.

She was also perplexed that her political help was so unwanted. "The thing that blows my mind," she texted, "is that some of these tight races have huge Latino or POC [people of color] populations, and nobody tries to pad their margins by expanding the electorate. TJ Cox won by nothing, and his race is crazy-low turnout, but [the] District is 40 percent Latino! I'm like, yo that's how we get to D+20 right there! In Florida the Dem party only put $100k (!!) into Puerto Rican outreach registration. But anywho, that's our path." (Cox lost reelection in 2020 by 1,522 votes.)

Her office began contemplating ways to operationalize a rival to the party's fund-raising structures. By pulling together the Squad members and Sanders, the group would have formidable fund-raising capacity, particularly if they invested time, resources, and their email lists to it. Sanders wasn't included to engage in intraparty warfare outside presidential campaigns, but the Squad had leverage over him, as he was eager for their support in his upcoming campaign. Yet no such fund-raising operation got off the ground.

Dan Riffle, her legislative aide, said the failure of the Squad to meet the expectations built for it flowed from a mismatch between, on the one hand, the approach preferred by Justice Democrats and much of the support base of the Sanders campaign, and on the other the approach preferred by the members of the Squad. "There was some real tension among the Squad," he said. "Ayanna, Rashida, and Ilhan were all previous elected officials, so they came there with a staff and an approach that was, like, we're here to make friends and influence people, notwithstanding our progressive views. And AOC was coming in, like, I'm gonna fuckin'—or at least her staff was coming in throwing Molotov cocktails."

From the outside, Justice Democrats and AOC seemed like one and the same, a perception strengthened significantly by two outspoken cofounders of the group joining as her chief of staff and head of communications. How could people think anything other than that they were joined at the hip? Yet nothing could have been further from the truth. "She ran against Joe Crowley," Riffle reminded me. "Anybody who ever has any hopes of working in or with the Democratic Party is not going to touch that. She had a marriage of convenience ready to go with Justice Democrats." As much as she needed them, they needed her. "They had this ridiculous grand scheme where they're going to replace all 435 members. Absurd. And so they were striking out left and right. And this was their best last bet," he said. "They put all their chips in this race and they have no choice but to wind up with each other. And then she wins. So now it's like, now what the fuck are we gonna do? And again, same sort of deal, given the fact that she had run with JD, given the type of race that she ran and who she beat, in terms of staffing, she had nowhere to go."

Meanwhile, she was being hit from two sides. Her congressional colleagues would routinely pull her aside and urge her to get those loud men in her office to pipe down so that she could speak for herself. And she was bombarded by misogynistic, right-wing media accusations that she was an empty-headed puppet of George Soros, recruited and trained by the Marxists at Justice Democrats. So she ran 180 degrees in the opposite direction, dismissing the help she had gotten as late and opportunistic. Using a phrase similar to Riffle's, she said that she had a "relationship of convenience" with many of the groups who'd backed her.

While Ocasio-Cortez may have been a pariah in the House, she was much sought after at the presidential level, and the same week Obama called her out, Warren invited her to lunch. "I really like her. She's the real deal," AOC said afterward. "I know the waters would part before this, but honestly if [Warren and Sanders] were both on the ticket and won, it'd be a best-case scenario. She has a policy focus and knows what levers to pull. And he has the organizing capacity and public sentiment."

AOC worried about the two senators' ability to connect with the rising racial justice movement, however. "Functionally, I feel like they need each other. But I also worry about the social/racial justice component with them and [their] ability to communicate it convincingly as a priority," she said. "Yet the idea of having an all-white ticket also seems like a huge gamble, too. So, it's tough."

She said that her own calculation was factoring in all the negatives that were piling up around her. "I get scared about the damage my endorsement could do," she said. "Like, I don't know if my endorsement would help [Sanders] in Iowa, haha.

"I'm excited to go to KY and some other places. We're gonna try to do better with white people," she added. "'Cause they reeeaaaally don't like me right now. 😆"

10

RUN AND HYDE

In early April 2019, freshman representative Katie Hill and Ocasio-Cortez were chatting during a break in a hearing of the Oversight Committee. The news outlet ProPublica had published a story reporting that a bill sponsored by Rep. John Lewis, the civil rights leader from Georgia, included a major giveaway to the company Turbo-Tax, a provision that barred the IRS from developing its own platform to allow taxpayers to calculate and pay their taxes electronically.

That the U.S. government would outsource such a basic function to a private company, and ban itself from performing that function, was as absurd as it was emblematic. Ocasio-Cortez's legislative aide Dan Riffle had missed it, as had the legislative operation for the Congressional Progressive Caucus. Riffle reached out to the legislative teams at the other Squad offices but got back no interest in opposing the bill, with the staff arguing that the ProPublica article was wrong. "I was pointing to all of these Columbia law professors who were saying, 'That's what's in there.' I believe them when they say it," Riffle said. But he got nowhere. "We couldn't really get a multimember operation against this. So, we went to AOC with it, and it's, like, you know, 'It's you, and it's Katie Hill, and that's it. And you guys need to stand up and request a recorded vote and point out that this [TurboTax] provision is in there.'"

Often, the kind of legislation that would be the most unpopular with the public—like legislation forcing people to pay TurboTax to file taxes while blocking the IRS from setting up a simple online system—doesn't get a recorded vote on the House floor. That way, nobody is on record specifically supporting it. The presiding officer asks for the "yays" and "nays," and if nobody requests a recorded vote, the bill passes unanimously. That's what both parties wanted to do with the TurboTax bill.

Lewis's office and aides from the Ways and Means Committee argued that a recorded vote was unnecessary, pointing toward all the good the bill would do outside of this one, perhaps unfortunate provision. Riffle told Ocasio-Cortez the way to rebut this was simple: "We don't have to do shitty things in order to do good things. Like, you can just do the good things. We are in control now."

On the way to the House floor, AOC and Riffle went over the arguments and counterarguments. "So, she goes to the floor, and immediately, John Lewis starts talking to her about her concerns. You know, he's fucking John Lewis. He's a civil rights icon. To stand up and say, 'This John Lewis bill is bullshit,' that's a hard ask. She, I think very understandably, was having second thoughts about doing it."

Ocasio-Cortez emerged from the cloakroom to find Riffle. "I talked to John Lewis, and there's all these other good parts of this bill, so, I don't know. He's making a pretty strong case that, on the whole, this bill is pretty good," Riffle recalled her saying, floating the possibility of speaking in favor of it.

Riffle proposed the option of just not saying anything. "I get it," Riffle said, "but just know that if you vote for this, that if you go up there and speak in favor of this bill, you're going to get annihilated on Twitter. People are going to be furious." A third option, he added, was just not saying anything.

She headed back to the House floor with Riffle not sure which option she'd choose. She rose to speak, thanking Congressman Lewis and the committee for the good work they'd done on the bill and lauding the laudable parts of it. Then she added that she was deeply concerned about the TurboTax provision. Once the speeches were done, the question was put to the full body. "The question was, 'Okay, so are we going to request a recorded vote so that people are on record on this?'" said Riffle. Requesting a vote wouldn't stop the bill—it had plenty of support from both parties. But it would put members on record when angry constituents came calling.

Ocasio-Cortez didn't request a vote.

Riffle said he couldn't judge her in the end for not demanding that her colleagues be put in a tough spot. "I don't have to sit next to them on a charter bus when they go to some summit somewhere and make small talk with somebody who hates my fucking guts," he said.

"I don't have to look them in the eye in committee hearings every day. So I totally get it. But the place wears you down."

He himself had no similar hesitations, however, and posted his frustration on Twitter: "Congratulations to @HRBlock and @turbotax for their successful acquisition of @RepRichardNeal and the entire Democratic leadership." In the thoroughly corrupt House of Representatives, the number one thing you are not allowed to say is that anybody makes any decision for any reason other than personal conviction or, perhaps, political expediency—but you can never imply that they are corrupted in any way by money. Riffle later deleted the post.

That spring of 2019, the budget process known as appropriations was getting started, and AOC's legislative director, Ariel Eckblad, tasked the staff with scouring the bill for areas that could be amended. Presidential candidate Biden was facing intense backlash at the moment for defending his position on the Hyde Amendment, which barred federal money from paying for abortion services. Women had formed the backbone of the resistance to Trump, and their votes, donations, and volunteer time had produced the Democratic wave that retook the House in 2018. Elizabeth Warren was surging in the polls. This was no time for Biden to be on the wrong side of the issue. And if the increasingly radical Supreme Court overturned *Roe v. Wade*, the Hyde Amendment would block a Democratic White House from offering abortion services on federal property.

Riffle noticed that despite Democratic alignment around repealing it, the Hyde Amendment was still included in the Democratic bill. Given that every presidential candidate opposed it and virtually every House Democrat, and given that Democrats controlled the House, they might as well vote to strip it out. The appropriations subcommittee was even chaired by one of the staunchest backers of abortion rights in the chamber, Rep. Rosa DeLauro. It seemed like an easy one. "Let's take it out," Ocasio-Cortez told her team.

Yet, in the effort to remove it, Riffle realized it hadn't been left in as an oversight. When he approached the subcommittee, he was met with a highly skeptical reception, and Ocasio-Cortez got a long phone call from DeLauro, who walked her through the politics behind the bill but shied away from saying outright that AOC shouldn't press forward with the amendment. The problem, DeLauro argued, was that she had won an increase of $12 billion in funding for her section of the bill and that Senate Republicans would never agree to nix the Hyde Amendment. And even if they did, Trump would veto the bill. So there was no point. It would just force people to take a tough vote for no reason.

AOC's staff reached out to natural allies on the issue, Planned Parenthood and NARAL Pro-Choice America, the biggest pro-choice players on the Hill. Publicly, they were strident opponents of the Hyde Amendment and had lambasted Biden for his support of it. Riffle first spoke with Jacqueline Ayers, the top lobbyist for Planned Parenthood, and was surprised to learn that the organization did not want Democrats to try to remove the Hyde Amendment. Planned Parenthood's reasoning was similar to DeLauro's: we don't have the votes in the Senate, so we'll lose.

But isn't it worth the fight? Riffle asked.

The problem, Ayers explained, was that Planned Parenthood would have to "score" the vote, because it's a publicly stated priority of theirs. In other words, because Planned Parenthood had been so public in its opposition to the Hyde Amendment, it would have to publicly push Democrats to vote to repeal it. A Democrat who voted the wrong way would then get a bad "score" from Planned Parenthood. Getting a bad score could then hurt that Democrat with some voters in the coming elections.

But, Riffle argued, isn't your mission to repeal Hyde and protect abortion rights?

Yes, she told him, but we can't do that if Democrats lose the majority, so protecting them is the first order of business.

Kate Ryan, the chief lobbyist at NARAL, told Riffle her organization was aligned with Planned Parenthood on the strategy.

"If you guys are against it," Riffle said he told Ayers, "we're not going to offer this amendment without your support. So we'll just table it. I can't say I agree with the strategy, though. And I'm discouraged to hear that that's your philosophy."

That evening, after a sustained barrage, Biden reversed his decades-old position in a speech at a Democratic National Committee gala in Atlanta, highlighting the gap between the politics of the campaign world and the realpolitik inside Congress. A similar dynamic was unfolding when it came to health care: candidates like Kamala Harris were vowing to ban private insurance and implement Medicare for All while, back in Congress, Democrats couldn't even get agreement on allowing Medicare to negotiate drug prices with pharmaceutical companies. "If I believe health care is a right, as I do, I can no longer support an amendment that makes that right dependent on someone's zip code," Biden said in his speech. "I can't justify leaving millions of women without access to the care they need and the ability to exercise their constitutionally protected right."

Ocasio-Cortez was floored. How was Joe Biden to the left of Planned Parenthood and NARAL on abortion rights? It made no sense. "They're 'one-daying' us," Eckblad said, explaining the tactic of tamping down action today in exchange for a pledge that, one day, the good thing will happen, as long as enough Democrats are elected.

Ocasio-Cortez continued to push internally. Meanwhile, the abortion rights groups reached out to lobby her directly. They set up a meeting with women of color who were leaders in the field of reproductive justice, which brought a racial justice lens to the politics of abortion, thinking that those activists would have some sway with her. It would have been an awkward meeting, with the abortion rights groups lobbying AOC *not* to push for more expansive abortion rights. At the last minute, AOC didn't show, sending an aide instead.

She was still intent on repeal. "We circulated to [the] Squad that we were going to do this amendment," Riffle said. "And then Ayanna's people got back to us and said no, no, no *we're* gonna do an amendment. And we were like, 'Okay, what's *your* amendment?'"

Their plan, Pressley told him, was to introduce an amendment, debate it on the House floor, and then pull it before a vote. That way, they could call attention to the issue but not put anybody in a difficult spot. Riffle suggested a wild idea: "I was, like, 'Okay, why don't we just vote on it?'"

Ocasio-Cortez spoke to Pressley, who was the chair of a caucus dedicated to promoting abortion rights, and agreed to cede the issue to her. Pressley ended up writing an amendment that, for procedural reasons, was expected not to get through the Rules Committee. That would allow opponents of Hyde to make a run at it without forcing a vote or even a debate on the floor. As expected, the Pressley amendment was rejected before it could get to the floor. A Planned Parenthood official followed up by complaining to Ocasio-Cortez's office that Riffle had been too gruff on the phone.

This was not remotely the first or last complaint she'd receive about her rambunctious staff. Part of the animosity that colleagues felt toward Ocasio-Cortez came from her unique approach to her team. On Capitol Hill, often even spokespeople won't speak on record by name, because the member of Congress wants to be the only voice or face of an office. There's an undeniable logic to this desire: voters sent the member, not the staff, to Washington. But Ocasio-Cortez empowered her staff—not just Corbin Trent, her spokesperson, though particularly him—to speak to the press and post on social media in ways that, in another office, would have been not just forbidden but unthinkable.

Given the common perception of Ocasio-Cortez as a coastal elite who didn't understand the white working class, the public would be surprised to know that both Riffle and Trent had been raised working class or rougher in Appalachia—Trent in Tennessee and Riffle in southern Ohio. Riffle was raised by a single mom who struggled, giving up two kids to adoption because she couldn't afford to keep them. "She was a waitress at a Red Lobster. Couldn't tell you my dad's first name," Riffle said. "Lights and water both being on at the same time was a treat, that kind of thing."

The sharp blade of his and Trent's class edge shone through. Riffle gave an early on-record interview to the *Washington Post*'s Jeff Stein that infuriated Capitol Hill. "I remember getting to the Hill thinking, 'The staffers here are going to mostly be activists and idealists,'" Riffle told the *Post*. "Then I got here, and I found out that's not true at all. These are careerists. These are people who grew up on the Upper West Side and went to Ivy League schools."

Ocasio-Cortez wasn't happy at all with the comment or the blowback to it, though she avoided confronting him directly about it. "We never talked directly about it but it was indirectly clear that she did not agree with that approach," Riffle said. "I gave a quote that I thought was the approach of the office. And after it came out and shit hit the fan, most people in the office were like, hell yes, that's well said, I agree. And people from other offices [said the same]."

Riffle said that as the leader of her staff as well as a movement, it was up to Ocasio-Cortez to make clear which approach she wanted to take, but she didn't do so, instead muddling forward with two contradictory strategies. "In retrospect, if I had a better idea of what her approach was I would not have given that quote, if we had a couple of heart-to-hearts or more direct conversations earlier about what the strategy is going to be," he said. "There was an opportunity in that first couple of weeks or months to say, this has happened, this is my approach, this is how we're going to do things, and it's not what you saw at Justice Democrats or what you read in the campaign. Now we're here, now we're governing. Now we have to make friends with people and so the approach is going to be different. That never happened."

Her staff and many of the backers of Justice Democrats wanted to go to war against the people they saw as in the way of progress, Riffle said. They wanted a real political revolution. "The difference of what Corbin and Saikat and myself and other people in the incoming AOC camp thought was, 'These are shitty people. And the reason that these policies are bad is that the party is being run by shitty people.' I don't think [the Squad] thought that," he said. "We thought you should burn it down because the house was occupied by shitty people. They thought we should burn it down because, you know, we can build a better house with better policies."

The back-and-forth barbs grew hotter, and AOC's staff even engaged publicly with Pelosi. Members of Congress shied away from using Pelosi's name, referring to her either as "the Speaker" or "Speaker Pelosi." Chakrabarti ditched this norm with a tweet. "Pelosi claims we can't focus on impeachment because it's a distraction from kitchen table issues," he wrote on Twitter. "But I'd challenge you to find voters that can name a single thing House Democrats have done for their kitchen table this year. What is this legislative mastermind doing?"

11

HALF A REVOLUTION

In mid-June 2019, a year after the world first turned its attention to Trump's policy of separating children from their parents at the border, the controversy lit up again in the wake of an Associated Press article reporting that up to 250 infants, toddlers, and teens were being kept in metal cages at an El Paso Border Patrol station in wretched conditions. Trump had officially ended the child separation policy, yet it was continuing in a different form.

U.S. Customs and Border Protection blamed a cash shortage, calling on Congress to appropriate new money the agency promised it would use to clean up the facilities and provide adequate food, clothing, and medicine to the migrants, while the government worked to reunite the children with family members. That all sounded nice, but at the same time, ICE was publicly threatening a nationwide roundup of undocumented immigrants, and Trump's hard-liners, led by outspoken nativist Stephen Miller, were girding for a battle.

Congress moved quickly, with the Senate putting together a bipartisan package that doled out $4.5 billion for the various agencies involved. In the House, Pelosi did the same, but her bill had virtually zero Republican support. Dozens of progressives—enough to sink it—were opposed, insisting that the bill include restrictions on how the money could be used and requirements that the government move children quickly into the custody of a family member. Pelosi met through the night with opponents and added a series of restrictions to the bill before addressing her caucus the next day, ahead of the vote. "The president would love for this bill to go down today," she said in the private gathering. "A vote against this bill is a vote for Donald Trump and his inhumane, outside-the-circle-of-civilized attitude toward the children."

Ocasio-Cortez had been the lone "no" vote against more funding for DHS and its immigration agencies at the beginning of the session, but this time, much of the caucus had been close to joining her. Pelosi's pressure campaign, coupled with concessions, persuaded the skeptics of the bill to support it. But the Squad voted in a bloc against it, the only four Democrats to do so.

The vote came on a Tuesday evening, and as the caucus convened on the House floor, the polls closed in New York, where local primaries were being held. It produced another jarring dislocation between the reality of the Squad's power in the House—4 votes against a bill that passed without them—and the surging potential of the movement behind them nationally. The key race being watched was a proxy battle between Hakeem Jeffries of Brooklyn and his ally Rep. Greg Meeks of Queens on the one side—the new bosses of the Brooklyn and Queens machines—and Ocasio-Cortez and the increasingly influential Democratic Socialists of America (DSA) and Working Families Party (WFP) on the other. Meeks and Jeffries had both gotten behind Melinda Katz, whose regrettable time as a lobbyist for Rupert Murdoch's News Corp made for awkward Democratic politics, but she was a loyal machine soldier and a known quantity. The left had rallied behind DSA member Tiffany Cabán, a public defender running to bring a radical approach to criminal justice to Queens.

Ocasio-Cortez had resisted entreaties to endorse Cabán throughout much of her campaign, concerned about the campaign's operational capacity and viability. The debate in her office over whether to do so was among the fiercest her team had and marked the only time she and Corbin Trent shouted at each other. "What are you in this for?" he demanded of her. She ended up endorsing Cabán through her political action committee about a month before the election.

As the returns came in, Long Island representative Tom Suozzi, whose slice of Queens had allowed him to beat out AOC for the city's Ways and Means seat, found Ocasio-Cortez on the floor. Startled that Cabán was in the lead, he marveled to AOC that he'd never seen off-year turnout in Jackson Heights, Astoria, and Long Island City like he was seeing that evening in the returns.

"Hey, you know where that came from, right?" AOC said to him, reminding him that she represented the district and had backed Cabán—though she had done so belatedly, much closer to the election than Cabán's team would have preferred.

Representative Meeks, who had skipped the border funding vote to be in New York for the election, was livid at the returns and lashed out at Bernie Sanders and Elizabeth Warren, effectively calling them racist for intervening in the election by endorsing Cabán, a curious charge given that Melinda Katz, the candidate Meeks was backing, was white and Cabán was not. What Meeks meant, though, was that Cabán's base of support in gentrified areas of New York—along with the politicians those areas preferred, like Ocasio-Cortez, Sanders, and Warren—was working in opposition to the Black areas of the district. Queens, meanwhile, is home to one of the more prosperous Black populations in the country, and that middle-aged and elderly community had indeed gone heavily against Cabán, even if their voting-aged kids were with her.

"This is wild. Like truly," Ocasio-Cortez texted as the lead grew. "I told her if she needed any help with the incoming deluge of texts and calls [let me know] but I'm pretty sure I still have unanswered texts from primary day." She sent an image showing 795 unread text messages. "Lol that's still from the primary. I hope she pulls it off," she said. "I'm sure a lot of the absentees will go to her too, but let's hope their senior center operation wasn't wild."

Their "senior center operation"—where machine officials hit up senior centers for absentee votes—turned out to be wild. Cabán held a 1.3-percentage-point lead at the end of the night, but absentee ballots put Katz ahead by just 20 votes. A recount, shot through with the controversy endemic to every poorly run New York election, finished with Katz ahead by 60.*

Back in Washington, the politics of the border bill got even hairier. Josh Gottheimer began making a move against the House bill Pelosi had gotten through, telling her he had the votes to block it. This was the bill the Squad had objected to for not having enough safeguards to make sure the money was actually used to improve conditions for migrants and speed up their liberation. Yet, for Gottheimer, Pelosi's bill went too far, and he insisted that Congress simply approve the Senate version instead.

Pelosi was asked Wednesday if she'd allow the Senate bill to be

---

* Cabán was elected to the city council in 2020, an election year that saw DSA and WFP candidates largely sweep Brooklyn and Queens at the local and state legislative levels.

voted on, and she rejected the idea, but Gottheimer kept pushing. That night, at the annual congressional softball game, Gottheimer urged his Problem Solvers Caucus allies to promise to tank the bill, and Pelosi caved to him the next afternoon. "In order to get resources to the children fastest, we will reluctantly pass the Senate bill," she wrote in a letter to her colleagues Thursday afternoon. Her reversal came days after a searing photo showing the bodies of a migrant father and his young daughter, Óscar Alberto Martínez Ramírez and Angie Valéria, who had drowned while trying to cross the Rio Grande, sparked international outrage.

The capitulation was so rapid that it took even Senate minority leader Chuck Schumer by surprise. Schumer made a rare trip across the Capitol to the House side for a private meeting with the Congressional Progressive Caucus, telling them that he hadn't expected the House to cave so fast and that the plan had been for progressive opposition to fortify Democrats in the Senate so they could extract a better deal from Republicans. "I truly didn't expect the House to pass the Senate bill unamended," he told those gathered. He said nobody in House leadership had communicated with him, so he wanted a direct line to the CPC going forward. From that meeting, Jayapal and Schumer struck up a relationship that would later become important during the Biden administration.

Gottheimer's move sapped the House's leverage. "The quote-unquote Problem Solvers Caucus, I think, threw us under the bus and undermined our position to actually be able to negotiate," said Rep. Ruben Gallego, a Democrat from Arizona.* This time, 95 Democrats voted "no," but Republicans gave the bill the votes it needed, and it passed 305–102. As Democrats argued off camera on the House floor, Abigail Spanberger, a former CIA official turned moderate Democrat, waved the House amendments around, saying she was tired of being forced to vote against her values. The right thing to do, she was insisting, was not to try to attach strings to the money, but to rubber-stamp the Senate bill and move the money quickly. Rep. Katie Porter was stunned. "What values?" she said. "Go be a Republican, then."

---

* In 2023, Gallego announced a primary challenge to Kyrsten Sinema, while No Labels moved to get a ballot line Sinema could use to run in the general election in case Gallego beat her.

Pocan, never afraid to let his contempt for Gottheimer show, fumed as well. "Since when did the Problem Solvers Caucus become the Child Abuse Caucus?" he asked. "Wouldn't they want to at least fight against contractors who run deplorable facilities? Kids are the only ones who could lose today."

Ilhan Omar said a vote for Mitch McConnell's border bill "is a vote to keep kids in cages and terrorize immigrant communities." Tlaib said, "If you see the Senate bill as an option, then you don't believe in basic human rights." Ocasio-Cortez noted that the Senate hadn't even bothered negotiating with the House. "We have time," she said in a tweet. "We can stay in town. We can at LEAST add some amendments to this Senate bill. But to pass it completely unamended with no House input? That seems a bridge too far."

"Can we stop calling the Blue Dog caucus 'fiscally conservative but socially liberal'? I missed the part of fiscal conservativeness or social liberalness that includes wasting $4.5 billion of taxpayer money to put kids in concentration camps," Chakrabarti tweeted, deploying a term Ocasio-Cortez had entered into circulation to describe Trump's border facilities. "Instead of 'fiscally conservative but socially liberal' let's call the New Democrats and Blue Dog caucus the 'New Southern Democrats.' They certainly seem hell bent to do to black and brown people today what the old southern Democrats did in the 40s."

Climate activist and writer Julian Brave NoiseCat pushed back, asking if everybody, including Sharice Davids, the Native American congresswoman who had been arrested standing up for the rights of Dreamers, needed to be lumped in as a white supremacist.

"I think the point still stands," Chakrabarti replied. "I don't think people have to be personally racist to enable a racist system. And the same could even be said of the Southern Democrats. I don't believe Sharice is a racist person, but her votes are showing her to enable a racist system."

The House failure led to widespread recriminations. Jayapal, Pocan, the CPC, and the Congressional Hispanic Caucus (CHC) were blamed for urging House Democrats to pull out of negotiations with the Senate earlier that spring; Chuck Schumer took heat for agreeing to a weak bill that left children vulnerable to abuse; Pelosi was slammed for caving; and Gottheimer's Problem Solvers Caucus was widely derided for its unhelpful intervention.

Responding to the criticism, Gottheimer simply denied that he had done what he had done. His case was undermined when No Labels, the dark-money group that sponsors the Problem Solvers Caucus, sent out a private note to supporters celebrating what Gottheimer had done.

In the end, the upshot was that the largely Republican-drafted bill, which showered money on immigration agencies with no strings attached, had been passed by a Democratic House. The next year, the U.S. Government Accountability Office would release a report finding that the Border Patrol had diverted its new funds to the purchase of ATVs, computers, and other products that didn't remotely fit the monies' intended purpose.

Having been beaten, the Squad and the CHC organized a trip for the next week to tour the Border Patrol facility that had sparked the controversy. Just before they left, ProPublica reported on the existence of a 9,500-person Facebook group of Border Patrol employees, including senior officials, passing around racist memes and otherwise glorying in reactionary online commentary. Sexualized images of Ocasio-Cortez were particularly popular, with one showing Trump forcing her to perform oral sex, another depicting her performing oral sex on a migrant through a fence, and so on. Another popular Border Patrol post suggested a GoFundMe to pay the legal costs of any officer willing to throw a burrito at the Squad during their upcoming visit to the facility.

It set a haunting tone for the trip. Even having seen the photos and read the descriptions, the members of Congress on the delegation, Squad and non-Squad alike, were horrified at what they saw there. Most, including the Squad, were blocked from taking their phones into the facility, but Rep. Joaquin Castro managed to get his in, and he captured shocking images of cruelty. Pressley tested a sink, the only source of fresh water, and found it broken. The refugees told them they had resorted to drinking from the toilet bowl. A mother cried in Ocasio-Cortez's arms, saying she didn't know if she'd ever see her child again.

Following the tour, the group was scheduled to hold a press conference about two hundred yards from the facility, but they found protesters blocking their path. Ocasio-Cortez asked for an escort, but Customs and Border Patrol turned them down. "CBP looked me in the eye, intentionally denying us protection before sending me into a crowd of Trump supporters with machetes and guns," she later told me. "This was after they found officers threatening to rape and harm us on that trip." Corbin Trent, who was along for the trip, found the local sheriff and asked for an escort, but he was similarly turned down. Hate was pulsing from the crowd, he said, and men were standing on rocks with AR-15s slung over their shoulders. The group of congresspeople waded into the crowd, made it to the microphones, and held their press conference, though the press could hardly hear them. The crowd jeered and shouted at them throughout it. "We don't want Muslims here!" a protester repeatedly shouted at Tlaib and Omar.

"You can all scream at me," Tlaib fired back. "I will never stop speaking truth to power."

Four German shepherds tugged at their leashes just feet in front of them. "You're a lawless bitch, a fake-ass bitch," one woman shouted, though it wasn't clear to whom.

"Members for sure thought I was going to get hurt or killed at that press conference. I went back into the van, and Corbin was crying," Ocasio-Cortez said, which Trent later confirmed to me, calling the trip one of the most searing moments of his life, adding that it was surely worse for those inside the facility.

"That was the first time I for sure thought I might be killed," Ocasio-Cortez texted. "It was a lot lol."

The day before, Pelosi had sat down at a restaurant by the San Francisco Bay for omelets with *New York Times* columnist Maureen Dowd to deliver her own critique of the Squad, though one unsullied by the profanity on display at the border. "All these people have their public whatever and their Twitter world," Pelosi said of their stand against the capitulation to Trump over the border funding. "But they didn't have any following. They're four people, and that's how many votes they got."

The comments were published that weekend in the *New York Times*, the same weekend I published an article in the *Washington Post* that explored the tensions between the left and party leadership. "Leadership is driven by fear. They seem to be unable to lead," Trent had told me for the article. "The greatest threat to mankind is the cowardice of the Democratic Party."

The quote had been approved by Chakrabarti, but not by AOC, who also commented in the same piece, "When it comes to defending why we don't . . . push visionary legislation, I hear the line so frequently from senior members, 'I want to win.' But what they mean by that is, 'I only want to introduce bills that have a 100 percent chance of passing almost unanimously.' But for new members, what's important isn't just winning but fighting. I don't care about losing in the short term, because we know we're fighting for the long term."

She added, "The older members really cling to the idea that things are going to go 'back to normal.' For us, it's never been normal, and before that the bipartisanship was shitty anyway and gave us the War on Drugs, DOMA"—the Defense of Marriage Act, which barred federal recognition of or benefits for same-sex couples—"and stripping the leg[islative] branch of everything."

But it was Corbin Trent's comment that made headlines. Most Hill spokespeople talk to reporters on background first, before issuing an on-the-record quote, but Trent saw this as dishonest and cowardly. Everything he said was on the record. Dan Riffle was the same way, as was Saikat Chakrabarti. They considered the anonymity-heavy culture of the Hill to be fundamentally deceptive.

Ocasio-Cortez and Omar both pushed back publicly against Pelosi's remark. "That public 'whatever' is called public sentiment," AOC responded, taking the fight to her Twitter world. "And wielding the power to shift it is how we actually achieve meaningful change in this country." Omar backed her up, tweeting, "Patetico! You know they're just salty about WHO is wielding the power to shift 'public sentiment' these days, sis. Sorry not sorry."

That's when Chakrabarti chimed in with his dig at Pelosi: "What is this legislative mastermind doing?"

The next week's caucus meeting turned heated. "You got a complaint? You come and talk to me about it. But do not tweet about our members and expect us to think that that is just okay," Pelosi told the caucus, making clear she was talking about Ocasio-Cortez's staff.

"It's a mess," Ocasio-Cortez texted. "It's a perfect example of how life and death situations—aka kids dying on our border—gets [sic] minimized to a caucus spat issue. It's not about the caucus. It's about the fact that we're totally fine with hurting kids behind closed doors, so long as we don't call it out in public."

Pelosi's lecture was intense, its focus broadened to include the rest of the Squad. "Some of you are here to make a beautiful pâté," the Speaker told her charges, "but we're making sausage most of the time." Ayanna Pressley told reporters afterward that it was demoralizing. "I am worried about the signal that it sends to people I speak to and for, who sent me here with a mandate, and how it affects them," she said. Ocasio-Cortez ratcheted the tension up by accusing Pelosi of singling out women of color, an identity-based defense increasingly being wielded by combatants in progressive debates. "When these comments first started," she said, "I kind of thought that [the Speaker] was keeping the progressive flank at more of an arm's distance in order to protect more moderate members, which I understood. But the persistent singling out . . . it got to a point where it was just outright disrespectful—the explicit singling out of newly elected women of color."

Right around this time, by coincidence, a profile of Chakrabarti ran as a cover story in *Washington Post Magazine*, complete with a splashy photo spread. It was the kind of coverage members of Congress—remember, there are 535 of them—dream of, and here was a chief of staff getting it. "Chief of Change," the headline blared, followed by an even more ambitious subhead: "Saikat Chakrabarti isn't just running [AOC's] office. He's guiding a movement." It was a more dignified profile than the one *Elle* had run earlier that year—headlined "You Need to Know Alexandria Ocasio-Cortez's Chief of Snacks Saikat Chakrabarti," which Trent had printed out and left everywhere around the office—and also more dangerous for Chakrabarti politically.

On Friday night, July 12, the same day the *Washington Post Magazine* profile of Chakrabarti was posted online, the official Twitter account of the House Democratic caucus controlled by Hakeem Jeffries went nuclear on him, using his earlier tweet about Rep. Sharice Davids as ammunition: "Who is this guy and why is he explicitly singling out a Native American woman of color? Her name is Congresswoman Davids, not Sharice," @HouseDemocrats posted, dredging up Chakrabarti's two-week-old conversation with NoiseCat and highlighting what so many on Capitol Hill consider a most serious offense: the use of a member of Congress's first name. "She is a phenomenal new member who flipped a red seat blue. Keep 🖐 Her 🖐 Name 🖐 Out 🖐 Of 🖐 Your 🖐 Mouth." Michael Hardaway, the hard-charging spokesperson for Hakeem Jeffries, who oversaw the Twitter account, posted a video of the drive-by shooting scene from the 1993 film *Menace II Society* from his personal account.

Chakrabarti tried to defend himself. "This tweet was in response to someone else's tweet where they specifically brought up Rep. Davids.

Why did you leave that out? I've known Rep. Davids for a long time, consider her a friend, and encouraged her to run for Congress back in the fall of 2016. I'm glad she did," he responded. "Everything I tweeted 2 weeks ago was to call out the terrible border funding bill that 90+ Dems opposed. It gave Trump a blank check to continue caging people in horrendous conditions. Our Democracy is literally falling apart. I'm not interested in substance-less Twitter spats."

Riffle said AOC's team watched the fight break out with delight, ready to charge back at the party leadership. "It became this huge Twitter blowup. That's the kind of shit that we were eager for. We're here to fight these fucking people. And so that match was thrown on a combustible stack and started to burn and she very quickly was like, 'No, no, no, let's not have this fight,'" he recalled. "You had all these people preparing for a fight and the fight breaks out and she's like, 'Let's not fight.'"

That same week, *USA Today*'s Susan Page, writing a biography of Pelosi, sat down with her for one of their regularly scheduled interviews and found the Speaker still bristling about the insults from the Squad and their backers, particularly the charge that she had caved.

"We're not the Republican Party; we're not a rubber stamp. I mean, that's not what we are," Pelosi said. "Nothing surprises me," she added. "Thirty years since I've been here. They've never seen any fights like what we had when we had Central America and the caucus was divided. NAFTA, and the caucus was divided. Iraq War, and the caucus was divided."

She then told Page she was done with the topic, saying sharply, "But did you want to talk about the book?"

Page tried one more question, asking about Pelosi's "beautiful pâté" remark. "With that, she became as openly agitated as I had ever seen her in an interview—and not with me," Page later wrote. Pelosi told her about how former Appropriations Committee chairman Dave Obey used to say that some of their colleagues merely wanted to "pose for holy pictures." Pelosi "changed her voice and mimicked a child," squeaking, "'See how perfect I am and how pure?'"

Pelosi would often burnish her progressive bona fides by telling members about her past activism. "The amount of times she told me that stupid 'I have protest signs older than you in my basement' shit," a frustrated AOC texted me. "Like yeah but mine don't collect dust."

The purity, however, would come with a cost, the Speaker declared.

"They'll understand when they have something they want to pass," she said. "If you don't want any results, you don't ever have to do anything. But if you have something that you want to pass, you're better off not having your chief of staff send out a tweet in the manner in which that was sent out. Totally inappropriate. I've never seen anything like it."

But just as the party leadership was moving in for the kill, Chakrabarti won a stay of execution from Donald Trump, who decided to wade into the fracas—on the side of Pelosi. Omar, Tlaib, and Pressley were joined by Rep. Deb Haaland, who would later become Biden's interior secretary, on a panel at the Netroots Nation convention, a gathering of progressive activists, organizers, and writers, held that year in Philadelphia. Ocasio-Cortez, who had already developed a reputation for declining invitations to appear at most events, stayed away.

The panel's conversation arrived at the battle with Pelosi, which was now well into its third week and showing no signs of abating. "One thing I tell women of color is that we never needed to ask for permission or an invitation to lead," Omar said. "There is a constant struggle with people who have power about sharing power, and we're not in the business of asking to share that power, we're in the interest of grabbing that power . . . We are not carrying the water for this cruel administration. We are doing the job that people in this country put us forward to do."

Trump also got his share. "We're gonna impeach that motherfucker, don't worry," Tlaib said, a throwback to her original forecast. "It's up to you, it's not up to us. We went from 'let's not talk about it' to close to eighty members of Congress coming out and supporting it."

Trump's subsequent response on Twitter would become one of the most infamous of his term, and there's an added layer of irony to the presence onstage of the Native American Haaland.

So interesting to see "Progressive" Democrat Congresswomen, who originally came from countries whose governments are a complete and total catastrophe, the worst, most corrupt and inept anywhere in the world (if they even have a functioning government at all), now loudly and viciously telling the people of the United States, the greatest and most powerful Nation on earth, how our government is to be run. Why don't they go back and help fix the totally broken and crime infested places from which they came. Then come back and show us how it is done. These places need your help badly, you can't leave fast enough. I'm sure that Nancy Pelosi would be very happy to quickly work out free travel arrangements!

Days later, at a rally, Trump would bask in chants of "Send them back!" It's highly unlikely he had known Haaland was onstage at the Netroots Nation gathering, or that she was Native American, but it was clear his tweet was referring to the four members of the Squad, only one of which, Ilhan Omar, had been born outside the United States. A few days later, he went after Omar directly: "There's a lot of talk about the fact that she was married to her brother. I know nothing about it. I've heard that she married her brother," he said on the White House Lawn.

Pelosi was humiliated to find herself being egged on in her fight by Trump. She quickly condemned his remarks and ended her public attacks on the Squad.

That week, the four women were invited onto *CBS This Morning* with Gayle King, where Tlaib reiterated the charge that Pelosi had singled them out. "Acknowledge the fact that we are women of color, so when you do single us out, be aware of that, and [of] what you're doing, especially because some of us are getting death threats," she said.

The way in which the fight had unfolded was a window into how Democratic politics was being reshaped. It had begun, as Ocasio-Cortez observed, over the life-and-death question of the treatment of migrants at the border. It had then moved to a question of power. Should Democrats take what they could from Trump? Did the Squad have any power, or were they just four preening votes? From there, it bounced over to questions of identity and the singling out of women of color. The party brass had one-upped them, indicting Chakrabarti for singling out a Native American woman. But while identity politics can be weaponized cynically, it derives its power in part from the reality that women of color are indeed singled out for particular abuse. Trump's lumbering into the ring was an unwelcome reminder of this.

The fight simmered down, and on July 26, Pelosi invited Ocasio-Cortez, a month after the war started, for a private meeting in her office. In the roughly thirty-minute talk, Pelosi—according to people who were told the rough contours of the talk—stressed the importance of being a team player and talked about the difference between activism and legislating. "It's like you're in a family. In a family you have your differences, but you're still a family," Pelosi told reporters. "We just had a meeting to clear the air." Her biographer Susan Page later reported that the Speaker "had blown up in private at AOC over her immigration vote."

Later that day, Pelosi showed the difference between her approach to Ocasio-Cortez and that toward Omar. When Omar's phone lit up with Pelosi's name, she pressed the green button with trepidation, bracing herself for a tongue-lashing, fully aware she had just blasted the Speaker on Twitter in defense of AOC. Yet Pelosi didn't mention it and instead invited Omar to be one of just fourteen members of a delegation to Ghana to commemorate the four hundredth anniversary of the slave trade from Africa to the North American continent. "We just can't go without you," Pelosi told her.

She accepted eagerly. "They said 'send her back' but Speaker Pelosi didn't just make arrangements to send me back, she went back with me," Omar posted.

Most members use the opportunity of joining a congressional delegation to buttonhole leadership over major priorities, but Omar passes out in moving vehicles, whether airborne or not, and slept the full way to Africa. On the flight back to the States, Omar and Joyce Beatty were having lunch—eating was the one way Omar stayed awake—and Pelosi came over to ask Beatty if she could have her seat and chat with Omar. Pelosi told Omar she marveled at how well Omar had been able to withstand the relentless criticism, talking about how she, too, has been the subject of vitriolic and misogynistic attacks for decades. But she mentioned the IstandWithIlhan hashtag that had trended on Twitter when Omar was attacked most recently and said she had been moved by it. "It's remarkable how much people rallied around you," she said, adding a comment that betrayed some vulnerability in her legendarily impregnable emotional armor. "No one's ever done that for me," she lamented—or, perhaps, simply observed. "I've borne the brunt of these sexist attacks from Republicans my entire career, and nobody had my back." Omar later ruminated on the closeness of her bond with Pelosi, which at times had been stronger than with other members of the Squad.

Back in town, Ocasio-Cortez talked with both Trent and Chakrabarti about their jobs. The blowup with the offices of Jeffries and Pelosi—the one that included a post of a drive-by shooting—had been just two weeks earlier. I was on the phone with Trent when AOC called him. "Welp, I'm done," he said when he rejoined the call, saying that she wanted him to leave the congressional office and work only as her campaign spokesperson, an offer he understood was in everybody's best interests. Things went more smoothly with Chakrabarti, who was ready to go. "She was getting the pressure to get rid of him," Trent said, "and he was like, 'No, I'm going, it's great, this works out for everybody.' She's like, 'Are you sure? I feel bad.' It was a more pleasant—it just was a better experience" than with Trent. "I'm just not very good at leaving things," Trent allowed. "I do poorly at it. I'm actually not that good at dealing with people, to be honest with you."

Ocasio-Cortez had barreled into Congress with more steam than any freshman perhaps in the lower chamber's history, even including former president John Quincy Adams, who finished his life as an abolitionist in the House. She had grown her celebrity and her public profile and had also faced ever-growing hostility from the right-wing media ecosystem. In the House, her celebrity hadn't, however, been paired with the kind of one-on-one glad-handing required to build a network of allies in Congress. "There are certain members where they would call her, and she didn't return their calls, which, as you know, is unprecedented in this business," one House Democratic leadership aide told me, asking for the customary anonymity. "Early on, when she initially won, and even when she came to DC, people would reach out to her, and she wouldn't return the call. And she just wasn't generally accessible to other members." Trent said it was a personality trait. "She just gets so freaked out when people see—when there's access, she's just real closed off," he said. "It's true. She never called anyone back." Dan Riffle, her aide, also confirmed that plenty of calls went unreturned, but added that the incoming volume meant doing so was physically impossible, that even some heads of state didn't get calls back.

The leadership aide said that the rest of the Hill staffers were glad to see Chakrabarti and Trent go. "That was a summer of her staff just being out of fucking control, and she wouldn't control them," he said. "I don't even really know what they did on a daily basis in that office, but they didn't come to any of our delegation meetings, they didn't really participate in a way that senior staff members participate with other members. A lot of us looked at [that]—particularly with the chief—as just kind of like this dickhead who wanted to tweet stuff for attention, but [who] wasn't actually doing the job that we were all doing for our bosses."

Riffle said that he understood the spot AOC was in, but that it came with the territory. "It was a dumb tweet," Riffle said of Chakrabarti's post. "But one of the things that we talked about when I interviewed for the gig with Saikat [Chakrabarti] was tolerance for mistakes. If you're gonna turn the table over and you're going to do things in a way that they've never been done, you're gonna fuck up more than once. And there has to be a tolerance for making mistakes. But, again, we're not the ones who have to bear the brunt of the consequences when we make those mistakes. She's the one who has to go answer those questions on the record."

Trent said the staff wasn't out of control, but was carrying out a strategy by design. But, ultimately, that strategy required them and the other left members of the House to fully take on the machine. Instead, they ended up trying to have it both ways, crashing through the gates but then expecting to be welcomed and thanked for being there. Half in, half out, they angered those on the inside for challenging them and those on the outside for not challenging those on the inside enough. In an effort to win over her colleagues, Ocasio-Cortez distanced herself from Justice Democrats and declined to endorse most primary challengers, but she did, in the 2020 cycle, endorse Jamaal Bowman, Marie Newman, Jessica Cisneros, and Alex Morse, all of whom challenged incumbents.

The problem, Trent said, was that they had tried to do half a revolution. "We talked about raising the profile of staffers deliberately, so that it would be more of a movement. But then we didn't do anything with it," he said. "The whole office got too big for its britches. If we weren't going to move fast and break things, if you're not trying to fuck with people, why are you fucking with people?"

12

DINNER WITH FRIENDS

It was an occupational hazard of working in the Senate: Bernie Sanders was late for dinner. That didn't typically bother the senator, who would much rather be in front of a crowd of thirty thousand than at a table of ten. But this one was important, and he knew it. He'd been invited to Elizabeth Warren's condo for a lasagna dinner, one that he knew would include a chat about each of their ambitions for the presidency.

But he was also in charge of the War Powers Resolution he had introduced with Republican senator Mike Lee, pushing for an end to U.S. support for the war in Yemen, the same issue Gottheimer had battled against in the House.

The arcane legislative process included what's known as a "vote-a-rama," which could be an all-night affair and often included endless amendments. As in the House, supporters of Israel's hard-line government were looking for a way to use the vote to embarrass Democrats on their issue and were proposing an amendment to do just that. Sanders aide Ari Rabin-Havt, while huddled with a group of senior staffers in the cloakroom just off the Senate floor, proposed a strategy for responding to the amendment. "Well, have you checked with AIPAC on that?" another staffer asked.

Sanders had been nowhere near, off fiddling with his phone. "He was in the conversation so fast, I swear, it was like he apparated in like Dumbledore," Rabin-Havt said. Sanders declared, "No staffer of mine will ever ask AIPAC for permission for anything."

Sanders was several hours late for dinner, but Warren was as aware as anybody about the nature of the Senate job. The pair were joined by her husband, Bruce Mann, a legal historian at Harvard, and what was said there that night would later become a source of high controversy during the Iowa caucuses.

Two weeks later, on New Year's Eve 2019, before the Squad had been sworn in to Congress, Warren announced that she was running for president in 2020 and would be officially launching her campaign with a February rally in Lawrence, Massachusetts, commemorating the 1912 Bread and Roses Strike led by seamstresses and other garment workers. Along with two later speeches—one in New York City, near the site of the 1911 Triangle Shirtwaist Factory fire, and another in Atlanta to honor the 1881 Washerwomen Strike—the focus on women organizing for better conditions in the workplace was her attempt to square the circle of her politics. Contemporary Democratic pressures nudged her in the "Nevertheless, she persisted!" direction of women's empowerment, but Warren's politics had long been aimed squarely at taking on the elites, and she was concerned about getting lumped in as a retread of Hillary Clinton, despite having oriented her politics directly against Clinton-style neoliberalism.

The launch, from a fund-raising perspective, was a dud, with her email list bringing in just a few hundred thousand dollars. But things were going much slower for Sanders, who was hemming and hawing about getting into the race, not pulling the trigger until February 19. When he did, though, he hauled in some four million dollars in just a few hours, a sign that the energy that had gathered around him in 2016 was still there.

Among the first issues Warren confronted was a staff unionization effort. Only a handful of campaigns had unionized for the first time in 2018, but it would become common by the next cycle. Professional office spaces had been changing since the 2010s brought a new generation into the workforce. These "Millennials," joined later by "Zoomers," felt a greater sense of urgency around climate and social justice questions than their elders and, more important for the workplace dynamic, believed deeply that the personal was political and that fights for the greater good couldn't be waged until justice had been achieved closer to home. The election of Trump had uncorked an unending stream of rage from all corners of the left and center-left, and much of it was channeled into resisting his administration and electing Democrats in the wave year of 2018. Now, with the presidential campaign in full swing, that contest drew in some of the bubbling energy, but much of it also began to turn in on itself, with progressive organizations beginning to implode in the kind of tumult that would truly burst at the seams several years later.

As every Democratic candidate must, Warren immediately said that she would recognize the union and voluntarily enter contract negotiations. She and the union organizers then proceeded to do roughly nothing for months, because negotiating a union contract while running or working on a presidential campaign is not easy. It's much easier to put it off.

The Sanders campaign, meanwhile, moved as quickly as it could to recognize its staff union and, in the process, flagrantly violated labor law. Two unions were competing to be the one to represent the campaign's workers—the Campaign Workers Guild (CWG) and the United Food and Commercial Workers (UFCW). The CWG, which had been formed only in 2017 to capture the rising militant energy among young people on campaigns and in progressive organizations, was known to be a bit edgier than the UFCW, which was a 1979 merger of two unions that dated back to the nineteenth century. But while the CWG tended to be more militant, it had also worked on campaigns before, which the UFCW had not. And writing a contract for a campaign is wildly different from negotiating one for grocery workers.

The Sanders campaign's senior officials hoped that the workers chose the UFCW, for multiple reasons. Working with the union could help win its endorsement, for one, but also it was thought that the union's longtime professional track record would be useful in maintaining good relations with staff. And the senior staff did more than just hope. Several senior campaign sources confirmed that there was a push by some near the top of the campaign to put their thumb on the scale of the vote between the two unions—a stratagem barred by labor law. Chuck Rocha, the senior-most consultant on the campaign, directly lobbied workers to go with UFCW, according to multiple sources familiar with Rocha's effort, even though labor rules insist that such decisions be made free of management pressure. (Rocha said he applied no pressure in either direction, but that workers may have assumed he preferred the UFCW because of his prior work with the union.)

Some workers complained about the pressure to officials at CWG, which very nearly released a public statement condemning the unfair labor practice, which had the potential to significantly damage the campaign, undercutting Sanders's image as an uncompromising backer of workers. Ultimately, CWG held its fire and backed away, and a contract was agreed to with the UFCW.

The contract, however, was riddled with contradictions and imprecision. It suggested, for instance, that the campaign would find housing for workers who had to relocate, though that rarely happened, leaving some staff sleeping in tents in Iowa. "It wasn't even clear how many days a week people were supposed to work," recalled one senior aide, calling the contract "a complete, unmitigated disaster."

Another problem arose as a result of Sanders's long-held skepticism of campaign staff. He worried (and had done so going back to the 1970s) that they would bankrupt his campaign and were unnecessary to what he needed to do, which was simply to communicate clearly and directly with the public. He didn't understand why so many people were needed to do this. At major rallies, staff were told not to introduce themselves to Sanders as his staff, lest he ask later why so many people had been hired to work the event. The 2016 campaign had gone to extreme and previously unreported lengths to keep the candidate from panicking about the size of his staff. In Burlington, the campaign staffed two separate headquarters, one with just a handful of people (the size Sanders thought reasonable) and the other with the rest of the workers (the number of staff actually needed to run a campaign that raised and spent a quarter of a billion dollars). This led to some awkward moments. Once, an email went out to all the staff in Burlington that Sanders would be at the headquarters the next day, and workers who'd come to idolize him arrived, finally believing they'd get a chance to meet him in person in an intimate setting. But Sanders knew about and visited only the smaller headquarters, leaving the rest of the staff feeling left out.

In 2019, Sanders hesitated for months before green-lighting the hiring of a field staff, hoping instead that volunteers could do enough of the legwork. By the time the field staff began arriving, the contract had been inked. Newer workers felt less bought into the arrangement, and the contract was largely unworkable as it related to field staff anyway, meaning months of new negotiations that ate up scarce time.

While the 2016 campaign had largely attracted entry-level staff who supported Sanders but were also simply looking for a job, the

2020 campaign lost out on those types of workers to campaigns like Warren's and South Bend mayor Pete Buttigieg's, who had staffed up earlier. And while, in 2016, there had been just three serious candidates, 2020 boasted so many that debate organizers needed two stages to fit them all. The upshot was that good help for a campaign hiring late was very hard to find. What the Sanders campaign was left with were activist true believers, and those activists brought their activism to the inside. The campaign eventually agreed to offer higher pay and better benefits for most workers, particularly after several worker actions. On the professional platform Slack, worker after worker lambasted campaign manager Faiz Shakir for not yet agreeing to their demands, and a worker or workers began leaking to the *Washington Post* and *Politico* a variety of grievances, some pay related, others not. Shakir, meanwhile, saw Sanders campaign workers as overly entitled and demanding. Leaking about the campaign in order to win internal advantage, he told them, was not just petty but also immoral. This wasn't just a job, he said, but was a vehicle for the hopes not just of the country but of all those around the world who needed the United States to be a leader and a force for good.

The battles with the staff would nearly destroy the campaign in Iowa, but first Sanders had to make it to the caucuses. Heading into the summer, however, Warren was climbing, while Sanders was stumbling along with what seemed to be his floor of hard-core support, roughly 15 percent. In a crowded field, it was enough to stay competitive, but he needed a jolt to break out. And he needed a break from the *New York Times*. No paper was more important to Democratic primary voters than the *Times*, and its coverage of Warren was celebratory, while the beat writer assigned to Sanders was seen by the campaign as openly hostile. The Sanders campaign, complaining to editors in New York, managed to get the person who reported on Warren, Astead Herndon, reassigned elsewhere, but there was nothing they could do with their own assigned reporter but bicker.

What they needed was a boost from the Squad, particularly Ocasio-Cortez. She had volunteered for the Sanders campaign in 2016, and her hesitancy to get on board again was becoming conspicuous. The campaign knew it was unlikely to win over Ayanna Pressley, who, as a Boston congresswoman, had her eye on the Senate seat if Warren vacated it. Ocasio-Cortez, too, had her eye on a Senate seat and was worried about her standing upstate if she endorsed Sanders. Corbin Trent made the case that Sanders was significantly more popular in Upstate New York than she herself was, so, if anything, allying with Sanders would redound to her benefit if she ever made a run for the upper chamber.

In mid-September, the Working Families Party, one of the largest electoral organizations on the left, officially endorsed Warren over Sanders, in what WFP leaders hoped would be a breaking of the dam, with other national progressive groups getting behind her as the most viable challenger to Biden. Warren was still climbing in the polls, and within a week, she'd be leading Biden both nationally and in Iowa, grabbing the role of front-runner, while Sanders was hovering in the low teens. But the endorsement exposed a bubbling rift on the left, with a divide emerging between what's been called the "professional left"—the ecosystem of nonprofit leaders, foundation-backed progressive organizations, and Washington-based membership organizations like MoveOn—and the base of active voters who considered themselves heavily progressive or socialist. The WFP's method of arriving at its endorsement came under scrutiny. It had relied on a combination of a vote of the elections membership plus leaders in the coalition, but it never released the membership vote tally.

Online, and particularly on Twitter, the Sanders army lashed out at WFP, launching a swarm of denunciations. Sanders himself thought the vote had been rigged. "We gotta make them reveal their membership vote," he told his senior staff.

Sources in the nonprofit and foundation world told me that heavy pressure had been put on organizations by their funders to rally behind Warren, and many of the leaders of those organizations were themselves strong supporters of Warren, having grown up professionally with her as their champion. And, as a good politician, Warren maintained strong relationships with many of them—phoning at the birth of a child and so on. Sanders, meanwhile, never did any of that. "I'm not good at backslapping. I'm not good at pleasantries," he told the *New York Times* editorial board during its endorsement process. "If you have your birthday, I'm not going to call you up to congratulate you, so you'll love me and you'll write nice things about me. That's not what I do. Never have. I take that as a little bit of a criticism—self-criticism. I have been amazed at how many people respond to 'Happy

Birthday!' 'Oh Bernie, thanks so much for calling.' It works. It's just not my style. I try to stay focused on the important issues facing working families in this country, and I fight for them."

The WFP in particular, sources said, had been prepping to endorse Warren for months. But the battle for the endorsements of the organizations that made up what Obama spokesman Robert Gibbs had derisively dubbed "the professional left" was a live one, because even though they were funded and led largely by Warren supporters, they were also staffed primarily by younger people backing Sanders, and to the extent they had grassroots memberships, a good chunk of those were Sanders supporters, too. (Neither Warren nor Sanders was phoning the younger folks on their birthday—though a young staffer had a better shot at a selfie with Warren, who made them a feature of her rallies.) The tension between the younger base and their leadership was too much.

The WFP's endorsement was the culmination of all that pressure breaking through, and it unleashed a torrent of toxicity in both directions. Reaching for the Bernie Bro playbook that had been developed by Hillary Clinton, Warren's backers organized a letter demanding that the Sanders campaign "denounce the racism in its ranks." The letter noted, "For the first time in its history, Maurice Mitchell, a Black man with decades of experience building movements and strengthening our democracy," was leading the WFP. "The virulent, racist attacks on these leaders are unacceptable and dangerous. What do we do when racism and sexism is [sic] present in progressive movements?" The attacks on Mitchell and the WFP were coming from Sanders supporters, the argument went, and therefore, Sanders needed to denounce them publicly.

The rhetoric got even hotter. "We refuse to concede to white terror from the Left as well as the Right," the letter read, adding moral authority with the appeal "As Black leaders in this movement . . ." Privately, the Warren campaign's senior leadership thought the missive was a death blow to the Sanders campaign. And they had good reason to think so. Not only was Warren well ahead of Sanders, with Biden fading, but the language of racial justice was increasingly able to dictate terms from the moral high ground on the left. And the notion that Sanders represented a base of young white men was starting to stick.

Warren gave Sanders a rare phone call, telling him roughly, "Bernie, it's going to be hard to unify with your people continuing to attack me."

Sanders rejected the premise. "Elizabeth, your people are just as bad, they're attacking me," he said.

"I think that the characterization, or the stereotype, has stuck," Pramila Jayapal told me in the heat of the campaign. "There are a lot of people who think about 'Bernie Bros' and think that it's a real phenomenon. And I think that it depends on what we're talking about. Are there people online that are nasty that are Bernie supporters? Yes, for sure. I'm not sure if they're really Bernie supporters or if they're just plants."

Demographically, Sanders was polling better among young people of color than any other candidate. And because he had such a strong following online, with millions of supporters, he had more angry and rude ones than anybody else. "Most of the characterization of Bernie Bros seems to come from social media. It doesn't come because there are vast majorities of Bernie supporters in person who are being nasty," Jayapal went on. "In the vast scheme of how many Bernie supporters there are, I think they are a tiny portion in real life."

Ocasio-Cortez was worried about the toxicity, too. "Bernie's supporters have been very, very damaging to him, and it's really frustrating to see and experience. They don't realize how influential they are. It's frustrating to feel like they are hurting him," she said at the time. "I feel like Warren is scooping up LGBT, progressives, women, & progressives of color because of how they isolate. And it makes agreeing with [Sanders] ideologically difficult. So it feels like they are forcing an unnecessary choice between class analysis and race analysis—again—through their behavior, not so much policy[,] and it creates issues." It wasn't just random trolls online, she worried. "It can be news because people with influence are acting this way," she said. "And the movement has centered quite a few problematic people with a culture that questioning them means you're not progressive."

Warren was able to read Ocasio-Cortez's hesitation, and she made the case to her that endorsing Sanders would be a mistake because of the divisive surrogates like Nina Turner around him. She had her staff send AOC a long dossier of mean tweets from aides and surrogates like Turner, David Sirota, Briahna Joy Gray, and Shaun King.

Ocasio-Cortez let Sanders know about the dossier. Still, she said, she wasn't giving up on Bernie. That weekend, she secretly traveled to Burlington to meet with him and his wife, Jane. Ari Rabin-Havt arranged the hotel room so that it wouldn't be in her name and made sure she got in without being seen. She had dinner at the Sanderses' home that evening, and the candidate and Shakir made the case for why Sanders still had a path to the nomination and why he could win the general election. Fifteen months ago, AOC had been an obscure, long-shot candidate and a bartender; now she held the fate of the Sanders campaign in her hands. The next day, she suggested brunch, and Sanders breathed a sigh of relief. They both understood that she'd be seen with him in Burlington—and that she was good with that. They went to the popular diner the Penny Cluse Café, and as expected, a customer snapped a photo of her, Shakir, Jane, and Bernie.

Sanders mostly got her name right that weekend, suggesting that the charm offensive was in full force. Shakir made the pitch that the sooner AOC endorsed, the bigger role she could play. He wanted her to be not just a surrogate but a strategic leader of the campaign. Partly, this sentiment flowed from Shakir's respect for Ocasio-Cortez's strategic abilities—but also from the vacuum at the top of the campaign. Sanders wouldn't let anyone set the campaign's strategy, and he wasn't doing it himself. Earlier that week, Shakir had given a quote to CNN, in an article about a staff shake-up, that appeared to be campaign pablum but that was revealing of the dynamic. "We all take our leadership and follow the direction of Bernie Sanders and he drives the strategy," it read. "I believe strongly that we all take our guidance from the top— and he is the one driving this train." With AOC on board, Shakir reasoned, if she set a strategy, the campaign could pursue it instead of waiting for Sanders.

Departing, Ocasio-Cortez left the clear impression that she was supportive but wasn't ready to endorse quickly; she wanted to see some upward movement in the polls first. The Bernie camp was frustrated by the reasoning, as an endorsement and campaign swing by Ocasio-Cortez would draw big crowds and media attention and likely prompt the boost in the polls she was looking for. She also wasn't interested, she made clear, in anything that looked like attacking Warren or drawing sharp contrasts with her. The target had to be Joe Biden.

On Sunday evening, the team regrouped for a conference call.

"She's so smart," Sanders marveled. He added, putting into words what the rest of the group had taken from the meeting, "She's wondering if we can win this thing."

Jane Sanders couldn't hold back. The polls had been driving her nuts, and now they were going to cost them AOC's endorsement at a time they needed it. A new *Des Moines Register* poll from the weekend before—one of those "gold standard" polls the press elevated above others—had Warren on top for the first time, at 22 percent, with Biden at 20 and Sanders all the way down at 11.

The *Des Moines Register* poll was bogus, Jane complained. "Do you know anyone who was polled?" Unskewing the polls wasn't going to be enough, the campaign knew, but it had to push ahead, hoping AOC would come through. Sanders flew to Las Vegas for a series of events in the state that would hold the second caucus of the campaign.

On Tuesday evening, October 1, 2019, Sanders was speaking to a small group of mostly Muslim supporters at Shiraz, a Mediterranean restaurant in Spring Valley, Nevada, when the "oh shit" moment hit Rabin-Havt. He'd been traveling with the candidate for several years at that point and had never seen him ask for a chair. Now he had. "He hates chairs at events," Rabin-Havt said. As the event wound to a close, Sanders told Rabin-Havt he was feeling uncomfortable—and that chest pain was involved. Rabin-Havt and Sanders's new body man, Jesse Cornett, looked at each other ominously. Sanders wanted to sleep it off, but Rabin-Havt—saving his life, as it would turn out—insisted on finding an urgent care facility. The first one said it was too busy, so they kept looking. At the next urgent care, Rabin-Havt went in and told them he had Bernie Sanders in the car and that the senator was in need of urgent, but private, attention. The attending nurse told him that if it truly was Bernie Sanders, he was welcome to come in the back, but if it wasn't he'd be kicked out.

The doctors there told Sanders he had a ninety-minute window to get to a cardiac catheterization clinic to get treated. They dropped a mouthful of medical terminology, none of which Rabin-Havt understood, other than the urgency.

Sanders stayed awake—and stayed classic Sanders—throughout the procedure, for which he never went under. A blockage was found in an artery, and two stents were inserted to clear it. It was by now after midnight on the East Coast, and Rabin-Havt, the only senior staffer there, struggled to get hold of Jane and the Sanders kids, not wanting them to wake up and see the news on CNN.

"He slept last night and I didn't," Rabin-Havt texted me in the morning.

He asked the doctors to describe precisely what they had done, so the campaign could release an accurate statement. Rabin-Havt didn't know it at the time, but his framing of the question was a consequential decision. The doctors described, as asked, precisely what they had done, but they said nothing about why—beyond chest pain and the blockage. But it was enough information for doctors to publicly begin speculating that Sanders likely had suffered an arterial infarction, the medical term for a heart attack.

Faiz Shakir, boarding the plane, assumed the campaign was over; Sanders, however, never for a second considered dropping out. The hospital, meanwhile, allowed a nearby room to be transformed into a makeshift campaign headquarters. Walking into the room, Shakir saw a spread of sodas and cookies the hospital had provided. "See, I even get comped in hospitals in Vegas," Rabin-Havt, a high-stakes poker player, joked.

The campaign spent the next few days trying to get the doctors, who worked in several different hospitals, in the same room, so they could put out a statement that included a diagnosis—not that they were in a rush to get it out. The hospital, meanwhile, was pushing Sanders to sign a privacy waiver so they could boast in advertising that they had treated the Medicare for All champion.

Ocasio-Cortez and her staff gathered on a conference call. In an emotional exchange, she said that the time had come to take the leap and endorse Bernie Sanders for president. He had fought his entire life for the progressive movement and had nearly lost that life, and they couldn't abandon him now. The decision had been made.

While still in the hospital, Rabin-Havt got a phone call from Trent, but he missed it. A moment later, Ocasio-Cortez called Shakir's phone; he answered it, started smiling, and handed the phone to Sanders. It was a very quick call, but it was everything Sanders had wanted. "You two should get on the phone with this woman Rebecca"—Sanders told them, referring to AOC's cousin, a top aide—"and Corbin and figure out how we're gonna do this." AOC was in.

The news of Ocasio-Cortez's pending endorsement was held tight until mid-October, and in the meantime, she traveled to Copenhagen to meet with an international conference of mayors to talk climate change, her first foreign trip as a member of Congress. The *Guardian*'s dispatch on her address was over the top: "From the moment she began speaking, the main hall at the summit became completely still, and when she finished, the ovation she received far exceeded that received by the veteran climate campaigner and former vice-president Al Gore; Denmark's prime minister, Mette Frederiksen; or the UN secretary general, António Guterres."

A little less than a week later, Sanders made a triumphant debate stage return—still alive. Warren, now the front-runner, was savaged from all sides and promised to release her own version of a Medicare for All bill that wouldn't raise taxes on the middle class. Sen. Amy Klobuchar left a memorable mark on Warren during the debate: "At least Bernie's being honest here in saying how he's going to pay for this and that taxes are going to go up." The moment played to Sanders's strength, his authenticity, and to the sense that he wasn't the kind of politician who would tell voters only what they wanted to hear. He'd been saying the same things for forty years. The debate on October 15 would mark the high point for Warren's campaign. Her campaign team identified in real time, and increasingly in hindsight, how pivotal the endorsement of AOC had been. Just days earlier, Warren had lunched with Ocasio-Cortez again, part of a concerted effort to win her over or at least keep her neutral. To the Warren camp, if AOC had urged Sanders, while bottoming out in the polls and recovering from a heart attack, to step aside and collectively endorse Warren, the nomination would have been a lock.

As the debate ended, Dave Weigel of the *Washington Post* broke the news that both Ocasio-Cortez and Omar would be endorsing Sanders. Initial reports included Tlaib, too, but that was withdrawn, as Tlaib wanted to make her own announcement later, in Detroit. Three weeks later, Pressley endorsed Warren, home state politics trumping her DC Squad. But losing AOC, Omar, and Tlaib to Sanders, as he returned from his heart attack, was a blow from which the Warren campaign never recovered, with its senior leadership believing the moment ultimately undid their chance at the nomination.

What followed from November through January was nothing short of miraculous, a campaign and a candidate brought back from the dead, so to speak, and surging into Iowa with a head of steam that threatened to snatch away the nomination. Part of the miracle had an earthly explanation: the Sanders campaign had saved enough money to go big on TV in Iowa, New Hampshire, and Nevada, but particularly Iowa, throughout the winter, while the other campaigns were more strapped from overspending earlier.

The race changed fundamentally on January 13, 2020. Faiz Shakir was asleep in Des Moines when he got an early morning call from the campaign communications director, Mike Casca. Early meant bad news. "So CNN is about to report that Bernie met with Elizabeth like a year ago, and she says—or, apparently, he said a woman can't be president," Casca told him. Shakir told Casca he wanted to go down the hall and tell Sanders in person. "It was important to me that I actually look at his face and see how this goes," he said.

Shakir told the candidate about the looming report, and Sanders just looked at him and then put his head down. Shakir let a moment pass. "You know, Senator, if there's any piece of that that's accurate, I totally understand. I just need to understand, like, what happened, what transpired there? Did you say that?"

Sanders's face jumped up, and he stared at Shakir. "Faiz, she called me to meet with me to tell me that she's running for president. Do you think in my right mind I would ever say something like that? Do you think I would ever tell her that a woman can't be president? How stupid would that be?" He put his head back down. "It was clear to me that he was just hurt, he was fundamentally hurt by that," recalled Shakir.

MJ Lee, CNN's Warren beat reporter, told the campaign that the comment had allegedly been made during Sanders's 2018 meeting with Warren and her husband in their Chinatown condo. Sanders had reportedly told her that a woman couldn't beat Trump. The Sanders campaign told Lee that Sanders would deny on the record that he had said such a thing, which meant Lee would have anonymous sources who weren't in the room against an on-the-record source who was. Sanders was convinced Warren herself would knock the story down, and tell CNN it wasn't true.

Lee stood her ground. "My fourth source matches yours," she said, calling one of her sources "unimpeachable."

The top staff on the Sanders and Warren campaigns had known

each other for years, and some had been longtime friends and former coworkers. "I'm pinging them, saying, like, 'Hey, are you going to shut this damn story down?'" Shakir said. "And they're, like, 'No. We're no comment.' The whole time they're sitting there, like, 'No. This story is cool with us.' I'm, like, I cannot believe that we're about to go through this. They're going to sit and let this thing happen."

A Sanders campaign official said the Warren camp saw the whole affair as revenge for the Bernie Bros. "When they decided to call Bernie Sanders a sexist, I felt—or heard from them—basically the justification: 'This is revenge. You guys have been initiating for months these kinds of sly hits on us on Twitter.' Like, wait a minute, what? How does that even compute? So, you're upset about some mean tweets, so then you go out and call him a sexist from the candidate's mouth?"

Sanders, instead of calling it a miscommunication, outright called it a lie. "It is ludicrous to believe that at the same meeting where Elizabeth Warren told me she was going to run for president, I would tell her that a woman couldn't win," he said in his statement to CNN. "It's sad that, three weeks before the Iowa caucus and a year after that private conversation, staff who weren't in the room are lying about what happened. What I did say that night was that Donald Trump is a sexist, a racist and a liar who would weaponize whatever he could. Do I believe a woman can win in 2020? Of course! After all, Hillary Clinton beat Donald Trump by 3 million votes in 2016."

At a debate that night, hosted by CNN, Sanders was asked about the story and again denied it, which led to a surreal exchange.

CNN moderator: You're saying that you never told Senator Warren that a woman could not win the election.

Sanders: That is correct.

CNN moderator [to Warren]: What did you think when Senator Sanders told you a woman could not win the election?

The audience, Sanders, and even Warren laughed at the slant of the question. "I disagreed," Warren said.

After the debate, Warren made a beeline for Sanders. "I think you called me a liar on national TV," she said.

"What?" asked Bernie.

"I think you called me a liar on national TV," she repeated.

"Let's not do it right now. You wanna have that discussion, we'll have that discussion," Sanders said.

"Anytime," Warren said.

"You called *me* a liar. You told me—" Sanders said, stopping himself. "All right, let's not do it now."

In tracking polls, the Sanders campaign saw their numbers with women, which had been climbing, plateau and then dip. "At that point, we lost about ten points with women," said a top Sanders campaign official, citing the campaign's tracking polls. "Where that really showed up in a big way was on Super Tuesday, when we lost by ten points to Biden among women. And I still think that's a vestige of Elizabeth Warren, a person with credibility, saying that my friend Bernie Sanders is a sexist. That hurt us in a way that it was almost impossible to recover among some women, because it just opened up the wounds of the Hillary thing all over again and made people fired up to dislike Bernie Sanders."

At the same time, the Senate was trying President Trump, who'd been impeached by the House for threatening to withhold weapons from Ukraine unless the newly sworn-in Ukrainian president, Volodymyr Zelenskyy announced a corruption probe into Biden's son Hunter. This kept Sanders and Warren off the campaign trail, leaving it open for Buttigieg and, to a lesser degree, Joe Biden, who was drawing embarrassingly small audiences, many of whom would tell reporters they had arrived noncommittal but had left vowing not to vote for him.

Democratic Majority for Israel went on the air with attack ads, going after Sanders's heart attack and arguing that he wasn't up to the task of defeating Trump. A dark-money group organized by a Silicon Valley doctor on behalf of Warren began running ads in the *Des Moines Register*—ironically praising Warren for refusing super PAC money—but the Warren campaign asked them to stop the ads, just as she had done in her 2012 and 2018 Senate campaigns.

The next jolt to the campaign would come from a surprising place: *The Joe Rogan Experience*. In an episode of the podcast that aired to millions of viewers and listeners in mid-January, the former kickboxer and comedian told guest Bari Weiss, a journalist, "I think I'll probably vote for Bernie." Rogan had interviewed Sanders, Tulsi Gabbard, and Andrew Yang on his wildly popular podcast, but he had turned down Warren and other candidates. He cottoned to Bernie. "He's been insanely consistent his entire life. He's basically been saying the same thing, been for the same thing his whole life. And that, in and of itself, is a very powerful structure to operate from," Rogan told his millions of listeners on January 20. Two days later, the Sanders social media team shared a clip of the "endorsement" on Twitter. The blowback was intense.

As the since-departed Michael Brooks, a leading progressive online broadcaster, put it at the time, Joe Rogan represented what could be called the political center far more than institutions like the *New York Times*, who try to claim that label. His astonishing listenership numbers—averaging more than ten million per show—still didn't do justice to his cultural influence, because not every listener listened to every show, and the program often ran longer than three hours. This meant that tens of millions of people were tuning in to Rogan with some regularity. They tended to be working class, partly because of the format of the show. For people driving for a living—whether piloting delivery vehicles, Ubers, or trucks or working in any other occupation with long stretches of "window time"—a three-hour podcast is far better than a thirty-minute one. The shorter one ends, and now you have to fumble around for the next one, which could be a dud. The same holds for people who work on construction sites, in kitchens, in warehouses, in hotels, or any place where the time goes by faster with your mind occupied. Rogan's show is basically without structure—his free-flowing interviews operate more as conversations. If you zone out or miss a chunk, you can dip back in wherever you want.

White-collar professionals can get away with listening to music, but trying to do your job at your desk while also listening to a podcast is much more of a challenge than it is for a line cook or an Uber driver. These are also the voters, overwhelmingly men, whom political operations have the hardest time reaching, because they're simply not regularly tuned in to politics. Most of Rogan's shows for years were about entertainment or fighting or sports or comedy. Rogan often described his politics as on the left—supportive of universal health care, a higher minimum wage, and so on. He was also socially liberal, supportive of causes like marriage equality.

But in the wake of his endorsement of Sanders, Rogan's critics insisted the podcaster was a "transphobe," circulating video of his commentary regarding mixed martial arts fighter Fallon Fox, a trans woman. *Vox*, in an article on the controversy, also cited Rogan's commentary, "I didn't have a dog in this fight," Rogan said of the politics of trans rights. "I was completely open and liberal about it—until there was a case where a man who had been a man for 30 years became a woman for a little less than two years and then started MMA fighting women. Beating the fuck out of these women, and then not proclaiming that he or she used to be a man . . . if you ever watch the fights, she wasn't winning because she was skillful. She was fucking manhandling these women, it was ugly."

For readers of *Vox* and critics of Rogan, it was an open-and-shut case of transphobia. "This very short paragraph contains all the classic tropes of transphobia: a denial of the authenticity of trans people's identity, an insinuation that they're a threat to cis folks, and a claim that they're using their gender identity to somehow get ahead in life," *Vox* wrote. But that assessment treats the handling of Fallon Fox's case as settled and unimpeachable. Within the fighting community, however, many women were clamoring for rules that would require a fighter to disclose a recent transition from male to female. Just before a sports journalist forced her outing as trans, Fox had taken thirty-nine seconds to dispatch her opponent, tossing her around the ring and then knocking her flat with a knee to the face. Mixed martial arts is a rough sport; everyone going into it knows that. But did Fox's opponent have a right to know that Fox had been born male, gone through puberty male, and built up the various biological advantages that come with it? Even asking that question in 2020 in progressive spaces was considered transphobic.

Rogan, an Ultimate Fighting Championship commentator, made clear he wasn't bound by leftist orthodoxies and argued that disclosure around the timing of the transition was appropriate, though his explanation for why wasn't one of the clips circulated by his critics. "We're not just talking about bike racing. We're talking about the most contact. We're talking about fucking fighting," he said. "If you think that's fair, you're fucking crazy. If you choose to fight her and you know that she's a trans woman, I'm totally fine with that, but that was not what was going on here. What was going on was this woman, who used to be a man for thirty-two years, transitioned to being a woman and then didn't tell anybody and fought two different women who thought they were fighting a woman and got fucking smashed. I was watching it, it was like watching a man fight a woman. She wasn't particularly skillful. It wasn't like she had some unbelievable background in judo like Ronda Rousey. It wasn't that. You were just literally watching a former man beat up women."

The *Vox* article, typical of the mainstream progressive response, said that the controversy raised the question, "What views should render someone unacceptable in polite discourse?" *Vox* went on:

> Throughout the 2016 campaign, Sanders was dogged by accusations of disinterest in identity issues—of having a monomaniacal socialist focus on economic inequality and class that led him to sideline other vectors of oppression. The Sanders campaign has worked to address this concern in 2020, building a strong base of support in minority communities (particularly among young voters) and putting forward highly progressive plans on issues like criminal justice and immigration.
>
> But the scars from 2016 aren't entirely healed over. Trumpeting Joe Rogan's support plays right into this axis of conflict. Rogan isn't particularly offensive to the left on class issues; his worst excesses all come on other identity-based concerns. Deciding to highlight his support so prominently will play to stereotypes, justified or not, about what Sanders really cares about.
>
> The fight over Bernie Sanders and Joe Rogan is, in short, not really a fight about Joe Rogan. It's a fight over the direction and identity of the Democratic Party at a moment when Sanders is rocketing up in the polls—a debate over who he is, and whether he has the right values and judgment to lead the party.

Ocasio-Cortez, watching the fracas unfold, considered it handled poorly, though she supported the idea of reaching Rogan's audience. "I thought the campaign making a video and amplifying [the endorsement] was not smart. Bernie going on was fine. But to make a whole video on an 'endorsement' that wasn't really an endorsement when [Joe Rogan] alienates so many people and platforms alt right figures was just signing up for an insane amount of blowback. And then the 'big tent' response made things worse instead of actually responding to the grievance," she texted. Twitter, AOC noted, was "probably the worst place to amplify that."

Rogan faced weeks of attacks for transphobia and vowed he would never again endorse a political candidate. His guest lineup already leaned toward the right, but after the Sanders fight, his political guests were nearly all conservative. By the end of the campaign, he told his audience that, unlike in 2016, he'd be voting for Trump.

The appearance on Rogan's show in August had been a revelation for Sanders. In April, he had appeared at a Fox News town hall in Bethlehem, Pennsylvania, an old steel town, where the mostly white and aging blue-collar audience gave him raucous applause for his socialist agenda, startling even the network's hosts. In mainstream coverage of the town hall, the takeaway had been the scandal of Sanders saying he supported the right of felons to vote—even, he said when pressed, the Boston Marathon bomber. But the event also demonstrated the appeal of Sanders and his agenda. The Rogan interview, though, had far more reach than the Fox town hall event.

Wherever Sanders went for the next several months after that, people would approach him and say they had heard him on Joe Rogan's show and been intrigued by this or that point he had made. He was used to young people treating him like a rock star at rallies—"I'm like Mick Jagger," he told his aide Ari Rabin-Havt once, half-joking, as young people swarmed his car outside the Capitol—but this was different. He traveled to Miami a few days after the interview for the National Association of Black Journalists conference and ate with Rabin-Havt that evening at a small Cuban restaurant. The owner, a Cuban American immigrant, told him she had heard the Rogan interview. Because of his self-description as a socialist, and her lifelong hostility to Castro, she had never liked Sanders, she said. But what he had said made sense, and she was going to take a closer look. "These conversations happened over and over again," Rabin-Havt said.

The decision to post the video of Rogan's endorsement had been made at a low level by Sanders's social media team, but it's likely the controversy would have raged whether Sanders promoted the clip on Twitter or not. The interview and the controversy, though, were a significant net positive for the campaign, and their internal polling showed his audience moving his way after the interview. Sanders had been hit in the fall by the Working Families Party controversy—including the letter denouncing racism in his ranks. Then, in January, he was hit as a sexist by Warren, and then as a transphobe less than two weeks later. The dustups had blunted his momentum. Yet, in the face of it, he was still climbing, which suggested that the attacks had less bite to them than bark.

A CNN poll published on January 20, the same day the Sanders campaign boosted the Rogan video, was typical of what others were finding: Biden was considered by Democratic voters to be the most electable and the most able to "unite the country," but Sanders was the most connected to the electorate. He scored top marks, by far, on "agrees with you on issues that matter most to you" and "best understands the problems facing people like you." People just weren't sure he could win.

Winning would put those doubts to rest, yet Sanders wasn't as well positioned to capitalize on his momentum as he might have been. He had waited so long to hire a field operation in Iowa that he was getting out-organized outside Des Moines by Pete Buttigieg. And the organizers he did hire were contemplating an open revolt.

Some of the field staff's complaints were about the long hours, some about the pay, and some about the hierarchical nature of the campaign. They started making demands for more time off in December and January, just weeks before the February 3 caucuses, but the demands were not met.

So they started organizing—not organizing voters to come to the caucus, but organizing among themselves to get time off and to redress other grievances. Several would-be open letters were written but not published. Some staff proposed a work stoppage and suggested they cease entering data into the campaign's system, which would have crippled the operation. This was their moment of maximal leverage, they argued. Fortunately for the Sanders campaign, they had a union contract already, if an imperfect one. Having a union meant there was a process set up to handle these kinds of disputes. A bargaining unit call was scheduled for a week before the caucus, to hash out their strategy. The state's regional field directors were also part of the union, and they knew about the brewing uprising. They got organized, too, and came to the call prepared with all the arguments against a work stoppage and against a public statement denouncing the campaign. Arguing for time off just days away from a caucus—a caucus that could determine the fate of the campaign—would be a wildly unsympathetic public demand to make, the regional field directors noted accurately. A vote was held, and a majority wanted to back down and not make the fight public.

Sanders, catching wind of the discontent, was frustrated by what he saw as a lack of focus. "Stop hiring activists," he told his leadership team, urging them to hire, instead, only people who wanted to do a good day's work and get paid for it.

A week later, in a caucus plagued by an app failure scandal, Sanders won slightly more votes than Buttigieg, but a software meltdown meant that the official vote total wouldn't be known publicly for days. The Sanders campaign released what raw numbers it had, showing a lead for their candidate, but Buttigieg went onstage and preposterously declared victory. The final tally would end up being 45,652 for Sanders and 43,209 for Buttigieg. Because of the way caucus math works—if a candidate has less than 15 percent at a precinct, their supporters then move around the room to support other candidates—a popular vote win doesn't guarantee a delegate win. Buttigieg was eventually declared the winner by a single "state delegate equivalent," but a cursory look under the hood found this not to be credible. Take Dubuque precinct 36, which was worth 7 delegates. At that location, 46 residents caucused for Buttigieg, 45 for Sanders, 30 for Biden, and 23 for Klobuchar. Because of the odd number of delegates at stake, the remaining delegate would go to the candidate who had been rounded down the farthest in the first calculation. In this case, that would be Biden, so the math would give 2 to Buttigieg, 2 to Sanders, 2 to Biden, and 1 to Klobuchar. Yet the talliers gave 3 to Buttigieg and 1 to Biden. Fix just that one math error, and Buttigieg and Sanders tied statewide.

Yet it shouldn't have been that close. The difference had come in rural Iowa, where the Sanders campaign often didn't have caucus captains to shepherd people through the bizarre in-person voting process that involved shuffling from one side of a gym to another and then reshuffling to another spot if your candidate got knocked out. Had a few more people shown up in a few more precincts, or had a few more precincts been better organized, even with all the app-fueled shenanigans, Sanders would have won both the popular vote *and* the delegate race.

The app debacle was a boon for Biden, as it obscured the extent of his loss. Heading into the campaign as the front-runner, he finished fourth in Iowa, barely edging out Klobuchar, with Andrew Yang on their heels.

New Hampshire, next door to Sanders's home state of Vermont, was considered a lock for Sanders, with the question being only by how much he would win it. Chris Matthews, the soon-to-be-former MSNBC host, following a New Hampshire debate, offered perhaps the most colorfully deranged response to the Sanders surge. "I have my own views of the word 'socialist,' and I'll be glad to share them with you in private," he said, and then proceeded to share them in public. "They go back to the early 1950s. I have an attitude about them. I remember the Cold War. I have an attitude toward [Fidel] Castro. I believe if Castro and the Reds had won the Cold War there would have been executions in Central Park, and I might have been one of the ones getting executed. And certain other people would be there cheering, okay? So, I have a problem with people who took the other side."

Biden finished a shocking fifth place in New Hampshire, somehow managing to do worse there than he had in Iowa.

After Iowa and New Hampshire came the Nevada caucuses, where the legend of the chair-throwing and English-only-demanding Bernie Bros had been etched into stone. The fight for the 2020 Nevada caucuses made the campaign up to that point seem downright genteel. The Democratic political machine in the state had been built from the ground up by the now-retired but still powerful Harry Reid. It was built on the back of the Culinary Workers Union and operated in tandem with the casino industry, which played both parties, but Reid made sure to keep them as at least a part of his operation. The culinary union had been built by a man named Donald "D." Taylor, who by then had become president of UNITE HERE! International. Reid had orchestrated Clinton's victory in 2016 by instructing Taylor to mobilize casino workers for Clinton and instructing casinos to give their employees time off to caucus.

Sanders didn't have an equivalent operation. In 2018, Reid wanted Sanders to come to Nevada to rally for his chosen Senate candidate, Jacky Rosen. Sanders, through Rabin-Havt, the former Reid aide, said he would come if Reid agreed not to interfere in the 2020 caucuses. Reid made that promise and, by all accounts, abided by it. The union leadership, however, did not. As Sanders staged events in Las Vegas, the union sent workers to take ambush videos of him and demand to know why he was going to take away the health insurance benefits they had fought so hard to win. The idea was that Medicare for All would be great for many people but that it would mean worse coverage than they already had. Sanders's bill included a provision labeled "maintenance of effort," which required employers to keep any existing benefits that were better than what the new law offered. Still, all of it was a fantasy. Under no circumstances would a President Sanders be able to marshal the 60 votes in the Senate needed to ban private insurance.

As the caucuses approached, Sanders continued to gain strength nationally, while Biden receded. On February 19, a *Washington Post–ABC News* poll found that 72 percent of Democratic voters thought Sanders could beat Trump, the highest percentage of any candidate. A SurveyUSA poll released that same day found Sanders leading not just among white voters, but with Black, Hispanic, and Asian voters, too. The opinion poll site FiveThirtyEight the next day published an analysis showing that Biden had lost 12 points of his Black vote share since Iowa, with much of it going to Sanders, leaving the two neck and neck nationally for African Americans.

On the Friday before the caucuses, the *Washington Post* reported that intelligence officials believed Russia was working to boost the Sanders campaign. No evidence was given to support the claim, but anonymous sources—most likely Democrats on the House Intelligence Committee or officials within the FBI—used an old trick to make the news public. Sanders, about a month earlier, had been briefed by intelligence officials about their conclusion. The briefing itself was news, whether the information Sanders was briefed on was true or not. The headline in the *Washington Post*: "Bernie Sanders Briefed by U.S. Officials that Russia Is Trying to Help His Presidential Campaign." The paper reported that the intelligence committee had been similarly briefed. Sydney Ember, the *New York Times* beat reporter following Sanders, asked the candidate what he thought of the timing. "I'll let you guess about one day before the Nevada caucus. Why do you think it came out?" Sanders asked.

For Sanders, it was confirmation that the nation's establishment was dead set against him and that the Bernie Bros were largely an artificial creation. "In 2016, Russia used Internet propaganda to sow division in our country, and my understanding is that they are doing it again in 2020," he told the *Post*. "Some of the ugly stuff on the internet attributed to our campaign may well not be coming from real supporters." Sanders was pugnacious in his response. "I've got news for the Republican establishment. I've got news for the Democratic establishment. They can't stop us," he posted on Twitter that Friday night.

The next day, he looked to be right. The caucuses concluded on the morning of February 22, a Saturday, and despite the culinary union leadership's aggressive effort, casino and hospitality workers—primarily Hispanic women—carried "Tío Bernie" to a crushing victory. He ended up with 47 percent of the delegates to Biden's 20 percent.

The win by Sanders, the national press reported, with as much surprise as anybody, made him the clear front-runner heading into South Carolina a week later, followed by Super Tuesday. In 1988, following a surprise victory in Michigan, Jesse Jackson had enjoyed a similar position in the Democratic nomination contest, a candidacy that was backed by the then mayor of Burlington, Vermont, Bernie Sanders. The Democratic establishment then went into full-blown meltdown mode, which resulted in a rapid consolidation behind Michael Dukakis and a collapse of support for Jackson. But, in the meantime, the party brass began cooking up backup plans for the potential that Jackson could storm into the convention with a plurality but not a majority of the delegates. The plan they hit on was to wrangle it from him there and crown New York governor Mario Cuomo instead. This time, out of fresh ideas, establishment figures began suggesting that Cuomo's son, New York governor Andrew Cuomo, arrive at the convention and wrest the nomination from Sanders. The absurdity of some of the plots to stop Sanders betrayed the panic on display. Unlike in 1988, this time, the public could watch the meltdown unfold in real time on MSNBC, CNN, and Twitter.

Chris Jansing, on hand at a Las Vegas caucus site while reporting for MSNBC, delivered an on-air sigh that would become legendary in Sanders circles. "These again are people who work on the strip," she said in a stand-up, with caucusgoers behind her, "within two and a half miles of the Bellagio, largely people of color. Of those, the majority are Latino, and they are clearly, at least from eyeballing it"—Jansing let out a loud sigh—"strongly in favor of Bernie Sanders, with Joe Biden coming in second."

James Carville blasted the media for not covering Sanders's campaign more closely. "It's obvious that he's the front-runner," Carville said. "We're in a whole new ball game here. This game could end a little after mid-March." Two weeks earlier, Carville had been sounding the alarm in apocalyptic terms. "It's gonna be the end of days," he foretold his cable audience. "I'm scared to death. I really am." Now Carville's worst fears were coming true. "The happiest person right now—it's about one fifteen Moscow time—this thing is going very well for Vladimir Putin. I promise you. He's probably stayin' up, watchin' us right now. How you doin', Vlad?"

Nicolle Wallace, formerly a Bush administration spokesperson, blasted Sanders voters as a "squeaky, angry minority," adding, "I have no idea what voters think about anything anymore."

Brian Williams, on the same network, was angry at the process. "What is going on here, and is this any way to pick a nominee?" he asked Chris Matthews.

"Well, I don't think so, but it's the way we're picking this one, and it looks like Bernie Sanders is hard to beat right now," Matthews said. "I think it's a little late to stop him, and I think that's the problem . . . I'm reading last night about the fall of France in the summer of 1940. And the general, Reynaud, calls up Churchill and says, 'It's over.' And Churchill says, 'How can it be? You've got the greatest army in Europe. How can it be over?' He said, 'It's over.' So I had that suppressed feeling. I can't be as wild as Carville, but he is damn smart, and I think he's damn right on this one."

Matthews earned himself a suspension and an apology tour by comparing the Nevada win to the Nazi blitzkrieg on France, but setting aside how inappropriate it was—much of Sanders's family was wiped out in the Holocaust—it did betray the fatalism that had consumed the establishment in the wake of the caucus. It was over. Bernie had won.

Jason Johnson, an MSNBC pundit who'd been among the most vitriolic opponents of Sanders, was called upon to apologize to Sanders's staff. "Earlier this week in a conversation about the Sanders campaign and the behavior of his staff and supporters I referred to his campaign spokesperson as coming from the Island of Misfit Black Girls," Johnson posted on Twitter, saying the insult had been directed at Sanders communications director Briahna Joy Gray. "It was a harmful and unnecessary comment and I apologize." Johnson, too, was suspended. Cable was scrambling; CNN even reached out to me to see if I was interested in doing on-air commentary, telling me they had been caught off guard and needed people who understood the progressive wing of the party with Sanders on the rise.

MSNBC had Anand Giridharadas, a visiting scholar at New York University, who used the opportunity to tell his colleagues to wake up. "Something is happening in America right now that actually does not fit our mental models. It certainly doesn't fit the mental models of a lot of people on TV," he told host Joy Reid. "You have someone talking about, in a way we have not heard, genuine, deeper democracy— popular movements, human equality—in a meaningful way, and a politics of love in the tradition of Dr. King and winning elections, in America! The United States of America! And I just have to say—and I've been encouraged watching you on air talk about your own rethinking of things, which I think we all have to do to be in this work—I think this is a wake-up moment for the American power establishment."

There was no sense of curiosity. "Many in this establishment are behaving, as they face the prospect of a Bernie Sanders nomination, like out-of-touch aristocrats in a dying aristocracy," he continued. "Just sort of: 'How do we stop this? How do we block this?' And there is no curiosity. '*Why* is this happening? What is going on in the lives of my fellow citizens in this country that they're voting for something that I find so hard to understand? What is happening?'" Giridharadas said, aiming his fire at the network directly.

"I think of this network, which I love, which you love, and I think we have to look within also," he continued. "Why is a lobbyist for Uber and Mark Zuckerberg on the air many nights explaining a political revolution to us? Why is Chris Matthews on this air talking about the victory of Bernie Sanders, who had kin murdered in the Holocaust, and analogizing it to the Nazi conquest of France? The people who are stuck in an old way of thinking in twentieth-century frameworks, in gulag thinking, are missing what is going on. It's time for all of us to step up, rethink, and understand the dawn of what may be, frankly, a new era in American life."

The biggest handicap for Sanders had been concern among Democrats that he couldn't beat Trump, but the act of winning produced confidence that he could be a winner, and Biden's three straight blowout losses undercut his major claim to the nomination. If Biden was so electable, why was he losing so many elections?

By mid-February, as the nation began tuning in, polls around Sanders's electability turned around, and primary voters rated him as the most electable of all the Democrats running, topping Biden on that all-important number. This gave Sanders a major boost among Black voters, particularly older ones, who told pollsters their top priority was beating Trump. It's often said that people become more conservative as they age, but often it's the case that people's politics stay the same as their willingness to take risks decreases. An *Economist*/YouGov poll from mid-February captured the dynamic. Asked whether they would prefer a candidate who aligned with their values or one most likely to win the general election, voters age eighteen to twenty-nine said, by a two-point margin, that they'd prefer somebody who shared their values. Voters over sixty-five, by a whopping 83–17 percent, said they wanted the most electable candidate. Voters ages forty-five to sixty-four said the same thing by a 3–1 margin. Some of that had to do with income: the higher up on the scale, the more electability mattered. By the time you're middle-aged, you have something to lose. Voters making less than fifty thousand dollars a year were the least likely to prioritize electability.

Once Sanders broke the electability barrier, he was able to bust through his ceiling. The media's long-trumpeted theory that Sanders had a strong base of support but a low ceiling that would keep him from a majority began to crumble. Polls showed that he was the second choice for most Biden voters, undercutting the notion that there might be a strong "Never Bernie" current, and the same mid-February *Economist*/YouGov survey found Sanders had the highest number of voters who had considered voting for him, a good proxy for a ceiling.

Matt Bennett, a top official at the corporate centrist group Third Way, declared Armageddon. "In thirty-plus years of politics, I've never seen this level of doom. I've never had a day with so many people texting, emailing, calling me with so much doom and gloom," he told *Politico*. The next primary was scheduled for that coming weekend in South Carolina, followed by Super Tuesday just days later. Time was running out for the party establishment, just as it had four years earlier for the Republican brass that had failed to stop Trump. Within hours of the caucus ending in Nevada, establishment figures were lobbying South Carolina representative Jim Clyburn, the state's most influential Democrat by a long shot, to weigh in on the race, and Clyburn made the Sunday show rounds the next day hinting that he would.

Sanders's momentum, however, didn't last through the weekend. On Sunday night, *60 Minutes* aired an interview Anderson Cooper had conducted with Sanders in which he grilled the Vermont senator on his previous kind words for Cuba under Castro and Nicaragua under the Sandinistas. "We're very opposed to the authoritarian nature of Cuba," Sanders said—but unlike other politicians, he didn't leave it there. "But, you know, it's unfair to simply say everything is bad. When Fidel Castro came into office, you know what he did? He had a massive literacy program. Is that a bad thing, even though Fidel Castro did it?"

Cooper responded by saying there were a lot of dissidents imprisoned in Cuba.

"That's right. And we condemn that," Sanders said.

The interview led to a round of headlines announcing that Sanders had defended Fidel Castro, all playing into the trope that the candidate was a crypto-Communist—with the goal of eroding confidence in his electability, the main concern primary voters had with his candidacy. On Tuesday, the remaining candidates—now including billionaire Michael Bloomberg, because . . . why not?—met for a debate. Earlier that day, Nancy Messonnier, director of the CDC's National Center for Immunization and Respiratory Diseases, said publicly that the novel coronavirus Covid-19 met two of the three criteria for a pandemic: a potentially fatal illness that was sustainably spreading from person to person. The virus was not yet worldwide, however, she added.

Onstage, the highlight of the debate was Warren brutally murdering Bloomberg's candidacy before his eyes. But the moderators also dwelled on Cuba and communism. "You've praised the Chinese Communist Party for lifting more people out of extreme poverty than any other country," anchor Margaret Brennan told Sanders. "You also have a track record of expressing sympathy for socialist governments in Cuba and in Nicaragua. Can Americans trust that a democratic socialist president will not give authoritarians a free pass?"

The next day, South Carolina representative Jim Clyburn, a legend of the civil rights movement and the third most powerful Democrat in the House, stepped in to endorse Joe Biden, arguing that only with a rapid consolidation behind Biden could Sanders be stopped. What followed was the largest swing in voter attitudes in a primary campaign in the shortest amount of time in American history, absent a crushing scandal. On the day Clyburn endorsed Biden, Sanders was beating the former vice president in national polls, according to the Real Clear Politics average, by more than 11 points. Sanders was sitting above 29 percent, with Biden at 18, Bloomberg at 14, Warren at 12, Buttigieg at 10, Klobuchar at 5.4, and Tulsi Gabbard and Tom Steyer both drawing above 2 percent.

Biden that week had gone negative on Sanders, while Sanders had resisted every entreaty from his advisers to go after Biden. The *Atlantic* had reported ahead of the Nevada caucuses that Sanders had contemplated a primary challenge to Obama in 2012, and Biden used this information against Sanders in an ad campaign. "When it comes to building on President Obama's legacy, Bernie Sanders can't be trusted," the ad jabbed. An article in the *New York Times* on February 27 was headlined, "Democratic Leaders Willing to Risk Party Damage to Stop Bernie Sanders."

What has also been lost to history is that coming out of Nevada, Biden was just 2 points ahead of Sanders in South Carolina, at 23–21, with Steyer, who'd spent millions of his own fortune in the state, collecting around 15 percent. By Election Day, polls had Biden up by about 15 points, but the polls had missed the velocity of the swing toward him. The actual results delivered Biden a 28-point win on Saturday, February 29. Clyburn was among the few people remaining in American politics who had the ability to move voters with a nod. An Edison Research exit poll found that 56 percent of South Carolina's primary voters were Black, and Biden had won 61 percent of them. Of those, 6 in 10 said Clyburn's endorsement factored as important in their decision. And among Black voters under age thirty, Sanders narrowly won them.

Steyer finished with 11 percent and dropped out that night. Buttigieg pulled in 8 percent and Warren 7, and both vowed to fight through Super Tuesday, just four days away, with Warren now enjoying the support of a super PAC with ads on air around the country.

Former President Obama, leading the pushback by the party establishment, began making calls. Pete Buttigieg dropped out the day after South Carolina, flying back to South Bend rather than to Dallas for a rally. He spoke to both Biden and Obama that night. Biden said publicly he had offered Buttigieg a job. "I warned him that if I get elected, I'm coming for him," as Biden put it, meaning he'd recruit Buttigieg into the administration, not that he'd attack him. ("That's called a quid pro quo, right?" Trump needled the White House Press Corps, fresh off his impeachment.) Obama, too, encouraged Buttigieg to use his leverage. Buttigieg endorsed Biden the next day, as did former candidate Beto O'Rourke. Amy Klobuchar also dropped out and endorsed Biden. Shakir, the Sanders campaign manager, could see on Sanders's face as he took the call from Klobuchar that the power of the establishment was on the move. The endorsements themselves may not have been enough to do it, but the tenor of the news coverage shifted radically, with endless airtime being given to the historic consolidation. Critical Mention, a media monitoring firm, estimated that Biden was on the receiving end of nearly $72 million in favorable media coverage in the days between South Carolina and Super Tuesday, and this was aside from the millions spent by Bloomberg to bash Sanders.

Democratic voters, who are highly tuned in to the political news, got the message. And although the day has gone down as a Sanders wipeout, and the moment when Biden put the race away, it very nearly did not.

Biden fairly easily carried Alabama, Arkansas, North Carolina, Tennessee, Virginia, and, to a lesser degree, Oklahoma. But he won Texas by fewer than 5 points, and Sanders had been polling ahead there since before Nevada. Sanders won easily in California, Colorado, Utah, and Vermont. Biden won by just 1 point in Maine. Sanders lost Maine by roughly the number of votes won by Tulsi Gabbard, who had endorsed him in 2016 but declined to drop out in 2020 and endorse him. (She later left the Democratic Party.) But the backbreaker for Sanders came in Massachusetts, where he had rallied and where he hoped the state's progressive electorate would turn out for him. Before the consolidation, he had led nearly every poll there, with Biden far behind. Now, Biden carried the state 33 percent to 27, with Warren finishing third in her home state, with 21 percent. Minnesota went for Biden 39–30 after Klobuchar dropped out. A poll prior to the consolidation had Sanders up by 5 points. Had the party leadership not consolidated behind Biden, of the fourteen Super Tuesday states, Sanders would have carried California, Texas, Colorado, Maine, Massachusetts, Minnesota, Utah, and Vermont, as well as a likely win in Oklahoma, leaving Biden just the southern states.

But they *did* consolidate, and Sanders went from expecting to have an insurmountable delegate lead to having an insurmountable deficit. The "what if" for many in the Sanders camp involved Elizabeth Warren—both her decision to stay in the race, made possible by a Super PAC infusion of cash, and her refusal to endorse Sanders, her closest ideological ally in the race. Some Sanders officials believed it wouldn't necessarily matter, arguing that internal polls showed a sizable number of her voters had Biden as their second choice, not Sanders. But Sanders had made appeals for her endorsement nonetheless, but their conversations left Warren nervous about his trajectory, sources familiar with their talks told me. In each conversation, Warren would ask what his exit plan was if he wasn't going to win the nomination, and each time he'd demur. "Elizabeth, we're going to win the nomination," he'd assure her. That gave her flashbacks to the dead-end run by Sanders from spring 2016 into the convention, and she dreaded being asked by reporters in the Capitol hallways on a daily basis whether she thought her endorsed candidate should just drop out already. She and those around her also harbored doubts about whether he would be a good president—not that his politics were lacking but that his gruff style of grievance politics wouldn't translate into executive chaos. That forecast may or not have been accurate, but the Warren team long considered themselves significantly more competent than Sanders and what they thought of as his motley crew—an underestimation that cost them in the primary. But combined, the two concerns were enough to keep Warren from endorsing Sanders.

If there was any doubt about the primary after Super Tuesday, Biden put it to rest a week later. Sanders hoped for a shock upset in Michigan like the one he had pulled off in 2016, and like Jesse Jackson had accomplished in 1988, giving both campaigns new life. Jackson himself even endorsed Sanders, and the two reunited for a poignant rally ahead of the vote. But with six states contested, Sanders won only North Dakota.

The next day, the World Health Organization declared Covid-19 to be a pandemic, and two days later, Trump declared a national emergency. The campaign effectively shut down, with Biden heading to Wilmington, where he'd stay through the election, and Sanders camping out in Burlington. Biden continued winning primaries throughout March, and Sanders decided to hang it up. He had come to the conclusion that he had no path to victory and, for the sake of defeating Trump, needed to drop out and consolidate behind Biden.

But two considerations pushed him forward into the April 7 Wisconsin primary. First, he wanted to make sure he could continue to cover the health care costs of his staff, unwilling to send them off into a deadly pandemic uninsured, and his campaign was still working out details. Also, in Wisconsin, there was an under-the-radar but unusually important election for the state supreme court that would take place on the same day as the primary. If Sanders dropped out, it was likely the Republican would win, and the GOP would have locked in control of the court in the state, with a radicalized Republican state legislature already in place. Instead, Jill Karofsky knocked off the conservative incumbent.

It's hard to overstate the importance of the 2020 election. In December, the Trump campaign challenged Biden's win in Wisconsin, moving to have 28,000 absentee votes thrown out in two Democratic counties. The state supreme court rejected the challenge, ripping it to shreds in the strongest terms. Yet that decision came down on only a 4–3 vote. Karofsky cast the deciding vote. Had she lost her election, the decision could have gone Trump's way.

The day after the primary, Sanders dropped out, and the next week, in a move that infuriated his die-hard supporters, including some on his campaign, he endorsed Joe Biden for president.

13

SUMMER TURNS TO FALL

Bill Moyer, a former organizer with Martin Luther King Jr.'s Poor People's Campaign who went on to lead the antinuclear movement, famously documented eight stages in what he called his Movement Action Plan. Others have subsequently simplified it to four "seasons" that roughly map to Moyer's stages.

Stage one Moyer called "normal times," the period before the public is paying much attention to an issue, when only a few activists are working to develop solutions and tactics. Stage two comes with the failure of institutions, as the public and activists more generally become aware of a problem and the need for change. This represents "early spring," which then evolves into stage three, "ripening conditions." To take the civil rights movement as an example, the Supreme Court decision on *Brown v. Board of Education* helped ripen conditions, as did a rising Black college student population after World War II and the return of Black veterans from the war more generally, along with a surge in anticolonial freedom struggles across Africa.

The 2008 financial crisis had broken up normal times, and the stirrings for change could be seen in the Occupy Wall Street encampments that sprang up in cities around the country. Black Lives Matter and the embrace of marriage equality radically reshaped attitudes around race, sexuality, and, a bit later, gender. The energy was nascent and forward-looking enough that Sanders was able to be a vehicle to channel it. A movement in retreat feels a sense of scarcity, and can devolve into infighting, but a movement on the march has room for everybody. When Sanders finally dropped out of the 2016 campaign, relations between him and his supporters and Hillary Clinton and her supporters were frosty at best. Sanders didn't officially endorse Clinton until July. Although Biden ran in 2020 as the un-Bernie—while nearly every other candidate endorsed Medicare for All and pretended to be a borderline democratic socialist—there was far less distance between Sanders and Biden than there had been between Sanders and Clinton. Part of this represented the growth of the Sanders wing of the party, the advent of the Squad showing Democrats the movement's potential. And some of that flowed from a coalescing of the party against Trump. For years, the center had fought off the party's left by warning of the right-wing barbarians at the gate. Trump had finally made those threats credible.

"I could not justify making a futile effort that might have undermined the united front we needed to build in order to defeat Trump," Sanders wrote in his memoir. It was April when he endorsed Biden, three months earlier than he had backed Clinton. This led to the creation of the task forces between Sanders's and Biden's teams, which produced open channels that, on the one hand, influenced the Biden administration when it came to personnel and policy and, on the other hand, pulled the party's left-wing figures, like Sanders and Ocasio-Cortez, inside the tent, working as a team with Biden rather than as critical outsiders.

The Warren camp, meanwhile, by continuing its campaign rather than dropping out and endorsing Sanders, had also won the favor of the Biden camp, leading to the appointments of Rohit Chopra at the Consumer Financial Protection Bureau, Lina Khan as chair of Federal Trade Commission, and Jonathan Kanter as head of antitrust policy at the Department of Justice.

All of a sudden, what progressives wanted mattered. Yet it came from losing, and for many, it felt like losing. They were in one of the key stages Moyer had described, one that often results in infighting as the movement loses direction amid its newfound success and splits develop among factions who are satisfied with nudging things in the right direction and factions that see such compromising of core values as a sellout of the original mission. The hard-core group of Sanders supporters who wanted to keep the fight going were in for more disappointments throughout April 2020. On the fifteenth, just days after Sanders dropped out, Ocasio-Cortez appeared on *The View* and said she'd be getting behind Biden. "The stakes are too high when it comes to another four years of Trump," she said. "I think it's really important that we rally behind our Democratic nominee in November."

Those calling for a third-party challenger should rethink, she said. "What's really important is that we do realize that, at the end of the day, one of these two candidates are going to be elected president of the United States. It's either going to be Joe Biden or it's going to be Donald Trump."

She framed her reluctance to give a full-throated endorsement of Biden rather than merely opposition to Trump in pragmatic terms. She needed to be able to honestly explain to her constituents why they should back Biden, she said. "There's this talk about unity as this kind of vague, kumbaya kind of term," she said. "Unity and unifying isn't a feeling, it's a process. And what I hope does not happen in this process is that everyone just tries to shoo it along and brush real policies—that mean the difference of life and death or affording your insulin and not affording your insulin—just brush that under the rug as an aesthetic difference of style."

When Sanders endorsed Biden, he had extracted a promise to create a series of "unity task forces" that would focus on six areas: climate change, criminal justice reform, economy, education, health care, and immigration. The committees drafting the new agenda would include representatives of the Sanders wing of the party, and on May 13, Ocasio-Cortez and Sunrise's Varshini Prakash were named to the climate task force, with AOC and former secretary of state John Kerry, who had been lead sponsor of the climate bill that flopped in 2010, serving as cochairs. The small task forces met over Zoom once a week for six weeks, hashing out their platforms. After Ocasio-Cortez and Kerry opened up their task force's first meeting, Kerry surprised Prakash by coming to her first, asking her to detail the top priorities of the youth climate movement she represented.

The climate task force ended up adopting many of those priorities. First among them was a demand for a Civilian Climate Corps—essentially, a redo of President Franklin D. Roosevelt's iconic Civilian Conservation Corps. CCC workers would be trained in climate-friendly work. Senator Schumer would go on to be the provision's lead champion. The group also won a commitment to abide by "Justice40," a directive that 40 percent of all funding go toward the communities most disadvantaged by climate change. The Biden campaign committed to making the electric grid 100 percent powered by clean energy by 2035. At the time, wind and solar made up roughly 5 percent of the production. By the end of the campaign, Biden's platform was more aggressive on climate than the Sanders campaign's had been in 2016. After the election, as the Biden transition staffed up, Sunrise was in position to help stack the White House climate office with allied climate hawks.

Shortly after Sanders endorsed Biden, American politics would go through its most seismic shift in several generations in the wake of the murder of George Floyd in Minneapolis. Much of the country had been locked down since mid-March. At the end of the month, Trump had signed into law the CARES Act, a more than $2 trillion piece of legislation that invested in public health, covered payrolls for companies that kept workers on staff but let them stay home, cut direct checks of $1,200 to individuals, and boosted unemployment. Sanders, who had championed the direct checks, held the bill up to demand an additional $600 per week for laid-off workers and won the money, which later became known, often affectionately for those receiving it and derisively by bosses struggling to find workers, as "the super dole."

Schools were shuttered, and anti-lockdown protests, mostly organized by the right, began bubbling up. Extreme measures that would later be conclusively understood to be counterproductive were implemented: parks were closed, beaches were shut down, and even dog walking was banned in some cities. Alcohol consumption skyrocketed. That May, the *International Journal of Environmental Research and Public Health* found that 60 percent of adults said they were drinking more out of stress, boredom, and the simple availability of booze at home. Overnight, office work shifted to home. This delighted some, but many workers lacked the space to work comfortably, sharing a bedroom with a partner or common areas with roommates, all while juggling endless Zoom meetings and wondering when the virus would infect them—all this against a backdrop of horror stories of patients tortured with ventilators before succumbing to the disease. By the end of May 2020, the CDC reported, more than one hundred thousand people in the United States had died of Covid-19.

On May 25, Minneapolis police got a call about a potential counterfeit twenty-dollar bill used at a corner store, and multiple cops ended up corralling George Floyd into the back of a police car. But then Officer Derek Chauvin dragged Floyd back out and pinned him to the ground for more than nine agonizing minutes, as a crowd formed and pleaded with police to ease off. Floyd gasped and called for his mother.

"I can't breathe," he said repeatedly, echoing the last words of Eric Garner on Staten Island. The next day, police announced that Floyd had died of a "medical incident" after resisting arrest. When video of the incident was posted shortly after the statement, the country was introduced to the reality that police can lie flagrantly.

The Black Lives Matter movement was by then well organized in the Twin Cities—Omar herself had been active in it for years—but the outpouring of support for Floyd and opposition to the police went far beyond what had come before. Minneapolis's Third Precinct police station was abandoned by police, and protesters burned it down. The Minnesota governor called out the National Guard as protests spread around the country. "When the looting starts, the shooting starts," Trump posted on Twitter, encouraging state governors both privately and publicly to crack down.

Chauvin was arrested, but the protests only grew, with some involving vandalism and looting. On June 6, half a million people turned out in hundreds of cities. By then, it was estimated at least 16 million people had participated in a protest. Anti-lockdown protesters were livid as public health officials said that racism was a dangerous enough phenomenon that it was better to be out in a crowd protesting than at home isolating. (It turned out that being outdoors was largely safe, as the virus has difficulty passing from person to person in such a setting. Studies found no link between protests or other major outdoor activities like sporting events and increased community spread of the virus.)

Even Mitt Romney, the Republican senator for Utah, marched for Black lives, and Democratic leaders, including Pelosi and Schumer, posed for a widely ridiculed photo, kneeling while garbed in kente cloth. The intensity of the cultural power of the protests can be best understood with one detail: Trump, after trying to walk back his "when the looting starts" comment, signed an executive order on June 16 encouraging police reform and establishing a database to track use-of-excessive-force complaints against officers, long an elusive goal of the reform movement.

The protests began reshaping the Democratic primary contests still under way. One of those was in Westchester and the Bronx, where two challengers had been taking on Eliot Engel, the House Foreign Affairs Committee chairman, a leading critic of Obama's nuclear deal with Iran and one of Israel's most outspoken defenders in Congress.

Engel, who represented a chunk of the Bronx and Westchester, had been living in Maryland, quarantining with Covid-19 while pretending to be in his home district, with his campaign regularly posting on Facebook that he had been at this or that event. His neighboring congressional representative Ocasio-Cortez was going door-to-door in her district, delivering food and medical supplies, and lawmakers across the country were throwing themselves into the Covid response with everything they had. Hiding outside the district and lying about it was a brutal look. A reporter knocked on Engel's door in Maryland, and a flustered Engel explained, "I'm in both places."

Engel likely didn't properly perceive the threat he was under because he was facing two primary opponents rather than a single one who could consolidate support. Both his challengers had sizable bases of support: Jamaal Bowman, a former school principal running with the support of Justice Democrats, and Andom Ghebreghiorgis, an activist organizing his campaign around Engel's foreign policy hawkishness.

But with just over three weeks remaining until Election Day, Ghebreghiorgis did what few progressives had done before. Instead of fighting a noble but futile crusade to the end, he dropped out and endorsed Bowman just as the protests were getting started. Engel was rattled, and returned to the district—though maybe, in hindsight, he'd have been better off in Maryland.

The George Floyd demonstrations in the Bronx had turned into sporadic vandalism, and local politicians called a daytime rally to support the protests but lament the property damage. Engel showed up and elbowed his way to the microphones. Bronx borough president Rubén Díaz Jr., a local machine leader, told Engel that the list of speakers was too long and that he didn't want every politician within miles parading through. Engel pleaded his case, and then, with microphones rolling hot to the media, set his campaign on fire by telling Díaz and the world, "If I didn't have a primary, I wouldn't care."

A gaffe is damaging only in proportion to how well it strengthens a narrative about a candidate. Obama's "cling to their guns and religion" remark stuck in 2008 because it fueled the belief that the Harvard-educated lawyer was suspicious of rural folk. Romney's "47 percent" gaffe—the private equity mogul had told an audience of wealthy donors that nearly half the country simply wanted welfare—added to the belief that he was a plutocrat who saw nearly half the country as leeches. Engel had been under fire for ignoring his district, and now here he was, admitting that his impending election was the only reason he had bothered to come to the Floyd rally.

The next day, June 3, Ocasio-Cortez jumped into the race, endorsing Bowman over Engel. For AOC to endorse a challenger to the dean of her congressional delegation was the kind of move that drove her House colleagues insane with rage, the kind of move that would guarantee she would never be accepted as one of the club, even as she hoped that not endorsing in most other races might still give her a way toward acceptance. Her backing of Bowman, as it had done for Sanders, was a major boon to his campaign.

Mark Mellman's organization, Democratic Majority for Israel, had been spending to defend Engel, but in the wake of the hot-mic moment, Mellman turned the spigot on full blast. As the barrage of ads attacking Bowman intensified, I reported at the *Intercept* that Republican donors were heavily responsible for the money being spent against Bowman. The stink of it, combined with the hypocrisy of Mellman's group calling itself Democratic Majority for Israel, backfired badly and led to a round of terrible press for Engel. And some of the ads themselves backfired as well. None focused on the question of Israel-Palestine, with some attacking Bowman for having owed several thousand dollars in back taxes. Attacking a working-class Black man for financial troubles before he'd risen to become a successful principal in the area would have been considered tone-deaf in a New York Democratic primary in any recent cycle, but it was particularly so with the Floyd protests flaring.

In late June, the Squad added another member, with Bowman winning by a landslide, carrying even heavily Jewish precincts where Engel had been expected to romp. The same day, Mondaire Jones, another Black progressive, though more moderate than Bowman, won an open primary against a field of well-funded candidates. Antonio Delgado, a lawyer and former rapper, had flipped a nearby district blue in 2018 and easily won the nomination for reelection, meaning that New York's Sixteenth, Seventeenth, and Nineteenth Districts, all of which leaned wealthy and were predominantly white, were all represented by Black men. Add in Jahana Hayes, who by then represented a wealthy white district in Connecticut, and a new path to Congress for Black candidates was opening up.

Mellman recalibrated and fired his fund-raiser, hiring instead the Bonner Group, run by Mary Pat Bonner, known for her fund-raising for Media Matters and other Democratic operations. A Bonner ally began consulting for AIPAC's super PAC.

The next contest was set for two months later, in St. Louis, Missouri, a rematch between incumbent Lacy Clay Jr. and Black Lives Matter activist Cori Bush, who had lost to Clay by 20 points in 2018. In the wake of that earlier defeat, it looked like Bush's role in the documentary *Knock Down the House*, which became largely about Ocasio-Cortez, might have been the peak of her career. She had had a rough time up to that point in her life. With two young children, she had experienced a bout of homelessness, living out of her car. "There were days that I had to go into my job with the same clothes that I had on the night before and go in and sneak into the bathroom and go and wash myself up before work," she told me. Bush would mix infant formula in McDonald's bathrooms and lived out of food pantries. With her two children in the back seat, she endlessly worried that she'd drift off to sleep and they'd get too cold, or that the police would arrive and impound her car. "You can just feel the judgment," she said, "where people are asking questions to see where they can find your error, because it's your fault that you ended up in those positions."

After her loss in 2018, Bush also lost her job at a local hospital. She was told that her firing was the result of pressure from Clay, she told me not long after it happened. I wasn't able to verify that claim, as doing so definitively would be impossible without something in writing, evidence unlikely to exist, but it wouldn't have been out of character based on the type of machine Clay and the local Democrats ran. Without her nursing work, she was back on very hard times—circumstances made worse when she landed in the hospital with terrifying Covid symptoms but without insurance. From those depths, she launched a second challenge to Clay. This time around, Bush knew more about raising money and running a campaign, and she had name recognition to start out. In the wake of the George Floyd protests, she started picking up serious momentum.

Bowman rallied for Bush, but nobody in Congress got behind her—not AOC, not Omar, not Tlaib, not Pressley. Their reluctance to get involved spoke to the evolving roles they were playing, willing to pick some fights while shying away from others they'd clearly have embraced in the past, even if this meant leaving Bush to fend for herself. Bush did get several hundred thousand dollars in big-money support from a foundation-funded dark-money group that focused on anti-monopoly work and was run by Faiz Shakir, fresh off his tenure as Sanders's campaign manager.

Shakir had just watched Biden crush Sanders with Black voters by calling his former boss disloyal to Obama for floating a primary challenge. Now Shakir would return the favor. While Obama was president, Clay had allied with Wall Street lobbyists who were trying to roll back a tough rule on investment firms being put forward by the Department of Labor. This put Clay on the wrong side of Obama, and Shakir's group hammered him for it. "When predatory Wall Street firms needed a favor, they turned to Congressman William Lacy Clay," the ad intoned. "Clay opposed President Obama's effort to protect working families' retirement savings from greedy financiers. What did Clay get for opposing Obama and siding with Trump? Tens of thousands of dollars in campaign contributions." The goal was to get the ad in front of persuadable voters, both white and Black, who were on the fence about voting, so Shakir skipped the normal route of blanketing cable news and broadcast TV. Instead, he saturated evenings by buying up space on A&E, Bravo, ESPN, TNT, TBS, MTV, BET, and other entertainment-focused channels.

On August 4, Cori Bush stunned the political world by upsetting Lacy Clay Jr. by fewer than 5,000 votes. Clay became a lobbyist and stuck around Washington. I bumped into him at a fund-raiser two years later and asked how he thought Bush would do in her 2022 primary against a new challenger. He said rightly that he thought she would win. "Incumbency has its advantages," he said, before pausing to add, with a self-deprecating smile, "until it doesn't."

I reached out to Ocasio-Cortez for her reaction. It was around 1 a.m. East Coast time, and Bush had been declared the winner. "It's incredible. This has brought things to a totally new level," AOC said of Bush's win that night. I asked how she felt about not having endorsed her. "It's actually way better this way. They pinned every single race on me, even when they weren't J[ustice] D[emocrats]. Now it's not a fluke, and now they also can't say progressive wins are just me, either. I could go on forever about the inside dynamics here, but ultimately this is just a very, very good thing."

In other words, Ocasio-Cortez had spent the last year assuring her colleagues that not *all* the primary challengers they were seeing around the country had anything to do with her. She wasn't even supporting all the Justice Democrats–backed candidates. But so far, she had backed Marie Newman in her successful bid against an incumbent and Jessica Cisneros in her failed effort, plus Bowman in New York. That was enough for her colleagues to assume she was behind everything.

In April, AOC said, the party establishment got a little too comfortable. Justice Democrat Morgan Harper had been running a challenge against incumbent congressional representative Joyce Beatty, one of just two challenges Justice Democrats launched against a member of the Congressional Black Caucus (both with Black challengers). Harper needed everything to go right for her. She needed Sanders to last until the Ohio primary, to draw young people out, and she needed there not to be a pandemic that kept college students away from the ballot box. She ended up losing by nearly 40 points, after which Hakeem Jeffries celebrated a win against his Squad rivals. "They started this. We'll finish it," he posted on Twitter, promising future victories ahead in primaries pitting progressive challengers against establishment incumbents.

Beating Morgan Harper had led the progressives to get overconfident, Ocasio-Cortez argued, which had allowed Cori Bush to take them by surprise. "I do think that they took Beatty's race the most seriously, and when she won that, they relaxed a little," she reflected. "They went in for Engel and got major pie in their face, but it still wasn't one of their members. And so, I do think they bought their own line that this was just a white gentrifier liberal thing. Even until right before my own primary, members still joked that I was only supported by young white people, which was both just categorically false but also really insulting. Anyways they really do talk themselves into believing certain fantasies. But most of that storytelling comes from Hakeem [Jeffries] and [Gregory] Meeks. And Hakeem noticeably took the foot off the gas after Engel lost. And me not going into this race didn't trigger the spend that they did against Bowman, for example."

The outside money swirling around these races had changed the calculation, she said. "They take me super seriously now, so, if I went in [for Bush,] they would have probably poured even more than they did for Engel [because] Clay is on FSC," she said, referring to the

Financial Services Committee, generally home for Wall Street–friendly lawmakers.

"They definitely did believe that this was largely confined to POC challengers against white incumbents in POC places," she said, referring to the dynamic that could describe the wins by her, Pressley, and Bowman, all of which had come against white men. "Because honestly that's been almost all of J[ustice] D[emocrat]s wins until today. This"—the defeat of Clay by Bush—"is the first C[ongressional] B[lack] C[aucus] member to fall. This has officially gotten way bigger than they imagined," she added, "and they do not have any idea what's going on nor how to 'contain' it."

The left was feeling confident and turned its attention to a final boss battle, scheduled for September 1. In the Senate, Sunrise and AOC had gotten heavily behind incumbent senator Ed Markey, who had made a pivot to the left and his sponsorship of the Green New Deal central to his argument for why he should be reelected over Rep. Joseph Kennedy, who was challenging him. In the congressional primaries, Justice Democrats had endorsed Holyoke, Massachusetts, mayor Alex Morse against Richard Neal, chair of the powerful Ways and Means Committee and an implacable foe of the Sanders wing. The same anti-monopoly group that had backed Cori Bush had also gone in for Morse. The year before, Neal had reluctantly agreed to allow a hearing on Medicare for All to come before his powerful committee—a product of the last-minute maneuvering by the Congressional Progressive Caucus and AOC at the beginning of the term—but before it began, he privately warned every Democrat on the committee not to utter the phrase "Medicare for All." His most high-profile fights during the 2019/20 term came against the push to allow Medicare to negotiate lower drug prices and against a separate effort to ban what was known as surprise billing—the practice by which hospitals or other providers surprised patients by treating them with an out-of-network doctor even if the facility was in-network. It was an ingenious scheme that had been pioneered by private equity firms, which extracted billions from patients with the maneuver. Neal's support for the practice wasn't just greased by campaign contributions; he also had part-time constituents to think about: over recent decades, private-equity moguls had flocked to buy vacation homes in Western Massachusetts, which Neal represented, with their winnings.

Bowman had endorsed Morse but, again, going up against the Ways and Means chair meant getting legislatively iced out, and he had no backers in Congress. On the Friday after Cori Bush's victory, Morse's surging campaign looked like it had blown up. Three weeks before the election, a week before the first debate, and just ahead of early voting, the local College Democrats of the University of Massachusetts at Amherst sent Morse a letter disinviting him from future events; it was quickly leaked and published by the college paper. The letter alleged that he had made students uncomfortable by making advances on them, though it didn't include names, dates, or specific incidents.

The Working Families Party and Sunrise announced that they were suspending their support for Morse; Bowman, too, said he was backing off. Within just hours, the candidate had seemingly been destroyed. Covering the race, I observed on Twitter at the time that the letter from the College Democrats did not include either a specific allegation or an accuser, either named or unnamed, and that perhaps further inquiry was merited. What followed was the most surreal few days of my career in journalism, as the fury that had been driving at Morse was aimed squarely at me, with endless suggestions being made publicly that the only possible explanation for my tweet was that I supported predatory abusers and likely was one myself. All the hatred directed my way, however, brought me to the attention of dissenting members of the College Democrats chapter, and several reached out with different pieces of evidence that exposed a shockingly cynical operation under way.

At the *Intercept*, we began publishing the first of four exposés that reported, first, that one of the students who had orchestrated the scheme against Morse was motivated by a desire to launch his own political career through Morse's opponent Neal; second, that the students had sought to entrap Morse and, having failed, had gone ahead with their vague allegations anyway; third, that the state Democratic Party had offered legal advice and media training to the students involved in preparation for their letter's being leaked; and fourth and finally, that the state party, once the scheme was exposed, had publicly ordered an investigation into the students' conduct while, at the same time, privately urging the students to delete any messages showing collusion with the state party.

The *New York Times* called the reporting "a cascade of head-spinning revelations" in its article about Morse's exoneration, but in the district, voters who relied on the local news were still treated with "he said, he said" coverage that made room for Morse's denial but gave little oxygen to the reality that the whole episode had been an orchestrated smear. Major damage had been done, as the race turned into a conversation not about corruption, but about gay sex. Morse's internal polling showed that even when told that the smear had been trumped up and the letter orchestrated by allies of Neal, the scandal still made 1 in 5 voters more likely to support Neal. The week of unmitigated bad press had driven up the number of voters who had a negative opinion of Morse, and without the local media covering the second phase of the story—and with early voting locking in tens of thousands of votes—Morse was in a deep hole. The Working Families Party got back into the race, as did other organizations that had backed away from Morse.

On August 20, Pelosi endorsed Rep. Joe Kennedy in his Senate race against Ed Markey, backing a challenger against an incumbent. Ocasio-Cortez, believing the same rules applied to rank-and-file members as to leaders, thought this gave her the green light to endorse Morse, which she did on August 25, the scandal now having been debunked. I asked her what her reasoning had been. "I just think he has a shot and there's a big progressive coalition behind him," she texted. "To be honest I feel like Pelosi's endorsement of Kennedy gave me a lot more wiggle room. I also think Morse could be within striking distance. And when I talked to him, Neal is the most similar to Crowley. Very progressive seat, apparently he has never seriously been challenged in 30+years, and he got the seat through machinery to begin with. And the whole corrupt setup thing just really pissed me off." She added that her Courage to Change PAC would be backing him. "The whole point of it is to support underdog/unlikely candidates," she said. But Justice Democrats had endorsed Morse back in August 2019, a full year earlier, giving him time to translate that support and the organization's resources into real help on the ground. Had AOC endorsed at the time, she'd have suffered an equal amount of vitriol from her incumbent colleagues, but her support would have been exponentially more valuable than in the closing days of the campaign. Justice Democrats, who paused support of Morse for three days after the scandal hit, had gone all in, raising $141,000 directly to the campaign from its members and spending an additional $715,000 independently.

Neal's supporters never backed off the smear, even after it was exposed as a plot, and made sure the conversation remained about Morse and his sex life, adding fuel to the fire with TV ads and robocalls. A super PAC backing Neal spent roughly a million dollars on attack ads, including one that, falsely, hit Morse for having sex with college students. The PAC apologized for the ad, claiming that it had been sent to stations by mistake, but the group continued airing the "accidental" ad right through Election Day. The American Hospital Association and the College of Radiology, looking to oppose public health care and protect the right to surprise patients with their billing practices, spent nearly $600,000 defending Neal. DMFI came through with just short of $200,000. And the decision by the coalition partners behind Morse immediately to denounce him or to pause support left a lasting mark. (Faiz Shakir's anti-monopoly group was one of the few to stand firmly by him.)

Neal won with a 17-point margin. Ocasio-Cortez had come for the Ways and Means chairman and missed; now she'd pay the price. But statewide, Markey romped over Kennedy—the first in that family to lose an election in the Bay State—a vindication of the former's move leftward and a sign to Washington that political gold could be found in progressive hills.

But mining that gold required a team of people willing to work together. Julian Cyr, a state senator in Massachusetts who had defended Morse, later told the *Times* that his case was the most vivid example of a phenomenon the left needed to get hold of. "This is the concern around a trigger-happy cancel culture, as it gives undue credence to the initial allegation without due diligence," he said. In the summer of 2020, it was getting increasingly difficult for progressive organizations, stuck in a cycle of accusations and counteraccusations, to do anything at all.

14

MARCUSIAN MELTDOWN

In 1999, as she recalls it, Tema Okun came home in a huff after a particularly upsetting client meeting. A Bay Area–based activist and consultant, she was running the type of training sessions that would evolve into the "diversity, equity, and inclusion" industry. Stewing about the way she had been treated in the meeting, and about the rationalizations offered in opposition to her ideas, Okun, a white woman, began to settle on the belief that the meeting's indignities were in fact the product of a culture of white supremacy. So she sat down and wrote what would become one of the most quietly influential documents to rip through the progressive world over the next twenty years, a description of what she called the characteristics of a white supremacy culture.

"I came home, and I sat in front of the computer, and the article literally came through me," she told me years later in her first interview about her paper. "It was not researched. I didn't sit down and deliberate. It just came through me. And I've never had that experience with my writing, before or since." She added, "It was spirit moving through me."

She shared the paper with two colleagues, one of whom, Okun said, suggested including antidotes for each white supremacy characteristic listed—which she did. She also added the name of a prominent Black man in the field, her mentor Kenneth Jones, to the byline and included the document in her organization's anti-racism training packet. Some people who came across the page posted copies of it online, and it began circulating in progressive spaces.

Calling it a paper is generous. Clocking in at under three pages, it's more a list of bullet points explaining how each quality given is a function of white supremacy and/or is used to uphold white supremacy.

Under "Urgency," for instance, Okun writes that "A constant sense of urgency":

- makes it difficult to take time to be inclusive, encourage democratic and/or thoughtful decision-making, to think long-term, to consider consequences;

- frequently results in sacrificing potential allies for quick or highly visible results, for example[,] sacrificing interests of communities of color in order to win victories for white people (seen as [the] default or norm community); [and]

- reinforced by funding proposals which promise too much work for too little money and by funders who expect too much for too little.

And then, under "Antidotes," she recommends:

realistic workplans; leadership which understands that things take longer than anyone expects; discuss and plan for what it means to set goals of inclusivity and diversity, particularly in terms of time; learn from past experience how long things take; write realistic funding proposals with realistic time frames; be clear about how you will make good decisions in an atmosphere of urgency; realize that rushing decisions takes more time in the long run because inevitably people who didn't get a chance to voice their thoughts and feelings will at best resent and at worst undermine the decision because they were left unheard.

Social media was not yet a thing, and Okun's paper circulated over the next decade, largely by email. In the early 2010s, though, it began a new chapter in its life, as it was embraced by the generation graduating into the rubble of the Great Recession and going through what became known as the Great Awokening.

At universities in the mid-2010s, the paper's claims increasingly became part of demonstrations against befuddled administrators, who generally responded to those protests by hiring new vice deans to run new departments and hire more diversity and equity consultants.

Inside progressive organizations, managers began to be confronted with Okun's document, and employees wielded it against everything from being expected to show up on time, to meeting deadlines, to undergoing annual performance reviews. When I first began hearing that staff were claiming that qualities like being able to meet deadlines or show urgency or respect for the written word were aspects of white supremacy culture, I waved it off as impossible. But interviews with dozens of managers and staff at progressive groups confirmed that the phenomenon was real. A few years later, after the murder of George Floyd, the ideas in Okun's paper had become commonplace. An email in 2021 sent by one of Oregon's Regional Health Equity Coalition program managers delaying an upcoming meeting was typical of the genre. "In being responsive to partners across the state, we're hearing that the timing of this meeting is not ideal," she wrote in an email later forwarded to *Reason* magazine. "We recognize that urgency is a white supremacy value that can get in the way of more intentional and thoughtful work, and we want to attend to this dynamic. Therefore, we will reach out at a later date to reschedule."

Okun told me that she would sometimes hear directly from people who'd had her paper used against them as a weapon. "I went on a retreat," she said, "and I was paired with someone who's a white leader of a large organization, and we had known each other, but we didn't know each other well. And we get in the room and we put our bags on the bed and, she turns to me and she says, 'Well, I've just been kicked out of my organization, and your article was used to do it.'"

"I gave her a wry smile. And I said: 'I'm sure it was.'"

The ground had been tilled for Okun's paper to flourish by a strain of politics—or, more accurately, anti-politics—dubbing itself, variously, the practice of anti-racism or the checking of one's privilege. The civil rights movement, in its most potent form, whether during the Civil War and Reconstruction or the 1960s, focused on attacking systems of oppression (slavery and Jim Crow) and supplanting them with systems of equality and dignity. To accomplish systemwide change required the collective force of a people's government—through the barrel of a gun, when necessary—whether it was the occupation of the South or the use of federal troops to implement desegregation. As the 1960s gave way to the '70s and '80s, and faith in the ability of people to collectively shape society receded, an ethos of individualism rose up.

The government wasn't the solution; it was the problem. And this left only the individual to solve systemic problems. On the environmental front, that might mean being a better recycler and using canvas bags instead of plastic; and on the political front, it meant interrogating and acknowledging your privilege. What to do with the results of that interrogation was rarely part of the conversation, but the trend took off in the Bay Area.

Author and journalist Christian Parenti participated as a young man in one of San Francisco's first anti-racist trainings, a workshop in which people were asked to take steps forward or backward based on qualities of race, gender, or intersecting identities subject to oppression. He wrote about the experience in an article called "The First Privilege Walk," in which he described how, by the end, straight white men were standing far ahead, demonstrating the ingrained advantages of white supremacist culture. The goal of the exercise was to interrogate the attributes that so advantaged one person over others.

The roots of the privilege walk are thought to go back to diversity consultant and feminist Peggy McIntosh, famous for her suggestion that "white privilege" acted like an "invisible knapsack," but McIntosh swore off responsibility to Parenti, saying the trainings were worse than useless. "They are too simple for complex experiences relating to power and privilege. I don't know where they originated," she said. "They seem to answer a craving for instant one-size-fits-all awakenings. I think they are counterproductive."

The true origin story of the privilege walk is suitably Freudian, Oedipal, or whichever psycho-narrative hue properly backgrounds it. It was developed, Parenti uncovered, by another Bay Area diversity consultant named Ricky Sherover-Marcuse—and yes, that's as in philosopher Herbert Marcuse; she was his third wife.

Sherover-Marcuse—who, like Tema Okun, was an Oberlin graduate—referred to herself, not inaccurately, as a "red diaper baby" but left out the fact that her father was fantastically rich, a titan of industry. He was instrumental in helping to finance—in full collaboration with the Roosevelt administration, despite U.S. official neutrality—the Republican forces in Spain who were battling the fascists in the civil war there in the 1930s. He later left the family, moving to homes in Venezuela and Israel.

"Father and daughter eventually reconciled[,] but the biographical sketches of Ricky Sherover-Marcuse that litter the web never mention that she was the daughter of a very rich man; the daughter of an actual capitalist, even if that capitalist was some fading shade of Red," Parenti writes.

In light of Ricky's efforts to change the subject from economic *exploitation* to the more general field of *oppression*[,] this omission seems to betray not only oedipal rage, but also a guilty conscience. The charge could be: Rich girl convinces people to focus on race and gender instead of class. As it turns out, that is also the story of Peggy McIntosh. Her mother was a blueblood, heiress, WASP, debutante. Her father was a wealthy inventor and manager at Bell Laboratories. By nominally devoting her life to purging the Left of its alleged class-first sins, Ricky indulged in a quintessentially New Left reaction against the Old Left of her father.

Sherover-Marcuse's husband, in his later days, rejected the notion that the working class in industrialized nations held any remaining revolutionary potential. Marcuse's alternative approach predicted— and, through his wife, trained and prescribed—the left of today, with its obsession with the revolutionary potential of language. "The new sensibility and the new consciousness . . . demand a new language to define and communicate the new 'values' (language in the wider sense which includes words, images, gestures, tones)," he wrote in his 1969 book *An Essay on Liberation.*

It has been said that the degree to which a revolution is developing qualitatively different social conditions and relationships may perhaps be indicated by the development of a different language: the rupture with the continuum of domination must also be a rupture with the vocabulary of domination. . . .

. . . The transition [to a revolutionary condition requires] the intensification and extension of the political work: radical enlightenment. It is precisely the preparatory character of this work which gives it its historical significance: to develop, in the exploited, the consciousness (and the unconscious) which would loosen the hold of enslaving needs over their existence—the needs which perpetuate their dependence on the system of exploitation. Without this rupture, which can only be the result of political education in action, even the most elemental, the most immediate force of rebellion may be defeated, or become the mass basis of counterrevolution.

In other words, only through radical enlightenment—what would become the interrogation of privilege and so on—could a revolutionary constituency be built. Sherover-Marcuse developed these themes further in her dissertation at a German university, which Parenti unearthed. "Marx considers the abolition of mystified consciousness only in terms of removing its external causes," she writes. "He fails to consider the possibility that the abolition of mystified consciousness may require an intentional practice which focuses directly on its continuing existence in the subjectivity of individuals." Oppression, in other words, is so fully internalized that overthrowing capitalism is impossible without first liberating the mind. The revolutionary work, then, is internal. Hence the privilege walk and its derivative ideology of personal anti-racism.

A consulting industry was built up around this idea, one that employed Tema Okun, Robin DiAngelo, and countless others, and they found ready audiences among corporate America. It's an easy sell to tell a company that improving material conditions through, say, a union or a better union contract or higher wages isn't the most important goal but, rather, that enlightenment is more pressing. Hiring anti-racism trainers doubled as a useful corporate response to allegations of actual racism inside a company. It counted as *doing something* without structural reform. Universities, who had just faced a generation of collective upheaval on campuses, were also delighted to hear about a revolution of introspection rather than administrative office occupation or solidarity with underpaid janitors. That the privilege brand of activism was ineffective was the very thing that enabled its rapid march through the institutions. Once it was inside those institutions, it was wielded ruthlessly in factional and interpersonal battles—office politics—that have been central to institutions throughout history.

Fed up at being clobbered by Okun's paper, a group of Black leaders of progressive organizations began lobbying Okun to clarify her document, to retract portions of it, or to otherwise signal to readers of it that it was not intended as a shield against assignments from managers. Okun quietly did so, burying some mea culpas in the bowels of a new website she built to promote the legacy of the article. In her updated version, she includes a section at the bottom headlined in red: "Please Do Not Weaponize This Tool."

"I want to offer a cautionary plea here about weaponizing this list," she writes. "I remember how, in my early years of working with Kenneth Jones to offer dismantling racism training, people would take the analysis and framework we offered and use it to beat each other up—'My analysis is better than your analysis,' 'I am/we are more righteous than you.' Similarly, some people report that this list gets used as a weapon to accuse, shame, and blame in ways that perpetuate disconnection."

She wrote that "a skilled facilitator" had told her,

"I could not possibly tally the number of hours I have spent over the last three years dislodging people from the reductive stance they construct based on the tool. In its current [1999] form, just to name one area, it tilts people towards a behavioral and ahistorical frame. And because it couches things in a way that can be read as absolutist, it can generate almost ridiculous orthodoxies of exclusion. I worked in one situation where the communications function had come to a grinding halt because a segment of the staff had decided that editing was white supremacist and, while yes, there are elitist and racist frames around proper language, the organization was locked in an either/or frame that was incredibly unhealthy and unproductive."

She also included a reference to "call-out culture," which had become bound up with privilege discourse.

The movement is currently engaged in important conversations about calling in and calling out. I lean on the words of the late and fabulous and fierce and funny Cynthia Brown, a social justice warrior and beloved friend, who told us with her last breaths that we should never throw anyone away. This does not mean we can't hold each other accountable (another word for supporting each other to be our best selves), set boundaries when people have not learned yet to take responsibility for themselves, apologize and take responsibility ourselves when we cause harm, and continue to grow and learn how to be with each other even when we are getting on each other's last nerve.

I will say that white supremacy wants us to attack each other as the problem. As we fight with and among each other, we fail to identify the actual problem.

One significant piece of information included on the new site: that Okun had fabricated the coauthorship of Kenneth Jones. "At the time I had been working closely for over half a decade with my mentor, teacher, and colleague Kenneth Jones," her new site reads. "When I originally published [my paper], I listed him as co-author because so much of the wisdom in the piece was a result of our collaborative work together. When he realized I had named him as a co-author, he demanded that I take his name off the piece, claiming he didn't want credit for something he didn't actually write."

Okun said she pushed back but that Jones won the debate. Still, she said she's glad the paper got out with his name on it. "We argued and, given his seniority and determination, he won the argument, although many versions of the original article are still circulating with both our names on it. I am totally thrilled about that[,] because his wisdom has informed any that I might have," she said. One wonders what possible argument she could have deployed in her favor—he was not, in fact, a coauthor.

"It's amazing to me that one of the biggest clubs that women of color leaders are being hit over the head with—by their white staff as well as staff of color—was created by a white woman who had shoddy craftsmanship and leveraged a Black man's name without his permission to give it legitimacy," said one of the women who lobbied Okun. "Then wiped her hands of the world of mess it has caused . . . and is still causing!"

I asked Okun what she says when she's hears such criticism.

"I say, 'I'm so sorry. It's not what it was meant for in any way, shape, or form.'"

The year 1968 saw an explosion of activism, capping more than a decade of progress that had been made in fits and starts. The Civil Rights Act of 1968, known as the Fair Housing Act, was signed into law during the uprising following the assassination of Martin Luther King Jr. The Democratic National Convention in Chicago turned into a police riot, and protests of the Vietnam War surged. The November election of Richard Nixon as president shifted the landscape. Demonstrations against the war continued, but they were never as large as those in the mid-'60s, and they included more radical elements advocating violent insurrection, further self-marginalizing. In 1969, a faction of activists took over Students for a Democratic Society, shut it down, and launched the Weather Underground in its place, declaring war on the United States and carrying out multiple attacks. The "back-to-the-land" movement saw young people dropping out of society and joining communes. The Black Panther Party was crushed and collapsed.

Mark Rudd, an early member of SDS, helped convert it into the Weather Underground, a role he now regrets. "After the war was over, a lot of the left went on a complete and total dead end," he said. "We don't want power. We're allergic to it. It's not in our DNA. We don't like coercion. We don't like hegemony."

Rudd spent seven years as a fugitive after the Weather Underground began to fall apart, and he later served a prison sentence. ("I was a total nutcase," he said of his previous politics.) He has since returned to activism, but no amount of history in the movement can immunize anyone from a callout. Asked about the turmoil engulfing left-wing organizations, he said he had personal experience. "I have myself encountered it multiple times in the last years. And in fact, I was thrown out of an organization that I founded because of my 'racism,'" he said. "What was my racism? When I tell people things that they didn't want to hear," he added, saying the disputes were over things like criticism he had leveled at a young, nonwhite activist around the organizing of a demonstration. "I mean, it's normal. It's what's happening everywhere."

What's new is that it's now happening everywhere, whereas, in previous decades, it had yet to migrate out of more radical spaces. "We used to call it 'trashing,'" said Loretta Ross, a Smith College professor and author who helped coin the term *reproductive justice*. The 1970s were a brutal period in activist spaces, documented most famously in a 1976 *Ms.* magazine article and a subsequent book by feminist Jo

Freeman, both called *Trashing: The Dark Side of Sisterhood*. "What is 'trashing,'" she asks, "this colloquial term that expresses so much, yet explains so little?"

It is not disagreement; it is not conflict; it is not opposition. These are perfectly ordinary phenomena that, when engaged in mutually, honestly, and not excessively, are necessary to keep an organism or organization healthy and active. Trashing is a particularly vicious form of character assassination, one that amounts to psychological rape. It is manipulative, dishonest, and excessive. It is occasionally disguised by the rhetoric of honest conflict, or covered up by denying that any disapproval exists. But it is not used to expose disagreements or resolve differences. It is used to disparage and destroy.

Erich Fromm, the renowned psychoanalyst and democratic socialist who fled Nazi Germany for the United States, covered much the same terrain as Marcuse in his 1962 book *Beyond the Chains of Illusion*, but Fromm diagnosed the psychic pull that would trip up the American left fifty-plus years later.

A sense of powerlessness on the left had nudged the focus away from structural or wide-reaching change, which felt hopelessly beyond reach, and replaced it with an internal target that was more achievable. One former executive director of a major nonprofit advocacy group told me he saw those in his organization turn inward out of desperation. "Maybe I can't end racism by myself, but I can get my manager fired, or I can get so-and-so removed, or I can hold somebody accountable," he relayed. "People found power where they could, and often that's where you work, sometimes where you live, or where you study, but someplace close to home."

Fromm saw the same phenomenon. "If a society or a social class has no chance to make any use of its insight because there is objectively no hope for a change for the better, the chances are that everybody in such a society would stick to the fictions[,] since the awareness of the truth would only make them feel worse. Decaying societies and classes are usually those which hold most fiercely to their fictions[,] since they have nothing to gain by the truth," he wrote.

In the absence of that collective pursuit of a better world, people find meaning by retreating into tribes and by proscribing membership in those tribes based on a common language and set of beliefs that lie outside the notion of truth. Maintaining membership in that tribe becomes an essential pursuit, ethically, morally, culturally, and politically.

"The herd is so vitally important for the individual that their views, beliefs, feelings, constitute reality for him, more so than what his senses and his reason tell him," Fromm went on. "Just as in the hypnotic state of dissociation[,] the hypnotist's voice and words take the place of reality, so the social pattern constitutes reality for most people. What man considers true, real, sane, are the clichés accepted by his society, and much that does not fit in with these clichés is excluded from awareness, is unconscious. There is almost nothing a man will not believe—or repress—when he is threatened with the explicit or implicit threat of ostracism."

In some important ways, the phenomena that define our culture and our politics today were easier to divine as they first emerged in the 1950s and '60s, amid the abundance of the postwar period and the new constituencies and ways of being it created. Augusto Del Noce was an Italian philosopher and political theorist, both antifascist and conservative Catholic, who spent his life engaged in conversation with Marxism. Del Noce predicted that the politics of vulgar Marxism, as enacted in everyday life, would ultimately move beyond politics and become an ethic in its own right. This would set the stage for politics to supersede and subsume culture and even reality itself, an observation that looks strikingly prescient of the way tribal politics now seeps into every facet of contemporary life. If politics is ethics, then building coalitions with those who don't share all our politics requires acting in ways that challenge our ethics.

Winning power requires working in coalition with people who, by definition, do not agree with you on everything; otherwise, they'd be part of your organization and not a separate organization working with you in coalition. Winning power requires unity in the face of a greater opposition, which runs counter to a desire to live a just life in each moment.

"People want justice, and they want their pain acknowledged," Rudd said. "But on the other hand, if acknowledging their pain causes organizations to die, or erodes the solidarity and the coalition building that's needed for power, it's probably not a good thing. In other words, it can lead to the opposite, more power for the fascists."

Loretta Ross said she often hears from people skeptical of her critique of callout culture. "The number one thing people fear is that I'm giving a pass to white people to continue to be racist," she told me. "Most Black people say, 'I am not ready to call in the racist white boy, I just ain't gonna do it.' They think it's a kindness lesson or a civility lesson, when it's really an organizing lesson that we're offering, because if someone knows if someone has made a mistake, and they know they're going to face a firing squad for having made that mistake, they're not gonna wanna come to you and be accountable to you. It is not gonna happen that way. And so the whole callout culture contradicts itself because it thwarts its own goal."

For many, the whole thing has felt like an op. "I'm not saying it's a right-wing plot, because we are incredibly good at doing ourselves in, but—if you tried—you couldn't conceive of a better right-wing plot to paralyze progressive leaders by catalyzing the existing culture where internal turmoil and micro campaigns are mistaken for strategic advancement of social impact for the millions of people depending on these organizations to stave off the crushing injustices coming our way," said another longtime organization head. "Progressive leaders cannot do anything but fight inside the orgs, thereby rendering the orgs completely toothless for the external battles in play. . . . Everyone is scared, and fear creates the inaction that the right wing needs to succeed in cementing a deeply unpopular agenda."

The type of politics being practiced by many self-described allies on the left results in people already gifted with privilege maintaining their place in the hierarchy. The sophisticated vocabularies constructed for the stated purpose of diversity and inclusion create a moat around a social class that maintains its status as homogeneous and exclusive. Such a result is surely unintentional on the part of individuals participating in the process, who think, on the surface, that they're pursuing social justice, but it's no coincidence that the system itself incentivizes the type of politics that reifies the status quo. As Fromm wrote, it's also unsurprising that those participating in the sham would refuse to recognize it.

> In all these instances the underlying and unconscious desire
> is so well rationalized by a moral consideration that the desire
> is not only covered up, but also aided and abetted by the very
> rationalization the person has invented. In the normal course

of his life, such a person will never discover the contradiction between the reality of his desires and the fiction of his rationalizations, and hence he will go on acting according to his desire. If anyone would tell him the truth, that is to say, mention to him that behind his sanctimonious rationalizations are the very desires which he bitterly disapproves of, he would sincerely feel indignant or misunderstood and falsely accused.

Whatever the sociological, spiritual, or material origins, the culture that had engulfed much of American life by the early 2020s was that much stronger inside progressive advocacy organizations and had brought many of them to a standstill. "My last nine months, I was spending ninety to ninety-five percent of my time on internal strife. Whereas [before] that [it] would have been twenty-five, thirty percent tops," a former executive director told me. He added that the same portion of his deputies' time was similarly spent on internal reckonings.

"Most people thought that their worst critics were their competitors, and they're finding out that their worst critics are on their own payroll," said Ross, the Smith professor, author, and activist who has been prominent in the movement for decades, having founded the reproductive justice collective SisterSong. "We're dealing with a workforce that's becoming younger, more female, more people of color, more politically woke—I hate to use that term in a way it shouldn't be used—and less loyal in the traditional way to a job, because the whole economic rationale for keeping a job or having a job has changed." This lack of loyalty is not the fault of employees, Ross said, but was foisted on them by a precarious economy that broke the professional-social contract. This has left workers with less patience for inequities in the workplace. "All my ED [executive director] friends, everybody's going through some shit, nobody's immune," said one who had yet to depart.

Augusto Del Noce may have been engaging with the left in good faith, but he's been dead for thirty years, and today's right-wing critics of social justice culture are doing nothing but exploiting its vulnerabilities to weaken the left. This means that anybody who criticizes the culture from inside the tribe has broken with the unspoken ethic that binds the tribe together—and is thereby excommunicated. The result is that no criticism can come from a friendly perspective, as the act of the criticism itself renders the critic unfriendly. Adopting the right wing's language and framing feels like surrendering to malign forces, but ignoring them has only allowed the issues to fester.

"The right has labeled it 'cancel culture' or 'callout culture,'" said one longtime movement leader, "so, when we talk about our own movement, it's hard, because we're using the frame of the right. It's very hard, because there's all these associations and analysis that we disagree with, when we're using their frame. So, it's like, 'How do we talk about it?'" For years, recruiting young people into the movement felt like a win-win, he said: new energy for the movement and the chance to give a person a lease on a newly liberated life, dedicated to the pursuit of justice. But that's no longer the case. "I got to a point, like, three years ago where I had a crisis of faith, like, I don't even know. Most of these spaces on the left are just not—they're not healthy. Like all these people are just not—they're not doing well," he said. "The dynamic, the toxic dynamic of whatever you want to call it—callout culture, cancel culture, whatever—is creating this really intense thing, and no one is able to acknowledge it. No one's able to talk about it. No one's able to say how bad it is."

This environment has pushed expectations far beyond what workplaces previously offered to employees. "A lot of staff that work for me—they expect the organization to be all the things: a movement, okay; get out the vote, okay; healing, okay; take care of you when you're sick, okay. It's all the things," said one executive director. "Can you get your love and healing at home, please? But I can't say that. They would crucify me."

The 2020 presidential campaign in many ways served as a distraction from the infighting and gave focus to a fractious movement. When turmoil did erupt, often it was kept within the organization by all factions in order not to undermine the group's mission. In August 2019, for instance, a group of Sunrise staffers sent a letter to their leadership complaining that Sunrise staff and people of color were often "tokenized" and held up at organizing events to make the group appear more diverse than it was. The letter, written by the BIPOC caucus, urged the group's guiding principles be rewritten so that Sunrise would be an explicitly "anti-racist, anti-classist and anti-oppressive organization."

In January 2020, another group of staffers registered similar complaints. "A lot of us are in Sunrise largely because it seems to do a better job at prioritizing equity and anti-racism than many other similar climate-oriented organizations," they wrote the leadership. "Some of us are wondering to what extent that is actually true, or at least are not seeing this being as dominant a part of the conversation as we want."

Things became even tenser in the progressive community because of Covid-19 and its associated lockdown. Jonathan Smucker, the author of the book *Hegemony How-To: A Roadmap for Radicals*, trains and advises activists across the movement spectrum. After the pandemic forced people into quarantine in March 2020, he noted, many workplaces turned into pressure cookers. "COVID has severely limited in-person tactical options, and in-person face-to-face activities are absolutely vital to volunteer-driven efforts," he said in an email. "Without these spaces, staff are more likely to become insular—a tendency that's hard enough to combat even without this shift. Moreover, the virtual environment (Zoom meetings) may be convenient for all kinds of reasons, but it's a pretty lousy medium once there's conflict in an organization. In-person face-to-face time, in my experience, is irreplaceable when it comes to moving constructively through conflict. I know this is not the full picture and probably not even the root of these problems or conflicts, but it's almost certainly exacerbating them."

In April 2020, another group of Sunrise staffers, running the distributed hubs around the country, wrote a letter to leadership. "We are constantly burning out and reliving trauma for this movement (many of us without access to proper mental health services) and we should receive fair compensation for such emotionally intensive work," it read. "If there is money for flying people across the country, for the salaries of white leadership, and money for retreats, then there is money for our communities and the grassroot leaders who do this work." After each letter, Sunrise management and its workers gathered for a long series of meetings, one-on-one, in small groups, and in larger settings, with the organization's Slack platform often serving as a forum for hashing out disagreements.

In June 2020, in the wake of the killing of George Floyd in Minneapolis, the rage spilled into the streets. The outpouring of opposition to the brutalization of Floyd was near universal in the early weeks and months. The rage was funneled into a slogan picked up by the media and adopted by many members of the Squad—"defund the police"—

that would later become a yearslong fulcrum of contention inside the Democratic Party. But by the fall, the street protests had simmered down, and the general election between Trump and Biden dominated the cultural and political landscape. Inside progressive organizations, infighting reached a fever pitch.

The histories of the organizations were scoured for evidence of white supremacy, and nobody had to look very hard. The founder of Planned Parenthood, Margaret Sanger, was posthumously rebuked for her dalliance with eugenics, and in July 2020, her name was stripped from the headquarters of the organization's New York affiliate.

At the Sierra Club, then executive director Michael Brune published a statement headlined "Pulling Down Our Monuments," calling out founder John Muir for his association with eugenicists. "Muir was not immune to the racism peddled by many in the early conservation movement. He made derogatory comments about Black people and Indigenous peoples that drew on deeply harmful racist stereotypes, though his views evolved later in his life," Brune wrote that July, adding, "For all the harms the Sierra Club has caused, and continues to cause, to Black people, Indigenous people, and other people of color, I am deeply sorry. I know that apologies are empty unless accompanied by a commitment to change. I am making that commitment, publicly, right now. And I invite you to hold me and other Sierra Club leaders, staff, and volunteers accountable whenever we don't live up to our commitment to becoming an actively anti-racist organization."

Brune had come to the Sierra Club, the environmental group founded in 1892, from Greenpeace and the anarchist-influenced Rainforest Action Network. In 2010, he was considered a radical choice to run the staid organization. He didn't last the summer of 2021.

Then the Sierra Club's structure, which has relied on thousands of volunteers, many empowered with significant responsibility, also came under scrutiny after a volunteer was accused of rape. The consulting firm Ramona Strategies was brought in for an extensive "restorative accountability process."

"Being a 'volunteer-led' organization, [Sierra Club] cannot stand for volunteers having carte blanche to ignore legal requirements or organizational values around equity and inclusivity—or basic human decency," the consultant's report stated. "All employees should be managed by and subject to the oversight of individuals also under the organization's clear control and direction as employees. There is no other way we can see."

The recommendation was the logical dead-end point of the inward focus. Having only employees and no volunteers—or, in the case of Everytown for Gun Safety, asking volunteers to sign nondisclosure agreements—would render moot the structure of most major movement groups, such as Indivisible, Sunrise, MoveOn, and the NAACP. Organizations across the board came to a standstill, reckoning with internal conflict. "If you [had] talked to me four months after George Floyd, I would have said, we are so fucked. No one's talking about this, and it's imploding all our organizations, and the left is just a toxic place," said one group leader.

At Sunrise, the internal disputes continued. In September, a newly organized group, the Black Sunrise Caucus, sent a letter to leadership. "We outsource the fight for racial justice to other organizations. We exploit Black images, symbolism, songs, culture, and ideas," they wrote. "We have dedicated, Black full-time organizers for the Sunrise Movement, and these folks are often unpaid, unrecognized, and lack any movement decision power. Let this serve as notice that we will no longer allow the Sunrise Movement to exploit our voices, body, and labor." More meetings ensued.

Amid all the fighting, Sunrise was actively working with the Biden transition team on its climate unity task force, run by John Kerry and Ocasio-Cortez. It didn't produce everything the left wanted, but it was far closer to something that could be called a Green New Deal than was remotely plausible two years earlier.

Outside the task forces, the Squad was kept on the sidelines. "The campaign was awful to us," Ocasio-Cortez said just after the election. "We had a group of young AAPI [Asian Americans and Pacific Islanders] for Biden volunteers ask me to speak to them for a Zoom call, and the Biden campaign called to ask me to decline. That's how hostile they were to our engagement. I tried to help them with Latinos, and they didn't want me anywhere near them. It's disgusting how they treated Ilhan, and now they won't even give her or Rashida credit for saving them. They held a 'national progressive town hall for Biden' and invited Bernie and others but didn't invite us. It's bad."

15

VIOLENCE

Heading into the final weeks of the 2020 presidential campaign, Congress contemplated doing something big. The CARES Act, passed in spring 2020 to rescue the economy amid the pandemic's shutdown, was running out, and something had to be done to both finance vaccine development and production and continue stimulating the sputtering economy. Democrats had initially proposed a $3 trillion pandemic-response plan, with Senate Republicans countering with just $500 billion. The Trump White House, always more eager to spend than McConnell, offered up $1.7 trillion—but Democrats rejected this, hoping to take full control of government and go for broke instead.

But as the votes were being counted, it appeared that full control was unlikely. Biden's reverse coattails had cost Democrats seats in the House, which they'd hold on to with a slim majority. But in the Senate, they had lost winnable races in Maine and North Carolina, plus long-shot bids they had hoped to grab in Iowa and Montana, where the popular former governor Steve Bullock was running. Their only hope of winning the Senate was to claw it to a 50–50 tie by winning both runoffs in Georgia and then having the vice president break the tie, and that seemed too far out of reach to hope for.

And so Democrats crawled back to the negotiating table and made an offer of $908 billion, hoping to salvage something. The White House was on board, as were a handful of Senate Republicans.

During the last round of stimulus, Bernie Sanders had teamed up with an unlikely ally, Missouri senator Josh Hawley, to push for direct stimulus checks. The idea of direct checks had originated with Sanders in the early 2000s, when he proposed it as an independent member of the House. George W. Bush, who could spot a winning idea, seized it and made the checks a sheen of populism on his gargantuan tax cuts for the rich. In December 2020, when Hawley and Sanders teamed up again, they called for a second round of checks to be attached to the bill.

It turned out that people *liked* free money landing in their bank accounts. Party leaders eventually winnowed the giveaways down to $600, but included them in the final package. Congress passed the bill and sent it to Trump, but before signing it, he posted a video on Twitter demanding that the amount on the checks be increased. "I am asking Congress to amend this bill and increase the ridiculously low $600 to $2,000," Trump said two days before Christmas, "and to send me a suitable bill or else the next administration will have to deliver a Covid relief package."

Ocasio-Cortez immediately agreed publicly with Trump and drafted an amendment that would add $1,400 to the balance, bringing the total of each check to $2,000. What few noticed at the time is that she also allowed $1,400 for each dependent, including adult dependents over age seventeen. A family of four was now looking at a tax-free check of $8,000.

McConnell responded with a decision that would haunt him and the Republican Party for years to come: he said no. "The Senate is not going to be bullied into rushing out more borrowed money into the hands of Democrats' rich friends who don't need the help," he said. Schumer saw gold in the opportunity and hammered away at McConnell, demanding a vote. He relentlessly highlighted what was shaping up to be an almost impossibly perfect scenario for Democrats: We want to give you $2,000, but mean Mitch McConnell won't let us. If you elect two more Democratic senators, McConnell will be pushed out of the way, and you'll get your checks. How's that for a deal?

In order not to make voters feel too scuzzy about the arrangement, party leaders pitched it as a matter of charity and altruism: We know that you wouldn't sell your vote for $2,000, but think of all the struggling people in your life who could really use that money. Do it for them. "If you send Jon [Ossoff] and the Reverend [Raphael Warnock] to Washington, those $2,000 checks will go out the door, restoring hope and decency and honor for so many people who are struggling right now," Biden said in January in Georgia, just ahead of the vote. "And if you send [the Republicans] back to Washington, those checks will never get there . . . It's just that simple. The power is literally in your hands."

Unlike many claims by politicians ahead of an election, this one was simple and true. (By then, Trump had signed the legislation, and the $600 checks had started to arrive, leading some on the online left to say that the promise of $2,000 could no longer count the $600 as a downpayment and that the $1,400 checks that were later delivered actually reflected the breaking of a promise. AOC would be dogged on Twitter by the criticism for years.)

Trump's second gift to Georgia Democrats had been his ongoing insistence that the vote in the state was rigged, which had the effect of depressing Republican turnout. Why bother casting a vote if Democrats were just going to steal it anyway? Equally important, however, in the most direct example in modern memory, economic populism, in its purest form, delivered results. On January 5, voters in Georgia elected Raphael Warnock and Jon Ossoff to represent them in the Senate.

The Squad, meanwhile, was facing pressure from a base of supporters online. On November 18, in leadership elections, Pelosi had run unopposed for Speaker and won the party's support. On November 27, the day after Thanksgiving, a left-wing YouTube personality floated an idea to his audience. Because Pelosi would need Democratic votes to be officially named Speaker on January 3, and she had only 222 members in her caucus, a united Squad, now expanded to include Bowman and Bush, had the leverage to block her. They could use that leverage, he argued, to demand a floor vote on Medicare for All. The vote would then be an organizing opportunity and a way to bring attention to the issue. The idea stayed in the background for several weeks but started picking up attention online in mid- to late December.

The idea of exploiting leverage for concessions at the beginning of the term was not new. The CPC had done so the term before, to win committee seats. And the threat to take down the rules package over PAYGO had won the first-ever hearings for Medicare for All. This time, they were using their leverage to try to strip PAYGO entirely, so that the party wouldn't need offsets to enact what they hoped would be the most robust spending since the New Deal.

The Squad lives on Twitter, so they couldn't miss the attention that the movement—which came to be called Force the Vote—was getting online. But they were skeptical of the demand for a floor vote on Medicare for All. It needed 218 votes to pass. There was already a list of people who supported it and people who didn't. Members of Congress who hadn't cosponsored it were the targets of organizations like National Nurses United. Putting it up for a vote would produce, say, 320 votes against it and 115 votes for it, not the type of showing that would build momentum. Instead, the CPC wanted to focus on extracting concessions in the rules package. Ocasio-Cortez engaged with people on Twitter, asking about the tactic, but nobody from the Squad went on any of the YouTube shows or podcasts pushing the idea to explain their rationale.

Meanwhile, the rhetoric on YouTube had turned increasingly dark. "We need to storm Washington, DC. We need to scare the fuck out of people," one YouTuber said in support of the "Force the Vote" tactic, telling a story about Richard Nixon. "When they were coming for Nixon, they were protesting, and they had set up around the White House these school buses, and he says, 'What are those for?' And he's with Kissinger, and he goes, 'That's in case they break through the fences, those'll slow 'em down.' [Nixon] said to Kissinger, 'Henry, I'm afraid if they get through there they'll come for us and kill us.' That's where they should be. That's how afraid they should be of us."

The effort was affiliated with a third party that had been launched in 2017, Movement for a People's Party, though it had yet to field a candidate. As of the 2024 cycle, it still hadn't, but it was collecting donations online, organizing a petition to "Force the Vote," and converting new party members into the audience for YouTubers promoting the strategy. Nick Brana, the head of the party, on several occasions said that he knew the idea would fail, but in its failure it would expose the Squad as sellouts to the Democratic Party and would encourage people to leave it and join his party. The idea tapped into a real desire for bold action on the part of the progressive wing of the party, and a live town hall on YouTube to discuss it at the end of December drew more than one hundred thousand viewers.

"We saw this fight happening, and we saw it as so much more than a fight over Medicare for All, as big as that is," Brana said at the town hall. "What is the point, as this debate is illustrating, of having progressives and politicians in the Democratic Party who don't take corporate money if, at the end of the day, they end up listening to the politicians who do take the corporate money . . . It's not because AOC is a bad person. It's not because the Squad are bad people. They are in a party that is thoroughly, irredeemably corporate, and that's why we took on this fight as a Movement for a People's Party."

On January 1, the rules package was unveiled. It included a concession the CPC had won but that progressives had been keeping quiet so as to not generate counterpressure from deficit hawks on the right of the party. Any budget items that addressed "economic or public health consequences resulting from Covid-19 [or] climate change" would not be subject to PAYGO—which, in practice, meant effectively everything.

The vote was set for Monday, January 4, and Ocasio-Cortez said she wasn't sure if the exception would stay in the package, but that the roots of the win dated back to the fight over PAYGO of two years earlier.

"McGovern gave a promise that we'd address it in the next rules package, and then CPC geared up early to make it a major centerpiece of conditioning votes for the incoming rules package for 117th," she texted, betraying some of the frustration at the criticism. "Blue Dogs have been losing their mind about it so it's not a sure thing with this margin, and we don't want to poke the bear taking a victory lap before the vote. It's made this force the vote thing extra frustrating too. Cause it's like I'M DOING IT lol and f-ing have been trying to clear the way for it for months but yeah I'm the sellout." Still, she couldn't resist celebrating the win. "One of the 1st votes I ever cast broke w/ my party over House rules that strangled transformative legislation for working people + climate. It was honestly terrifying," she wrote on Twitter. "Now, CPC has pushed these critical rule changes in House negotiations."

She framed it as a win that related to Medicare for All and the Green New Deal. "One of the first deep lessons I learned in the House [is] that process IS policy. If you pass M4A, GND [Green New Deal], etc. w/ messed up process/rules, then it can be weaponized into austerity leg[islation] by rules requiring it to have insane tax hikes or service cuts tied to it that aren't applied to others," she tweeted. "So these rule changes are a big deal—& not only on healthcare. They are structural changes in the House that level the playing field for a full SUITE of flagship legislation, locks in that field for the next two years, & establishes precedents for after. This was not easy." She then turned to her critics. "And to be 100% honest, it was hard during this to be targeted+marred as some sellout-enemy of the people over a late tactical disagreement over 1 floor vote," she posted in the thread. "Also a bummer to see figures excuse comments like 'f-her and f-anyone who protects her.' That's not tone, that's violence."

Her equating of the criticism with "violence" is another thing she continued to get hit with for years. "On one hand, I am no stranger to abusive rhetoric and know that taking knocks comes w/ being an elected official," she said. "But as someone who prioritizes movement-building and winning, creating something joyful that people actually want to be a part of is an imp[or]t[ant] organizing principle. BUT, let us celebrate this achievement! We need the energy of celebration to keep pushing! These rule changes are a b[ig]f[ucking] d[eal]. Breaking austerity mindset + rules, esp on climate, is a major tenet of the Green New Deal. We will learn, build, uplift & advance together. ♡"

But the sense that the joy was fading from her role was increasingly evident in her public persona. She had come into office dancing—quite literally, when a video of her dancing on a rooftop in college surfaced and was circulated on the right, she leaned into it by dancing outside her congressional office—but it was becoming a slog. And her calls for civility clashed with her previous defense of protesters who had disrupted the dining experiences of Trump officials or whose clashes with police had developed into riots. Mainstream Democrats increasingly called for Big Tech firms to more tightly moderate and censor content on their platforms, and AOC's posture seemed more akin to that approach than to the more traditional support on the left for free speech, even the ugly kind.

Years later, reflecting on the fight, Ocasio-Cortez said she had sensed there was a hostile, reactionary element intertwined with the democratic socialist movement. "I felt this early before the Force the Vote stuff," she said. "I may have forced the confrontation too early, but I started quietly warning people about it in 2020."

Brana and other backers of Force the Vote called for a rally in Washington on January 2 and 3, a Saturday and Sunday, to pressure lawmakers directly. "We need to pressure the people who are the closest to us if they can be moved," Brana said at the town hall. "And if they can't be moved, then we need to have a conversation that's much deeper than this about electoral politics and the Democratic Party, something that we've begun as the Movement for a People's Party." The rally drew only a few dozen protesters, the online energy failing to translate amid the holidays into on-the-ground action. Pelosi was approved unanimously by Democrats that Sunday, and the rules package cleared the House with the CPC's PAYGO concession intact the next day.

I asked CPC chair Pramila Jayapal why they decided against asking for a vote on Medicare for All. "Well, I'm sympathetic, obviously, as the lead sponsor of the bill, to people who are frustrated that we have not moved to a single-payer system yet," she told me. "But the reality is, this is a very slim margin. The vote for Speaker was between Kevin McCarthy and Nancy Pelosi, and throwing the entire chamber into chaos would have been very detrimental for the Electoral College vote and everything else."

Jayapal's critics blasted her, arguing that as long as Pelosi's opponents voted for somebody other than McCarthy, McCarthy couldn't become Speaker, and the vote would be deadlocked until somebody blinked. But that's not what Jayapal was saying, as the second half of her sentence was missed. The vote for Speaker was scheduled for January 3, the rules package for January 4, the Georgia Senate runoffs for January 5, and the certification of the Electoral College votes on January 6. Two years later, watching right-wing Republicans hold up Kevin McCarthy's election to the Speakership for a week, advocates of the Force the Vote idea were convinced they had been dead right the last time and that the Squad deserved all the scorn that had been sent their way. But Jayapal's point is worth considering. If the Squad had withheld their votes and pushed the vote to the next day, January 4, would they have had more leverage or less? Now imagine if they had held firm, like the Freedom Caucus Republicans, and pushed it to January 5? The House would have been required to certify Biden's win the next day. How much popular support would the Squad have had in blocking that from happening as tens of thousands of Trump supporters marshaled in Washington?

Except, they wouldn't have had to withhold their votes. Pelosi would have readily consented to a vote, as it would have cost her nothing. Jayapal has said that it wasn't that she was unwilling to use her leverage, but she actively did not want a vote that she felt would set the movement back. "From my perspective, as the lead sponsor of the bill who's done so much to try and build momentum and gain sponsorship and move the bill forward in the legislative process, I didn't think it was a smart idea. I mean, for us to force a vote on Medicare for All before we are sure that we have the support, I think, is a bad strategy," she said. Getting intel on where members stood wasn't hard to do, either, she said. "You already know."

The days after the Speaker vote confirmed Jayapal's doubts of the wisdom in engineering new chaos at that moment. Ocasio-Cortez said the Capitol grounds and surrounding neighborhood were starting to buzz. "I knew since Monday something was going to happen—when I saw the barricades," she told me. Trump's protesters were filling the city in advance of the "Stop the Steal" rally. "Every protest I've been to of any notable size has layers of those waist-high fencelike barriers, at least two to three deep. They only had one. The one that's always there—so there were essentially no changes. And these people started to gather and bully us during votes as early as Monday. And by Tuesday at noon, it absolutely was no longer safe," she said.

Ocasio-Cortez lives in the Southwest Waterfront section of Washington, DC. With its faux-luxury condos populated by Republican staffers and operatives, it's the only area of the city where a significant number of precincts went for Trump. Her neighborhood filled up with more MAGA hats than normal, she said, and she could feel them eying her everywhere. "The threat was very obvious and escalating for two days prior to Wednesday," she said.

Her colleague Abigail Spanberger, a former CIA operative—if "former" truly ever applies to that role—warned AOC to be on high alert on the sixth and suggested she dress like a tourist rather than in her recognizable style. "The days before the sixth I asked for a USCP [U.S. Capitol Police] officer to escort me to votes on the 6th because the threats were so high. They told me no," Ocasio-Cortez said. "When they said no, we asked if I could hire my own security so they could escort me. They said no to that too." She said they told her that "elevated security limited Capitol access to approved personnel. They wouldn't approve our own security." It brought her back to the border in the summer of 2019. "There was definitely a lot of fucked up things that day (and before)," she texted after January 6.

Hostility toward Ocasio-Cortez inside the Capitol was real. Later that year, Pablo Manríquez, then a reporter with the outlet Latino Rebels, glanced down at the desk of one of the Press Gallery directors, an ex-military guy in charge of credentialing journalists, and did a double take at a printout. The desk sits down a hallway roughly six feet long, without a door, making it a semipublic area that reporters routinely drift into and out of, particularly to use it for cable TV appearances.

It was an internet meme brought to life, featuring a photo of Rep. Alexandria Ocasio-Cortez, Democrat of New York, with the caption "I Don't Always Speak My Mind, But When I Do, I Sound Like a Damn Idiot." Manríquez snapped a photo of the printout and complained. Days later, he went by again, and it was still sitting there.

On the morning of January 6, the city was thrumming with nervous energy, with tens of thousands of Trump supporters preparing for the president's "Stop the Steal" rally near the White House. As Trump spoke, reciting his litany of grievances about the election, his supporters began marching toward the Capitol, where Trump told them they needed to stiffen the spines of wobbly Republicans. "You have to show strength, and you have to be strong," he told the crowd. "We have come to demand that Congress do the right thing and only count the electors who have been lawfully slated, lawfully slated. I know that everyone here will soon be marching over to the Capitol Building to peacefully and patriotically make your voices heard." His suggestion that they remain peaceful was not taken as a direct order by many of them, as protesters forced their way past the minimal outer ring of security and smashed their way toward the Capitol doors and windows.

Because Ilhan Omar had been the subject of so many credible death threats, the Speaker had given her her own security detail in the fall of 2020. That meant six Capitol Police officers and three cars providing round-the-clock protection. Her proximity to the officers, and in particular their radios, gave her insight into the potential for unrest on January 6 that other members of Congress didn't have, and that apparently higher-ups in law enforcement also didn't have, leaving the Capitol shockingly poorly defended that day.

Omar also had her finger closer to the pulse of the MAGA movement, since she had long become a stand-in for all they hated about Democrats. She put on comfortable shoes and clothes that day, in case running would be on the day's agenda, and her husband Tim decided to come with her. Her detail encouraged her to stay home for as long as possible, easier to protect there. By the time she got into her car, news of a pipeline was making the rounds, and crowds were massing outside the Capitol. She still had easy access to her office on the seventh floor of the Longworth Building, and there she met Kelly Misselwitz, her legislative director.

Omar's office has a large window that opens to a flat roof. She and Misselwitz stepped out to watch the action and could see the endless stream of protesters. "There was not a single visible cop, anything like National Guard, no Capitol Police that we could see from up here. And I was like, this doesn't look good," she said later in an interview in her office, peering through the window at the roof.

The cops were growing increasingly nervous, she said, but continued to insist she stay put, that the office was the safest possible location. But then a new set of officers arrived, and issued a new order: it was time to evacuate. She, her husband, and her legislative director piled into the cars and were rushed to a military base she would later learn was Fort McNair.

Back in the Capitol, rank-and-file members of Congress were trapped. Covid-19 restrictions limited the number of people who could be on the House floor, so Pramila Jayapal was in the gallery overlooking the chamber. She was watching Republicans object to the certification of the Electoral College votes as text messages started to come in, each one more ominous than the last. Rioters had broken into the Capitol, and her husband suggested that she evacuate to her office for safety. But the fifty-five-year-old had just had knee surgery, and she couldn't imagine hobbling through a mob and making it in time. Besides, she told her husband, she was in the safest chamber on earth, with the House Speaker and the majority leader. They would be well guarded, she assured him.

Then she saw the Speaker being taken out by security. So much for that assurance.

Spanberger, seated next to her, showed her a photo on her phone. It was of a man carrying flex cuffs (also described as zip ties); he looked to be on the hunt for congressional prey. By now the mob was smashing glass and trying to push through to the chamber. One rioter, climbing through a window, was shot and killed.

Only a heavy wooden door separated the gallery from the hallway outside, and the hallway was now teeming with angry rioters trying to smash that door down. With the roughly dozen members of Congress in their gallery section were two confused Capitol Police officers, struggling to find a key to the door to lock it. The members of Congress were all handed gas masks. Her mask was heavy enough, Jayapal decided, that she could throw it at the first attacker coming her way, then start flailing away with her cane. She made the determination that if she was going down, she was going down swinging.

But the attackers didn't breach that door. Capitol Police reinforcements arrived in time and cleared a space in the hallway. Once the officers convinced the police inside the gallery that they were real, the latter opened the door, and Jayapal saw her would-be assailants splayed out on the floor. There weren't enough officers to escort everyone inside to safety and also guard their detainees, so the lawmakers were told to remove the pins that identified them as members of Congress and make their way to a congressional hearing room through the Capitol Hill Tunnels. Jayapal and freshman representative Mondaire Jones of New York contemplated the decision. Leave the pin on and be discovered by the mob. Take the pin off and be attacked by police who might not realize they're members of Congress. They left the pins on.

Then came the trouble of the long flight of marble stairs. Jayapal stared at them, knowing her knee couldn't make it. Rep. Mikie Sherrill, a New Jersey Democrat, held her up as the two hopped down the stairs. They made it to the hearing room, and as Jayapal opened the door it immediately dawned on her: she had tested negative for the coronavirus that morning, but this airless room was teeming with people. I'm going to get Covid, she forecast accurately to herself.

Ocasio-Cortez was in her office with one other staffer when the lockdown notice came. She heard a banging on her door and bolted for the bathroom. She then thought that a nearby closet might be a better hiding spot and cracked the door to her office, seeing in the hallway what she described as a "white man with a beanie. . . . And then I realize that it's too late for me to get into the closet—and so I go back in and hide back in the bathroom, behind the door. And then I just start to hear these yells of 'Where is she? Where is she?'"

"I didn't think that I was just going to be killed," she said later. "I thought other things were going to happen to me as well." She then heard her aide calling for her, and she learned that the man she had glimpsed was a Capitol Police officer who hadn't identified himself. He urged her to get to a safer location.

She raced to Katie Porter's office and barreled inside, startling Porter, who wasn't nearly as concerned that the mob would go from office to office. "She was opening up doors, and I was like, 'Can I help you? What are you looking for?' And she said, 'I'm looking for where I'm going to hide,'" Porter recalled later in an interview on MSNBC.

"Well, don't worry. I'm a mom. I'm calm, I've got everything here we need. We could live for like a month in this office," she told Ocasio-Cortez.

"I just hope I get to be a mom. I hope I don't die today," AOC responded, regretting her decision not to take Spanberger's advice on her attire. "I knew I shouldn't have worn heels. How am I going to run?" she wondered. Porter managed to find a pair of sneakers for her.

Ocasio-Cortez also wondered whether her colleagues on the Republican side of the aisle were actively involved with the mob. Several months earlier, Republican representative Ted Yoho had called Ocasio-Cortez a "fucking bitch." He apologized but claimed he had muttered that she was "fucking bullshit," not a "fucking bitch," though he continued stalking her around the Capitol afterward. During the transition the months prior, Republican representative Madison Cawthorn, known for his insistence on carrying a firearm—he would later be charged with gun possession at an airport—visited Ocasio-Cortez's office multiple times, creeping out her staff. "He was pretty insistent," she said, though she hadn't been there the times he came by. "[Rep. Lauren] Boebert had also been chasing me around a few days beforehand with her camera, for what appeared to be a selfie photo op or something," she told me. "Swalwell and the sergeant [at arms] kept yelling at her to put her phone away and stop tweeting locations, and she wouldn't stop," Ocasio-Cortez said, referring to California representative Eric Swalwell. "I also think [Marjorie Taylor] Greene was probably in on it, too."

At Fort McNair, Omar was soon joined by the leadership members of both parties and both chambers, each of them giving Omar an odd look, appearing to wonder why she was there but unwilling to ask. Pelosi, Omar recalled, was panicking because she had been rushed out of the House chamber with her phone still on the dais. Now she was left to coordinate the response without the tool that had been most valuable to her over her career in politics.

Omar and her aide, off in a corner, began drafting an article of impeachment, and she shared it with Majority Leader Steny Hoyer. Republican tempers were running so hot against Trump that forcing them to choose sides in the Senate that week could easily have resulted in his actual impeachment, conviction, and disqualification from any future run for the White House.

Sen. Lindsey Graham even urged the Capitol Police to open fire. From his somewhat secure room, he looked over and saw the Senate sergeant at arms in there with them. Graham yelled at him, according to several different books about January 6, "What the hell are you doing here? Go take back the Senate! You've got guns . . . USE THEM!" He then called White House attorney Pat Cipollone and warned that Republicans would remove Trump from office using the Twenty-Fifth Amendment if he didn't call off the mob.

Omar wasn't alone this time among Democrats in wanting to act quickly on the opportunity. The first member of Congress to begin drafting an article of impeachment other than Omar was Rep. David Cicilline, a Democrat from Rhode Island, who—according to the book *Unchecked: The Untold Story Behind Congress's Botched Impeachments of Donald Trump*, by Karoun Demirjian and Rachael Bade— scribbled his on scratch paper while locked down in the Rayburn House Office Building.

Rep. Ted Lieu, a Democrat from California—who had been forced to evacuate because of his office's proximity to pipe bombs that had been discovered—joined Cicilline in Rayburn, and the two worked on the article of impeachment together. They lobbied other members of the House Judiciary Committee, with Lieu texting them that they "should start drafting articles of impeachment now, regardless of what leadership says." Lieu and Cicilline confirmed the account to me, but said they no longer had the scrap of paper they had used.

Cicilline reached out to Democratic reps Jamie Raskin of Maryland and Joe Neguse of Colorado. Raskin recommended going for the

Twenty-Fifth Amendment—in which the cabinet deems Trump unable to carry out his duties—and if that didn't work, impeachment. Cicilline and Lieu worked on a Twenty-Fifth Amendment letter to Vice President Mike Pence but kept pushing on impeachment.

They then reached out to Judiciary Committee counsel Aaron Hiller for help fine-tuning the impeachment draft. Hiller called his boss, Rep. Jerry Nadler's chief of staff, Amy Rutkin, and told her, "I'm about to do something that's completely unauthorized by leadership. Should I tell you or not?"

"Do it," she said.

"Go find two hundred cosponsors right now to get it done," Hiller told Cicilline. "Don't wait for a blessing from leadership."

That evening, once the Capitol had been cleared and the House returned to finish its business, Cicilline found Hoyer on the floor, *Unchecked* reports. Hoyer, as majority leader, controls the floor schedule. Cicilline handed Hoyer the impeachment resolution and implored him to allow a vote right then and there. Hoyer hemmed and hawed and passed the request on to Pelosi.

Pelosi's staff first tried to tell Cicilline that there were technical reasons an impeachment vote couldn't be done, arguing that the House was in joint session and, therefore, couldn't impeach. But of course they could adjourn the joint session after certifying the election and gavel in a new session.

Bringing the House back into order to continue the business of certifying the election produced a surreal session. Broken glass was still being swept up, and there was blood staining the marble floor just feet from the House chamber, but Republicans stepped over it to continue making speeches objecting to the legitimacy of the election. Nothing had changed. With the election affirmed, Pelosi gaveled the chamber closed, adjourning without impeaching, and everybody went home.

The pro-impeachment group kept pushing over the next week, and Pelosi deputized Rep. Adam Schiff, a Democrat from California, to argue against them. By the end of the week, Schiff had come out publicly in support of impeachment, but on a critical call the next day, a Saturday, with Nadler and others pushing for impeachment, he again made the case, at Pelosi's behest, against it. Eventually, the pressure became too great, and the House impeached Trump on January 13, but not before Republicans had closed ranks and the window to convict had been shut.

Two days earlier, Cori Bush had introduced a resolution, her first legislative action of her congressional career, joined by the rest of the Squad and 42 other Democrats, calling for Republicans who had voted against certifying the election to be investigated for treason and expelled. Republicans quickly pointed out that two years earlier, citing Russian interference in the election, some House Democrats, including Jayapal, had voted against certifying Trump's election.

Throughout the past congressional cycle, when it came to issues such as the war in Yemen, civil liberties, government surveillance, antitrust policy, and corporate power, the left flank of the Democratic Party had found some uneasy alliances with the right flank of the GOP, both wings united to cause problems for their respective party leaderships. It fit with the confusing realignment and populist upsurge coursing through American politics and culture. January 6 put a cork in that for several years, with the violence driving the politicians inside the parties closer together, blue against red, and the parties themselves farther apart. This increasing partisan polarization would drain much of the energy from the Democratic civil war that had kicked off with Sanders's first campaign.

16

ENTER THE PARLIAMENTARIAN

The January 6 riot may not have saved Trump's presidency, but it did preserve the job of the Senate parliamentarian, Elizabeth MacDonough. Because there was an impeachment trial under way, Senator Schumer saw no feasible path to removing MacDonough, who'd been appointed by Majority Leader Reid and kept on by McConnell.

Coming into the Congress, Schumer sensed he could become majority leader. Starting that fall, he had expanded his outreach into the progressive world, meeting and taking calls with organizations who had long been intraparty adversaries, and he was sounding very much like one of them. The problem in 2009, he told group after group, was that Democrats didn't go big enough with the stimulus, and they let cynical Republican foot-dragging slow them down. He wanted to get rid of the filibuster, he said, as soon as he had 50 votes to do it. He wanted to cancel fifty thousand dollars in individual Americans' student debt, legalize marijuana, and do a major climate bill, he said, to lock down the youth vote for a generation. Adding sweeping voting rights reform, he said, would produce an unbeatable coalition. He told the progressive groups with whom he met that he had gotten into politics in order to oppose the Vietnam War, presenting himself as a political ally of the left. With climate groups, he would begin every meeting or call with the same joke: that his name was "Charles E. Schumer," so, therefore, he was the world's greatest champion of a "strong, clean electricity standard," or CES. (You had to be there.)

It was lost on nobody that Schumer was up for reelection in 2022. The summer of 2020 had shown that political conditions can change dramatically in a short span of time. The wins by Jamaal Bowman and Mondaire Jones in suburban districts suggested that the appeal of the new progressive energy extended beyond the boroughs. Schumer couldn't afford to be the next Joe Crowley, to look like he had taken his seat or progressive support for granted.

His first test was a stimulus bill called the American Rescue Plan. Democrats proposed a $1.9 trillion package that included the new checks, extended unemployment, a $300 monthly child tax credit payment for families, subsidies for health care, and money to cover Covid-19 treatment and vaccinations. Republicans countered with a fraction of that, which typically would be the moment that the two parties engage in endless negotiations before agreeing to something close to the Republican terms. Instead, Biden and Schumer simply dismissed the GOP, pledging to move forward without them. Ocasio-Cortez's amendment was adopted as written, with the increased checks for kids and adult dependents included.

"It's huge, and I'm glad it wasn't a huge point of contention. For now lol. I don't count anything until Biden signs it," she texted as the bill moved through the process. Her push for $2 billion in money for FEMA to cover $10,000 in funeral expenses for Covid-19 victims—her impoverished district had the highest rate of Covid-19 deaths—was also included. "It's funny how they don't attack my legislative record almost ever aside from GND [Green New Deal] b[e]c[ause] they will look bad even for them." Republicans and their allies in the conservative media may have had a better chance of noticing that Ocasio-Cortez had slipped billions in extra relief money into the package, but in a spasmodic eruption that would foreshadow the right's future direction, the GOP spent nearly all of its energy during the debate over the $1.9 trillion American Rescue Plan lashing out about Dr. Seuss. The estate representing the children's book author had announced that some titles were being discontinued for ethnically insensitive drawings or lyrics, and the issue took center stage for conservatives, who paraded to the House floor to denounce the decision. That a spending bill nearly three times the size of Obama's 2009 stimulus moved through Congress with little attention from Republicans reflected a drastic change in the priorities of the political parties.

Though AOC's own wins were secured, the fight for a $15 dollar-an-hour minimum wage was set back when the Senate parliamentarian advised Schumer it couldn't go through under the complex rules of reconciliation. The parliamentarian's role, legally, is only to advise, but a Senate that preferred a villain to blame when things couldn't get done had empowered MacDonough to essentially issue rulings. She had grown so comfortable in that position that her entire "ruling" on the minimum wage consisted of a single line simply stating that it couldn't go through. It would have been as if the president or attorney general asked their top legal counsel for an advisory opinion on an issue—say, the legality of indefinite detention at Guantánamo Bay—and the counsel came back with a simple "yes" or "no." Still, an interlocking set of institutional supports rendered MacDonough's ruling final. Specifically, Sen. Joe Manchin—as well as traditionalists like Sen. Pat Leahy, MacDonough's patron from Vermont—would vote to affirm her opinion on the floor, no matter what it was, as would every Republican, if the ruling went against Democrats. But because MacDonough's opinion had no legal bearing, the real decision would be left to the presiding officer of the Senate—Vice President Kamala Harris. If the administration chose that path, Harris could simply disregard the parliamentarian's opinion and rule the wage increase in order. Opponents would then need 60 votes to overturn the ruling. Trying to add it as an amendment required 60 votes.

Democrats didn't have 60 votes, and the dirty secret was they didn't have 50, either. Had the measure been included in the underlying package, there probably wouldn't have been enough Democrats who opposed it strongly enough to force it out. But asking them affirmatively to put it *in* was a different story.

Sanders forced a vote on the issue—rekindling the fight on Twitter over forcing a vote on Medicare for All—but this gambit failed, with 8 Democrats defecting, meaning he was 18 short of the 60 needed. The theory on forcing a Medicare for All vote had been that the theater of it would attract national attention and dramatically advance the cause. Instead, the vote on the minimum wage came and went with only cursory mention. Sanders, concerned that some in the Squad might vote the whole package down because it didn't include the increased minimum wage, pleaded with Jayapal to make sure nobody on the left voted against the bill. As Budget Committee chair, Sanders had jammed an enormous number of his priorities into the bill and considered it one of the crowning achievements of his political career. He saw no path to getting the higher wage into the bill with those Democrats against it and was worried that unemployment benefits would begin to lapse. Manchin might walk away from the deal, returning only at a price of, say, cutting the size of the spending bill in half, Sanders worried.

On March 4, I asked Ocasio-Cortez if there was much talk of voting the American Rescue Plan bill down. "There has been discussion about it, but grassroots groups don't have appetite for a public fight so for now we are in direct convos w/ the senate and WH," she texted.

> As been reported they're also trying to cut UI [unemployment insurance]. There's also a joint letter that either went out or is going out between CPC and some other caucuses objecting to the stimulus check phaseout changes. What adds pressure is how soon UI is expiring. It's a really delicate spot because in some ways it's too far gone but in other ways we can use leverage to preserve as much as we can, we just don't know how much. Senate Dems are way more conservative than even I imagined. It's pretty shameful—it's not just Manchin and Sinema. People think it's Manchin vs a handful of House votes but it's actually much more than Manchin. He's just taking all the heat for it I think. Still seems weird to take heat for denying people money though. I get the policing and cultural issues but the UI/stim checks/min wage seems weird from an electoral perspective.

The "stimulus phaseout" referred to an effort by Manchin to more tightly restrict who could get the checks and of what size the checks should be. Manchin was also threatening to tank the whole bill over the size of unemployment benefits, demanding significant cuts.

Jayapal made the case that it was a deal worth taking, as the pressure on the Squad online to vote the bill down was visible in both the House and Senate. Jayapal was in regular contact with Schumer, having developed a relationship after the fight over Trump's border funding. She told him that if he bent on the unemployment benefits, she'd lose the Squad, and the bill would go down. Schumer relayed the threat to Manchin, telling him he simply couldn't make the cuts Manchin was demanding. In an extraordinary example of the power of outside pressure creating a credible threat of action on the inside, Manchin caved. The American Rescue Plan bill passed late at night, by which time Arizona senator Kyrsten Sinema was slurring her words as she cast her vote.

But there would be no $15 minimum wage in the bill. As far as a chunk of the online left was concerned, it wasn't an instance of outside pressure working in tandem with inside operators. It was all just bullshit. The instances of capitulation were stacking up. First, the Pelosi vote; then the $2,000 checks that became $600 plus $1,400; and now the $15 wage on the cutting room floor. The argument around Force the Vote eventually morphed into a claim that Medicare for All could have been passed into law using the tactic, but that the Squad had blown it up, as the online critics drifted farther from reality. "About 18 months ago we made a plan to get Medicare for All and asked you to support it," Movement for a People's Party Brana told Ocasio-Cortez in a typical Twitter post. "It was called #ForceTheVote. You called it violence."

Yet among the public at large, Biden's approval rating surged. Never was he more popular than when he was riding roughshod over Manchin, Sinema, Gottheimer, and the rest of the corporate wing of the party. Up next was round two of the reconciliation fight, over what could become the biggest climate investment in world history.

17

WU & KHAN & KANTER

Elizabeth Warren's 2016 plan to stack a Hillary Clinton administration with her lieutenants was foiled by Trump, but a Biden administration gave her a new opening. Warren had cut her political teeth opposing Biden's bankruptcy bill in the 1990s. Reflecting on the fight in her 2003 bestseller *The Two-Income Trap*, she contrasted his credit-card company capitulation with his good work addressing violence against women. "In a statistic with special significance for Senator Biden, more women will be victimized by predatory lenders than will seek protection from an abusive husband or boyfriend," she wrote. "Senators like Joe Biden should not be allowed to sell out women in the morning and be heralded as their friend in the evening."

In the later phase of her political career, as bailout watchdog and then as senator, she had made up with Biden, so much so that by 2016 he told her that if he ran for president, he wanted her on the ticket as vice president. That, and her refusal to endorse Sanders, put her in a prime position to stack the administration with her allies, and she made a major play on the consumer protection and antitrust front.

In prior presidential transitions, much of the effort made by progressive organizations was around policy commitments, while corporate lobbyists worked on getting their preferred allies into positions of power. In 2020, the Washington progressive world finally started mimicking the tactics of K Street amid the transition. One reason the left had hardly tried the approach in the past was that there simply wasn't a base of progressive staff to push into positions of power, but a multi-cycle effort had closed some of that gap. The organization Demand Progress had spent years building a list of vetted staff, and during the transition it organized multiple letters and pressure campaigns on behalf of specific candidates—and also against particular nominees. Progressive opposition managed to block Gina Raimondo, a former banker turned conservative Rhode Island governor, first from being treasury secretary and, next, from Health and Human Services. Raimondo wound up with the concession prize of the Commerce Department. (As the Biden administration drifted rightward in 2023, her name began being floated again for treasury secretary.)

Lina Khan and Jonathan Kanter were among Warren's highest priorities for administration jobs. The same year he had sat down for a pivotal dinner with Elizabeth Warren, antitrust attorney Kanter joined the corporate law firm Paul, Weiss, where he represented smaller companies, like Yelp, that were targeting bigger companies, like Google, hoping not to be swallowed up like so many Yelp-like firms. Lina Khan had gone on to the House Judiciary Committee, where she led a landmark investigation into Big Tech. The heat from Congress, the Trump administration, and some state attorneys general, all of whom were taking a closer look at monopolies, meant that big companies suddenly needed antitrust attorneys. For this, they turned to Paul, Weiss, which started creating issues for Kanter's clients. A law firm can't take clients on both sides of a case, and the Goliaths were footing much higher retainers than the Davids. So Kanter was told he had to either drop his little clients or leave the firm. In 2020, he left to form his own firm.

She wanted Khan at the Federal Trade Commission and Kanter as the assistant attorney general at the Department of Justice's antitrust division. The problem was that business groups were implacably hostile to even the hint of such crusaders with so much power, and White House chief of staff Ron Klain had his eye on his longtime friend and ally Karen Dunn—who happened to be one of the top lawyers at Paul, Weiss, having brought in so much business from monopolists that Kanter had had to go.

Warren often repeated her "personnel is policy" mantra, but there was no clearer case than this one. The choice between Dunn and Kanter was a choice between a Justice Department that would continue to go light on monopolies and one that would aggressively move to prosecute companies. A source in Warren's diaspora, made up of aides who moved in and out of her orbit and formed a loose network of anti-corporate operatives, tipped off *HuffPost* reporter Zach Carter about the fight. When Carter reached out to Dunn for comment about her potential conflicts of interest, she asked if the story would still be worth running if she pulled her name from consideration. He told her the piece was about her potential nomination and that if there were no longer such a potential, there would be no story. She withdrew.

Next, Renata Hesse, a former Justice Department official under President Barack Obama who had worked alongside Sen. Ted Cruz defending Google a decade earlier and had helped shepherd through the Amazon/Whole Foods merger, was reported by Reuters to be a leading contender. The *Intercept* published a story highlighting Hesse's corporate ties and monopoly-friendly approach, relying heavily on research done by the organization Revolving Door Project, a part of Warren's diasporic empire. Hesse, amid pressure from Warren on Klain, faded from contention. Next up was Jonathan Sallet, another attorney who the Warren world worried was far too friendly to big companies—but another story in the *Intercept*, followed by pressure from Warren, bumped him from consideration, too. Eventually, only Kanter was left standing, and he won the job, becoming the top antitrust prosecutor.

Lina Khan, meanwhile, was appointed to the FTC and even made its chair. Rohit Chopra, a firebrand commissioner and Warren ally who'd been waging a lonely fight up to that point on the FTC, was named to run Warren's baby, the Consumer Financial Protection Bureau. Tim Wu, one of the nation's leading critics of corporate power, who had coined the term *net neutrality* and was loathed by Big Tech, was named special assistant to the president for technology and competition policy. The anti-monopoly movement, in celebration, began slinging coffee mugs honoring the mock law firm of Wu & Khan & Kanter. Over the next two years, the *Wall Street Journal*'s editorial page would run more angry screeds directed at Khan than any other official in the Biden administration by far—one less than every two weeks.

Adding insult to the injured *Journal,* labor economist Jared Bernstein along with Heather Boushey, a pioneer in advocating for increased financial support for children and families, were named to the Council of Economic Advisers. Both had long tangled with Larry Summers, who was shut out. Janet Yellen was named treasury secretary, about as progressive an economist as you could get in that position, and Wally Adeyemo, a former Warren lieutenant at the CFPB, was named deputy treasury secretary. Bharat Ramamurti, a longtime Warren lieutenant, was named deputy director of the National Economic Council; Julie Siegal, a veteran Warren banking adviser, was made deputy chief of staff at the Treasury Department; Graham Steele, a Banking Committee aide who was close with Warren and Ohio populist senator Sherrod Brown, was named assistant secretary for financial institutions at treasury. The legions of Larry Summers had been thoroughly routed in the transition.

In August 2021, the Federal Trade Commission sued Facebook. A year later, the agency sued Google amid reports it was preparing a suit against Amazon. Kanter, from his perch at the Department of Justice, launched a landmark suit against Google in 2023.

18

COUNTERINSURGENCY

In May 2021, the Israeli government began pushing ahead with evictions of Palestinians in the Sheikh Jarrah neighborhood in East Jerusalem. It was one more creeping step forward in an occupation and annexation process that had been under way for decades, but what was new this time was the reaction of Hamas, the government in Gaza. If the Palestinian Authority wouldn't stand up for the homeowners in Sheikh Jarrah, Hamas announced, they would do it themselves if Israel didn't back off its plan to evict the families.

The Israeli government did not back off, as was to be expected, and Hamas responded by launching rocket attacks into Israel, attacks that were intercepted by the U.S.-built Iron Dome air-defense system or that otherwise crashed to the earth. Israel launched an assault on Gaza, and what became known as the Gaza War of 2021 broke out.

In Gaza wars past, the Washington ritual had always been repeated. Israel had "a right to defend itself," each statement began, even if the support for that right was occasionally caveated with a hope that Israel might decide to respect human rights and, perhaps, if it saw fit, limit civilian casualties.

This war was different. In the United States, the tenor of the coverage was far less sympathetic than it had been, with images of Israeli police attacking protesters in East Jerusalem and reports of widespread casualties from the Israeli strikes. Mark Pocan, the Madison, Wisconsin, congressman who'd previously cochaired the CPC, reserved an hour of time on the House floor on May 13, and Democrats paraded through to denounce the assault.

It was like nothing the U.S. Congress had ever seen. Omar, standing in the well of the House, bluntly but not inaccurately called Israeli prime minister Benjamin Netanyahu an "ethno-nationalist." Tlaib added, "I am a reminder to colleagues that Palestinians do indeed exist."

Omar recalled her own experience as an eight-year-old huddled under a bed in Somalia, hoping the incoming bombs wouldn't hit her home next. "It is trauma I will live with for the rest of my life, so I understand on a deeply human level the pain and the anguish families are feeling in Palestine and Israel at the moment," she said.

Pressley, the elder of the Squad and the least inclined to challenge the status quo on Israel-Palestine, spoke directly to the political guardrails put up around members of the House of Representatives—and then ran right through those guardrails. "Many say that 'conditioning aid' is not a phrase I should utter here," she said, "but let me be clear. No matter the context, American government dollars always come with conditions. The question at hand is should our taxpayer dollars create conditions for justice, healing, and repair, or should those dollars create conditions for oppression and apartheid?"

Ocasio-Cortez hit hard, too. "Do Palestinians have a right to survive? Do we believe that?" she asked, reminding the House that Israel had barred Omar and Tlaib from traveling to the country. "We have to have the courage to name our contributions," she said, referring to the U.S. role in perpetuating and funding the fighting.

The clerk of the House addressed Cori Bush: "For what purpose does the gentlelady from Missouri rise?"

"St. Louis and I today rise in solidarity with the Palestinian people," Bush responded.

The Squad was not alone. Rep. Betty McCollum of Minnesota rose to slam the assault on Gaza, as did Reps. Andre Carson of Indiana, Chuy Garcia of Illinois, and Joaquin Castro of Texas.

As chair of the House Appropriations Defense Subcommittee, McCollum had influence over U.S. foreign military aid. "The unrestricted, unconditioned $3.8 billion in annual U.S. military aid . . . gives a green light to Israel's occupation of Palestine because there is no accountability and there is no oversight by Congress," McCollum said. "This must change. Not one dollar of U.S. aid to Israel should go toward a military detention of Palestinian children, the annexation of Palestinian lands, or the destruction of Palestinian homes."

Castro thanked Tlaib for her presence, agreeing with her statement "My mere existence has disrupted the status quo." He seemed to address Israeli leaders directly when he said that "creeping de facto annexation is unjust." "The forced eviction of families in Jerusalem is wrong," Castro said from the floor, offering what would have been an uncontroversial assertion most anywhere else, but that was a foreign one to the House floor.

Marie Newman, who had been beaten by the combined force of No Labels and AIPAC donors in 2018, had come back and won in 2020, and she joined her colleagues on the floor. Newman had started right away. In January 2021, she spoke out publicly against Israel's unequal distribution of the Covid-19 vaccine, demanding that the country vaccinate people in the Palestinian territories it was occupying and allow the vaccine to get to Gaza through the blockade. She organized a letter sent to Secretary of State Antony Blinken demanding that he act. "They ended up negotiating that the vaccine would go through. And so, as a freshman, that was kind of a big coup," she said. "Never before on any matter that engaged on Palestine, on any letter, resolution, legislation, did you get 23 or 25 members of Congress to sign up something, it just didn't happen. So, we felt like, Oh, gosh, this is so good. Then that's when the DMFI first was like, 'Oh, shit, she's a pain. She's a problem.'"

Newman was warned that being outspoken on the issue would come with a cost. "A couple of folks in my delegation, and then a couple of folks in Congress that were Democrats—more conservative than I am, said, you know, you need to be careful, because it's really going to ruffle some feathers," she told me. Speaking against the Gaza War on the floor brought out more opposition. "That's when I started getting donors that had given to me in 2018, and even some of them in 2020, saying, 'This is going to really hurt you, Marie, just so you understand.' And it did; they were correct."

The hour of speeches critical of Israel's bombing of Gaza was a sloshing together of watery metaphors—a high-water mark and also a watershed moment, one that unleashed a flood of money that would erode the foundation on which the Squad had built its power to date.

After the success of Sanders, Democratic politicians began to recognize that voters were in a progressive mood. This early recognition had saved Ed Markey's Senate seat and produced the environment in which progressive Democrats—and groups like the Sunrise Movement—had so much influence over legislation. If Sanders had led a self-described political revolution, the Gaza speeches galvanized the counterrevolution and brought tens of millions of dollars off the sidelines and into Democratic primaries, with the express purpose of blunting the progressive wave. "We're seeing much more vocal detractors of the U.S.-Israel relationship, who are having an impact on the discussion," Howard Kohr, head of AIPAC, told the *Washington Post* in a rare interview. "And we need to respond."

Throughout the 2020 cycle, AIPAC had been content to let DMFI run the big-money operation in Democratic primaries. To encourage support for it, AIPAC donors were even allowed to count money given to DMFI as credit toward their AIPAC contributions, which then won them higher-tier perks at conferences and other events. But the unprecedented display of progressive Democratic support for Palestinians amid the Gaza War, as seen on the House floor, was triggering.

The problem, Kohr said, was "the rise of a very vocal minority on the far left of the Democratic Party that is anti-Israel and seeks to weaken and diminish the relationship. Our view is that support for the U.S.-Israel relationship is both good policy and good politics. We wanted to defend our friends and to send a message to detractors that there's a group of individuals that will oppose them." The organization began making plans for that "group of individuals" to be able to deliver their message.

Coming out of the 2020 cycle, Democratic Majority for Israel had recalibrated. It had spent *only* about two million dollars against Bowman to support Engel. Aside from making sure it relied on *Democratic* millionaires and billionaires, to avoid the bad press that came from Republican money, the organization also vowed not to underspend again.

The first chance of the 2022 cycle to test its power came when Biden named his cabinet. He owed Jim Clyburn big time—the South Carolina Democrat's endorsement had delivered his home state and set Biden up for a knockout blow on Super Tuesday—and Clyburn lobbied for top jobs for his allies, among them, Rep. Marcia Fudge, who represented the district that includes Cleveland. Just don't pigeonhole the Black woman as the housing and urban development secretary, Clyburn told Biden, referring to the role Trump had assigned for brain surgeon Ben Carson, who knew nothing about housing. Fudge repeated the request, saying HUD was the one place she didn't want to be named. Biden sent her to HUD, and that freed up a seat.

Nina Turner, who had represented large parts of the district as a state senator and who came to national prominence as a surrogate for Sanders, quickly jumped into the race. Turner had been on quite a journey, having marched along a fairly conventional political career path until the first Sanders campaign: an aide to a state senator and then to the Cleveland mayor, a lobbyist for the local school district, then a city councilor and a state senator herself. Bill Clinton had supported Turner's failed bid for Ohio secretary of state, and Turner had been active with the Ready for Hillary super PAC and was otherwise organizing on behalf of Clinton's presidential bid. Then, in November 2015, Turner switched sides and endorsed Sanders. As she told the local press, her husband had turned her on to Bernie. She went all in. Whatever allegiance she had felt to the party establishment didn't hold her back, and she quickly became Sanders's most popular national surrogate, a position that owed partly to the lack of many others, but also to Turner's soaring, morally charged oratory. Adding Turner to the Squad had long been a fantasy draft dream of Sanders supporters.

Turner coupled her national fund-raising base with her popularity in the district—she was immediately endorsed by a slew of establishment figures, who hadn't been turned off by her turn toward political revolution—and jumped out to a 30–40 point lead over the crowded field. By any standard measure, the race was over: nobody had the combination of support on the ground and fund-raising capacity to compete.

But for the Squad, these were no longer standard elections, as Turner would learn. Shontel Brown, the chair of the Cuyahoga Democratic Party, entered the race (without stepping down from her party position) and emerged as Turner's most viable opponent. Brown knew things had changed, and engaged in one of the more flagrant acts of political panhandling in the post–Citizens United era. The one guardrail the five Supreme Court justices had established when it came to unlimited money in campaigns was around "independence." The idea was that if a person or company was spending money "independently" of their candidate, there could therefore be no quid pro quo and no appearance of corruption. To maintain this alleged independence, a super PAC was barred from coordinating directly with candidates' campaigns. People quickly found ways around the ban, as indirect coordination was allowed. For instance, a campaign could post raw footage of the candidate on its website, and the super PAC was free to use that footage. The campaign could also post opposition research and point toward the messages that worked for them and against their opponent. Campaigns would often put these messages inside a red box on their websites, to make them easier for the super PAC to find, and this information dump soon took on the simple name "red box."

Brown's campaign had its own red box, linked to a document collecting dirt on Turner. This was standard practice, but underneath it was the real tell: three rotating quotes from prominent advocates for Israel validating Brown's support for the state. The first was from Mark Mellman, and though he wore many hats—most prominently as head of the Mellman Group—the site labeled him "DMFI PAC President." DMFI had endorsed Brown in February but had not spent on her behalf yet. Brown clearly wanted this to change.

Amid the Gaza War, Turner retweeted a Jewish advocacy group, IfNotNow, that is the bane of right-wing "pro-Israel" groups. The news outlet Jewish Insider flagged the post in an article, noting the divergence on the issue between Turner and Brown. "Advocacy groups such as Pro-Israel America and Democratic Majority for Israel," reported Jewish Insider, "have also thrown their support behind Brown, who has had to contend with Turner's substantial war chest with less than three months remaining until the August 3 primary, according to the latest filings from the Federal Election Commission." Brown would not have to contend with that disadvantage for long.

DMFI had spent $6 million in the 2020 cycle, across all races—a big sum, but not the kind of thing that an organized and growing movement couldn't contend with. At the end of June 2021, DMFI came into the Turner race with its first ad buy of more than $300,000. The group kept up that spending until Election Day in August, bankrolling TV and digital ads, direct mail, phone banking, and billboards and newspaper ads throughout the district. Much of the money—totaling more than $2 million by the end—came from Stacy Schusterman, chair of an oil and gas company.

The spending brought Brown back from the dead, and in a straight-up contest between the two candidates, Turner's previous rhetoric about the party establishment came back to bite her. After Sanders had dropped out, it's unlikely Turner envisioned a Cleveland congressional seat opening up in a few months. Otherwise, she probably wouldn't have said, in an obscure online interview, that voting for Biden was like "eating half a bowl of shit."

After the passage of the American Rescue Plan, Biden was riding high with Democratic voters, and DMFI blanketed the district with Turner's "bowl of shit" comment. Hillary Clinton, paying Turner back for her disloyalty, endorsed Brown, as did Rep. Jim Clyburn and, painfully for Turner, the Congressional Black Caucus. The machine of Hakeem Jeffries, of which DMFI was a party, swung into action.

DMFI also preposterously hit Turner for allegedly opposing both a fifteen-dollar-an-hour minimum wage and universal health care. The ads were flat-out lies, attempting to rest their claim on the fact that Turner had voted against the DNC platform as a delegate, arguing that it was too moderate. The platform, partly thanks to Turner, had included support for the fifteen-dollar wage and the aspiration of universal health care—so, therefore, DMFI argued, Turner opposed both.

Even though DMFI's ads never mentioned Israel, back home in the district, the intensity of the Gaza War heightened focus on Turner's race in heavily Jewish communities. She said she was told that she ought to distance herself from members of the Squad—particularly Muslim representatives Tlaib and Omar—or face an onslaught. "I was told by a prominent Jewish businessman that 'We're coming at you with everything we got. You need to disavow the Squad,'" Turner told me, and "if I didn't do it, they were coming for me; and that also [the] Palestinian community didn't have rights that were more important than the State of Israel." She continued: "I even have emails right now, to this day, of local, primarily business, leaders in the Jewish community, where they were encouraging Republicans to vote in this primary and were saying things like 'We must support Shontel Brown. In no way can we let Nina Turner win this race,'" Turner said.

She forwarded some of these to me.

"This is a very important election for our community!" wrote one Turner opponent in an email to neighbors. "Shontel's main opponent, Nina Turner, was the honorary co-chair of the Sanders 2020 presidential campaign, as well as the leader of 'Our Revolution,' the post-2016 organization of Sanders enthusiasts. She has raised money proclaiming her desire to join 'the Squad' and has been endorsed by Congresswoman Ilhan Omar (see Turner fund-raising emails attached below)."

Another neighbor forwarded the email to still more folks, adding, "Many of us wouldn't bother with this primary election but this one is really important and electing Shontel Brown is a must. Whether a R or a D[,] you can elect to vote in the D primary."

On August 3, 2021, Turner lost to Brown 45 to 50 percent, falling short by roughly 4,000 votes. The deluge of money following the Gaza attacks was one difference. "Had that race been in May, you would be interviewing Congresswoman Nina Turner, that's irrefutable," she said. Another difference was turnout. The progressive case had long been that unapologetic support for working people would draw those people to the polls. Nobody was less apologetic than Turner, yet turnout was a typically anemic 17 percent in the special election. Brown singled out the city of Beachwood's and nearby Shaker Heights's heavily Jewish areas, where an impressively organized effort had seen turnout climb above 30 percent—double the rest of the district, an unheard-of disparity. Those votes alone made the difference. "I thank my Jewish brothers and sisters," Brown said during her victory speech, pledging unwavering support for Israel.

Turner's own Election Night speech decried the big-money intervention. "I am going to work hard to ensure that something like this never happens to a progressive candidate again," she told her dejected supporters. "We didn't lose this race—the evil money manipulated and maligned this election." The characterization of the funding as "evil," mixed with the notion of manipulation, brought out fresh charges of anti-Semitism against her. Around the country, would-be Squad members watched the race closely, with some calibrating accordingly and others bracing for what was coming.

In September 2021, a month after Turner's loss, Congress prepared to cut Israel a fresh check. It was considering its latest bill to both avoid a government shutdown and raise the debt ceiling—a legislative maneuver needed to avert both default on the debt and a global financial crisis—and Pelosi decided at the last minute to add a billion dollars in new money to the bill to replenish Israel's Iron Dome, which had been depleted by the Gaza War. The round number had a symbolic, slapped-together feel and was well out of whack with what the

United States had previously provided, representing 60 percent of the total funding given to the Iron Dome over the entire last decade. Sen. Pat Leahy, who chaired the Appropriations Committee, which doles out the money, told reporters the request wasn't remotely an urgent one. "The Israelis haven't even taken the money that we've already appropriated," he said. Democrats, though, were making a billion-dollar point, whether the money was needed or not.

But so was the Squad. Jayapal, backed up by the now six members of the Squad and by Minnesota's Betty McCollum and Illinois's Marie Newman, threatened to take the bill down if the money were included. Pelosi relented and pulled the bill from the floor on a Tuesday. The Washington insider outlet Axios described the stunning development for its readers: "Why it matters: There has never been a situation where military aid for Israel was held up because of objections from members of Congress."

Mark Mellman's client Yair Lapid, not yet prime minister, was serving at the time as Israel's foreign minister. According to a readout later provided by the Israeli government, Lapid called Steny Hoyer to demand to know what had happened. Hoyer assured him that it was a "technical" glitch and that the House would get Israel its money quickly.

Making good on his promise, Hoyer moved to schedule a new vote, suspending the House rules so the bill could hit the floor on Thursday of that week. Omar spoke with him the night before and pleaded for a delay, arguing that a spending increase that large needed to at least be discussed and that there were other ways to move the legislation. Why use this moment, Omar asked him, to force a fiery debate on the House floor? Doing it this way would put a target on the backs of the opponents, she said—with part of her aware that this was the precise purpose of hurrying with the vote. "Israel wants a stand-alone vote to show the overwhelming support for Iron Dome," Hoyer told Omar.

Bowman and Ocasio-Cortez both lobbied Hoyer for a delay or for a different legislative vehicle, but both were told the same thing. The vote was going ahead. In a floor speech, Rep. Ted Deutch charged Tlaib with anti-Semitism for accurately referring to Israel's government as engaged in apartheid. Pelosi made an unexpected appearance to claim that the proposed money was part of a deal President Obama had cut with Israel to fund Iron Dome. Voting against the funding, speaker after speaker said, would be tantamount to killing innocent Israeli civilians. "All of this framing starts to cross a new line—that we are now removing and defunding existing defense, when the bill is actually just shoveling on more," Ocasio-Cortez texted from the Capitol, trying to lay out her frame of mind. "Meanwhile the vitriol started to really heat up—AIPAC has escalated to very explicit, racist targeting of us that very much translates to safety issues. This is creating a tinderbox of incitement, with the cherry on top being that *Haaretz*'s caricature of me holding and shooting a Hamas rocket into Jerusalem with Rashida and Ilhan cheering on." Back at home in New York, she said, rabbis from City Island who were typically progressive and on her side were sending out mass emails warning that her vote would put people's lives at risk. She had even been banned from attending High Holidays in her district.

Ocasio-Cortez walked onto the House floor and voted against the Iron Dome funding. She and Bowman, in the neighboring district, had gotten a barrage of calls and emails to their offices urging them to support the funding, but almost nothing at all from constituents telling them to vote it down. "Those on the 'yes' side were very clear, and very loud, and very consistent with why they believed the vote needed to be 'yes,'" Bowman told me. "And that's why I'm saying there needs to be much organizing on the left around this issue and others." But back in the cloakroom, Ocasio-Cortez was shaken. For the first time in her life, she had been trailed that week by her own private security detail, the Capitol Police having refused to offer protection, even as the FBI was investigating four credible threats on her life, one of them a still-active kidnapping plot.

The other three members of the original Squad—Pressley, Omar, and Tlaib—had all cast "no" votes. The two newest additions, though, were split, with Cori Bush voting "no," but Bowman voting to approve the funding. In the cloakroom, AOC began to tear up while telling Omar and Tlaib that she felt she had to go out there and change her vote.

"Alex, it's fine," Omar said, embracing her. "Just don't go out there and cry." Omar was a big believer in the mantra that you couldn't let them see they'd hurt you.

Tlaib cut in. "Ilhan, stop telling people not to cry!" They all laughed, knowing Rashida's penchant for letting her emotions flow freely down her cheeks.

It may have been good advice from Omar, but Ocasio-Cortez didn't put it into practice. On the floor, she saw Pelosi, who knew AOC was angry at being forced to vote on the funding. Pelosi approached her, telling her she hadn't wanted this stand-alone vote, that it was Hoyer, who controlled the floor schedule, who had forced it. "Vote your heart," she told Ocasio-Cortez.

AOC broke down, this time on the floor, with tears flowing in full view of the press and her colleagues, some of whom gave a shoulder of compassion, others giving awkward back pats as they slid past. She switched her vote to "present."

Speculation about the tactical designs behind the vote quickly shot through the press. Did this nod toward the pro-Israel camp mean AOC was angling for a New York State Senate bid? Was she worried that redistricting would bring heavily Jewish New York suburbs into her territory? Or was all of it just becoming too much?

Her "present" vote was the epitome of Ocasio-Cortez's effort to be the consensus builder and the radical all at once. Voting her heart, she felt, would have permanently undermined her ability to serve as a peacemaker on the issue. "While I wanted to vote NO[,] the dynamics back home were devolving so fast that I felt voting P[resent] was the only way I could maintain some degree of peace at home—enough to bring folks together to the table[,] because all this whipped things up to an all out war," she said.

Omar and Tlaib held firm, though, and the threats of violence ratcheted up. "For Muslim members of Congress, it's a level no one understands," Omar messaged me when speaking about the death threats the next day. "The anti-American rhetoric is a violent beast and our vote yesterday makes it 10x worse."

Marie Newman also faced serious pressure after she had announced her opposition. Ahead of the vote, she said she got a call from a member of party leadership, and from other from rank-and-file members, urging her to reconsider. Pressure had been applied in the run-up to the vote, too. "I was like, well, it is what it is. It's done. And I feel good about it," she said. The resistance was fiercest on the floor during the vote. "I got bullied on the House floor. Two of AIPAC's members—congressional members—came over and literally yelled at me," she said, demanding to know why she had voted the funding down. "First of all, my husband is an engineer, and from an engineering standpoint, there's no way that battery system costs a billion dollars," she told them. But also, she said, her district was opposed to it and would rather the billion dollars be spent here, in the United States.

The next day, Ocasio-Cortez sent a long note of apology to her constituents. "The reckless decision by House leadership to rush this controversial vote within a matter of hours and without true consideration created a tinderbox of vitriol, disingenuous framing, [and] deeply racist accusations and depictions," she wrote. "To those I have disappointed—I am deeply sorry. To those who believe this reasoning is insufficient or cowardice—I understand."

Turner soon announced that she'd be seeking a rematch against Brown in the spring of 2022. That's when DMFI's reinforcements arrived—in the form not just of AIPAC, but also of crypto and Silicon Valley money, which flowed in. AIPAC finally stepped into the super PAC game in April 2022, funding what it called the United Democracy Project. It would go on to spend thirty million dollars, with its first broadside being launched against Turner.

A third group joined in, called Mainstream Democrats PAC, funded by LinkedIn billionaire Reid Hoffman. Mainstream Dems and DMFI were effectively the same organization, operating out of the same office and employing the same consultants, though Mainstream Democrats claimed a broader mission. Strategic and targeting decisions for both were made by pollster Mark Mellman, according to Dmitri Mehlhorn, a Silicon Valley executive who serves as the political adviser to LinkedIn's Hoffman. DMFI also funneled at least five hundred thousand dollars to Mainstream Democrats PAC. Together, Mehlhorn and Mellman controlled the kind of money that could reshape any race they targeted.

"Our money is going to the Mainstream Democrats coalition, which we trust to identify the candidates who are most likely to convey to Americans broadly an image of Democrats that is then electable," Mehlhorn told me, saying he relied on the consultants linked to DMFI to make those choices. "I trust them. I think Brian Goldsmith, Mark Mellman—they tend to know that stuff."

The constellation of super PACs and dark-money groups around No Labels, the political vehicle for Josh Gottheimer and Joe Manchin, kicked into gear, targeting progressives in primaries around the country. And then came the crypto. Hoffman's super PAC spent heavily, while crypto billionaire Sam Bankman-Fried, his Ponzi scheme having yet to collapse, chipped in a million dollars against Turner. SBF, as he became known, seeded his Protect Our Future PAC with nearly thirty million dollars and began spending huge sums.

Mehlhorn, Hoffman's right-hand man, was explicit about his purpose. "Nina Turner's district is a classic case study, where the vast majority of voters in that district are Marcia Fudge voters. They're pretty happy with the Democratic Party. And Nina Turner's record on the Democratic Party is [that] she's a strong critic," he told me. "And so, this group put in money to make sure that voters knew what she felt about the Democratic Party. And from my perspective, that just makes it easier for me to try to do things like give Tim Ryan a chance of winning [a U.S. Senate seat] in a state like Ohio—not a big chance, but at least a chance. And he's not having to deal with the latest bomb thrown by Nina. So anyway, that's the theory behind our support for Mainstream Democrats."

Mellman, in an interview with *HuffPost*, acknowledged that his goals extended beyond the politics of Israel and Palestine. "The anti-Biden folks and the anti-Israel folks look to [Turner] as a leader," Mellman said. "So she really is a threat to both of our goals." His remark was itself a case study in the strength of Washington narratives to withstand reality. The party's right flank, led by Manchin, Sinema, and Gottheimer, was actively undermining Biden's agenda, while Turner's allies in Congress were the ones fighting for it.

In response to DMFI's spending in 2020, the group J Street, a rival of AIPAC that takes a more progressive line on Palestinian rights, launched its own super PAC to compete. Its leaders guessed DMFI would spend somewhere between five and ten million dollars. If the advocacy group could cobble together two million, said J Street's Logan Bayroff, that would at least be something of a fight, given that AIPAC and DMFI had to overcome the fact that what they were advocating for—unchecked, limitless support for the Israeli government, regardless of its abuses—was unpopular in Democratic primaries. "We're always gonna expect the right to have more money, given that they're operating off of the basis of big donors. But that's a little bit more of a fair fight," he said of the disparity between J Street and DMFI. "But now you add to what DMFI is doing, 30 million [dollars] from AIPAC—that's just in a whole other realm," he said. "It's been a radical transformation in the politics of Israel-Palestine and the politics of Democratic primaries."

Going into 2022, Turner was joined by the biggest number of boldly progressive candidates running viable campaigns in open seats since the Sanders wing had become a national force. There was Gregorio Casar in Austin, Delia Ramirez in Chicago, Maxwell Alejandro Frost in Orlando, Becca Balint in Vermont, Summer Lee in Pittsburgh, Nida Allam and Erica Smith in North Carolina, Donna Edwards in Maryland, Andrea Salinas in Oregon, Marie Gluesenkamp Perez in Washington State, and John Fetterman and Mandela Barnes running for Senate in Pennsylvania and Wisconsin, both, coincidentally, their respective state's lieutenant governor. Also in Oregon, Jamie McLeod-Skinner was challenging incumbent Kurt Schrader, one of the most conservative Democrats left in Congress, who had made it his personal mission to block the Build Back Better Act and to stop Medicare from negotiating drug prices.

Redistricting had also produced two progressive-on-centrist primaries between sitting Democratic members of Congress, as Marie Newman and Andy Levin were both crammed in against centrist incumbents. On January 31, kick-starting the primary season, Jewish Insider published a list of fifteen DMFI House endorsements, nearly all of them squaring off against progressive challengers.

"In Michigan and Illinois, Reps. Haley Stevens (D-MI) and Sean Casten (D-IL) are, with support from DMFI, waging respective battles against progressive Reps. Andy Levin (D-MI) and Marie Newman (D-IL), who have frequently clashed with the pro-Israel establishment over their criticism of the Jewish state," the Jewish Insider piece read.

Levin was a scion of a powerhouse Michigan family that included Carl Levin, his uncle and a former lion of the Senate, and former Ways and Means chair Sander Levin, Andy's father. Any Levin had been redistricted into a primary against another incumbent Democrat, Haley Stevens, who became conspicuously outspoken about her unwavering support for Israel, becoming one of just 18 Democrats casting public doubt on the wisdom of Biden's reentering the Iran nuclear deal. To include Levin among an anti-Israel cohort stretched the definition to a breaking point. Wrote Jewish Insider, "While Levin, a former synagogue president, describes himself as a Zionist and opposes BDS, the Michigan political scion has frequently clashed with the pro-Israel establishment over his criticism of the Israeli government, including the recent introduction of legislation that would, among other things, condemn Israeli settlements while placing restrictions on U.S. aid to Israel."

The attack on Levin helped define what DMFI meant by pro-Israel. It included support for expanding settlements and ruled out criticism of the Israeli government. That Levin couldn't be written off as anti-Semitic made him that much more of a threat. That he was willing to defend colleagues like Omar and Tlaib was intolerable. Accusing Tlaib of anti-Semitism is made difficult if a former synagogue president has her back. AIPAC CEO Kohr, asked by the *Washington Post* why Levin was targeted, said, "It was Congressman Levin's willingness to defend and endorse some of the largest and most vocal detractors of the U.S.-Israel relationship."

But it was no coincidence that Levin was also known as the most pro-labor member of the House, not a friend of the super-wealthy donors who backed DMFI, AIPAC, and Reid Hoffman's PAC. Marie Newman also understood that it wasn't all about Israel. "DMFI, just to be clear, did not enjoy my pro-worker stance, my health equity stance," she said. "They did not like any of that, because it's a very corporate group."

In January, DMFI released its first list of fifteen endorsements, the start of the year's battle to shape what the next Democratic class would look like. A consultant for Maxwell Frost texted the Orlando candidate to let him know his opponent was on the list. "Didn't think they would hop in so early," Frost, vying to be the first Zoomer Democrat in Congress, texted back. "They hate progressives lol."

The constellation of progressive groups that played in Democratic primaries scrambled to respond. Their loose coalition consisted of J Street, Justice Democrats, Sunrise Movement, Indivisible, the Working Families Party, the Congressional Progressive Caucus PAC, and Way to Win.

This last group was its own big-money operation, organized largely by Leah Hunt-Hendrix, who had descended from a Texas oil fortune and had a knack for bringing together wealthy liberals and channeling their energy into efforts to drag the party leftward. The number of rich people in the country interested in doing this was severely limited, but it didn't take many to have an impact. In the 2022 cycle, Way to Win's PAC raised $5 million and used it to back candidates directly; it also funneled several million dollars to Justice Democrats and the Working Families Party. Its 501(c)(4) and 501(c)(3) spent even more heavily but spread the money around to organizations as well as campaigns. Way to Win and its donors weren't limited to supporting progressives in primaries; they also spent significant resources in Arizona and Georgia in particular, laying the groundwork for pivotal Senate and Electoral College wins there. In total, according to a year-end report circulated to donors, Way to Win "moved" $82 million—meaning it raised and spent the money itself on—or advised one of its 178 individual donors to direct it to—429 progressive organizations, from local ones to state and national.

Because Justice Democrats had been unable to form a collaborative relationship with the Squad, it hadn't been able to raise the kind of small dollars that AOC or the Sanders campaign could. This meant it was increasingly relying on the small number of left-wing wealthy people who wanted to be involved in electoral politics and were okay angering the Democratic establishment. This left the organization without many donors, but with enough to stay relevant.

Collectively, the groups would be lucky to cobble together ten million dollars, up against well more than fifty million in outside spending, and that's before counting the money that corporate-friendly candidates could raise themselves. Remarkably, the Squad and Bernie Sanders were conspicuously absent from this organized effort to expand their progressive numbers.

In the summer of 2020, facing down their most intense opposition from within their party, the four members had created a PAC called the Squad Victory Fund. But in the 2022 cycle, it raised just $1.9 million, and a close look at the finances show that it spent nearly a million dollars to raise that money—renting email lists to hit with fund-raising requests, advertising on Facebook, and so on. The remaining million was doled out mostly to the members of the Squad.

Had the Squad worked collaboratively with the coalition of organizations—lending their name, attending fund-raising events, and the like—several million dollars could have been raised. If Sanders had turned on his fire hose, the resources available to the left would have been considerable. As it was, the left had to find a way to even the playing field, and, to a handful of progressive operatives, Sam Bankman-Fried seemed like the only path left.

After SBF was arrested, he texted with a reporter at *Vox*, saying his effective altruism evangelism and woke politics was all a cover. "It's what reputations are made of, to some extent. I feel bad for those who got fucked by it," he said in a series of direct messages the reporter published, "by this dumb game we woke westerners [*sic*] play where we say all the right shib[b]oleths and so everyone likes us."

The coalition had data scientist and activist Sean McElwee on the inside, and he was adept at wielding those shibboleths. Organizers in the coalition decided to try to make use of the connection. The head of Data for Progress, a polling firm with lefty branding, McElwee was working closely with Bankman-Fried. The former was a polarizing figure in progressive circles who had burst onto the scene in 2018 hosting a series of progressive happy hours in New York City, boosting the campaign of Ocasio-Cortez, a happy hour attendee, and popularizing the phrase "Abolish ICE." He would then pivot to become a pundit-pollster who decried phrases like "Abolish ICE" as too fringe and harmful to the party. McElwee fancied himself an operator, and in 2020 he had bucked the New York socialist world by championing an eccentric city councilor from the Bronx, Ritchie Torres, for Congress over a DSA- and AOC-backed candidate. Torres, Afro-Latino, openly gay, and the product of public housing, became the most vocal critic of the rising socialist movement energy in New York, aligning himself with the crypto world and with the hard-line pro-Israel community.

"In New York City we've seen the rise of the Democratic Socialists of America, which is explicitly pro-BDS," Torres said in a private meeting with DMFI after winning his 2020 primary, video of which was leaked to me. "The democratic socialist left endorsed in about eleven races and won every single one except mine. So, it's proven to be effective at winning elections, and I worry about the normalization of anti-Semitism within progressive politics."

Torres went on to say that his own identity as a gay man influenced how he approached the question of Israel: "If the message to those who are both progressive and pro-Israel, especially to those of Jewish descent, is that in order for you to be part of the progressive community you have to renounce your identity and your history and your ties to your own homeland—and you have to be in the closet—that, to me, is profoundly evil; that's a perversion of progressivism."

A DMFI board member told Torres in the meeting that "it was so beautiful and almost—not other-worldly, but amazing the way you speak with such honesty and conviction about Israel . . . I just wish we could clone you so there were a million Ritchies running around talking about Israel." In other words, Torres was an ideal messenger to both DMFI and the crypto crew—if they could get to him. To start, they connected Frost, also Afro-Latino, with Torres for a conversation.

Rasha Mubarak, a Palestinian American consultant who'd marched with Frost to free Palestine, warned him away from Torres. "I said, 'Do you know that this person is not progressive at all?' I go, 'He *seems* progressive, but he's actually very problematic, not just on Palestine.'"

To reassure his early and most energetic supporters, Frost sat down on a Zoom call on March 9 with several dozen activists with the Florida Palestine Network for a conversation about his views. A former state senator, Dwight Bullard, joined the call. "My hope was, in being on that call, that he would feel a sense of camaraderie, if you will: 'I'm letting you know publicly I'm an ally of Florida Palestine Network, and it's okay to speak your mind,'" said Bullard.

In the legislature, Bullard had been introduced to the issue of BDS when Florida lawmakers pushed to strip state contracts from any company that endorsed the movement. Bullard was not himself a BDS supporter, but he believed the right to boycott was central to any struggle for dignity or civil rights and certainly was no business of the Florida Senate. "To me just on its face, it sounded like a repressive anti–First Amendment kind of thing. If students at Florida State wanted to boycott Coca-Cola, we wouldn't even be having this conversation, but here we are making this part of our legislation."

On the Zoom call, Bullard came away believing that Frost was in sync. "I heard him say he was in alignment with that group, that he would be an ally if elected to Congress," Bullard said.

A year earlier, Frost had signed a Palestinian Feminist Collective pledge that was to be delivered to Rep. Val Demings. Among its propositions, it pledged to "heed the call of Palestinian civil society for Boycott,

Divestment, and Sanctions" and called "for an end to US political, military, and economic support to Israel, and to all military, security, and policing collaborations."

According to four Florida Palestine Network members and allies on the call, Frost was clear he still stood with them. "I support BDS, which is a grassroots movement," he said. Though there is no recording of the call, Ahmad Daraldik of FPN, who was on it, added the quote to a group text going on at the time, and others on the call remember Frost saying it. "AWESOME!! Good job everyone," Maram Al-Dada texted the group in response to Daraldik's transcription. Frost later confirmed to me that he had made the promise. Perhaps even more important, he had said it as he was crafting his official Israel-Palestine policy position, in direct collaboration with his long-time allies in the Florida Palestine Network.

As far as political organizing in America is supposed to go, the Florida Palestine Network had done everything right: build an association of like-minded people, project power through rallies and lobbying of local officials, and back a candidate for Congress, holding that candidate accountable for positions he had staked out. Alexis de Tocqueville himself would easily have recognized their work as a quintessential element of democracy in action in the United States. But Tocqueville knew nothing of super PACs.

That's where Torres came in. Frost told me the two bonded over their shared identity when they spoke later in March. "We mainly just spoke about being young and Afro-Latino," Frost said. "[Torres] said that he was really excited to get more Afro-Latinos in Congress, and especially young men of color, and that's when he offered up his endorsement and his help and support."

Torres told me the same in an interview in the Capitol. "What I found most compelling about [Frost] was his youth. I remember running for the city council at age twenty-four, and I was drawn to the notion of the first Gen Z member of Congress. And then, when I met him, he's just incredibly impressive," he said.

I asked Torres if he had talked to Frost specifically about the Israel-Palestine issue. "We spoke about a variety of issues, and it is not my place to tell either a present or future colleague how to think or what to think," he said. "You know, I might encourage him to keep an open mind, listen to every side of the debate. But ultimately, when you're a member of Congress, you have to be your own person. You have to come to your own conclusions, and he's going to be fiercely independent."

DMFI had already endorsed Frost's opponent in the race, Randolph Bracy, and I asked if Torres had helped talk them out of spending actual money on behalf of Bracy. "We had a difference of opinion in the race," he said. "I'm convinced that Maxwell [Frost] represents exactly what we need in Congress," he added. "Those organizations are going to do what's in their interests. It's not my place to tell people whom to endorse or what to endorse," he repeated. "Just like I want others to respect my right to act independently, I would extend other individuals and institutions that same courtesy."

I also asked if he had put in a good word with the crypto world on behalf of Frost. "I don't tell them what to do, and you have to be careful," Torres said, referring to campaign laws around super PACs and coordination. "But obviously, it was known that I had publicly endorsed him."

Rachel Rosen, a spokesperson for DMFI, told me that Frost reached out to them "to hear our views on Israel related issues," she said. "We had several conversations with him and his team and were pleased to see the way his views evolved on U.S.-Israel policy as he learned more about the substance."

When it came to crypto, most candidates didn't need to "evolve" a past position because, given that crypto was so new, they didn't *have* past positions.

In early April, in the wake of Torres's endorsement of Frost, the fight for crypto support was on. Bracy, Frost's opponent, who had DMFI's stated support but not its money, made a play for crypto. A state senator, Bracy announced the formation of a legislative caucus that would include federal and state lawmakers interested in crafting crypto policy. Frost followed on April 27 by announcing a "national council" to advise him on "cryptocurrency and blockchain technologies." The council included experts as well as straight-up crypto advocate Adelle Nazarian, CEO of the American Blockchain PAC. It also included both Sean McElwee and Leah Hunt-Hendrix.

On May 10, Frost appeared on a crypto podcast hosted by one of his crypto council members, and that evening, at a bar in the Adams Morgan neighborhood of Washington, DC, he held a fund-raiser hosted by McElwee, Hunt-Hendrix, and Ben Wessel, campaign director for the Emerson Collective, a for-profit corporation founded by Laurene Powell Jobs. Gabe Bankman-Fried, the brother of Sam Bankman-Fried, spoke at the fund-raiser and was handling much of the political spending.

According to sources inside Bankman-Fried's political operation, a deal was cut whereby DMFI and AIPAC would agree not to spend money to support Randolph Bracy and Bankman-Fried would pay DMFI $250,000 for staying out. The deal was struck, the sources said, by operative Dave Huynh, a former Kamala Harris aide who goes by the nom de guerre "Delegate Dave."

The check was cut and showed up in federal disclosure forms as a quarter-million-dollar contribution from Sam Bankman-Fried directly to DMFI. When a Bankman-Fried operative saw the monies pop up on the FEC's page on May 25, 2022, he shook his head, telling me later, "Republicans are so much better at doing dark money." SBF's team had forgotten to cloak the payoff.

McElwee and Hunt-Hendrix worked over the Bankman-Fried team in a broader effort to keep the new crypto king from wiping out progressive candidates elsewhere on the map, successfully persuading him not to come after Summer Lee, Donna Edwards, or Jasmine Crockett, a progressive who managed to win her Texas race thanks in no small part to signing on to a broad crypto-friendly agenda. "We kept them out where we could," said one operative who helped block some of the crypto flow.

Crypto money linked to SBF and his firm, FTX, flowed into Vermont, backing progressive state senator Becca Balint, who was running to become the first out lesbian to represent Vermont in Congress (and the first woman of any sexuality) against a corporate-backed establishment Democrat for the Green Mountain State's only House seat. In a rare bit of progressive consolidation, Kesha Ram Hinsdale dropped out and endorsed Balint. The crypto money was routed through the LGBTQ+ Victory Fund, disguising its true source.

SBF's Protect Our Future PAC announced on May 17 that it would be spending at least a million dollars to back Frost. Former representative Alan Grayson, competing with Frost for progressive votes, didn't buy the rationale that it was all about pandemic preparedness. "I don't think you'll ever see a more clear-cut example of somebody putting themselves up for sale," Grayson said, noting the proximity of the creation of the advisory board with the influx of crypto money from what he called "the Bahamas guy." He would hammer Frost for SBF's backing in the closing weeks of the campaign. "He auditioned for the role of corruption, and he won the part," said Grayson, who, before the deluge of money, had been polling competitively.

Frost had started the race an opponent of military aid to Israel and a supporter of the BDS movement and finished a candidate who wanted no strings attached to military aid to Israel and who considered BDS "extremely problematic and a risk to the chances of peace and a two-state solution." The length of Frost's journey was unusual only because he had begun as someone so vocally supportive of Palestinian rights, but other candidates wound up where he was under the same pressures.

John Fetterman was locked in what threatened to be a tight primary race with Rep. Conor Lamb for a Senate nomination, and Lamb's campaign was openly pleading for super PAC support to put him over the top. Early in the year, Jewish Insider reported, Mellman had reached out to Fetterman with questions about his position on Israel. "He's never come out and said that he's not a supporter of Israel, but the perception is that he aligns with the Squad more than anything else," Democratic activist Brett Goldman told the news outlet.

Mellman said the Fetterman campaign responded to his inquiry and "came with an interest in learning about the issues." Following the meeting, the campaign reached out again. "Then they sent us a position paper, which we thought was very strong," Mellman said. But it wasn't quite strong enough. Jewish Insider reported that DMFI emailed back some comments on the paper, which "Fetterman was receptive to addressing in a second draft."

In April, Fetterman agreed to do an interview with Jewish Insider. "I want to go out of my way to make sure that it's absolutely clear that the views that I hold in no way go along the lines of some of the more fringe or extreme wings of our party," he said. "I would also respectfully say that I'm not really a progressive in that sense." Fetterman, unprompted, stressed that there should be zero conditions on military aid to Israel, that BDS was wrong, and so on. "Let me just say this, even if I'm asked or not, I was dismayed by the Iron Dome vote," he added. DMFI and AIPAC stayed out of his race.

When the January list of races around which DMFI was building infrastructure came out, the progressive campaign ecosystem breathed a sigh of relief that Austin, Texas, was not on it. Progressives were backing a would-be Squad member there in the form of thirty-three-year-old city councilor Gregorio Casar. Frost said he watched Casar's race, adding, "We watched all the races, keeping up to date on everything that was going on across the country as far as voting trends, especially looking at the youth vote, different stuff like that that we thought might give us some trend information to help us in our race."

Casar's absence on DMFI's list, it turned out, came after a letter he had sent that month to a local rabbi, Alan Freedman, laying out his position on Israel. He was opposed to BDS, he promised, and supportive both of a two-state solution and of military aid to Israel. His letter to the rabbi was published by Jewish Insider the day after DMFI's endorsement list was unveiled. "The letter was in response to a lot of people continuing to insinuate that progressives," Casar said, "are anti-Semitic. That is just not true. And, in particular, I also mean really progressive members of Congress, who fight for Palestinian rights, I do not believe are anti-Semitic. But I have a certain policy position, which is, I do not believe we should be writing a blank check on military aid. I think that we should provide some amount of aid, but we should also make sure we're not funding human rights violations anywhere in the world. So that's what I told folks when I was asked privately. People pushed for me to think about things differently, and learn more, and I'm always open to learning more."

He decided to put this position down on paper. "I said, 'You know what, let's just write this down, so that Rabbi Freedman can share this with people.' And that means that there's a very decent chance it'll become public. I did not share it with J[ewish]I[nsider], but I'm not, you know. I don't hold it against journalists to get hold of things however you guys do it."

Casar's colleagues at the Democratic Socialists of America were shocked and began the process of rescinding their endorsement. To avoid a nasty fight, Casar voluntarily rescinded his request for DSA backing. "We have a long history of working with Greg Casar on health care, paid sick time, police budgets, homelessness, housing justice, union rights, and more. We will continue to discuss this issue within our chapter and many individual members will continue to support the campaign, but we will no longer be working on this campaign as an organization," the Austin chapter said in a statement. Justice Democrats, which does not have an Israel-Palestine litmus test, despite the protestations of DMFI, continued to back Caar, spending just over one hundred thousand dollars in support.

Summer Lee, in Pittsburgh, also saw the DMFI and AIPAC money coming. Among the incoming class, she and Casar had the most overlap with the already embedded Squad members. In 2018, Lee ran for the Pennsylvania House of Representatives as an unapologetic democratic socialist, unseating a member of a powerhouse Pittsburgh political family in a house race. Her win made national news but was overshadowed by her allies winning at the congressional level.

I asked Lee if she considered moderating her public views on Israel-Palestine to try to stay out of the crosshairs. She said that it would have been pointless. "I'm being very honest. There was no world in which I did not think this was gonna happen," she said. "From the moment I saw the ways in which the four Black and brown women who came in in 2018—which is the same year that I came into the state house—watching the way that they had to navigate the issue, knowing the way that they had to navigate money and politics, then seeing Nina Turner—it was a very clear trend to me."

The irony, she said, is that Israel was never an issue that she had made a significant part of her politics—much the same point Ocasio-Cortez had made four years earlier when she herself stumbled on it. "It's really funny because, for me, as a Black woman who is a progressive, Israel is not, at the state level—it's not an issue that we ever had to talk about, that we broached," she said. Yet she was told by allies that her campaign was going to have an "Israel problem," she told me. "We heard people in the establishment talk about it—you know, 'Summer's gonna have an Israel problem,' We honestly knew on day one—and before. So, on day zero, it was something that we were thinking about," she said. "The question was always, *when* does it come in, but I didn't think that I would have the privilege of avoiding it."

DMFI came out early for Lee's opponent, attorney Steve Irwin. "There's a context here that I think we ought to take cognizance of, which is to say that we have had some organized groups out there that have said they are attempting to execute, in their words, a hostile

takeover of the Democratic Party," Mellman told Jewish Insider, referring to the organization Justice Democrats but expanding his discussion to include DSA.

During the Gaza War in 2021, Lee had once posted support for
the Palestinian plight. "It was really one tweet that kind of caught the
attention of folks," she said. "Here, this is it, we got you. And it was
really a tweet talking about Black Lives Matter and talking about how,
as an oppressed person, I view and perceive the topic. Because the
reality is—and that's with a lot of Black and brown progressives—we
view even topics that don't seem connected, we still view them through
the injustice that we face as Black folks here and the politics that we
see and experience here, and are able to make connections to that."

Lee had written on Twitter: "When I hear American pols use the
refrain 'Israel has the right to defend itself' in response to undeniable atrocities on a marginalized population, I can't help but think of
how the West has always justified indiscriminate and disproportionate force and power on weakened and marginalized people. The US
has never shown leadership in safeguarding human rights of folks
it's othered. But as we fight against injustice here in the movement for
Black lives, we must stand against injustice everywhere. Inhuman-
ities against the Palestinian people cannot be tolerated or justified."
That was the extent of her public commentary on the question.

But the comment was shocking to some in Pittsburgh. Charles
Saul, a member of the board of trustees of the *Pittsburgh Jewish Chron-
icle*, was later quoted by the paper saying he was concerned about Lee
because "she's endorsed by some people I believe are antisemites [*sic*],
like Rashida Tlaib." He went on: "Another thing that worried me was
her equating the suffering of the Gazans and Palestinians to the suffering of African Americans. That's one of these intersectional things.
If that's her take on the Middle East, that's very dangerous."

In January 2022, AIPAC transferred $8.5 million of dark money
to the new super PAC it had set up the previous April, United Democracy Project. Private equity mogul and Republican donor Paul Singer
kicked in a million dollars, as did Republican Bernard Marcus, the
former CEO of Home Depot. Dozens of other big donors, many of them
also Republicans, along with more than a dozen uber-wealthy Democrats, kicked in big checks to give UDP its thirty-million-dollar war
chest.

The Bracy campaign, concerned that there had yet to be independent expenditure to them by either DMFI or AIPAC, reached out to
officials connected to both to ask what was up, according to a source
with direct knowledge of the exchanges. Bad news came back: Torres
and other influential figures had weighed in on Frost's behalf; Frost's
new position had made super PAC spending unnecessary. Bracy had
been a loyal pro-Israel soldier throughout his career, counted many
friends among the community, and had even gone to Israel on an
AIPAC-sponsored trips. But he was disposable, and Frost would do.

Relations between Frost and his earliest backers deteriorated
further, even as, that week, he received a number of endorsements in
Congress—from Bernie Sanders, Elizabeth Warren, Ed Markey, Pramila Jayapal, and the Congressional Progressive Caucus. On May 11,
Israel Defense Forces sparked global outrage, first, by killing Palestinian journalist Shireen Abu Akleh and then, again, days later at her
funeral procession, by attacking her mourners and pallbearers and
nearly toppling her casket. His consultant Rasha Mubarak reached
out to Frost, asking why he hadn't spoken out yet. "A journalist was
murdered," she texted him. "This is an easy time to speak out in solidarity for Palestine."

He texted back that he had seen the horrifying video of the funeral
and was willing to do a post. She asked him to send her a draft first,
but when he did, she was underwhelmed, to say the least. "You're not
even using the word Palestinians? That's part of an erasure in itself,'"
she said she told him, flagging his use of *folks* instead of *Palestinians*. "In how people message things, it erases us as Palestinians and
doesn't name our oppressor. That's a reason why this continues to
happen. Because the world lets them get away with it by misleading/
reporting the reality."

She continued: "Then he said he was gonna quote-tweet Secretary
[of State Antony] Blinken. And I said, 'Maxwell, you would never quote-
tweet Secretary Blinken or align yourself with Secretary Blinken on
any other issue. Why on Palestine are you choosing a watered-down
approach?' And I sent him Marie Newman's tweet, I sent him Bernie
Sanders's tweet." Her examples were apparently not persuasive—or,
perhaps, were persuasive in the opposite direction, as Newman and
Sanders were among those on whom DMFI had unloaded.

On May 15, Frost quote-tweeted a two-day-old Blinken post,

leaving in the word *folks* and adding a reference to *Palestinians* at the end as people who deserve the right to mourn without facing violence. Mubarak knew she had lost him.

That Tuesday in May was a day that DMFI, AIPAC, and Mainstream Democrats had been hoping would be a death blow to the nascent insurgency that had been gaining traction in the primaries. In April, AIPAC had begun its furious barrage of spending, tag-teaming with DMFI, Mainstream Democrats, and Sam Bankman-Fried to make sure Nina Turner's second run against Shontel Brown never got off the ground. Turner was smothered. Reid Hoffman's PAC had spent millions to prop up conservative Democratic representative Kurt Schrader, who was facing a credible challenge from Jamie McLeod-Skinner in Oregon.

Nida Allam, a Durham County commissioner and the first Muslim woman elected in the state, ran for office after three of her Muslim friends were murdered in a gruesome Chapel Hill hate crime that drew national attention. AIPAC would spend millions to stop her rise. Elsewhere in the state, it spent two million dollars against progressive Erica Smith in another open primary. United Democracy Project, for its part, began hammering away at Summer Lee, whose Pennsylvania primary was held the same day as North Carolina's.

Justice Democrats, the Working Families Party, Indivisible, the Congressional Progressive Caucus PAC, and the Sunrise Movement worked in coalition with J Street on a number of races in which DMFI and AIPAC played. Where the progressive organizations could muster enough money, the candidates had a shot. "If you look at the races we lost, we were outspent by the bad guys six, eight, ten to one. If you look at Summer's race, it was more like two to one," said Joe Dinkin, campaign director for the Working Families Party.

In a Chicago-area district, DMFI and Mainstream Dems backed Gilbert Villegas against progressive Delia Ramirez. But DMFI put in only $157,000, while Hoffman's PAC chipped in $65,000. VoteVets, an organization that almost exclusively backs corporate, centrist veteran candidates against progressives when it comes to Democratic primaries, was the big spender, putting in more than $950,000. But the progressive coalition made Ramirez's primary race a major priority, spending nearly $1.5 million to back her. She ended up winning by more than 40 points.

AIPAC and DMFI did manage to win their rematch against Marie

Newman, who had beaten the incumbent Democrat Dan Lipinski in 2020. That win had been critical, as Lipinski would certainly have been a "no" vote on Biden's Build Back Better and the Inflation Reduction Act. In 2022, Newman was redistricted out of her seat, with much of her former area being sent to a new district, the one Ramirez claimed. This forced Newman into an incumbent-on-incumbent contest with a centrist. AIPAC and DMFI also knocked off the synagogue president Andy Levin.

Nida Allam lost a close race, and Erica Smith, who also faced more than two million dollars in AIPAC money, was beaten soundly. And in Texas the following week, Jessica Cisneros was facing Rep. Henry Cuellar in a runoff she would lose by just a few hundred votes. But McLeod-Skinner knocked off Schrader, and progressive Andrea Salinas overcame an ungodly $11 million in Bankman-Fried money through Protect Our Future PAC to win another Oregon primary.

The marquee race, however, was in Pittsburgh, where AIPAC and DMFI combined to put in more than three million dollars for an ad blitz against Summer Lee in the race's closing weeks. In late March, Lee held a 25-point lead before the opposition money came in—and that amount of money can go a long way in the Pittsburgh TV market. As AIPAC's ads attacked Lee relentlessly as not a "real Democrat," she watched her polling numbers plummet.

But then she saw the race stabilize, as outside progressive groups pumped more than a million dollars in and her own campaign responded quickly to the charge that she wasn't loyal enough to the Democratic Party. Her backers made an issue of the fact that AIPAC had backed more than one hundred Republicans who had voted to overturn the 2020 election while pretending to care how good a Democrat Lee was.

"When we were able to counteract those narratives that [voters] were getting incessantly—the saturation point was unlike anything you've ever seen—when we knocked on doors, no one was ever saying, 'Oh, hey, does Summer have this particular view on Middle Eastern policy?' Like, that was never a conversation. It was, 'Is Summer a Trump supporter?'" she said. "We were able to get our counter ad up, a counter ad that did nothing but show a video of me stumping for Biden, for the party. When we were able to get that out, it started to really help folks question and really cut through [the opposition messaging]."

On Election Day, Lee bested Irwin by fewer than 1,000 votes, winning 41.9 percent to 41 percent, taunting her opponents for setting money on fire. Had she not enjoyed such high popularity and name recognition in the district, AIPAC's wipeout of her 25-point lead in six weeks would have been enough to beat her.

John Fetterman, meanwhile, was able to face his centrist opponent in an open seat for the U.S. Senate without taking on a super PAC, too, and won easily. In Austin, Casar and the progressive coalition behind him had known he was within striking distance of clearing 50 percent in the first-round election, which would avoid a May runoff—and avoid the opposition money that would come with it. They spent heavily in the final weeks, and Casar won a first-round victory, another socialist headed to Congress. Once sworn in to the House, one of his first major acts as a legislator was to support Betty McCollum's bill to restrict funding of the Israeli military. He quickly became one of the leading progressive voices critical of U.S. adventurism abroad, likely producing regret among DMFI and AIPAC that they had allowed him to slip through.

The big-money coalition had not gotten the knockout win in the spring it had hoped for. But AIPAC itself posted impressive numbers. It spent big against nine progressive Democrats and beat seven of them, losing only to Summer Lee and an eccentric, self-funding multimillionaire in Michigan. Without their intervention, Turner, Donna Edwards (who saw AIPAC spend more than six million dollars against her), Nida Allam, and, potentially, Erica Smith would have joined the progressive bloc in Congress, in districts that are now instead represented by corporate-friendly Democrats. And many of the ones who did make it through had been forced to moderate their stances on the way in. Still, the Squad of AOC, Omar, Tlaib, Pressley, Bowman, and Bush was being joined by Summer Lee, Delia Ramirez, Greg Casar, Maxwell Frost, and Becca Balint. On a good day, that was ten. But what kind of ten?

Summer Lee, reflecting on her near-death experience, was pessimistic. I asked if the amount of spending had gotten into her head and influenced the way she approached the Israel-Palestine issue. "Yes, absolutely, and not just with me. I see it with other people. I see people who are running for office or thinking of running for office in the future, and they feel deterred because this is a topic that they know will bury them," she said. "There's absolutely a chilling effect . . . I've heard it from other folks who will say, you know, we agree with this, but I'll never support it, and I'll never say it out loud."

More broadly, though, it makes building a movement that much more difficult, Lee added. "It's very hard to survive as a progressive, Black, working-class-background candidate when you are facing millions and millions of dollars, but what it also does is then, it deters other people from ever wanting to get into it," she said. "So then it has the effect of ensuring that the Black community broadly, the other marginalized communities, are just no longer centered in our politics."

Her narrow win, coupled with some of the losses, began to crystalize into a conventional Washington narrative that the Squad was in retreat and that voters wanted a more cautious brand of politics. "It's a way of maintaining that status quo," Lee told me. "But also it's just disingenuous when we say that we're not winning because we're not winning on the issues. No, we're not winning because we're not winning on the resources."

Whatever the fears of hard-line Israel hawks, the rise of the Squad did not materially slow the expansion of Israeli settlements into occupied Palestinian territory. In 2019, the Squad's first year in office, Israel added more than 11,000 new settlement units. In 2020, the figure doubled to more than 22,000, many of them in East Jerusalem and deep into the West Bank. "As stated in numerous EU Foreign Affairs Council conclusions, settlements are illegal under international law, constitute an obstacle to peace and threaten to make a two-state solution impossible," said an EU representative to the United Nations in a report chronicling the increase. The settlement expansion included multiple "outposts"—seizure of farmland and pasture—which puts any semblance of Palestinian independence or sustainability farther out of reach. In 2021—despite Israeli prime minister Lapid's campaign promise not "to build anything that will prevent the possibility of a future two-state solution"—settlement expansion in East Jerusalem doubled in 2021 compared with the year before, threatening to fully slice the remaining contiguous parts of Palestinian territory into small, prisonlike enclaves.

On August 5, 2022, without the support of his cabinet, Lapid launched air strikes on the Gaza Strip, agreeing to a truce on August

7. Palestinian militants fired more than a thousand rockets, though no Israelis were killed or seriously wounded. The three-day conflict left forty-nine Palestinians dead, including seventeen children.

Israel's initial denial of any role in the killing of reporter Abu Akleh gradually morphed under the weight of incontrovertible evidence into admission of possible complicity. Partnering with the London-based group Forensic Architecture, the Palestinian human rights organization Al-Haq launched the most comprehensive investigation into her death. On the morning of August 18, at least nine armored Israeli vehicles approached the group's headquarters in Ramallah and broke their way in, ransacking it and later welding shut its doors. An attempt by the Israeli government, headed by Mellman ally Yair Lapid, to have the European Union label Al-Haq a terrorist organization was rejected by the EU, which reviewed the evidence Israel provided and found it not remotely convincing.

On August 23, 2022, voters went to the polls in Orlando and cast their ballots. Frost won 35 percent of the votes, Bracy pulled in 25, and Grayson—who, by the end of the campaign, had taken to calling Frost "Maxwell Fraud"—took in 15 percent. In the end, neither DMFI nor AIPAC nor Hoffman's group had to spend a penny on the race. Bracy lost, but they had won. "That's the goal," a source close to AIPAC observed after the election. "That's the whole point."

With the primaries over, Bankman-Fried's PAC, AIPAC, and DMFI had mostly stopped spending to help Democrats. In September 2022, the Democratic National Committee refused to allow a vote on a resolution, pushed by DNC member Nina Turner and other progressives, to ban big outside money in Democratic primaries. Leah Greenberg, cofounder of Indivisible, said it was absurd that Democrats continued to allow outside groups to manipulate Democratic primaries even though they clearly had little interest in seeing the party itself succeed. Their goal is to shape what the party looks like; whether it's in the minority or majority is beside the point. "For a group called Democratic Majority for Israel, they don't seem to be putting much effort into winning a Democratic majority," Greenberg said.

Rep. Elaine Luria, a Democrat from Virginia whose race was listed as "key" by AIPAC, had been one of the organization's most outspoken and loyal allies since her 2018 election and had regularly teamed with Gottheimer as he made his various power plays. Her first significant act as a member of Congress had been to join him in confronting Rashida Tlaib with their white binder of damning quotes. Still, AIPAC's United Democracy Project had declined to help her, and Luria was among the few incumbent Democrats to lose reelection in 2022.

Instead, AIPAC's first foray into the general election had been to spend its money in a Democrat-on-Democrat race in the state of California. According to Jewish Insider, "a board member of DMFI expressed reservations over [David] Canepa's Middle East foreign policy approach, pointing to at least one social media post viewed by local pro-Israel advocates as dismissive of Israeli security concerns." The allegedly dismissive message, which Canepa posted on May 13, 2021, as the Gaza War raged, had read, "Peace for Palestine."

But AIPAC saved the rest of its energy for Summer Lee. Because the Republican in the race had the same name, "Mike Doyle," as the popular retiring incumbent Democrat—deliberately, no doubt—voters thought that a vote for Doyle was a vote for the guy they'd known for decades. After spending millions of dollars attacking Lee for not being a good enough Democrat, AIPAC spent millions in the general elections urging voters to elect the Republican. Lee won anyway.

At the end of 2022, Bibi Netanyahu, at the head of a right-wing coalition so extreme that mainstream news outlets had dubbed it fascist, was once again sworn in as prime minister, ousting Yair Lapid, the prime minister backed by DMFI's Mark Mellman.

19

HOLD THE LINE

With the American Rescue Plan written into law in early March 2021, the White House turned its attention to drafting Biden's American Jobs Plan and his American Families Plan. The latter was focused on social policy—support for parents raising children, affordable housing, more affordable health care, and so on. The former included labor protections, infrastructure spending, and an enormous investment in combating climate change.

The earliest stages of the legislative drafting phase are arguably the most important, as that's where the contours of a bill are defined. Afterward, everybody from the right to the left negotiates based on that starting point, trying to nudge the proposed legislation in their direction.

Evan Weber, serving as Sunrise's political director, found himself in the truly disorienting position of being listened to by the White House at the most important moment of its legislation-drafting phase. Sunrise had been a lead backer of Sanders and had even given Biden's climate platform the grade of F, even though, by all accounts, it was quite a strong program. But Biden, sensing the growing energy on the party's left, had invited Sunrise, as part of the unity task force project, to help draft a new climate policy agenda, and the new White House chief of staff, Ron Klain, had become enamored of the organization. But just as the drafting of the new plan got going, Sunrise, like so many other organizations, began to implode.

At the end of March 2021, Alex O'Keefe, among the first Black hires of the Sunrise Movement and a member of management, dropped a long manifesto, signed by three others, into the organization's Slack account, indicting the leadership for a culture of white supremacy. It wasn't the first internal brushfire the group had seen, but none during the presidential campaign had come this close to becoming public or had been drafted with such intensity. By posting the manifesto in the organization's main Slack channel, it became visible to all the staff and many volunteers, a significant ratcheting up of pressure.

"We are calling on Sunrise Movement organization to publicly reckon with the movement-wide crisis we are in; dismantle our white, owning-class culture: and to publicly commit to using the tens of millions of dollars we have to equip our base, and build multi-racial, cross-class community power for a Green New Deal," the manifesto read, calling for "a public reckoning and public transfer of power."

The entire organization began grappling with the memo. The political team tried to negotiate among rival factions. The communications team responded with its own manifesto. The organizers met in one-on-one sessions, hoping to organize their way back to functionality. Weber was pulled away from the White House. "The few weeks leading up to the rollout of the American Jobs Plan—a key moment, peak Sunrise access with the White House—I was spending over fifty percent of my time dealing with internal strife, trying to prevent our organization from im- or exploding, when I could have been extracting as much policy concessions as possible from the legislative document that would end up forming the basis for the reconciliation package, basically, and the infrastructure bill," said Weber.

This meant that somebody else would be making inroads where Weber had been attempting them. "People like to sneer and cringe at access politics and things like that, but for the people who sneer and cringe at that, we're the only group they even halfway like," Weber said. "And with the access that we had at that time, if I wasn't there in those conversations, fighting for environmental justice, fighting for workers' rights, fighting for the most ambitious climate plan possible, it was gonna be left to the old stodgy legacy greens or business interests or whomever else." It wasn't just about him, Weber worried as the process dragged on. "I was representing millions of young people—it was my job to represent the voices, aspirations, and hopes of millions of young people in those conversations in the White House," he reflected.

The role of a movement is to build outside pressure that reshapes what is considered doable by insiders, but a movement needs allies on the inside, to move the policy the final few inches over the finish line. Wording or decimal point tweaks at the last moment can have profound long-term implications, and Sunrise was positioned to be in the room to make sure the bill was as strong as possible.

Unless the group's people don't make it into the room because they're occupied elsewhere. "There were definitely meetings that I missed, that I had to show up to some other internal shit for instead," Weber told me. "Most of the work doesn't happen in the big group meetings that are formal and on the record. Most of the work actually happens through one-on-one meetings and the relationships. And so, you have to be proactive about that. At every moment that I wasn't doing that, I was letting other people have that access instead, or just letting the White House do their own thing."

Given the Biden administration's unexpected desire to play nice with the party's left flank, private meetings with key White House officials routinely led to concessions being made. Meetings that didn't happen left policy wins on the table. Instead, Weber was facilitating Zoom sessions to sort through his organization's culture. "That's what the political director of arguably, somehow, the most powerful climate organization in the country—certainly the most powerful climate organization on the left—was doing in the lead-up to the rollout of that piece of legislation. It's hard to look back and be, like, 'I shouldn't have been doing that.' I certainly wish I wasn't doing that."

There were times, he added, when he pushed the internal strife aside to focus instead on strengthening the legislation. "You've got to try to keep your organization from imploding, because the stakes of that are pretty freakin' high. But, you know, if I thought that it was all inevitable, yeah, maybe I would have just said, 'Fuck this, this is our only moment,' and certainly there were times where I made those [prioritization decisions] as well."

Many other climate groups were sidelined during the later negotiations, too. Before Sunrise, the most effective youth climate group was 350.org, which organized civil disobedience against pipeline projects and pressured universities to divest from fossil fuel investments. But by 2021, it had completely collapsed into internal ruckus. A climate leader at a different organization reached out to 350 in May 2021, to collaborate on a climate messaging campaign related to Build Back Better that was right up the group's alley. It didn't go well. He was told that 350.org was "taking 'an eight week pause to focus on internal issues' right at the moment mobilization was actually most needed. Devastating."

"Just stunning," he said. "Please do your jobs and not whatever that is."

One senior progressive congressional aide said the Sierra Club infighting that led to Michael Brune's departure was evident from the outside. "It caused so much internal churn that they stopped being engaged in any serious way at a really critical moment during Build Back Better," the aide said.

As the year went on, and various compromises narrowed down the scope of the legislation, many of the groups responded not by working to salvage as much as possible, but by abandoning the entire project to focus on bills that had no chance of going anywhere. It made no sense from the outside but had an internal logic to it.

"I've noticed a real erosion of the number of groups who are effective at leveraging progressive power in Congress. Some of that is these groups have these organizational culture things that are affecting them," the staffer said. "Because of the organizational culture of some of the real movement groups that have lots of chapters, what they're lobbying on isn't relevant to the actual fights in Congress. Some of these groups are in Overton mode when we have a trifecta," he said, referring to the Overton window. The idea, in theory, is that pushing their public policy demands farther and farther left widens what's considered possible, thereby facilitating the future passage of ambitious legislation. Those maximalist political demands can also be a by-product of internal strife, as organization leaders fend off charges of not embodying progressive values inside their organization by pushing external rhetoric farther left.

But, the aide pointed out, there was legislative potential being lost. "There are wins to be had between now and the next couple months that could change the country forever, and folks are focused on stuff that has no theory of change for even getting to the House floor for a vote," the aide said about two months before Build Back Better ended up passing as the slimmed-down Inflation Reduction Act.

"There's a universe where people are on the outside, focused on power and leveraging power for progressives in Congress. Instead, they're spending resources on stuff that is totally unrelated to governing. Nobody says, 'Hey guys, could you maybe come and maybe focus on this?'"

Big money, though, wasn't sitting it out. In mid-June, Joe Manchin joined a Zoom call hosted by the group No Labels, the big-money operation associated with him and Josh Gottheimer that funnels high-net-worth donor money to conservative Democrats and moderate Republicans. The call included several billionaire investors, corporate executives, and other assorted moguls, and was led by Nancy Jacobson, the No Labels cofounder. Manchin told the assembled donors that he needed help flipping a handful of Republicans from "no" to "yes" on the creation of a bipartisan January 6 Commission in order to strip the "far left" of its best argument against the filibuster. The filibuster was a critical priority for the donors on the call, as it bottled up progressive legislation that would hit their bottom lines. The January 6 Commission had gotten 56 votes, four short of the 60 needed to overcome a filibuster—a thorough embarrassment for those like Manchin who claimed bipartisanship was still possible in the divided Senate chamber. Manchin told the donors he hoped to make another run at it to prove that comity was not lost, "so at least we can tamp down where people say, 'Well, Republicans won't even do the simple lift, common sense of basically voting to do a commission that was truly bipartisan.' It just really emboldens the far left saying, 'I told you, how's that bipartisan working for you now, Joe?'" (It did not work for Joe, and Pelosi instead created the House Select Committee to Investigate the January 6 Attack on the United States Capitol.)

The extent to which Washington had become accustomed to bribery, legal and otherwise, became clear amid a discussion of the best way to win over the vote of moderate retiring Republican senator Roy Blunt. Manchin casually suggested that a future payoff be dangled in front of hm. "Roy Blunt is a great, just a good friend of mine, a great guy," Manchin said, according to an audio of the gathering we obtained at the *Intercept.* "Roy is retiring. If some of you all who might be working with Roy in his next life could tell him, that'd be nice, and it'd help our country. That would be very good to get him to change his vote. And we're going to have another vote on this thing. That'll give me one more shot at it." Manchin was suggesting—without, perhaps, quite explicitly saying so—that the wealthy executives on the call could dangle future financial opportunities in front of the outgoing senator while lobbying him to change his vote.

In the background, Nancy Jacobson was plotting for 2024. She was in the process of raising seventy million dollars to get a federal ballot line for a corporate-friendly centrist politician to challenge both parties, with Manchin as her top recruit. On the call with Manchin, Jacobson boasted about how much money her organization had raised for politicians who backed its agenda. "We did over five hundred thousand for [Republican representative] Brian Fitzpatrick, which took us two weeks, to put that together," she said, adding that the group planned to raise and direct some twenty million in "hard" dollars this cycle, referring to money that goes directly to a member of Congress's PAC; that means the member of Congress has control over it, rather than having to rely on an outside super PAC.

"There's no other group in the center that's putting the hard dollars together," Jacobson said. "You may see these big numbers with the campaigns, but that's a lot of soft dollars, it's a lot of super PACs, it's things [candidates] don't control. They love the hard dollars, and I would be hard-pressed to think of any other group that can raise that sort of money. Our hope is at least twenty million dollars over the cycle with this group, and hopefully keep doubling it as we go."

In case there was any confusion about what the money was for, she spelled it out, saying that her organization would dole out its money to members of Congress who aligned with it on "this next vote," by which she meant the looming fight over the infrastructure bill, tax increases, and Build Back Better. It was, on the one hand, an admission that business in Washington is done just as people suspect it is. But it was remarkable to hear it said out loud. "So, we're waiting, right, Andy? We're gonna see what happens with this next vote. And we want to reward those people that, you know, get to bipartisan solutions."

Andy agreed. "It's dollars that they control, hard-money dollars," said Andrew Bursky, another cofounder of No Labels and the founder and managing partner of private equity firm Atlas Holdings. "I will tell you that I participated in the last cycle, when we handed out checks to a number of our members of the House in the range of fifty thousand dollars. And in many cases that was the single largest check they received, overall, in their campaigns."

Later in the call, Bursky, while helping Manchin field questions from the Zoom audience, noted that No Labels hoped to mobilize many more donors around pivotal votes. "We've been working hard to build a coalition. Most recently, the Chamber of Commerce has agreed to lock arms with us," said Bursky. "We're building out the No Labels Team One Thousand," he said, referencing a group of donors who could be tapped to give anywhere from five thousand to fifty thousand dollars a year in support of No Labels candidates.

The Zoom call also focused on the infrastructure bill, a sweeping set of proposals to pour investments into broadband, sustainable housing, electric vehicles, transportation, research, workforce development, manufacturing, and community-based care for the elderly and disabled. The Biden administration had called for a slew of tax hikes to pay for the legislation.

Manchin and the donors saw the battle over the infrastructure bill as the key clash of Biden's first term. If the party's left flank had its way, Biden would work with Democrats in Congress to craft a multitrillion-dollar piece of transformational legislation along party lines, using the process known as reconciliation. This would put Manchin and Gottheimer under enormous pressure to vote with their fellow Democrats. To relieve that pressure, they hoped to team up with Republicans to pass a trimmed-down infrastructure-only bill, heavily but not exclusively skewed toward fossil fuel projects. If they could break that off, they hoped to drain the energy away from the bigger legislation.

Manchin laid the strategy out on the call. "I'm not going to sign off on reconciliation, giving up on bipartisanship, until you give it a try," he said. The unseemly pairing of money with votes among a Zoomful of millionaires and billionaires meeting with the country's most powerful senator was met mostly with a shrug by the rest of the media after the *Intercept* reported the details of the call. That week, Ocasio-Cortez was invited on to MSNBC's *Morning Joe* to talk about the party's agenda, and she brought up the No Labels meeting with Manchin and his billionaires. "They didn't show the whole table, so I will just tell you people were squirming in their seats when I brought it up," she told me afterward. "It clearly made everyone physically uncomfortable."

The fight over the Biden agenda was on. And out of the gate, the Squad found itself in the unusual position of being aligned with party leadership—a spot they'd increasingly find themselves in as they evolved into more inside players. In late May, seeing the dynamic with Manchin, Sinema, and their GOP allies unfold, Schumer proposed to Pelosi and Biden that they move the process along on a two-track strategy. Let the bipartisan talks continue, and if they strike a deal, good for them, but it can't move through the House or be signed by the White House until there's a pledge to do a reconciliation package—with only Democratic votes needed—to pass what was left out. One way the deal was put in place was through public pledges by Democrats not to vote for one if the other wasn't happening, too. The leadership of the Congressional Progressive Caucus was formulating a similar plan at the same time. Ro Khanna was the first to go public in support of the strategy, saying that without a robust climate bill, he'd vote down the infrastructure bill. He had been talking with Ocasio-Cortez about the idea, and she also made the vow. Rank-and-file members of Congress began joining them, pledging that it was both or neither.

When the White House announced in late June 2021 that the bipartisan infrastructure bargain had been agreed to, Pelosi followed the next morning by saying that the House would not pass it without a reconciliation package. "There ain't gonna be no bipartisan bill unless we're going to have a reconciliation bill," she told reporters at her weekly press conference. "We will not take up a bill in the House until the Senate passes the bipartisan bill and a reconciliation bill. If there is no bipartisan bill, then we'll just go when the Senate passes a reconciliation bill."

Joe Biden echoed her strategy. "If this [bipartisan deal] is the only thing that comes to me, I'm not signing it," he said.

Schumer took the credit. "About a month ago, I laid out a two-track strategy to move the whole process forward. I talked to both President Biden and Speaker Pelosi, and they agree with that strategy, so now all three of us are on that page. Today was a big step forward for the two-step strategy," he said.

The CPC surveyed its members to see how many would hold firm and found "overwhelming support." Those results were relayed to the White House and leadership.

Republicans went wild at Biden and Pelosi's claim that they'd hold one piece of legislation hostage for another. Stung, Biden relented, though Pelosi held the line. Schumer, for his part, struck an unusual and private deal with Manchin. The two signed a document that listed $1.5 trillion as Manchin's top line, along with a demand that the spending be fully offset by revenue increases and that inflation be kept in mind as the bill was crafted. Schumer didn't share the document or its contents with Pelosi or the White House; the political world carried on with the number $3.5 trillion as the target. (The document didn't surface until somebody leaked it to *Politico* in late September.)

In late July, as Congress was heading toward recess, the White House announced that it would be allowing the pandemic-era eviction moratorium to lapse at the end of the month. Some harshly worded statements of protest emanated from Congress, along with a half-hearted attempt at legislation, but the issue seemed lost, and Washington began to move on. But Cori Bush had other ideas. Recalling the time she spent living out of her car with her children, she vowed that she wouldn't let the moratorium die without a fight. She told Ocasio-Cortez that instead of going back to her district for recess or to Cleveland to campaign for Nina Turner, she was going to sleep out on the Capitol steps, a show of solidarity with those insecure in their housing. AOC joined her. As it became clear what she was doing, Hill staff and other supporters from the DC area flocked to the steps to join the sleep-in. The Capitol Police told those gathered that they were free to assemble, but there were rules against sleeping. They could stay as long as they stayed awake. Some managed to sneak catnaps in nooks and crannies around the face of the Capitol, while others rotated in and out to keep the numbers up. The press descended on the spectacle, soon joined by Mondaire Jones, sporting a Working Families Party shirt, Elizabeth Warren, and a slew of others.

By Tuesday afternoon, pressure on the White House was so great that the administration announced, through the Centers for Disease Control and Prevention, that the moratorium was to be extended. The exhausted protesters let out a roar of celebration, and the remaining lawmakers called a snap press conference. As representative Jimmy Gomez praised Bush and talked about the struggles that informed her politics, she broke down in tears.

The next day, I asked her what emotions were coursing through her in that moment, because it had appeared from the outside that they were not simply tears of joy, but something deeper. "The tears came from feeling like I felt in those moments when I was unhoused.

I could still feel the way that I felt. I remember being in the car, and my babies being in the back seat, and just wondering what day this ends. What day this ends. How will it end? And: Will I ever end up back in this position again?" she said. "There's something that comes with standing in the line at a food pantry. Something happens to you, something happens when you have to explain how you're poor enough to be able to receive these resources, why you ended up in this position. You have to explain it, and I just remember feeling that and how it felt every time I pulled out my WIC vouchers in the grocery store. And whenever I paid for something with food stamps, all of that was just flooding back."

She could feel the eyes of people on her, wondering what mistakes she had made to wind up in that desperate situation—but desperate themselves to identify the mistakes, so they can go on believing that poverty is a personal failing, not something that could happen to *them*. The truth—that it quite easily could—is too difficult to bear, and so the impoverished must be othered. "You can just feel the judgment," Bush said. "Or where people are asking questions to see where they can find your error, because it's your fault that you ended up in those positions . . . I remember feeling like people don't understand, and how can I make them understand. It's not that we are bad people. It's not that we don't deserve to have a home or we don't deserve to have a better quality of life, getting people to understand that. And so that's where some of that emotion was coming from."

A month later, the Supreme Court overturned the moratorium.

On the climate and social spending front, Jayapal was nervous that the CPC was being asked to do more than it was capable of without backup. She dialed Bernie Sanders in early August and urged him to get on board with the strategy of holding the line by stalling the Senate from approving the bipartisan infrastructure bill without a commitment from Manchin and Sinema for a robust Build Back Better. He initially agreed but came back to her later after talking to Schumer, who argued that if the Senate didn't move the infrastructure bill to the House, Manchin would walk away from both. The House, Schumer argued, was where to make the stand—a convenient position for a couple of senators to take. "I'm gonna trust Chuck," Sanders told Jayapal.

"Please don't do this," she pleaded.

Jayapal warned Sanders that having so many progressive senators support the infrastructure bill started House progressives off in an impossible situation, without the Senate having made much progress on Manchin or Sinema. How could they credibly threaten to vote "no" when all 50 members of the Democratic caucus, including Sanders, had already voted "yes"? On August 10, the infrastructure bill passed, with 69 votes in favor, including Sanders, and just 30 against.

This gave Josh Gottheimer an opening to get into the game, and he announced just three days later that he had organized eight other Democrats who would be demanding the opposite of party leaders and the progressive bloc. He called his group the "Unbreakable Nine" and insisted that they would block the $3.5 trillion budget resolution from passing the House—a necessary step toward passing the final bill, which was by then known as the Build Back Better Act—unless the infrastructure bill were passed first. No Labels, the group backed heavily by hedge fund and private equity moguls, produced an ad applauding Gottheimer's self-proclaimed Unbreakables.

As the infrastructure bill was making its way through the Senate, the Taliban was steamrolling its way across Afghanistan. Italian media would later report that in July the government of Qatar, where the Taliban had its political headquarters, had paid the president of Afghanistan $110 million to turn the country over without a fight and, similarly, paid two top warlords $61 million and $51 million, respectively. After twenty years and $2 trillion, the United States lost control of the country with barely a shot fired. On August 15, the Taliban walked into Kabul without resistance. Chaotic scenes at the airport dominated cable news for days, with crowds chasing cargo planes down the runway. One man climbed aboard a moving plane but couldn't hang on as it took off. His fatal plummet to the ground was played on a loop, a tragic bookend to the scenes of falling men and women that had precipitated the war on September 11, 2001.

What was supposed to be Biden's most courageous decision as president—standing up to the combined might of the security state and the Pentagon to push through a withdrawal that Trump had been unwilling to oversee—turned to political ash. Inside the White House, Chief of Staff Ron Klain was livid that the president was getting no backup externally from the Squad or the progressive caucus, most of whom either stayed quiet or criticized the execution of the withdrawal while commending it in principle. The White House put out the suggestion privately that a little support might be nice but, effectively, nothing was coming. Biden's poll numbers crashed and never recovered. The Biden administration seized Afghanistan's foreign central bank reserves, producing a humanitarian catastrophe of biblical proportions that went essentially unmentioned by a media that had gone into fits of rage at the way the withdrawal put at risk Afghans who had collaborated with the United States.

Back in Washington, Biden was drained of capital as Gottheimer and Manchin went on the offense. They seized on inflation numbers showing prices rising in July at a 5.4 percent rate year over year. The bigger problem was gas prices, which had been at around two dollars a gallon when Biden was elected and had now climbed above three.

The forces now arrayed against Biden and his $3.5 trillion package appeared as isolated obstacles—Manchin in the Senate, Gottheimer's gang in the House, inflation and spiking gas prices—but they were working in concert for the same purpose: to block what would legitimately be transformational legislation. The gas price increases came directly from decisions made by Saudi Arabia's Mohammed bin Salman and Russia's Vladimir Putin—who we now know was busy preparing for an invasion of Ukraine less than a year later—to cut output. Bin Salman held a grudge against Biden for calling him a "pariah" and refusing to meet with him. MBS, as he was known, had a tight relationship with Trump and his family. As he was hiking gas prices on American drivers, he was also handing over two billion dollars to a new investment fund managed by Trump's son-in-law Jared Kushner. A Republican takeover of Congress and a Republican back in the White House were clear aims of MBS, and he used the tool he had at his disposal to push things in that direction. (Chances are high he'll do the same in mid-2024.) Corporate America, meanwhile, had the same interest as MBS. The nation's CEOs and private equity executives didn't hold a secret meeting to decide to take advantage of the pandemic reopening and the supply chain problems by jacking up prices in order to hurt Biden and stop the tax increases included in Build Back Better, but in practice that's precisely what they did. The Kansas City Fed, looking back two years later, found that "markups"—price increases that are above the cost of production—grew in 2021 by 3.4 percent. Inflation that year was only 5.8 percent, meaning that more than half of inflation was simply firms raising prices because they thought they could get away with it. It didn't hurt that those same price increases drained support for Biden's spending bill, with corporate America, right-wing media, and conservative Democrats like Manchin and Gottheimer blaming the American Rescue Plan for inflation.

Into these headwinds, Pelosi had scheduled a vote on the outline of the $3.5 trillion reconciliation bill for late August, and she hosted a major fund-raiser in Napa Valley the weekend before it. That's when No Labels began to play serious hardball. The organization offered to raise $200,000 for two of the so-called Unbreakable Nine—Reps. Carolyn Bourdeaux of Georgia and Vicente Gonzalez of Texas—if they canceled an appearance that Saturday at Pelosi's fund-raiser, according to two congressional sources familiar with the proposal.

Both had been scheduled to appear at the event, which was being jointly hosted by Pelosi and the Democratic Congressional Campaign Committee. Bourdeaux attended Pelosi's fund-raiser, but Gonzalez canceled his appearance. On Monday, Pelosi and her leadership team put the screws to Gottheimer and his crew, deploying a range of threats Gottheimer described later, including cutting candidates off from campaign funds. No Labels put out another ad defending the Unbreakable Nine, characterizing them as heroes of our time and comparing them unironically to a hodgepodge of politicians, from Abraham Lincoln to Margaret Chase Smith and John McCain.

The progressive caucus continued to insist that the bills move in tandem, couching their position as in support of Pelosi and Biden. But, on Tuesday, deciding she was unable to break the Nine, Pelosi cut a deal that would have the House vote on the infrastructure bill by September 27 if the group released its reconciliation hostage. That afternoon, Gottheimer; Bourdeaux; Rep. Jared Golden, a Democrat from Maine; and Rep. Kurt Schrader, a Democrat from Oregon, gathered over Zoom with dozens of No Labels donors for a victory lap. "You should feel so proud. I can't explain to you, this is the culmination of all your work. This would not have happened but for what you built," Gottheimer told the donors, according to leaked audio. "It just wouldn't have happened—hard stop. You should just feel so proud. This is your win as much as it is my win."

The call was led again by private equity mogul Andrew Bursky, who operates heavily in the construction and development sectors. "When it comes to their ringleader, this is about one thing and one thing only: blocking tax increases on the private equity guys who fill his campaign account," said one House Democrat, reflecting the broadly held view among the party that the effort by Gottheimer and No Labels was singularly focused on preventing tax increases on the wealthy, corporations, and tax-advantaged sectors like private equity and hedge funds. "No Labels professes to value bipartisanship, but from my experience, they value 'buy partisanship,'" said Rep. Mark Pocan, a Democrat from Wisconsin, the former No Labels member who resigned from the group when it declined to disclose donor identities and who had dubbed it the "Child Abuse Caucus" during the Trump border funding fight. "Clearly they want to advocate for their donors more than good government, and that means things like corporate tax breaks and the like."

Aside from Bursky, the Tuesday evening donor call was attended by a slew of some of the country's richest people. Gottheimer told the donors that both the White House and congressional leadership had put intense pressure on the Nine, but the support they had from the group on the call was key to bucking them up. "We got on the phone every single day for a conference call, and everyone stuck together. And they beat the shit out of us. Excuse my language. They really, really were tough on us. I mean, they used every single thing, every tool they had to put pressure on us, and you know it, and they wanted us to break apart, and we wouldn't break apart," he said during the Zoom meeting. "You had people from the DCCC threaten our members, to cut them off financially. People threatened redistricting, people threatened primaries—our own people, our own leadership. Justice Democrats, which is the Squad, are running ads against me and my colleagues in our district right now. But we fought back, and you all really helped us."

Kurt Schrader, the former chair of the Blue Dog Coalition, told the group that the win gave them leverage to target the reconciliation package. "This is a big deal. I just wanna thank you guys so much for your support, having our backs, being a big part of why we are, where we are today," he said. "Let's deal with the reconciliation later. Let's pass that infrastructure package right now, and don't get your hopes up that we're going to spend trillions more of our kids' and grandkids' money that we don't really have at this point."

Marie Newman, who'd beaten Dan Lipinski in a 2020 rematch with the help of Justice Democrats, was shocked by what Gottheimer was doing. "I just want to be clear. Josh Gottheimer is an astronomical liar and fabricator," she told me. "And I can't tell you how manipulative he and his Gang of Nine are. He's so beholden to the four million dollars he gets from corporate PACs every year that he promised to do that. I mean, he's evil," she said. "Sinema has the same problem. She's so beholden to Wall Street that she'll do whatever she's told. And Manchin, honestly, while he's beholden to Wall Street, too, it is also partly that he just doesn't like dramatic movement. He just doesn't. It scares him. He is a little bit more principled than those other two. The other two are just straight-up prostitutes to Wall Street."

The progressive caucus, in the face of the deal, insisted it was not party to it and that it would continue to hold the line.

"Try us," said Jayapal.

Pelosi scheduled the vote for September 27, as promised, and this time she put the full weight of her whip operation to get it over the line. The CPC whip, Omar, was confident in her caucus.

On Monday, the caucus held its ground, as Democrat after Democrat announced that they'd refuse to go along. The hashtag HoldThe-Line trended on Twitter. Progressives watching from the outside finally had something to cheer, and members of Congress, unused to being cheered, celebrated their fortitude. Was this what power felt like? Defeated, Pelosi announced that she would delay the vote to Thursday while she worked over her caucus. Thursday came, and she was still short.

Pelosi met privately with her caucus and ripped Gottheimer's group. "We read in the paper that there are members of our caucus joining with members of the Senate that reject the three-point-five," she said, referring to the $3.5 trillion reconciliation bill. "The very same people who are demanding a vote on a certain day are making it impossible for us to have a vote on a certain day."

Gottheimer's gang had been texting throughout the day, and their chain lit up as they sat in the meeting. Reporters Jonathan Martin and Alex Burns, for their book *This Will Not Pass*, got a look at the group text.

"Oh dear lord this whole thing is going to collapse," Bourdeaux texted the other eight members.

Kurt Schrader, who opposed the reconciliation bill all along, shot back, saying that Pelosi was a "truly terrible person." With progressives holding the line, Pelosi pulled the bill.

Toward the end of October, she made another run at it, but neither Manchin nor Sinema had committed to backing the reconciliation bill and were even making hints they'd walk away altogether. "How does zero sound?" Manchin asked Sanders at one private caucus meeting, touching his index finger to his thumb.

On October 28, with off-year elections in New Jersey and Virginia looming, Biden prepared to depart for a Group of Twenty summit in Rome, but he wanted to take a major infrastructure win with him, hoping it would coax other countries to make similar investments in climate spending. (Never mind that the bill included huge fossil fuel subsidies.)

Ron Klain called Jayapal and urged her to get behind the bill and give the president a win, but Jayapal countered with her own request: Please don't send the president up here. We don't want to embarrass him by voting the bill down. But we will vote it down.

Biden split the difference. He came to Capitol Hill and met privately with the progressive caucus, but he didn't ask them to pass the bill. He left that to Pelosi, who urged the CPC members to trust her and the president to deliver the climate and social spending bill even without the leverage of the infrastructure bill remaining. The meeting adjourned and Biden flew to Europe, while the CPC convened in a different room nearby to debate the way forward. Jayapal began that meeting by noting how conspicuous it was that Biden did not ask for their vote, which she argued gave them room to maneuver. As Representative Mark Takano was speaking, the door swung open, and there was Pelosi. A still fell over the room. "I'm just here to listen," she said, and walked toward Takano, sitting down two feet from the microphone. Takano, who represented Riverside in Pelosi's home state of California, took a breath and continued with his speech, encouraging his colleagues to hold the line. "He was really nervous, but he kept going," said one Democrat in the room. "He was incredibly emotional," said Jayapal. "Here's a chairman of a committee, who had just become a chair, from her home state, who was standing up and saying what he believed."

After Takano, Jan Schakowsky of Illinois spoke. She had been in office more than twenty years and had been a loyal Pelosi lieutenant and close confidante for just as long. With Pelosi inches away, she delivered the same message: Hold the line. "That was one really important thing, for people to see somebody like Jan stand up," said Jayapal. "When Pelosi came into the meeting, I could just see everyone's face, and I was like, 'Oh my God, nobody's gonna stand up and speak because she's here.' But person after person got up." When it was AOC's turn, she took the unusual step, for her, of confronting Pelosi directly. Unlike many others, she said, she would likely still be alive in fifty years and have to live with the consequences of their capitulation if they threw away their last opportunity. "She did this whole thing about not trusting her and I said it's not that I don't trust you it's that I don't trust Manchin. And no one has given me a reason to," she said. Pelosi left. Asked how long she had stayed in the room, one Democrat said, "It felt like forever," later guessing it might have been just twenty minutes.

Once Biden was in the air, a CPC whip count found that strong support remained for holding the line. Progressives used Biden's decision not to make an ask to decline to vote for it. "Today was hard, the hardest," Ocasio-Cortez reflected that evening in a text. I asked who took the brunt of the pressure from the White House. "There were a little over 30 that got whipped hard, even got personal calls from the White House including VP. It was incredible to see them not move. I think the public fight of values is helping," she said. "Our members have been amazing and brave."

I asked what arguments the party leaders were making to rush the bill through. "Something about the president traveling abroad, it was just weird," she texted back.

Just before six o'clock in the evening, Pelosi pulled the plug again. Biden would land in Rome without his bill. "To put our whip efforts against the White House and Pelosi and win is something I never expected us to do. But here we are," AOC texted. "Today was a big test no one expected we would pass and I am still exhausted from it." Sanders, she said, was helping buck people up: "Bernie is doing an incredible job working this with some members on our side."

In the upcoming off-year elections, Democrats had nominated Terry McAuliffe, a former governor of Virginia, for another go at it after Lt. Gov. Justin Fairfax was effectively disqualified thanks to a MeToo scandal he vigorously denied but couldn't overcome.

As the election approached, Manchin put out more signals that he was simply opposed to Build Back Better, and Cori Bush unleashed on November 1: "Joe Manchin's opposition to the Build Back Better Act is anti-Black, anti-child, anti-woman, and anti-immigrant," she said. "When we talk about transformative change, we are talking about a bill that will benefit Black, brown, Indigenous communities."

The next day, Ro Khanna and Rep. Joe Neguse, a young Black progressive rising star from Colorado, walked the few hundred feet over to the Senate floor and found Manchin. It was highly unusual for rank-and-file members to make that journey. "We don't wanna ambush you," Khanna told him. "We're just trying to lower the temperature."

"Oh, you don't have to worry about me," Manchin said. "I've been around the block. I've been in politics since before your daddy was born."

The three of them argued about climate, with Manchin making his arguments about China—if they're not doing carbon emission reductions, the United States shouldn't, either. He also attacked the effort by Gottheimer and other wealthy-district Democrats to get tax breaks for the rich into the deal—and Khanna and Neguse were happy to agree with him. Manchin said that he had gotten a flurry of text messages over the weekend from House progressives urging him to get on board and said he wanted to keep negotiating but didn't want to be "boxed in."

Khanna went on Fox News that day and was asked about Bush's comment. He told the host that Manchin wasn't racist. Bush reached out to Khanna. "You sided with Manchin over me?" she wondered. Khanna asked if they could go out for ice cream that night, and Bush agreed. Over cones, he made the case to her that the point she was making wasn't invalid, but that it was too overly intellectual to land the way she wanted it to and that her broader point was getting lost. It may be true that Manchin's position was doing the work of upholding the structures of white supremacy, but all he or the press would hear is "Manchin is racist," and that would sidetrack the conversation.

McAuliffe managed to lose to Republican Glenn Youngkin, a defeat that was pinned in Washington on progressives for holding up Biden's infrastructure bill. The notion that voters would have seen the bill pass and been so moved that they'd have elected McAuliffe was taken seriously in the Capitol. As absurd as all that is, it's worth absorbing that the progressive stand also did not help. If there was a silent majority of disaffected voters just waiting for progressives to show some backbone in Congress, they would have responded in Virginia and New Jersey by delivering big wins for Democrats. But the reality is that as much buzz as these Beltway battles generate on Twitter, they don't tend to filter down to a broad enough public to move the needle. People who aren't paying attention aren't paying attention. Bernie Sanders learned that lesson the hard way, when he banked his presidential candidacy on the increased turnout he hoped would come from his unapologetically speaking truth to power. That's not a reason not to fight, but it's worth understanding what outcomes are possible and what aren't.

Two days after the election, on November 5, House leaders were back at it, this time determined to break the progressive opposition. Biden picked up the phone and made the first of two calls to Jayapal, telling her he had won a pledge from Manchin to back the reconciliation bill and that he needed the CPC to let the infrastructure bill go. They had taken it to the end of the line, he told her. She told him she'd have to confer with her caucus. As House leaders met that day in an effort to reach a final deal on both the Build Back Better Act and a bipartisan infrastructure bill, House majority whip Clyburn suggested that the Congressional Black Caucus could be helpful in ending an impasse between the group of holdouts, given how many CBC members were also in the CPC.

The suggestion was dismissed out of hand by Gottheimer's crew, Clyburn would later tell allies, with the Black Caucus being written off as irrelevant in a changing Congress. Once known as "the conscience of Congress," the CBC, founded in 1971 by thirteen members, drew its power from the legacy of the civil rights movement and its ability to speak with one voice and vote as a bloc. That unity had been chipped away over the past two election cycles, amid a generational and ideological struggle that played out in party primaries.

After the meeting, a livid Clyburn summoned the CBC leadership, telling chair Joyce Beatty, Rep. Maxine Waters, and others about the disrespect being leveled at the caucus. It was incumbent on them to prove the doubters wrong, he said. How much disrespect was real and how much he was ginning up to motivate the CBC is a matter of dispute, but the effect was clear, as was the strategy: use the Black caucus to break the progressives. Beatty pledged that the caucus would move swiftly. Shortly before 2 p.m. she and Reps. Steven Horsford of Nevada and Sheila Jackson Lee of Texas left Clyburn's office and told reporters that the CBC would support the effort to split the two bills—though the caucus had yet to meet on the question.

Beatty quickly scheduled a caucus meeting and urged the group to back the leadership strategy, telling members that the credibility of Clyburn and the CBC was on the line. The meeting overlapped with a gathering of the Congressional Progressive Caucus, which was debating the same questions, with some members who served in both caucuses shuttling back and forth. At the CPC meeting, members were banned from bringing phones into the room, as the caucus was worried that some of its members were in fact moles for Pelosi, feeding her intelligence.

Back in the CBC meeting, Rep. Emanuel Cleaver, a Democrat from Missouri, made a motion that the caucus unify behind Clyburn and party leadership, and Horsford, who'd also been in the Clyburn meeting, seconded it. Reps. Bonnie Watson Coleman, Ayanna Pressley, and Omar all pushed back against the strategy, asking that the motion be withdrawn, which it eventually was. No vote was held. "We were adamant that there was no agreement, but they put out a statement anyway," said one frustrated CBC member.

Beatty then journeyed from the CBC meeting to the CPC one, where the progressive caucus was still gathered. She told reporters outside in the hallway that she was acting on her own initiative—but she was conspicuously accompanied by a staffer easily recognized as a senior aide to Pelosi.

Beatty stood outside awkwardly as she was refused entry under the reasoning that only CPC members could attend the meeting. "I think it was a mistake for CPC not to be in better dialogue with CBC and [a] joint strategy. Having Joyce Beatty wait outside to address the CPC was arrogant and wrong," said one CPC member.

One nonmember was allowed to join by speakerphone, however: Joe Biden. A week earlier, after lengthy negotiations with Joe Manchin that had followed the successful CPC effort to hold the line and keep the two bills paired, the Biden administration released a new framework, which Manchin praised.

During the CPC meeting, Biden, on speakerphone, beseeched the caucus to give him a win on the infrastructure bill, asking them to trust that he had a commitment from Manchin to get Build Back Better done. The day before, Manchin had appeared on *Morning Joe* and said he was in agreement with a $1.75 trillion top line for the bill. Was that good enough?

After the call with Biden, a tearful Jayapal spoke, arguing the caucus had held the line as long as it could and that, at this point, they needed to trust the president. The most vociferous supporters of the holdout strategy were shocked at her reversal.

"Even after that call, twenty-seven people were still willing to vote no," said one angry CPC member, arguing Jayapal capitulated too soon. But others involved in the vote counting said it was a fantasy to think that many progressives would hold the line directly against the president's pledge that he had worked out a deal with Manchin.

Jayapal and Gottheimer got together, and Jayapal told him that she'd deliver the votes for the infrastructure bill if Gottheimer and his crew made a firm commitment in writing to vote for the new $1.75 trillion Build Back Better. Gottheimer made the pledge, which, to Jayapal, fulfilled the original purpose of the CPC's holding the line: the House would pass both pieces of legislation, and it would be up to the Senate to put up or shut up. "Pelosi's use of the Black Caucus was important on that day [as was] the president's multiple entreaties. And then the negotiating that actually got us to an agreement," Jayapal said, referring to the deal struck with Gottheimer to move the bill through the House. "There wasn't any agreement to move Build Back Better forward before that day. And so that negotiation was happening at the same time. . . . Don't get me wrong, I was worried," Jayapal said. "I was texting Josh every day just to make sure."

Whether House Democrats had the votes still remained an open question, however, and five members of the Squad—Omar, Bush, Ocasio-Cortez, Tlaib, and Bowman—told me they would be voting "no." "I'm a no," Ocasio-Cortez told me that evening. "This is bullshit."

Without those five, Pelosi needed Republican votes, and GOP leadership had previously said it would force Democrats to pass the majority threshold on their own before Republicans helped. Jayapal went from stiffening the spines of her caucus, urging them to vote "no," to whipping the Squad to vote "yes." She pulled Ocasio-Cortez into a room with a handful of progressive caucus members who were also in leadership, and made a passionate case to vote "yes." House leadership had promised that the first vote would be on the Build Back Better framework, followed by the infrastructure vote. "Several people in the Squad said that they were going to vote for it, that they would vote for both. And then when Build Back Better got delayed by a week there was a lot of distrust," Jayapal said.

Jayapal and the other progressives began arguing that it was essential for their midterm prospects that they pass the bill that night. Ocasio-Cortez flagged the contradiction. On the one hand, Democrats were saying that the direct checks and the child tax credit payments included as part of the American Rescue Plan would be totally forgotten by the election, yet voters would somehow all remember that the infrastructure bill passed or didn't pass in November 2021. Party leaders had said the House would vote on a motion first and then move to the main bill, and Ocasio-Cortez looked up and saw that they had skipped one and moved directly to the second. How can we trust the Senate to do the right thing, she asked, if we can't even trust House leaders on a thirty-minute procedural promise? "The president has no path to getting the Build Back Better votes that he's promising," she warned, and left the room, committed to voting "no."

But not long after the vote opened, several moderate Republicans voted "yes," ensuring the bill's passage. Ayanna Pressley ended up joining her Squad colleagues in their "no" votes.

Gottheimer, it must be said, was true to his word, and the reconciliation outline passed on schedule, two weeks later, on November 19. But without a solid commitment from Manchin or Sinema to move forward on it, progressives had no cards left to play. Jayapal had alienated many of her centrist colleagues by holding the bill up for more than two months, even sending Biden to Europe empty-handed. Now she was alienating her progressive flank by letting it through. "Everybody was feeling good about what we had become, and we're back to square one," said one CPC member. Everything for her was riding on Manchin's good-faith follow-through on his pledge to support something in the $1.75 trillion range.

For the next month, Manchin negotiated with the White House. Those negotiations, Jayapal later argued in her defense, were made possible only by House progressives holding the line, adding that the Senate had already acted without any commitment from Manchin. "The Senate passed the infrastructure bill without any commitment on the Build Back Better Act, and it fell to the progressive caucus, against the push of our own leadership, political pundits and eventually the White House, to hold the line," she said. Her argument had merit: the CPC had indeed gotten Biden and Manchin close to the finish line.

"I believe we were able to put him in a box with that framework where he would either have to uphold his commitment to the president or—and I do believe the president when he said to us, and to me personally, that he got a commitment from Senator Manchin—or he'd have to go back on his word," Jayapal said.

The job of House progressives, she said, was to get both bills through the House and get a commitment from Manchin, beyond which the responsibility lay with the president to finish it. "We held the line not just once, but twice, and even a third time for a very long day at the end to insist that we get what we needed to pass both bills through the House, and pass both bills through the House we did," she said.

Then things got even weirder. On December 14, a Tuesday, Manchin and Biden met, and Manchin offered to back a $1.8 trillion package, while Biden also made some concessions. A deal was close. Both sides said they'd put out a statement. The White House drafted a statement, and sent it to Manchin. It included a mention of his name. "I had a productive call with Speaker Pelosi and Majority Leader Schumer earlier today. I briefed them on the most recent discussions that my staff and I have held with Senator Manchin about Build Back Better," the president's statement read. "In these discussions, Senator Manchin has reiterated his support for Build Back Better funding at the level of the framework plan I announced in September. . . . My team and I are having ongoing discussions with Senator Manchin; that work will continue next week."

That was the only mention of Manchin. Manchin's chief of staff asked the White House to remove Manchin's name or add in Sinema's, but it didn't do so, and on Thursday, it released the statement. Manchin flipped his lid. That he lost it over something so small suggests the enormous pressure he was feeling. He complained to the White House that singling him out "puts my family at risk."

What the White House didn't know was that Gail Manchin had been at home recently in West Virginia and heard a noise outside. She turned on the lights, and whoever was there fled. Protesters with Sunrise and other groups had paddled kayaks out to Manchin's houseboat in the Potomac and surrounded his Maserati in his parking garage. He wasn't rattled enough to stop pressing forward then, but when it came to his wife, he responded intensely.

On Sunday, December 19, Manchin took to Fox News and let the world know he was "done." A frantic White House tried to reach him before he went on the air, but he refused their calls. The political world was in shock, wondering how a deal that was so close had suddenly vanished. On Monday morning, Manchin called Jayapal to talk, and she lit into him. Later, in a conference call with reporters, she said that she had been blunt with him. "That lack of integrity is stunning," she said, "particularly in a city where your word is everything."

She said Manchin denied ever having made a commitment to Biden. "I don't know what to make of that," she said. "I still believe the president got that commitment."

Asked if she regretted the decision to break up the two pieces of legislation and give away leverage, she said she had pondered it since. "This is the question I've gone over in my head a million times," she said, concluding that she didn't regret the decision because, she argued, there was no particular tactic that could have overcome what she now believed was always Manchin's plan to walk away. "I don't believe the senator actually wanted to pass Build Back Better," she said. If Democrats had held the line again that evening and blocked passage of the infrastructure bill, she argued, Manchin would have used that moment as his excuse to bolt. "I think he was looking for a way to not do it, and that would have been the day that the Build Back Better Act died," Jayapal said, referring to November 19, the day the infrastructure bill passed the House with majority support from the CPC. "That would have also been the day that we turned the country against us," she added. "So, no. I don't have regrets."

Those who objected to the strategy in real time, however, saw Manchin's move as the danger they had predicted. "Alexandria warned it could happen," read an email Ocasio-Cortez sent to reporters. "Yesterday, it did."

In hindsight, what Manchin was doing was clear. He had been publicly and privately pleading to slow the negotiations down, to wait until mid-2022, to see how inflation was running, before Congress passed another big bill. Democratic leaders knew from the 2009/10 session that dragging things out was disastrous, so they had pushed to get it done as soon as possible. Manchin, unable to win the "strategic pause" concession he'd been asking for, simply created his own pause by appearing to kill the deal. He also got the White House out of his hair. Sunrise Movement, which had been bird-dogging him in his parking garage and from the stern of his boat, threw in the towel, largely shutting down its federal operation, reasoning that it had no cards left to play against Manchin and, besides, was engulfed in so much internal turmoil that it couldn't play them even if it did.

Insults flew between Manchin and Klain, and the two stopped speaking, with Biden dispatching his old lieutenant Steve Ricchetti to deal with him instead. In mid-February, Schumer and Manchin finally sat down in person again, dining at a divey Italian institution, Trattoria Alberto, that was long the favorite restaurant of former Speaker John Boehner.

Manchin agreed to reopen negotiations, but he wanted to wait until April, and he wanted to deal directly only with Schumer. Just days later, Putin launched his invasion of Ukraine, sending energy markets into turmoil. With cheap Russian gas no longer a guarantee, the European Union moved quickly to pledge hundreds of billions of dollars in clean-energy investments. All of a sudden, there was more demand for solar than China, which had cornered the market, could produce. Manchin saw this as an opportunity to make huge investments in clean energy in the United States, and couple them with big upgrades to the fossil fuel industry. "That is the catapult that basically launched me," Manchin later told *Politico* of Putin's invasion.

Manchin and Schumer spent the next few months hammering out the contours of a deal, bringing back the measure to allow Medicare to negotiate lower drug prices, which had been a main focus of objections from Gottheimer's gang, who were flush with Big Pharma cash.

Mitch McConnell, who had spent the last decade being hailed as a tactical genius by the Washington press, had far outlived the description. At the end of June 2022, as word began to leak out that Manchin might finally be serious about getting a deal done, McConnell committed a major blunder, threatening to block a bipartisan bill to invest money in the domestic semiconductor industry, known as the United States Innovation and Competition Act, or USICA, if Manchin continued his talks with Schumer. "Let me be perfectly clear: there will be no bipartisan USICA as long as Democrats are pursuing a partisan reconciliation bill," McConnell said on Twitter.

Manchin took the threat as a personal affront. If McConnell didn't like the CHIPS bill, he should say so, but the idea that even having discussions about one bill meant McConnell would kill a different one was outrageous. It pushed Manchin away from Republicans and closer to Schumer.

Schumer then pulled off a move that screwed over McConnell and boxed in Manchin all at once. On July 14, again griping about inflation, Manchin told Schumer during a Zoom call that he just couldn't get on board with what Schumer was pushing. Schumer that night announced that Manchin had abandoned talks. It's unknowable if Schumer really believed Manchin meant to walk away from the talks. But the effect of his claiming so brought the fury of the world down upon Manchin, who turned out to be unable to handle the pressure. The next morning, he did an interview with a West Virginia radio host, saying he wasn't done, but nobody believed him.

The haymakers from Sanders and the Squad were expected, but rank-and-file senators came for Manchin, too, with New Mexico's Martin Heinrich suggesting he be yanked as chair of the Energy Committee. "Manchin's refusal to act is infuriating," he tweeted. Sen. Tina Smith, the Minnesota-nice replacement for Al Franken—who in 2018 resigned as senator after being caught up in the MeToo callouts—posted, "This is bullshit." The West Virginia senator heard even worse in private.

"He unleashed the dogs," Manchin said of Schumer.

Chris Coons, a Delaware senator close to Biden, told Manchin that many of their colleagues were concerned that he had sold them out for personal profit, his ownership of a coal brokerage company becoming too glaring a conflict of interest to overlook. "There are folks in our party who are saying all sorts of terrible things about you, who believe you were stringing us along for a year and that you were never going to come to a deal because of your state or because of your conflicts of interest," Coons said, according to *Washington Post* reporting at the time. "I can't think of a better way for you to prove them all wrong than to sign off on a bold climate deal. Prove every critic wrong."

Manchin paused to think and then responded, "It would be like hitting a homer in the bottom of the ninth, wouldn't it?"

If Schumer's move had been calculated, he had calculated correctly. The next day, Manchin was back, meeting privately with Schumer in a Capitol basement office, with a Schumer aide keeping Sinema abreast of the talks. McConnell, believing the package was dead, finished negotiations on the semiconductor bill known as CHIPS—no small bill, it spent $280 billion on research, development, and production of chip technology—and passed it on July 27. Just hours later, Manchin and Schumer announced their astonishing deal. Republicans were livid, issuing new threats to shut down the Senate and on and on, but the threats were empty. They'd been outplayed. Progressives in the House took solace in Manchin's return, believing that their willingness to hold the line allowed the process to ripen in a way it wouldn't have otherwise. Ron Klain told me he didn't buy that argument. "It delayed getting something done. I understood their viewpoint but did not agree with it," he said. But, he added, fighting to the bitter end had convinced progressives that the new deal with Manchin was worth accepting. "It was part of a process that helped build acceptance of a lesser BBB bill as worth supporting. We needed to bring CPC along all the way to the finish line. They had a lot of votes and we needed their votes on CHIPS and what became IRA. And they felt like the White House had treated them fairly and respectfully."

What remained in the package, and what got cut out, was in many ways the end product of the effort that began with Bernie Sanders strolling out of the Capitol Building in early 2015 to casually announce that he was running for president. In that campaign, Sanders drew laughter during a debate when he called climate change the greatest national security threat. Two years later, in occupying Pelosi's office, Sunrise, Justice Democrats, and AOC had put climate change at the center of the conversation, making it required for 2020 presidential candidates to one-up one another on how aggressively they'd go after it. Even as Sunrise imploded and AOC distanced herself from Justice Democrats, the impression on the political class remained that if you wanted to be the progressive in the race and you wanted to win the youth vote, you had to be a climate champion. When White House aide Anita Dunn met with frustrated advocates of the care economy provisions of the package, she urged them to study the climate movement's success.

Even if the climate provisions were the only pieces Manchin wanted to strip out of the package, that wasn't an option for him given the political structures that had built up in the previous few years. He *was* able to slice out the care economy provisions and the housing policy. Democrats who had celebrated cutting child poverty in half would now be letting it double again. And the crisis that was tearing the country apart—runaway rent and housing costs—would go unaddressed.

20

OVERTURNED

On the evening of May 3, 2022, everything changed. According to a draft opinion leaked to *Politico* reporter Josh Gerstein, the Supreme Court had privately decided to overturn *Roe v. Wade* and *Casey v. Planned Parenthood*, stripping women of the constitutional right to abortion. The *Dobbs* decision, as it became known, was the culmination of decades of right-wing resistance to *Roe*, the fulcrum of a political movement that had organized behind the Reagan Revolution, bringing business elites and cultural conservatives into an uneasy alliance. Now they were on the cusp of getting what they had claimed they wanted, but the Court opinion flinched, stopping short of the maximalist goal of outlawing abortion. "It is time to heed the Constitution and return the issue to the people's elected representatives," the Court's majority decision read.

Neither party, it turned out, was ready for what that meant. Kyrsten Sinema quickly put out a statement rejecting calls to reform the filibuster and quickly codify *Roe* into law legislatively with the party's waning majority. Sinema, who specialized in making arguments so preposterous that she'd leave her opponents spitting with confused rage, said that her defense of the filibuster was in fact rooted in her support for abortion rights. Eliminating the filibuster, she warned, could allow a future Republican Congress to ban abortion. The claim wasn't pulled from thin air. For years, that had been the position of major pro-choice groups in Washington, but they had long since abandoned it, recognizing that defense was no longer the primary goal. Ocasio-Cortez slammed Sinema. "She should be primaried," AOC concluded. Manchin, too, said he'd oppose reforming the filibuster, and that was that.

The right's long-standing fear that a public wave of revulsion would bring hundreds of thousands of people into the streets in protest—as had happened the day after Trump's inauguration—was fully allayed. Protesters gathered at the Supreme Court and in pockets around the country, but largely, the response was confined to angry posting on social media. Abortion rights groups couldn't have been any less prepared for the moment, having spent the last several years locked in the kind of generational struggles over race and gender described in chapter 14. At one major reproductive rights organization, the staff demanded that their organization prepare healing rooms for the day the official ruling came down, along with grief counselors and loosened work obligations. In a break with past practice, the organization's leadership finally said no. The staff's job was to defend the rights of the millions of people under attack, and they needed to do their job that day more than any other, they were told.

The upside of the leak of the ruling was that it gave Democrats the opportunity to prepare. Yet when the ruling on *Dobbs v. Jackson Women's Health Organization* finally came down, on June 24, 2022, it was as if the Biden administration had missed the earlier memo.

That wasn't for a lack of available ideas. At a rally on the Supreme Court steps, Ocasio-Cortez listed a few of them. "There are also actions at President Biden's disposal that he can mobilize," she told the crowd. "I'll start with the babiest of the babiest of the baby steps: open abortion clinics on federal lands in red states right now." She and others also called on the federal government to protect access to FDA-approved medication abortion and contraception. Instead, the White House did . . . nothing. Two weeks later, Biden issued an executive order tasking other parts of his administration to study the question and get back to him with potential ideas. Kamala Harris, a vice president who had complained she had no good role in the administration, was nowhere to be found. Democratic voters were accustomed to the party's letting them down, but this was a new low. Yet it had a familiar feeling, reminiscent of the Democratic establishment's response to the election of Trump in 2016. Flat on their back, it took an explosive, organic mobilization of resistance by its voters to put life back into the party.

In 2022, people took over again and rescued the Democratic Party from itself. Republicans gave them the opening. Abortion foes in Kansas had put a constitutional amendment on the ballot to allow the state to ban abortion. They had scheduled it for the doldrums of August 2, hoping only "pro-life" zealots would come out to vote. But the overturning of *Roe* had changed the calculus, and suddenly it became do or die for abortion defenders. Kansas was surrounded by states that had banned abortion or were in the process of doing so, meaning that if Kansas fell, too, women there would need to drive up to a full day to find reproductive health services.

Washington thinks of Kansas as hopelessly Republican, but the state had a Democratic governor, and its grassroots organizations knew how to compete, leaning into the Kansan appreciation for individual liberty. Covid-19 vaccine mandates were increasingly unpopular among conservatives at the time, and the "Vote No" campaign there deployed a strong argument: If you don't want the government telling you what to do with your body, then don't let it tell us what to do, either.

Because American elections arrive on set dates rather than being called in a snap as in many parliamentary systems, there's often a significant gap in time between a policy decision and public input, draining some of the democratic character of the system and contributing to a lack of engagement. But, coincidentally, Republicans in Kansas had set up a real referendum on abortion rights, producing a verdict just six weeks after the Supreme Court ruling. Facing the threat of a concrete right being taken away, voters overwhelmingly stood up for that right. An election that had been uncertain turned into a landslide, with the "no" side winning 59–41. Data analysts noticed that women and young people had registered to vote in the race at unprecedented rates. The analysts found similar patterns in other states where the elections could affect abortion rights, but they didn't find the pattern in states such as New York, where rights were safe for the time being no matter what happened.

California and Vermont also had upcoming ballot measures, though in neither was the outcome in doubt. This wasn't the case for Michigan, Kentucky, or Montana. Yet, in all three, abortion rights won convincingly.

Michigan saw the most behind-the-scenes drama ahead of the election. The state had been home to a long-running clash between foundation-funded local reproductive justice organizations and the major national reproductive rights organizations, also funded by foundations and wealthy people supportive of abortion rights. The issues were the same ones tearing other organizations apart. The local organizations, charging that the national ones perpetuated white supremacy, urged nearly all funding to go toward abortion rights rather than toward political work. To the extent that political work was worth doing, the local groups argued, it should be done to destigmatize abortion and to celebrate it as a positive good rather than a difficult or complex decision. The national groups argued that while there was virtue to shifting the narrative around abortion, when it came to elections the notion polled terribly. The movement, the national groups said, should go with what worked. At an impasse, the national groups largely declined to fund the local organizations' efforts to win the Michigan referendum, but they also declined to go around the organizations, for fear of looking like they were bigfooting marginalized communities. They would rather sit it out.

That's where Barbara Fried came in. The mother of the crypto-billionaire Sam Bankman-Fried—not yet in federal custody—Fried was a successful professor of law at Stanford. Partly with her son's money and partly with her own connections, she pulled together millions in funding for the Michigan election. The local organizations were presented with a deal: you can come on board, but we're using message-tested tactics. Because Fried and her allies weren't embedded in the nexus of the Democratic Party and its allied organizations, the local groups had no leverage and went along with the plan. Abortion rights won by more than 10 points in Michigan and more than 5 in both Kentucky and Montana.

In August and then in October, Biden also delivered on two policies that had flowed out of the Sanders campaign: on canceling student debt and legalizing marijuana. The August announcement saw ten thousand dollars of student debt canceled for all borrowers and twenty thousand dollars for anybody with Pell Grants. In October, he pardoned everybody with a federal conviction for simple possession of marijuana and, perhaps more important, instructed the government to study the question of whether weed ought to be a Schedule I drug (the most restrictive category) or should be rescheduled or desched-uled, which would allow states to fully legalize, tax, and regulate it without worrying about federal law. That study will come back in time for the 2024 election.

Dmitri Mehlhorn, the Reid Hoffman adviser and tech executive who had spent millions trying to beat back the Squad during the primaries, worried that the group was an albatross around other Democrats' necks, grudgingly agreed after the election that student debt relief may in fact have been helpful to the party. "For now, I am willing to concede that the student debt relief might have generated some net gains for Democrats by comparison with not doing it—still not sure, but possible," he offered. A few months later, he allowed, after looking at data, that turnout among young people seemed to have been "driven entirely by the *Dobbs* decision and related discourse." But the Squad was no longer his only beef, he added. "I do agree that some members of the Squad are behaving reasonably, but the Squad is not the only problem. People like Pramila Jayapal and Ro Khanna are good people, and very smart, but their theories of politics are fantastical if you move outside of heavily Democratic enclaves—and in my view are entirely wrong in their theories of Trump." The campaign against the Squad, he said, had been so successful at marginalizing and taming them that they wouldn't be the focus of his 2024 big money strategy. "I think we're okay now," he said. "In terms of general voters, I don't think it's a problem anymore, and I don't think we need to do more to fight back against it, at the moment."

At the heart of Mehlhorn's analysis is the question that will shape Democratic politics in the coming years. Going back to the Jesse Jackson campaigns of the 1980s, the left argued that if Democrats could credibly promise to improve the material conditions of the lives of voters, those voters would remain loyal, as they did with the New Deal coalition for decades. The Sanders campaign came after forty years of neoliberalism, and Sanders had little he could point to that the party had actually accomplished—outside of the New Deal and Great Society era—so his campaign rested on ambitious promises, as did the Squad's campaigns in 2018 and the second Sanders run in 2020.

Across the world, advanced democracies were seeing the same realignments reshaping their politics, as voters shifted along cultural lines defined by education. People with a college degree and beyond drifted to the left, and those without degrees drifted right. Sanders, in his 2020 campaign, hoped to excite working-class voters and bring previously checked-out people into the process. He and Ocasio-Cortez both articulated this at a rally at Chaparral High School in Las Vegas at the end of 2019. "We're not here to be spectators in our democracy. We're here to fight for it. So, we need to decide: Are you going to bring someone with you to the caucus?" Ocasio-Cortez asked, saying that even posting about the election on Facebook mattered. She quickly added, cognizant of the Bernie Bro criticism, "But don't get into any arguments with people. That's not productive." The goal, she said, was to find people who hadn't voted before and make the case to them that it was worth it. "The swing voters that we're most concerned with are the nonvoters to voters. That swing voter is going to win us this election and the general election," she said, arguing that it was inaccurate to say nonvoters were apathetic.

"What we need to communicate is that this, this year, for two days—your primary and the general—it's worth it to believe. Just suspend your disbelief for two days out of the year. That's all I'm asking."

Sanders picked up on her theme. "Alexandria a few minutes ago made the point, and I want to make it again," he said. "There are a whole lot of folks out there who have given up. You know them. Some of you are in this room—given up on the political process, 'My vote doesn't mean anything. Politics is bullshit. Why do I wanna vote?'" He said that when they left and told friends they'd gone to a Bernie Sanders rally, they should be ready for those friends to wonder why they'd bothered. "'Why'd you waste your time getting involved in that stuff?' You explain to them you're sick and tired. Tell them to stop complaining and get involved in the political process." If they do, he said, they can win. "The truth is we can win this election if we have the largest voter turnout in the history of this country," he said. "We are strong in Iowa, we are strong in New Hampshire, we can win here in Nevada, I believe we're going to win in California, do very well in South Carolina. We can win this Democratic nomination, but we can't do it without increased involvement in the political process."

Increasing the size of the electorate, said Sanders, was everything. "On caucus night, turn on the TV early, and if the moderator tells you there's a large voter turnout, we win. If they tell you there's a low voter turnout, we lose. It's really as simple as that."

Simply put, it didn't work. Caucuses, low-turnout affairs, were the places where the Sanders campaign could do best, because the candidate's passionate supporters were more likely to go through the hassle of attending one. But the campaign wasn't able to find enough of those nonvoters-to-voters to move the needle. The apathy and disaffection were too deep to be overcome with a campaign that lasted just a few months at its height and spent nearly all its money on advertising—ads that nonvoters simply glossed over if they got anywhere near them. This would seem like a point for the Mehlhorn argument, indicating that, therefore, Democrats should search out the policies that polled the best and run on those—a philosophy that became known as popularism. One of the leading practitioners of that type of politics back in the 1990s and 2000s was Chuck Schumer, who loved to rail against the major annoyances of modern life. No airline bag fee was safe from the scrutiny of Schumer. But what the new Schumer had concluded was that passionate supporters also needed to see the party fighting and seeing it deliver.

Dobbs answered the question that both wings of the party had been asking, but not in the way anybody was expecting—anybody, that is, outside operatives inside reproductive rights organizations who'd been screaming that, if done effectively, abortion was a winning issue for Democrats, not something from which to squeamishly run.

In Michigan, when Democrats got beaten in the 2014 midterms, voters under age thirty made up just 15 percent of the electorate, according to the Center for Information and Research on Civic Learning and Engagement (CIRCLE). In 2022, they made up 36.5 percent, an unheard-of increase. That was more than a 10 percent increase even against 2018, which had been a banner year for Democrats. In every state where a vote to support abortion rights could plausibly matter—by flipping a statehouse, approving or rejecting a referendum, or electing a governor—youth turnout in general and turnout among women surged. Clearly, it *was* possible to turn nonvoters into voters. A ballot measure is straightforward: the law is self-executing—whereas when it came to supporting a political party, voters had to believe the candidates would do what they said they'd do, or at least get caught trying.

The related fundamental shift that Schumer had observed but Mehlhorn had missed was around the kind of policies that worked in swing districts and purple states. Mehlhorn and other self-described pragmatists were fond of pointing out that the Green New Deal and Medicare for All might poll well as general ideas, but once they were hit with counterattacks support dropped quickly. Mehlhorn mistakenly concluded that, therefore, the underlying policies were actually not very popular and merely benefited from good marketing. In reality, the concepts underlying the Green New Deal and Medicare for All are wildly popular, but the brand names had suffered from an onslaught of demonization by both conservative media and the Democratic establishment. In Georgia and Pennsylvania, Jon Ossoff, Raphael Warnock, and John Fetterman all ran on policies that amounted to versions of Medicare for All and a Green New Deal, even while avoiding the labels. Fetterman, previously a Sanders supporter, had backed Medicare for All in an earlier campaign and didn't shy away from it in 2022, but he didn't lead with it, either. Instead, he talked about getting to universal health care as quickly as possible in whatever way was possible. In Wisconsin, Mandela Barnes ran for the Senate as an unapologetic progressive. Despite Republicans being able to credibly link him to "defund the police" rhetoric, he fell just 27,000 votes short of unseating Ron Johnson, despite the party's having abandoned him for a crucial stretch during the campaign. Patty Murray and Maggie Hassan, incumbent Democrats running in Washington State and New Hampshire, panicked in the summer, demanding that Schumer divert money their way. He complied. They each won by double digits, meaning the diversion of resources away from Barnes wasn't necessary, and likely cost him the race. Otherwise, senators running on progressive platforms won in those critical purple states, not just holding the Senate but adding a seat.

In the House, the world had fundamentally changed since the last similar legislative session, 2009/10, when Democrats passed the Affordable Care Act and the House passed a climate bill. Every vulnerable Democrat who voted for the latter did so knowing it would hurt them in the next election, and they were pretty sure Obamacare would, too. In 2021, New Democrats, the caucus made up of business-friendly Democrats from wealthy districts, led the charge on the child tax credit, complaining furiously to leadership that Manchin's allowing it to expire would hurt them electorally. When the Inflation Reduction Act passed, the climate spending, subsidies for Obamacare, and cheaper drug prices became key reelection themes rather than drags on their popularity.

With a Senate divided 50–50, Congress pushed through well over four trillion dollars in new spending, including its historic climate investments and an expansion of Obamacare that made the program genuinely affordable (though only through 2025). Inside the White House, Warren's antitrust agenda was on the move, with her lieutenants having colonized every possible consumer-oriented position. And voters rewarded Democrats for it.

But as it is for every movement that shifts into the phase where an agenda is starting to be incorporated into the power structure and implemented as law, it was disorienting for people who considered themselves outsiders and agitators to be insiders, to be members of the team. As committees were being formed for the next Congress, Ocasio-Cortez was made vice chair of the Oversight Committee, while Republicans moved to throw Omar off the House Foreign Affairs Committee. Josh Gottheimer voted with his party to oppose that move, but the attempt was the culmination of years of his work.

Democrats had been expected to lose the House by a wide margin, but the surge in turnout, the revulsion against the *Dobbs* decision on *Roe*, and support for what Democrats had gotten done made it a nailbiter on Election Day. The results weren't called for more than a week, with even Colorado's Lauren Boebert going to a recount in her heavily Republican district. The difference had come in gerrymandering—Georgia, for instance, sent only five Democrats to Washington, even though the state had fourteen seats and had gone blue in recent elections—made easier by the new census, which Trump had overseen, telling his Commerce Department to put a thumb on the scale against Democrats. New York lost a seat, while Florida gained one and Texas picked up two. Both of the new Texas seats went red, and Florida went from a five-seat margin to a twelve-seat margin. But even in the face of all that, if Democrats had done better in New York, they'd have had a much better shot at holding the House.

New York lost its seat in the census by just eighty-nine residents—a deficit that wouldn't have existed had Gov. Andrew Cuomo and Mayor Bill de Blasio not been warring constantly. In 2020, the party had an eleven-seat congressional margin. In 2022, this was knocked down to just four. Cuomo-appointed appeals court judges ordered a last-minute redistricting, one that turned out badly for Democrats. But the same thing had happened in Ohio, with the state supreme court deeming the GOP gerrymander there illegal, but Republicans simply ignored it. Democrats complied, and this pushed the primaries back to the end of August, giving voters and the media just weeks to track the general election—and allowing a con artist calling himself George Santos to flip a Democratic seat.

Had Democrats simply maintained their margin in New York, Republicans would have had just a 218–217 margin in the House. (Add in the fact that both Jim Clyburn and Joyce Beatty worked with Republicans in their home states of South Carolina and Ohio to draw safer districts for themselves at the expense of fewer Democratic seats overall, and you can account for the full loss of the House in 2022.) Even DCCC chairman Sean Maloney, after leaving his district to run in a bluer one, was wiped out. "If Democrats do not hang on to the House, I think that responsibility falls squarely on New York State," Ocasio-Cortez told me shortly after the election. She argued that New York politicians were too reactive to Fox News and too corrupt. "If we're going to talk about public safety, you don't talk about it in the frame of invoking defund or anti-defund, you really talk about it in the frame of what we've done on gun violence, what we've done to pass the first gun reform bill in thirty years. Our alternatives are actually effective, electorally, without having to lean into Republican narratives," she said.

"Cuomo may be gone, but his entire infrastructure, much of his infrastructure and much of the political machinery that he put in place is still there," she added. "And this is a machinery that is disorganized, it is sycophantic. It relies on lobbyists and big money. And it really undercuts the ability for there to be affirming grassroots and state-level organizing across the state."

One of the biggest players in that machine, I pointed out, was Hakeem Jeffries, who was planning to turn the Democratic defeat into a personal triumph by becoming party leader amid Pelosi's resignation.

"I think there has been a multiyear strategy to try—it's essentially been a campaign within the Democratic Party to undermine progressive politics and try to mischaracterize [them] as toxic," AOC responded. "And I think a continued insistence on that is going to hurt the party. Because I think one of the big things that we learned last night is that not only is it not true, but that candidates who refuse to overcompensate and overly tack right were actually rewarded for sticking to their values." She continued: "I personally do think that there should be a political cost to being heavily backed by big money." Jeffries had won his 2018 race against Barbara Lee promising vague "generational change," and Ocasio-Cortez alluded to that but didn't mention Jeffries specifically in her answer. "Regardless of who it is in this discussion about generational change in the Democratic Party, I think we also need to be looking at donor bases," she said. "We shouldn't be shifting in a direction where the party or our party leadership becomes even more dependent on large donors and corporate backers, not less dependent, especially in a time when more Democrats are being elected independent of that and where the infrastructure for small-dollar fund-raising has only grown and become more vibrant."

She said she hoped the election results would temper some of the hostility directed toward progressives. "I do hope that there really is reflection on some of the strategies that went awry in New York, and how that was different from other places in the country. And I do hope that there is a reflection on being outwardly antagonistic toward a very enthused progressive base, especially one in which young people delivered these wins," she said.

While she was speaking, Hakeem Jeffries was sewing up the votes to be party leader. Jayapal had contemplated running for leadership but hadn't gotten her operation together in time. No other progressive bothered to challenge him.

Jeffries—after going to open war with the progressive wing of the party, after his top aide had posted a video of a drive-by shooting while taking down Ocasio-Cortez's chief of staff—ran unopposed to replace Pelosi, with the Squad all casting votes for him.

This humiliation came at the same time that Democrats sat back and watched Republicans battle over the rules package and the Speaker's gavel in the way many progressive activists had hoped the Squad would do. Right-wing provocateurs Matt Gaetz and Lauren Boebert—who had just won reelection by a too-thin margin of 546 votes—and more than a dozen other holdouts pledged to block Kevin McCarthy from the Speakership after Republicans narrowly won the majority. They had no support for an alternative, so the fight dragged on for days. On January 3, Gaetz ventured across the center aisle to find Ocasio-Cortez, confiding in her that McCarthy had been telling Republicans that he'd be able to cut a deal with Democrats to vote "present," enabling him to win a majority of those present and voting, according to Ocasio-Cortez. She told Gaetz that wasn't happening and also double-checked with Democratic Party leadership, confirming there'd be no side deal. "McCarthy was suggesting he could get Dems to walk away to lower his threshold," Ocasio-Cortez told me of her con-versation with Gaetz on McCarthy's failed ploy. "And I fact-checked and said, 'Absolutely not.'"

Rep. Paul Gosar, a Republican from Arizona, another McCarthy opponent and one of the lead organizers of the Stop the Steal efforts on January 6, also huddled with Ocasio-Cortez in the chamber, where they discussed the possibility of adjourning the House. She was non-committal on the tack, as an adjournment strategy would require party leadership, and for this play, she was marching in lockstep with leadership.

That alliance, which required public vote after vote for Hakeem Jeffries, juxtaposed with the rebellion under way across the aisle, brought out a response from Ocasio-Cortez on Instagram Live. Her analysis of the Freedom Caucus revolt was revealing for how much it said about her approach to politics inside the House chamber. "When people say, you know, why don't we do this? First of all, there's a lot of cost and dysfunction," she said. "Second of all, those people who are holding out right now, they may have made certain structural gains, but they have also made incredible reputational and relational harm within their caucus. And so, if you are trying to get something done within your caucus moving forward, you still need members of your caucus. And that, at the core, is an element of electoral politics that is simply inescapable. Even when you look at someone like Bernie Sanders's tenure in the House, where he was the amendment king, you needed your party to pass your amendments."

The rebels would pay a price, she argued. "You have this faction that is in a lot of trouble moving forward, despite having made cer-tain structural gains," she said. "When people say, 'Lauren Boebert has more spine than you'—Lauren Boebert won her race by five hun-dred votes. Lauren Boebert took a Trump plus—what?—nine district [meaning Trump won the district easily against Biden] and nearly lost it to an up-and-coming Democrat as an incumbent member of Congress. Lauren Boebert is dramatically weakened, dramatically weakened. And the people of Colorado nearly sent her packing. If five hundred people voted differently that day, this would not be happen-ing right now."

Boebert, she argued, had hurt herself in front of normie Repub-licans, just as Ocasio-Cortez was winning over normie Democrats. A poll around that time found AOC to be the most popular Democrat in the crucial state of New Hampshire. "If you're a hard-standing Republican, [Boebert] almost cost you your majority," AOC said.

She also argued that it was easier for the Freedom Caucus to push a nihilist agenda than it was for them to actively construct a positive one. "The Freedom Caucus is not organized around any core policy issue. Progressives, we organize around Medicare for All, we organize around a Green New Deal," she said. "Even if it's not all the whole farm all at once, but the building blocks to get us there, that's what we fight for and fight toward. But these folks, they're negotiating around committee assignments for themselves, certain rules changes. Not all of the [rules changes] are bad, mind you, but not all of them are good, either. And they're really organized around grievance."

She added a plea for people on the outside to help her internally, rather than chase the YouTube algorithm. "The idea that you can push and emphasize legislative goals without an outside [base of support]—that part, I think, is untenable," she said. "The right wing of the Democratic Party also organizes on the outside for their internal goals, but they do it with money. And as progressives, we have to do it with people. And so, when you have a base that focuses most of its ire toward the people on their side, because YouTube algorithms reward that, you're just playing into the hands of the capitalists who run those algorithms. And so, I'm not saying that all these folks in these media outlets who stir these things up are bad. Far from it. There are incredible people doing very thoughtful work. But there are also a lot of people who make and determine what they're going to make their videos on based on YouTube views and based on algorithms, and those algorithms, almost always, reward left infighting. That's what's gonna get you your clicks."

There were just four of them when she first came to Congress, she reminded her supporters, speaking of the progressive caucus. "We're getting a little closer to that double-digit representation. And that's when things start to get really interesting should we win back the House in '24. But, you know, this is a team sport, and I think a lot of times people think elections are just about 'set it and forget it': 'I'm just gonna pull my lever for someone and let them do the work.' And if you're that kind of person, I'm not sitting here to knock that. But if you are a left, or if you are a progressive organizer, what we need the most is support during game time, during legislating. And I can't tell you how common it is for us to look to the grass roots for guidance. And sometimes you don't hear anything until after something bad happens."

She finished with some historical context, situating the left despair partly as the product of long-running sabotage and suppression. "The fact of the matter is that the left in the United States has been persecuted at different points in history for a very long period of time. And as a result, [it] has been really winnowed very much," she said. "From the civil rights movement, or from other types of activist movements throughout American history, they have been surveilled, jailed, et cetera, for a very long period of time. And so I just think that we are at a point of increasing and ascending organizing awareness in the United States. But we have more to go. And the more we talk with each other, the more we organize, the more that we can do it."

Her second term, as she faced increasingly vitriolic criticism from elements of the left, had been a low point for her, Ocasio-Cortez told me. "That time really forced me to kind of sit with who my base was," she said. "Because for a while it did not feel like the left. Like I was left but the left didn't really support me, it felt like more a relationship of convenience and the moment I stopped being as useful I'd be dumped. And you can't movement build with your most fickle supporters."

I asked what she meant, and whether she had found a better base of supporters. "I don't think it was figuring out a 'better' base but more figuring out who my base actually was/is," she said. "Like as much as I love them, I did not win my election because of DSA. Or even JD. Or any of these orgs. They all either abandoned, ignored, or fought with me and then swooped in at the last moment when I busted my whole ass for a long time to become even remotely viable."

Because she had spent so much time being called a puppet, she seemed to have written the help she had gotten out of the story. "They all had important contributions but to be honest they were pretty much nowhere until the month before the primary," she said. "Really it was [Alexandra] Rojas at JD that arguably helped the most. But we had built everything from scratch and did the hardest parts and then when it looked appealing enough they jumped in."

Yet Brave New Congress and its later offshoot, Justice Democrats, had been there from the beginning. Shahid had helped set up her operation, sticking with the campaign from summer 2017 to March of the next year. And when Justice Democrats made the decision, following Shahid's argument, to cut off all other candidates and focus on Ocasio-Cortez following their December 2017 retreat, it had come at a cost. Staff were laid off to focus resources on her. The organization's email and donor list was used exclusively to find recruits and raise money for her. Chakrabarti moved to New York in January to volunteer full time as campaign manager. Trent and Rojas, when they joined him in the spring, slept on floors and couches. The film made about her campaign documents the herculean effort and captures the bedraggled organizers setting aside their personal lives and the organization's earlier mission to go all in on her race.

In her mind, the contributions of Justice Democrats, which were real and pivotal, were blending with those of DSA, which were late but useful, and then mingling in a toxic stew with the hostility she was getting from the broader online left. And all of that was caught up in the question of whether she was part of a movement, merely a product of a movement, the leader of a movement—and, importantly, what kinds of values that movement practiced. "There is a certain faction of the left that thinks they own or are responsible for electing a candidate just because that candidate happens to be ideologically left on their own. But in the actual work of getting elected, like it's just these armchair people who talk shit but don't do shit. And listening to people who don't do shit is how you lose whatever you've built," she said.

She thought back to her first campaign for Congress, when she was scrambling for endorsements. "Every endorsement vote was basically all the white guys voting no and women and [people of color] voting yes, and the places where we had the numbers we won and the places we didn't it got slow-walked or denied," she recalled. "I didn't even get endorsed by the Queens OurRev chapter! Which is why there is no longer one. But I did get support from the Bronx one.

"I think I had to reflect on the fact that that's what the actual experience was, and there are aspects of that relationship with the . . . let's call it the more dogmatic left even when I was a nobody that still persist now. I take it less personally now. It used to really hurt," she said. "But ultimately the people that were the harshest were never the ones that signed up for canvassing shifts or knocked any real amount of doors or really had convos with people because the ones that did got it."

Watching the members of the Squad come in for harsh criticism for things Bernie Sanders was also doing was demoralizing. "I was most depressed at the time by the misogyny I saw within the left and how differently we were treated," she said.

Onetime Sanders supporters had hoped that when the political revolution came to Congress, guillotines, or at least metaphorical ones, would accompany it. Those folks hadn't paid close attention to the career of Sanders to that point, who lived and legislated his values, but who also behaved as pragmatically as any other politician when it was advantageous. He was far from a left version of the Freedom Caucus. But the rallying behind archrival Hakeem Jeffries consummated a marriage of two wings of the party, each coming toward the other with uneasy steps. The civil war that had simmered inside the party for decades, and that erupted in full in 2016, seemed to be subsiding, with the establishment securely in place, but having co-opted enough of the Squad agenda to pacify and incorporate the left energy that had given rise to Sanders. In the spring of 2023, several months into the tenure of Jeffries as party leader, AOC was startled to find herself enjoying her job much more than she had previously. "I thought things would get worse," she texted. "I thought a lot of my misery was more due to leadership more broadly having a thing against me. But literally like . . . my life has completely transformed. It's crazy. And it's that that made me realize it was kind of just [Pelosi] the whole time. Which I couldn't really tell bc it's not like we talked much and other people talked way more smack, Clyburn, etc." She was finally able to operate as any other member. "Now senior members talk to me, chairs are nice to me, people want to work together. I'm shocked," she said. "I couldn't even get floor time before. They wouldn't even move my suspensions that I had GOP on for," a reference to uncontroversial bills that Republicans had agreed to cosponsor, yet Pelosi would still keep off the House floor.

Looking back to the early days of the birth of Brand New Congress and then Justice Democrats in Knoxville in early 2016, some of the founders of the groups couldn't help but regret the lost opportunity. Influencing the Democratic Party was good, and the hundreds of billions of dollars in climate spending may never have happened without them, but the ambition had not been to nudge power in a decent direction but, rather, to *take* power. And they hadn't. "Progressives don't want power," Corbin Trent concluded.

In the spring of 2023, Trent, the food truck operator who became AOC's pugnacious communications director; Saikat Chakrabarti, her chief of staff whom the *Washington Post* had called the leader of a movement; and Zack Exley, the flip-the-tables activist who helped Chakrabarti recruit Ocasio-Cortez, got together again to sort through what went right and what went wrong.

Their initial strategy, to recruit 435 everyday people to form a "brand new congress" had gotten bogged down in recruiting. They spent too much time combing through teacher-of-the-year lists and reading local articles, trying to find the right targets and then do the impossible: persuade them to give up everything for a job most normal people wouldn't want. When they ran out of time for that, and pivoted to Justice Democrats, their most promising candidates were, unsurprisingly, already politicians. Pressley had been elected citywide to her at-large Boston council seat. Omar and Tlaib had both served in their state legislatures. Of the remaining people who came from outside the system, only Ocasio-Cortez had made it through the primary, with Justice Democrats going all in on her campaign, bringing essentially their entire team to New York and putting the full weight of their fundraising and organizing power into that one campaign.

But, from there, the Squad did catch fire. Looking back, Trent charted out a counter history that might have gone differently. With the media attention that came AOC's way, they could have built a durable base of financial power. To Trent, the media's fascination with Ocasio-Cortez from 2018 through 2020 disproved the belief in the Sanders campaign that the corporate media were implacably hostile to the left.

With Ocasio-Cortez, everything she touched turned into ratings gold, and the networks went wild with it. "Why? Because it was good ratings. It clicked. Literally anybody would have fucking taken anything from her, and it didn't matter what she said. They would have printed it, they would have put it on the air. Actually, the farther she went, the better," said Trent.

Still, structurally, several things were missing. First, the Squad was not a real thing. "There is no such entity," one member of the nonentity told me, speaking on background. "You know that, right?" Rather, the Squad was a product of media branding that took off from one AOC Instagram caption and fit a girl-power aesthetic ascendant at the moment. But the Squad members did not know each other well; Justice Democrats hadn't done the work of intentionally and deliberately building enough bonds. "We didn't build any relationships," Trent said. "Like, Cori Bush didn't really know AOC that well, and then, across the board, none of these candidates were that well connected.

They also hadn't built a tight enough connection with Justice Democrats to survive the pressure of combat on Capitol Hill. From the outside, the bond seemed tight, with Trent and Chakrabarti installed in key leadership positions inside AOC's office. But by the first summer they were both out.

And while AOC and Tlaib joined a conference hosted by Justice Democrats in order to recruit future challengers, the collaboration effectively stopped there. Anytime any Squad member mentioned or appeared with Justice Democrats, their colleagues assumed this meant they were coming from them. That was power, but it complicated internal caucus relationships, and Justice Democrats as an organization was left floating in the wind. It wasn't provocative enough on its own to consistently regenerate a small-dollar fund-raising base, but it also wasn't close enough with the Squad to get their help raising money.

The two PACs eventually set up—Squad Victory Fund and AOC's Courage to Change—were initially intended to tap into outside support and translate it into hard dollars that could then be translated into power. To be truly effective, though, they'd have needed to team up with Sanders, "which is going to be tough, because he's very much an institutionalist. But [AOC] had a good relationship with Bernie," Trent noted. "You just took Crowley down, right? Nobody knows what the fuck is gonna happen, nobody feels safe. If Bowman had done what he did, and you kept perpetuating this fear cycle, and then you show the capacity to raise a shit-pot full of money. You actually do start a PAC that's going to be out there being competitive, that's doing IEs." Those IEs— "independent expenditures" made on behalf of candidates—could then compete with the outside money that flowed in to slow the Squad's rise.

The Sanders campaign had learned that getting attacked by the right people was lucrative. Each time Hillary Clinton came at him in a way his supporters felt was unfair, hundreds of thousands of dollars, sometimes millions, would pour into the campaign. Building a bucket to catch that rain would have made it costlier for the party leadership or for Gottheimer to attack the Squad, if each insult meant another one hundred grand in their coffers.

And the capacity was there. Single emails from AOC in 2019 were raising some forty thousand dollars a pop. Even tweets were bringing in money. During one two-week stretch, as AOC attacked Trump's "concentration camps" and visited the border, some two million dollars came in just from Twitter. "Who does that? Nobody. Nobody does that," Trent marveled.

The PACs did get created, but not with Sanders's support, and the funds from the Squad Victory Fund went mostly to support the Squad members themselves, while the Courage to Change PAC cut five-thousand-dollar checks and paid for some travel. "There was talk about [AOC] and Bernie just doing something like AIPAC," Trent said. "If you want to fight AIPAC, you can. I think you could blow them out of the water as far as fund-raising capacity goes, but their [email and text] lists became less useful because they didn't really have anything to go for."

And that was the fundamental problem that came before everything else, Trent came to believe, faulting himself and his organization for not building a coherent economic vision into the DNA of the project.

He said all this crystalized for him during the Covid-19 pandemic, when progressive lawmakers, including the Squad, began criticizing Republicans for "putting the economy over people's lives." It struck Trent that too many progressives viewed the economy as merely the province of Wall Street—some money moving around for no reason other than to enrich the elites. "This phrase, 'We're prioritizing the economy over people's lives,' sort of stuck with me," he said. "The economy is not Wall Street. The economy is the food that we eat, the clothes that we wear, the power that we utilize; it's all these things."

The economy and the discontent it produced across racial and gender categories had been at the heart of the first Sanders campaign and had animated the energy behind the Squad, which was bent on transforming the Democratic Party into a vehicle for the hopes of a multiracial working-class movement. Amid the endless clashes with the racism, sexism, and xenophobia of Trump, coupled with the rise of a left-liberal politics more oriented around culture, the fight over the shape of the economy had faded off center stage. And a left that had felt organized around a collective agenda had disintegrated into infighting.

With the climate crisis intersecting with endemic financial precarity, Justice Democrats had set out to radically transform the country and the world as rapidly as possible. By accident, instead, they may have produced a future president. In January 2023, the University of New Hampshire kicked off the next presidential cycle by putting a major poll into the field. The top line that it came back with couldn't have been pleasant for Biden. His transportation secretary, Pete Buttigieg, despite being mired in port, rail, and airline controversies, was polling ahead of Biden in the first-in-the-nation primary. But digging a little deeper into the numbers revealed a startling new reality: the most popular Democrat in New Hampshire was Alexandria Ocasio-Cortez. She came in with a 66 percent approval rating, with 9 percent of respondents saying they had an unfavorable impression, and another 22 percent positing themselves as neutral. Among self-identified socialists, a surprising number for New Hampshire, AOC's unfavorable number was zero, suggesting the online post-left turn against her either wasn't resonating on the ground in New Hampshire or hadn't been picked up in the poll. Among "progressives," her negative number was just 1 percent.

Sanders wasn't far behind in the New Hampshire poll, at 61–9. Warren, Raphael Warnock, and Buttigieg were all also above a net approval margin of more than 50, an indication that Democratic voters liked a lot of Democrats—no surprise there. But while Ocasio-Cortez and the Squad spent much of 2019 in conflict with party leadership, and spent the first half of 2020 trying to nominate Sanders for president, AOC had been a team player in the general election, and through Biden's term, she had consistently framed her advocacy as in support of his administration and his agenda. "In any other country, Joe Biden and I would not be in the same party, but in America, we are," she famously said in 2020. Yet they were in the same party, and now that party's voters were rating her more favorably than him. "I saw it and do not believe it 😆," Ocasio-Cortez said, when I asked if she had seen the survey.

Perhaps a part of her does believe it. In the early summer of 2022, in the depth of the Biden doldrums, when inflation ran hot and Build Back Better had been left for dead, Jamaal Bowman was growing antsy and began talking with his comrades about how to shake things up. In the House Democratic cloakroom, he found Ocasio-Cortez and told her he thought somebody from the Squad should run for president in 2024—not to dethrone Biden, but merely to get their message out, much as Sanders had planned to do eight years earlier.

It was worth a shot, he argued, and if nobody else wanted to do it, he was willing to try. Hold that thought for a minute, Ocasio-Cortez responded. She might just run herself. But, she added, she had little faith in her prospects. "I had kind of felt at the time that the left was so bad in its double standard of its own female candidates that there was no way we could get united enough under someone like me for a bigger fight," she told me of her cloakroom conversation. "I was really going through it at that time. But I feel like things are better now than they were then."

AUTHOR'S NOTE

The best way to think about this book, particularly in the era of the Avengers, is as essentially a sequel to my 2019 book *We've Got People: From Jesse Jackson to AOC, the End of Big Money and the Rise of a Movement.* That one begins with the transformation of the Democratic Party in the 1970s and 1980s, as corporate PAC fund-raising began to replace labor money and energy as its driving force. Pushing against that realignment was a factional coalition of civil rights activists, environmentalists, feminists, and union reformists—dubbed the Rainbow Coalition—coalescing around the presidential candidacies in 1984 and 1998 of the Reverend Jesse Jackson, who came stunningly close to claiming the prize during his second bid. Playing a leading role in delivering Vermont's delegates to Jackson was Burlington mayor Bernie Sanders; it was his first foray into Democratic politics. *We've Got People* runs through that period and—spoiler alert—it ends with the occupation of incoming House Speaker Nancy Pelosi's office by the Sunrise Movement, Justice Democrats, and Representative-elect Alexandria Ocasio-Cortez. This new book picks up in 2015, with the launch of the first Sanders presidential campaign and runs through the 2022 midterms. For the sequel to stand alone as its own unit, the narrative for *The Squad* starts before the end of *We've Got People*, allowing me to give the backstories of the characters we meet. In doing so, in some early chapters I occasionally draw liberally and verbatim from passages in *We've Got People* or from my reporting in the *Intercept*, with gratitude to Strong Arm Press and the *Intercept*, respectively.

ACKNOWLEDGMENTS

This book wouldn't have been possible without the great privilege I've had to do daily reporting on Democratic politics and the progressive movement over the past nearly two decades. I'm indebted to everyone who has helped me along the way. Early chapters in this book draw on my reporting for the *Huffington Post* on the nascent Black Lives Matter movement and the first campaign of Bernie Sanders. The team of reporters and editors there—including Nico Pitney, Sam Stein, and Amanda Terkel—were and are invaluable friends and colleagues. I joined the *Intercept* in 2017, and the book draws on my reporting on the Democratic civil war that erupted that election cycle, which I was fortunate enough to cover with my editor Nausicaa Renner, along with Maryam Saleh, Roger Hodge, Betsy Reed, Lee Fang, Glenn Greenwald, Ali Gharib, Aída Chavez, Akela Lacy, and Briahna Joy-Gray. The reporting on the campaign of Alex Morse was done in collaboration with Daniel Boguslaw and Eoin Higgins. Reporting on the first campaign of Alexandria Ocasio-Cortez was done with my colleagues Chavez, Greenwald, Joy-Gray, Jeremy Scahill, and Fang. The chapter on the 2020 Sanders campaign was greatly assisted by research Nicholas Marchio did into the media's relentlessly adversarial coverage of him. It does sources no favors to mention or thank them, but just know that if you shared your story for this book I'm deeply thankful for the trust you placed in me, and I hope that I earned it.

Endless thanks to my family for supporting me through this process, above all my wife, Elizan Garcia, and our kids, Iris, Sidney, Virginia, and George, all of whom handle my unusual work schedule with grace. Thanks to my parents, George Grim and Cindy Quinn, for pointing me in the right direction. And my love and gratitude go to Mimi

Hook, who not only is the editor of my Substack newsletter *Bad News*, but has also become a devoted grandma.

My agent, Howard Yoon, provided helpful feedback and deftly maneuvered the book into position to be published. I was lucky on that front to wind up with Serena Jones as my editor at Holt, who shared my vision for the book and guided it masterfully. And by the end of it, somehow, we didn't even hate each other. Chris O'Connell, the book's production editor, and Jenna Dolan, my copy editor, were patient and professional. Anita Sheih shepherded the book expertly through the process, while Carolyn O'Keefe in publicity and Laura Flavin in marketing went above and beyond to make sure it had every chance to be read. And thanks to publisher Amy Einhorn and editor in chief Sarah Crichton for taking a chance on the book.

INDEX

Muilenburg, Dennis, 79
Muir, John, 210
Murdoch, Rupert, 135
Murray, Patty, 302
Mynett, Tim, 221

NAACP, 111–13, 211
Nadler, Jerry, 225
NAFTA, 24, 143
NARAL Pro-Choice America, 68, 73, 130–31
Nazarian, Adelle, 255
Neal, Richard, 129, 191–94
Neguse, Joe, 224, 285
Netanyahu, Benjamin, 100, 102, 236, 267
New Jim Crow, The (Alexander), 28
Newman, Marie, 68–70, 148, 190, 238, 244–50,
　261–63, 282
Nixon, Cynthia, 39
Nixon, Richard, 203, 215
NoiseCat, Julian Brave, 138, 142
No Labels, 59, 68–70, 137n, 139, 238, 247,
　272–74, 280–81
Norcross, Don, 64
Norman, Jim, 65–66

Obama, Barack, 1, 4–5, 9–12, 17–18, 41, 55–56,
　60–62, 79, 84, 88, 102, 110, 121, 126, 155,
　177–78, 185–86, 189, 234, 244
Obama, Michelle, 60
Obey, Dave, 143
Ocasio-Cortez, Alexandria (AOC)
　abortion rights and, 129–31, 295–96
　Amazon HQ2 and, 51–53
　ambitions of, 119–20
　attacks on, 98, 126, 139–40, 147, 245
　Biden and, 118, 182–83, 211
　border and, 97, 134–47
　Build Back Better and, 274–76, 284, 288–91,
　　294
　climate and, 49–57, 93, 110–20, 160, 211, 294
　committees and, 78, 86–90, 109, 119, 303
　early life of, 9–12
　election of 2008 and, 9
　election of 2020 and, 311
　election of 2022 and, 304–7
　election of 2024 and, 315
　fund-raising and, 76, 122–25, 251–52, 312–13
　grassroots and, 307–11
　House colleagues and, 57, 72–74, 121–32,
　　140–41, 147, 310–11
　House freshman orientation and, 76–80
　House rules and, 91–95, 214–18, 231
　Israel-Palestine and, 45–47, 237, 244–47
　January 6 riot and, 219–24
　Keystone XL Pipeline and, 11, 26
　Obama and, 11, 121
　Pelosi and, 42–43, 58
　popularity of, 45, 311–15
　primaries and, 26–42, 45, 56–57, 71, 135,
　　187–94, 264
　Sanders and, 153, 156–60, 166–67, 299–300
　Squad term coined by, 43–44
　staff and, 109, 125, 132–33, 146–48
　stimulus and, 213–14, 228, 230
Ocasio-Cortez, Blanca, 10, 12
Ocasio-Cortez, Gabriel, 10–11, 26
Ocasio-Roman, Sergio, 10
Occupy Wall Street, 1–2, 11–12, 41, 181
O'Keefe, Alex, 268–69
Okun, Tema, 195–202
Omar, Ilhan, 17, 44, 79–86, 93, 98–108, 119,
　125, 138–41, 144–46, 160, 185, 188, 211,
　220–25, 236–37, 242–46, 250, 264, 282,
　287–88, 303, 311
O'Rourke, Beto, 178
Osman, Abdihakim, 83
Ossoff, Jon, 213–14, 302

Page, Susan, 94, 143, 146
Pallone, Frank, 94
Palma, Annabel, 35
Parenti, Christian, 198–200
Pascrell, Bill, 63–64
Pelosi, Christine, 42, 87–89
Pelosi, Nancy, 26, 39–43, 49–59, 64, 68,
　70–73, 77–79, 84–94, 105–6, 110, 118, 123,
　133–47, 185, 193, 214–15, 218–19, 224–25,
　231, 243–46, 272, 275–76, 280–84, 287–90,
　294, 304, 310
Pence, Mike, 79, 225
Penn, Mark, 59–62, 69–70
Percy, Charles, 69
Perez, Tom, 4, 84
Perriello, Tom, 76–77
Pitcock, Josh, 79
Pocan, Mark, 85–87, 94, 107, 138, 236, 281
Podesta, John, 4
police brutality, 13–17, 19, 184–85
Porter, Katie, 90, 137, 223
Power in Words (Gottheimer), 61
Prakash, Varshini, 51, 118, 183
Pressley, Ayanna, 38, 44–45, 76, 79–80, 90, 93,
　108, 125, 131–32, 139–44, 153, 160, 188,
　191, 237, 245, 264, 287, 289, 311
Primus, Wendell, 85, 87, 89
Problem Solvers Caucus, 59, 70–71, 137–39

ABOUT THE AUTHOR

Ryan Grim is the *Intercept*'s Washington bureau chief and the cohost of *Counter Points*. He was previously the DC bureau chief for *HuffPost*, where he led a team that won a Pulitzer Prize. Grim has been a staff reporter for *Politico* and the *Washington City Paper* and a contributor to MSNBC and *The Young Turks*. He's the author of the books *We've Got People: From Jesse Jackson to Alexandria Ocasio-Cortez, the End of Big Money and the Rise of a Movement* and *This Is Your Country on Drugs: The Secret History of Getting High in America*. He is the host of the podcast *Deconstructed* and lives in Washington, DC.